Therefore Choose Life is the first of a series of volumes in preparation which together will comprise the intellectual and spiritual legacy of Rabbi Silver. The emphasis of the first volume is on his interpretation of the Jewish faith, the meaning of its traditions, and its application in life. Forthcoming selections in the series will center around his understanding of the Bible and Jewish thought, his concern with social issues of the day, and his struggle to create a Jewish homeland in Palestine.

Abba Hillel Silver was a beloved rabbi, a noted scholar, a vigorous champion of human rights, a speaker and writer who helped transform the life of our time with the power of words. The permanent value of his message is everywhere evident in *Therefore Choose Life*, for he spoke to the needs of men in every age. This anthology will be welcomed by all who knew or heard Rabbi Silver during his lifetime and by all who seek a faith that makes sense and gives strength in an age of crisis.

HERBERT WEINER, editor of *Therefore Choose Life*, is Rabbi of Temple Israel of the Oranges and Maplewood, N. J.

SOLOMON B. FREEHOF, who has provided the Introduction, is Rabbi Emeritus of Rodeph Sholem Temple, Pittsburgh, Pa.

THEREFORE
CHOOSE LIFE

"... I have set before thee life and death, the blessing and the curse; therefore choose life, that thou mayest live, thou and thy seed. . . ."

—Deuteronomy 30:19

THEREFORE CHOOSE LIFE

Selected Sermons, Addresses,
and Writings of

Abba Hillel Silver

VOLUME ONE

EDITED BY HERBERT WEINER,
WITH A MEMOIR BY SOLOMON B. FREEHOF

THE WORLD PUBLISHING COMPANY
CLEVELAND AND NEW YORK

Published by The World Publishing Company
2231 West 110th Street, Cleveland, Ohio 44102

Published simultaneously in Canada by
Nelson, Foster & Scott Ltd.

Library of Congress Catalog Card Number: 66–25890

Printed in the United States of America.

Grateful acknowledgment is made for permission to
reprint the poem "*If*," copyright 1910 by Rudyard
Kipling. Reprinted by permission of Mrs. George
Bambridge, The Macmillan Company of Canada, Ltd.,
and Doubleday and Company, Inc.

CONTENTS

I. THE VISION

"Choose Life That You May Live"

"The Lord Is My Shepherd"

II. THE WAY

"What Does the Lord Demand of You . . ."

"If I Am Not for Myself, Who Will Be for Me?"

"If I Am Only for Myself, What Am I?"

PREFACE

This is the first in a series of volumes which will present the intellectual and spiritual legacy of Rabbi Abba Hillel Silver.

Its contents may surprise the reader who thinks of Dr. Silver in terms of a meteoric public career, a distinguished American citizen and a leader of the Zionist movement. For it is not a record of blazing statements attempting to rally the resources of a people and nation, or designed to influence the course of large public events. Such statements were made, and they will be presented in the later books of this series. In this volume will be found words which Abba Hillel Silver addressed to the individual as an individual. The sermons and addresses here collected are concerned with the basic needs and hungers of a human being for life, comfort, courage, and meaning. They attempt to offer the individual guidance in his confrontation with life's mysteries, in his attempt to form viable relationships within the context of his family, his community, and his people. The reader will find that the points of view expressed have clear relevance for his own life. Furthermore, though most of them were oral pronouncements, they bear the test of attentive reading.

Perhaps there is no reason for surprise—if we remember the central commitment of Abba Hillel Silver's life. He was a rabbi who ministered to the needs of a large congregation for almost fifty years. The fact that he was also an important leader of men and movements during this turbulent half-century was never allowed to blur this basic commitment. Wherever he spoke, whether at a university, a meeting of the Cleveland City Club, or a convocation of the United Nations, he spoke as a rabbi. That is to say, he consciously tried to confront the issue at hand not only in terms of his own personal analysis or the context of the moment, but also from the perspective of a moral tradition which had been tested in the crucible of Jewish history. The phrases "I think" or "in my opinion" are rarely found in Rabbi Silver's discourses. It is rather the opinion of the

Bible and of the rabbinic tradition that we are asked to consider in these sermons and addresses. For a rabbi must call upon "the values which are from everlasting to everlasting," emphasizing those aspects of modern truths which can help men meet "the particular crisis and urgency of their age." Rabbi Silver's effort to think and speak in such terms makes many of his statements expressions of the classic Jewish view rather than purely personal observations. This is one reason why his sermons withstand the test of time. Another reason is Rabbi Silver's determination not to succumb to the temptation of his natural gifts.

He was unusually gifted. Nature had endowed him with a tall, handsome, and impressive presence. He had a magnificent and perfectly controlled voice. His family had provided him with an unusually rich Jewish education, and his talents as a student enabled him to complement this heritage with an equally deep knowledge of all aspects of Western culture and thought. He had a natural flair for the poetic and striking phrase, a sense of the dramatic, and the instinct of the actor who can rivet the audience's attention by a gesture. He was gifted. But he did not rely on his natural gifts. He insisted on hard work and severe, self-imposed discipline. In his public talks he never depended upon inspiration, lest "the lady come too late." He carefully prepared even his casual public utterances. It was not unusual for him to spend two or three days researching and writing down every word of a sermon, then memorizing the whole. He knew how to approach the pulpit, then stand there polishing his glasses until the expectant hush deepened to the point of high drama. But when he spoke, it was the thought, the logic, the carefully worked out phrase that carried the listener along until the desired conclusion appeared inevitable to the mind as well as the heart.

The fruit of this work was hundreds of manuscripts, most of them carefully written and recorded—a legacy of high value in terms of what they can offer both the individual reader and the historian.

It is hoped that the full scope of Abba Hillel Silver's oral and written works will be revealed in volumes to be published over the next few years. The second volume will comprise a collection of addresses on the high moments of the religious and civic calendar. Rabbi Silver's remarkable gift for illuminating Biblical themes and characters will be the focus of the next book in the series. Finally, there will be one or two volumes presenting his statements and addresses as spokesman and leader in the broader community—as citizen, statesman, and Zionist.

Obviously, any attempt to compartmentalize a man's ideas and work into thematic sections is artificial. It is particularly difficult in the case of Abba Hillel Silver, who was a remarkably integrated personality. He was many-sided in his interests and talents—poetic, interested in mysticism, but also fascinated with politics on both a local and international level; a splendid administrator; and a highly self-disciplined scholar. Yet his thought and work in all of these worlds were unified and harmonized by some simple basic convictions. These convictions he found early in life and maintained without fundamental change. These "root beliefs," out of which opens a many-branched and exceedingly fruitful tree of life, form the central theme of the present volume.

The privilege of being called "editor" of this series deserves a speedy confession. My work was made possible by the gracious help of several people. More than half a century of speech-making, teaching, and writing resulted in many hundreds of manuscripts and articles. All of these have been carefully filed in the Abba Hillel Silver Memorial Archives at The Temple in Cleveland. Responsible for this immensely helpful resource are Miss Miriam Leikind, Librarian at The Temple, and Miss Fay Zipkowitz, in charge of the Archives. I am grateful to them for their cooperation and suggestions.

Rabbi Silver's beloved wife, Virginia, has been kind as well as helpful. His sons, Raphael and Daniel, along with many good friends in the congregation, made possible the publication of this and future volumes. I am especially indebted to Rabbi Daniel Jeremy Silver, who has guided every step of this project with understanding and proud love.

HERBERT WEINER

RECOLLECTIONS OF ABBA HILLEL SILVER

A Memoir by SOLOMON B. FREEHOF

IN SEPTEMBER, 1962, the Congregation Rodef Shalom of Pittsburgh invited my classmate, Abba Hillel Silver, to speak at a celebration organized in honor of my seventieth birthday. A few months later, I went to Cleveland to speak at the celebration held by The Temple for Abba Hillel Silver's seventieth. This exchange of visits had become a sort of tradition; I had been going to Cleveland and he to Pittsburgh for our respective anniversary celebrations for a number of years.

At this seventieth celebration in Pittsburgh, Abba Silver spent the first part of his address talking of our school days. He spoke of the time when he had first met me, of the essay prizes for which we had competed with each other, the first of which he had won and the second of which I had won. Our student days, so long ago, were brought to living memory by his speech. It was worth discussing those days, because the unusual nature of life at the Hebrew Union College in those years explains much of his career and his relationship to his rabbinical colleagues.

The Hebrew Union College in those days had nine classes. The total student body was between forty and fifty, so most classes had only five or six students. It was an exceptional class that had ten students. It was therefore impossible for a person not to know his classmates well. It was evident at the very beginning that Abba Hillel Silver was different in temperament from most of us. We were often serious, but we were boys and rather lighthearted. We saw at once he was more mature, or at least much more adult than most of us. There were certain boyish or post-adolescent characteristics which he seemed to lack entirely or which he had outgrown. As young people, we were capable of sudden new enthusiasms, friendships, quarrels, excitement over matters which soon proved to be trivialities. He seemed already at nineteen to have grown away from the excitability, the frothiness of youth. He never just babbled for the sake of self-expression. He would express a strong opinion, but would never excitedly snatch at passing ideas. He had, it seemed to us then, a premature reserve. He had the capacity, characteristic of mature leadership, for listening patiently and in silence. He could not or would not make sudden friendships and get into minor quarrels. There seems to have been no triviality about him from the very first time we met him. We were rather boyish and he was already in temperament a man.

That does not mean that he was solemn or dour. He had a hearty sense of humor. He could tell and be delighted by some characteristic anecdote. He was capable of making some brilliant plays on words or twisting a well-known sentence or quotation into a new and charming idea. He could laugh heartily, but not giggle. He had humor but very little playfulness.

Much of his quiet maturity, his reserve, may well have been due to basic temperament or to the mood of the life of his family in New York; but certainly a great deal of it was due to the fact that when he came to Cincinnati to attend the college, he already had a serious goal in life, in addition to the rabbinate and his personal career. He was a strong and convinced Zionist. In the last ten or twenty years in American life, being a Zionist represents an almost normal or average Jewish attitude. But in those days, fifty-five years ago, it was an exceptional attitude, especially in this new environment to which he had come to study for the Reform rabbinate.

The general tradition of Reform Judaism had been anti-Zionist; or, more correctly, Reform Judaism, which preceded Zionism by two generations, had a world attitude which was bound to become anti-Zionistic. The Reform movement was an outgrowth of the universalistic hopes of the Enlightenment; it was rooted in the conviction that the future would bring a diminution of the differences between peoples. Therefore the new nationalism that arose in Europe seemed to the leaders of Reform Judaism to be a retrogression. Of all the literature of the Jewish past, they stressed the universalistic dreams of the Prophets. Therefore when Jewish nationalism arose in parallel to the new forces of modern history, it seemed to the leaders of Reform to be a grave error, a backward step, almost a denial of the idealism of the universalist-prophetic dream. Therefore anti-Zionism or anti-nationalism to the earlier generation of Reformers was a matter of principle, an idealism. It then developed into a sort of prejudice, for Jewish nationalism seemed to them to be an anti-cultural movement, an anti-modern movement, a strange ideology springing from the mass of life of oppressed Jewry in eastern Europe.

Into such an environment compounded of ideals and moods, Abba Silver came with his warm and passionate Herzlian Zionism. In this he differed not only from the opinion of most of the faculty but from the average students who came from the Middle West. The boys from the Eastern Seaboard were often sympathetic to Zionism, but they were in this regard much less serious than he. If a student became devoted to some practical cause, it would generally be the cause of social service and social advance, for this was the logical expression of the traditional prophetism of Reform Judaism. Abba Silver was exceptional as a nationalist devotee, a Zionist activist.

One or two of our schoolmates came from the same group as he did, and his brother Maxwell came to the college the next year; and we learned then of the background of his strong and convinced Zionism. His father was one of the earliest Hebrew teachers making use of modern Hebrew, and he influenced his sons and his pupils in modern Hebrew conversation and Herzlian Zionism. He was a pioneer in this new method of Jewish education, which later became almost universal. We learned how these pupils founded the Herzl-Zion Club from which many of the later leaders of the Zionist movement came; how they wrote plays in Hebrew and gave them in a public hall; how Abba went to the meetings of the various lodges and unions to persuade the organizations to buy tickets. All this early pioneer Zionistic enthusiasm gave a direction to his life from which he never deviated.

Many of us had come from families which were Zionist or in which there was a member who was interested in Zionism; but Zionism was a minor movement in American Jewish life in those days, so there were none of us whose whole family life was organized in so firm a Zionist devotion as his was. Certainly our Hebrew education at home was then of the cheder or the Talmud Torah type of those days, without the many changes which the use of conversational Hebrew later brought about.

I think it was in the first year that Abba Silver was at college that a famous Zionist world leader came to Cincinnati and was invited to address the students at the chapel service. I am no longer sure who the speaker was; it may have been Nahum Sokolow. After he spoke, Abba was asked to give a response and thanks on behalf of the students. To our astonishment, this new student from New York made the response in fluent, modern Hebrew. I know that very few, if any, of the other students could have done that. We recognized at once that Abba Silver had a new type of Jewish background, different from ours, and that his interest in Zionism was much more single-minded and devoted than ours.

Perhaps this was one additional reason for his quiet thoughtfulness. He had some very strong thinking to do. Those of us whose sympathy with Zionism seemed at variance with the non- or anti-Zionism of most of our teachers had only to adjust a sentiment to a doctrine. But he had two strong doctrines to adjust and to harmonize. He must have spent a great deal of quiet time weighing the two points of view and seeking an inner harmony.

Being reserved in mood and having much to think about, he could easily have kept aloof from his classmates and schoolmates and gone on alone on his chosen road through life, except for contact with his family and intimate co-workers. But this was the Hebrew Union College, the school in which forty to fifty young men saw each other for hours every day and for many years. We were a family in which temperamental differences were recognized and generally respected, and yet in which all the members knew that they belonged together. So Abba Silver, the devoted Zionist, the serious, reserved, thoughtful man, never withdrew or could withdraw from his classmates or his colleagues. He became an intimate part of our college life, participating in the concerns of our student meetings and playing an active part in our college enterprises, except athletics. Sports never interested him at all.

In our meetings, he rarely argued about procedural matters or the trivia of organizational politics. He would therefore not speak frequently but, as might be expected of a man of his temperament, he would wait till a thought was matured in his mind (a patience not easy for young people), and then when he knew precisely what he wanted to advocate and how to advocate it, he raised his hand for the floor, slowly unfolded his tall, lanky frame, and began to speak. We had never before heard such eloquence at our student meetings. We had plenty of good men, bright men, who could express themselves; but none of us could speak in his particular way. Heaven knows where he learned these secrets of eloquence! He did not throw away emotion by hot, excitable speech; but quietly, with steady march, and in his magnificent clarion voice, expressed his ideas with firm tread, giving weight to every sentence.

Abba had decided that what the student body needed was a literary magazine. He advocated the idea and we all adopted the enterprise. He became the first editor of the *Hebrew Union College Monthly,* the magazine which has continued for over fifty years with only occasional interruptions.

The intimacy which kept this reserved and thoughtful man close to our college life and activity continued as it did with all of us in the Central Conference of American Rabbis, for when we entered the Conference almost half of the membership were former schoolmates. He could easily have kept his membership in the Conference down to a nominal, professional affiliation, much as a busy physician might belong to the American Medical Association without taking part in its organizational activities or even attending its conventions. If that had happened with Abba Silver, it would have been understood—regretted but forgiven—because very soon he became deeply involved in significant Jewish work outside the scope of our direct rabbinical professional concerns. He became very quickly the outstanding young man in the Zionist movement in America, soon one of the coming leaders, and after a while, the leader. He contributed more than any other American Jew to the establishment of the independent State of Israel. All this work of his involved him in endless political battles in the Zionist organization, constant involvement with the raising of money, frequent visits to Washington for discussion with government officials, great rallies and protest meetings all over the country, and participation in the World Zionist Congresses. This could understandably have taken away from our professional organizational contacts. Yet he never permitted it to do so; the rabbinate meant too much to him as a life calling, and the intimacy of our family life at the college put the impress of brotherliness upon him. For very many years, he always managed to come to our Conference, if only for a day or two. He never failed to give a paper or a sermon or a lecture when the program committee asked him to do so.

Of course, in his attendance at the conferences, he could frequently serve the Zionist cause which was so dear to him. Every year we had resolutions which tried somehow to balance the traditional anti-Zionism of the older generation and the growing interest in Zionism of the younger. We constantly had debates on the wording of our resolutions on Palestine and Zionism. All this was important to him, but that was not the reason for his attendance at conferences. He never regarded the Conference as merely or primarily one more institution which he could use to further the Zionist cause. The Conference itself was precious to him as a professional organization of the Reform rabbinate, his beloved calling, and also because of the boyhood friendship and comradeship which our college life instilled in him and in us all. Therefore he continued in his attendance and his service to the Conference and, when the time came, became our president and served magnificently as the leader of our profession.

Abba Silver entered into a career in which he delivered a new address twice (or at least once) a week. An ordinary lecturer may prepare two or three lectures for a year, and go around the country repeating them in city after city. Of course, in his rabbinical life, from the very beginning, he had to travel throughout the nation to speak for the Zionist cause and for other causes. This experience of nation-wide lecturing came to him earlier than to most, because he entered the rabbinate already in command of a grand eloquence. But in addition to the two or three lectures which could be given over and over again in different parts of the country, as all traveling speakers must necessarily do, he was an active rabbi and had to speak to the same congregation once or twice a week. A man can prepare two or three lectures as an objective task. He has a theme to express and he expresses it. Some of his personality, though not necessarily much, will be revealed in these lectures. But a man who has to speak to the same congregation week after week cannot possibly be entirely or chiefly objective. Inevitably he will soon begin to reveal his deeper attitudes and his own basic temperament. A good selection of Abba Silver's lectures and addresses is more than an exposition of his ideas; it is a revelation of his personality.

Thus there can be no secret of what Abba Silver believed, thought, and advocated. And when we put together his thoughts from college days with the thoughts in his writings of later years, it is astounding how consistent his personality and his ideas are. There is, of course, growth and broadening with greater knowledge, and deepening with the richer understanding which the years bring to a fortunate person. But the basic principles and the basic moods remain the same. It is not that the set of ideas which he brought to the Hebrew Union College remained fixed all through his life. They were, of course, always there, but were deepened and enriched and were taught, as it were, to stand side by side with certain convictions and life attitudes that came to him at the Hebrew Union College and with others which came to him as he lived and worked in Cleveland and became a leading force in that great metropolis. He brought from New York a powerful, deep-rooted Jewishness. He added to it in Cincinnati an idealistic Judaism, and expanded it in Cleveland to an active, practical vision of social betterment. All these ideas were interwoven into his personality because he, in his deliberate thinking and meditation, had himself woven them into a consistent unity.

And a unique unity it was! He came, as we have said, to the Hebrew Union College with a powerful sense of Jewish nationalism which was some day to be translated and realized in a Herzlian sense into a Jewish State. In Cincinnati he came into contact with a third generation of leadership of the Reform movement (our president, Mr. Kohler, was a pupil of Geiger), and he saw the world idealism which breathed through it. He always appreciated and never mocked that prophetic idealism. In his own thinking, he made an extraordinary merger of both moods, one inward toward Jewish concentration and the other outward toward world brotherhood. He achieved it through his re-thinking of the prophetic message. Whereas the early Reformers emphasized only the vision of world unity, he saw in the prophets the vision of Israel's redemption as an instrument for human brotherhood. Therefore his first constructive thinking was in the realm of Messianism, the redemption of Israel leading to the redemption of the world. His first book was in that field. Herzlian Zionist though he was, and convinced that nationalism was indispensable for the redemption of the people of Israel, he nevertheless looked forward to the time when the nationalism of each separate nation would outgrow parochial self-worship and become a force towards world unity. What the early Reformers dreamed of for the world, he dreamed of attaining through Jewish nationalism, a redeemed Israel, as a servant and exemplar to the world.

There is a constant danger in eloquence. The ability to move an audience by the pageant of stirring mental pictures can become an intoxicating joy to the speaker, until he begins to rely more and more on the success of a technique. This never happened to Abba Silver. Perhaps it was his father who first trained him to honest study. At all events, from his college days he was an earnest and devoted student and remained so all his life. The content of his addresses and sermons was always more important to him than the manner in which they were given. The Jewish content, in addition to the ideas from a general world culture, was rather extraordinary and surprisingly original. From some semi-obscure cabalistic work, from some medieval Jewish historical chronicle, he would produce an illustration that was enlightening and brilliant. Perhaps more astonishing was his use of Scripture. Innumerable men know the Bible well and can quote it aptly; but it might well be said that he never actually quoted Scriptural verses, or rarely did so. He had absorbed Scripture so completely through constant and thoughtful and receptive reading that Scriptural verses or fragments of verses appeared interwoven into the texture of a sentence, to produce a most original and, to those who knew the Bible, a stirring effect.

The only analogy that comes to mind to illustrate his absorption of Scripture is the way William Shakespeare used the Bible. Shakespeare almost never quotes a verse from Scripture as it is, but Scriptural phrases suddenly loom up in the texture of his language. The Book of Proverbs speaks of the soul of man being the candle of the Lord. The Psalm speaks of man's life as a moving shadow. Shakespeare had these verses in mind and he also saw before him in his daily experience the footlights of the stage, which in those days were lighted candles casting the shadows of the moving actors onto the stage floor; and he embodied Scripture and experience into the words in *Macbeth:*

"Out, out, brief candle!
Life's but a walking shadow, a poor player
That struts and frets his hour upon the stage. . . ."

In some such way, Abba Silver made Scripture part of the texture of his public speech and turned the letter of the Bible into the living word. All of which indicates that he was a constant student. He believed in the discipline of study, and often when he spoke on education, he referred to the primary duty, almost the moral duty, of teaching students early the discipline of concentrating the mind on a problem and not relaxing until the problem is solved.

It was certainly the Biblical influence which led to his great emphasis on social justice. He was a fearless advocate of the rights of Labor and that, too, in his original way. He did not make his social ideals the reflection of a political or doctrinal radicalism. I do not remember ever hearing from him, even in our student days, any expression of an idea that could properly be called Marxist. Somehow political radicalism did not attract him. It may be because he was a strong Herzlian Zionist, and in the environment of his boyhood Socialists were anti-religionists and anti-Zionists and frequently mocked the intense Jewishness of their fellow Jews. This was long before a merger was made between Socialism and Zionism in the Labor Zionist movement. So in his original and independent fashion, he could combine political conservatism with social reform. He believed that religion should never be an apologist for any social system, but should always, through the terms of its own inner mandate, work to allay the injustices of the world.

So Abba Hillel Silver was his own man. His opinions matured and developed from within; and once they developed, they received the superb advocacy of his magnificent eloquence. Because his opinions developed from within, being the outgrowth of syntheses which he himself created through his thought and study, he was firmly rooted; and when he spoke, he spoke from a firm conviction. This must be considered his most conspicuous characteristic. It was noticeable in his boyhood at the college and apparent all through the years in his public career. If there was an issue upon which he was not convinced, he would not speak upon it. I do not ever remember him, in any of his speeches, weighing one alternative against the opposite and trying to arrive at a conclusion while he stood upon his feet. When he was not yet convinced, he would either dismiss the subject as one on which he had no opinion, or else he would weigh the matter in silence until he achieved an opinion. When he achieved it, he believed in it and advocated it with power. I never heard him give a trivial or a shilly-shallying speech. He always gave the impression of strength, of fearless strength.

It is not the purpose of these few words to enumerate Abba Hillel Silver's many achievements—some of them unforgettable—or to list his books, or analyze his addresses, or try to find the secret of his remarkable eloquence. These lines are meant to convey the impression he made upon a classmate and colleague and to tell what his personality meant to his friends and colleagues in all these years. He was an original. Whatever thoughts he had learned from people or books were reworked and remade into new forms and ideas. He was an embodiment of the best of our Jewish literature. He was a man of ideals and powerful conviction. While he lived, he was a tower of strength to us all, and his honored memory will, we pray, remain to enhearten and to bless.

I. THE VISION

I BELIEVE in myself. I believe in the dignity and the nobility of the soul which God has implanted within me.

Even as I believe in myself I believe in my fellowmen, for they are like unto me in gifts and capacities.

I believe in work.

I believe in the adventure of life.

I believe in saving my soul from wealth and from poverty, and from all the physical circumstances of life. They must not touch my soul.

I believe in never growing old.

I believe in never growing surfeited with life, in never drinking too greedily and too hastily of the cup of life.

I believe in disciplining myself to hunger for things.

I believe that I owe a debt to my God and my fellowmen for the soul which God has given me and for the education which society has afforded me.

I believe in service, first as a payment of a just debt, and secondly, as the only avenue by which men and women ever can find or ever have found real soul contentment and happiness.

I do not believe in being ordinary and average and commonplace. The one ambition of my mortal days would be to break through all the confining circumstances of my world to rise above the dead level of mediocrity, and to raise others; to lead, even as I first am content to follow, to be a pathfinder, to blaze a trail through life. . . .

FROM A SERMON, THE TEMPLE
FEBRUARY 1, 1920

"Choose Life That You May Live"

We begin with two addresses—delivered almost forty-five years apart, yet trying to evoke the same mood. Between the valedictory sermon delivered at the Hebrew Union College in 1915 and the 1959 address at the University of Virginia, the world saw two disastrous global wars, and the development of armaments which could annihilate the human race. But the mature Abba Hillel Silver clings to the same root conviction that he held as a young man. It is the song of his life, his portion in the Messianic faith of his people—namely, that the future can be wondrously good.

This is Abba Hillel Silver's root affirmation—a full-hearted "Yes" to the possibilities of life. Wherever he looked, he saw the "irresistible upsurge" of creation. All nations on earth should participate in this upward thrust. America must continue to be the "land of the rainbow promise." Judaism must ever renew its dream of a new heaven and a new earth. Jewish communities in all lands must have faith in their ability to build a vibrant and creative existence. The ancient land of Zion was destined for a new birth of body and soul.

This kind of optimism would not have been extraordinary in the nineteenth century. But it was Rabbi Silver's lot to speak and lead during an age which witnessed bitter economic depressions, global conflicts, and the annihilation of six million Jews. An optimism which could survive such events had to be based on something deeper than visible surface phenomena.

Abba Hillel Silver drew his faith from a commitment to the classical tenets of Judaism—its command to choose life; its belief in the existence of a Supreme Designer who wanted His creation to be based on foundations of justice and mercy; its assertion that man could and must help God to complete His design. The proofs he offered for his commitment also ran along classic lines. He sought testimony from man's intuition, from the example of great souls and the lesson of history.

Of course, with Rabbi Silver as with any strong and creative personality, these fundamental Jewish doctrines took on the flavor of his own temperament, a temperament which William James would have quickly classified as "healthy-minded." And it was a youthful brand of healthymindedness that Silver called for—called for with as much vigor in his sixties as he did in his twenties. He rejected morbidity and despair. He called again and again for the "lift" which goes with youth. He fought old age wherever it appeared, whether in the tendency of an individual to surrender dreams, or the inclination of a religion to settle in "deep grooves of habit." Rabbi Silver liked the Hasidic interpretation of the Biblical phrase ". . . And Abraham traveled." "Yes, Abraham traveled—he traveled and traveled—from level to level."

This vision of life as a constant reaching for a new, a higher level appears in Abba Hillel Silver's earliest sermons. It is maintained with unyielding tenacity to the end of his life.

H.W.

Man's Hopes in the Atomic Age

BACCALAUREATE
UNIVERSITY OF VIRGINIA
JUNE 14, 1959

This age in which we live is a truly great age, one of the greatest in human history. We are too near our times properly to appraise them. One requires distance in order to see great objects in their proper perspective. We ourselves are too much involved in the turmoil, the fears, and the conflicts of our day to see objectively the amazing new patterns of life which are emerging. In a generation or two, when mankind will have entered quieter waters and a period of consolidation will have followed this explosive and revolutionary age of ours, men will be able to look back upon it and evaluate it properly.

Many people today are filled with dark forebodings and are quite pessimistic about our times. They are quick to describe them as materialistic, as lacking in idealism, aim, and purpose, and as drifting helplessly to disaster in a flaming sea of atomic horror.

I am persuaded that ours is truly a great age. Great and historic things are coming to pass in our day. I am not thinking at the moment of the new worlds which science is continually disclosing, the new insights into the nature of matter and energy, the new sources of power and wealth, the new methods of production, distribution, transportation, and communication. I am not referring to the amazing progress in the medical sciences, nor to the marvels of engineering and the miracles of construction all over the globe. Inventions and discoveries come in such rapid succession in our day that they no longer excite any unusual comment. We take it all in our stride—the flying age, the television age, the atomic age—and now the interplanetary age.

5

In characterizing our age as great, I am thinking in terms of human advancement and civilization. More is being done in our day for the improvement of the conditions of the life of the common man, for the raising of his standard of living, his health, his education, and for his protection against the disabilities of sickness, unemployment, and old age than in any generation—than in any five generations in the past. Never have peoples and governments been so much concerned with the improvement of the lives of men. Never have more determined efforts been made to bring about a fairer sharing of the wealth produced and a better way of life for all.

Never have the submerged races and peoples of the earth, who for centuries groaned under foreign or native tyranny, risen as they have risen in our day to demand and to achieve freedom and self-determination. Within the last fifteen years, one-fourth of the earth's population—more than five hundred million non-self-governing people—have obtained sovereignty and self-government. Imperialism and colonialism are in their death throes. Backward peoples are pressing forward into the light of a new day, and the exploitation of the dark races of the earth is rapidly drawing to a close.

What we are witnessing in our day, if we have eyes not only to see things but to see into the heart of things, is not social disintegration, but a radical new reintegration of humanity, a profound change in the social evolution of man, a change not free, of course, from dangers, but one of boundless and immeasurable potentialities.

I do not wish to overdraw the picture. I am not suggesting that the millennium is just around the corner. There is no country on earth, including our own, which is altogether free from class conflict, from bigotry, intolerance, slums, and privation. It will take centuries, not decades or generations, before all the peoples of the world will possess even that measure of well-being, far from the optimum, which some of the most favored peoples of the world already possess.

The important thing to consider, however, is not whether we are on the eve of the millennium, but whether the major trends of our age are moving toward the hoped-for good society, or away from it. Is our age purposefully trying to eradicate poverty and illiteracy and to raise the standard of living of all peoples, regardless of race or color or creed? Is it trying to satisfy the legitimate aspirations of peoples to national freedom and independence? Is it trying to organize the world for peace and for international cooperation? I believe that in all these major trends, our age has given welcome evidence of serious determination and of considerable progress. It is moving purposefully in the right direction—the abolition of war, the reduction of poverty, and the elimination of racial barriers and inequalities. These are the three major trends of our century. And because they are the major trends of our day, there is great hope for man in this atomic age.

What we need is a strong faith which will sustain us in the long, hard struggle to establish this good society toward which we all wish to move.

Such a faith, in my judgment, is built upon three postulates: the reality of purpose in the universe, the significance of the individual, and the sanctity of method. Within such a faith man will find that measure of dignity, confidence, and courage without which the struggle for social progress cannot long be maintained and the promise of human life must be abandoned to defeat.

In *The World As I See It,* Albert Einstein wrote: "What is the meaning of human life or of organic life altogether? To answer this question at all implies a religion. Is there any sense, then, you ask, in putting it? I answer, the man who regards his own life and that of his fellow creatures as meaningless is not merely unfortunate, but almost disqualified for life."

As man develops in awareness of himself and of the world about him, and gains in sensitiveness and comprehension, he acquires also glimpses of purpose in the universe. He comes to sense what the Prophet Isaiah sensed when he declared: "He is a God who created the world not for chaos, and formed it to be inhabited." Like all human insights into fundamentals, this sense of purpose and meaning is not clear beyond any peradventure of doubt. It is seen as through a glass darkly, but it is sufficiently persuasive and responsive to basic human needs to be enheartening and strengthening.

Addressing the Harvard Law School Association of New York back in 1913, Justice Oliver Wendell Holmes gave expression to just such a strong, mystic, conviction: "I think it is not improbable that man, like the grub that prepares a chamber for the winged thing it never has been but is to be—that man may have cosmic destinies that he does not understand. And so beyond the vision of battling races and an impoverished earth, I catch a dreaming glimpse of peace." And he voiced his faith "in a universe not measured by our fears," but one "that has thought and more than thought inside of it."

A confident faith in a controlling and beneficent purpose unfolding in the universe, of which we and our struggles and our aspirations are an integral part, is, in my judgment, an essential ingredient of that faith which will serve us best in the long struggle for the building of the good society and the attainment of man's hopes. It is the conviction of purpose which alone can bridge for man the gulf between his isolated and homeless self and the apparently alien and indifferent world about him. Man will feel at home in the cosmos only if he believes that it is his Father's house. "Lord, Thou hast been our dwelling place. . . ." Without this faith, he will fall victim to one or another form of moral nihilism as his mind comes to the edge of the wilderness. Atheism has never built any great civilization. It has been responsible for breakdowns, not for breakthroughs.

Belief in the significance of the individual is another essential element of that faith which will serve us best in our propulsive age. In one of his published *Unpopular Essays*, Bertrand Russell writes: "The importance of Man, which is the one indispensable dogma of the theologians, receives no support from a scientific view of the future of the solar system." To which one is prompted to reply, so much the worse for the so-called scientific view, which doubtless will go through many revisions and corrections in the future, as it has in the past. Time and again science has been tardy in arriving at conclusions which the intuitive religious genius of mankind postulated long before.

But Bertrand Russell is entirely correct when he states that "the importance of Man is the one indispensable dogma of the theologians." It is also the one indispensable dogma of democracy; and it is at the heart of the terrible crisis which is tearing our world apart today.

To the religions of the Western world, man has immense significance in the scheme of things. Man is important to God in the unfoldment of His purposes—each man, every man, rich or poor, wise or simple, black or white, saint or sinner. Sin is voluntary abandonment of status, self-degradation, descent into unworthiness and the lower life from which man has emerged. Religion challenges man to live and act always as if his life were tremendously significant and endlessly ascendant.

Religion demands much of man in terms of duty and sacrifice, but it also gives much to him in terms of high and independent status, dignity and inherent rights. "Every man has the right to say," declared an ancient teacher of Israel, "for my sake was the whole world created," and another teacher declared that "man is a co-worker of God in creation."

Religion has endeavored to give man a sense of greatness in a universe in which he physically is small. The world of the ancients was, of course, far smaller in scale than our world of expanding immensities—"one hundred thousand million galaxies in space and each galaxy containing on an average of one hundred thousand million stars," wherein man's racial history is less than a moment in geologic time. Yet, even in relation to their vastly smaller universe, man appeared pitifully puny, lost, and unimportant. "When I look at Thy heavens," declared the Psalmist, "the work of Thy fingers, the moon and the stars which Thou hast established— What is man that Thou art mindful of him, and the son of man that Thou dost care for him?"

Moral aspiration is impossible in man as long as he regards himself as of little account. No moral aspiration ever springs from the soil of belittlement and disesteem. Hence, the Psalmist climaxes his hymn with an apostrophe to man's unique distinction and the assurance of his worth in the world which God created for him. "Yet hast Thou made him little less than God, and hast crowned him with glory and honor. Thou hast given him dominion over the works of Thy hands; Thou hast put all things under his feet." Man's high and noble estate imposes upon him the obligations of aspiration. "Be ye holy for I, the Lord your God, am holy!"

In primitive society the individual counted for little. But as life moved on, the despotism of the organized group was slowly attenuated. The individual began to discover his own private life. As against his heritage of mass tradition, he became aware of personal sources of judgment and sanction.

But man's hard-won victories against corporate authority are never permanently secure. We have witnessed in our lifetime the most massive and ruthless onslaught of *Gleichschaltung*, of *Vermassung*, and of totalitarianism ever experienced by man within historic times. Fascism and Nazism scored terrifying victories before they were broken on the battlefield. But their ideologies are not dead. And Communist dictatorship is today established in a fourth of the globe.

Men are being handled in many parts of the world and in many departments of life impersonally in the mass. Increasingly they are becoming statistics in the hands of a predatory collectivism. They are shunted about like herds of cattle. They are coordinated and subjugated to the state until the last vestige of their freedom and their rights vanishes. Because the religious basis of our society has been widely denied, and materialistic theories of life and history have taken hold of the thoughts and actions of many men and governments, the stature of the individual, and with it, his rights and inherent dignity have suffered tragic abatement and diminution. Every precinct of his life is invaded and violated. Denied the image of God, man is being given the mask of the robot.

The faith that will serve us best, as free men in this great age, is faith in the worth and significance of the individual, and his inalienable rights. Without such faith, written as a dogma into the heart of our Declaration of Independence and our Constitution—"We hold these truths to be self-evident, that all men are created equal and that they are endowed by their Creator with certain inalienable rights"—man's stature will be progressively reduced, the free domains of his mind and spirit will speedily come under ironclad controls, and man's dignity will be dragged into the dust. With such a faith, we will be strong enough to accept all necessary social controls and still remain a free society. It will help us to set our course by a dependable compass.

One of the evil forces at work in the world which tend to undermine the individual and destroy his intellectual integrity is the force of organized propaganda, whose objective is to stampede men to think uncritically and emotionally in the way some special interest wants them to think. Through slogans, catchwords, clichés, and cleverly coined half-truths, it drives men or panics them into attitudes and actions which they would not take if they were given accurate information upon which to base judgments and attitudes. Propaganda in our day has been developed into a dangerous pseudo-science. Through the readily available mass media of communication, it can undo overnight, as it were, generations of slow, patient, and painstaking work of education. Our gravest danger today is not illiteracy. The overwhelming majority of our people know how to read and write. The danger of our day is propaganda, whose aim is to confound, confuse, and misdirect our literate population.

The third element in the faith which will serve us best in our exciting new age is faith in the sanctity of method—the method of human progress. Spiritual religion defined a method by which men might attain morally desirable ends, a method worthy of such ends. It outlawed the notion that moral ends justify immoral means. Each single step on the way toward the realization of a worthy objective must, as far as is humanly possible, be a worthy objective in itself. To establish justice or freedom or peace, men must employ the ways of justice, freedom, and peace.

The more exalted human goals are, the less likelihood there is of their early or complete attainment. Accordingly, when ruthless, brutal, impatient, and desperate measures are employed, they not only make the attainment of these goals impossible; they also turn man's long journey toward them into one of unmitigated misery and horror.

The classic way of religion has never been fully tried in the world. Today in an evolving atomic age wherein man's power is vastly augmented, including the power of self-destruction, religion is being ignored more thoroughly than at any time in human history. State and class autocracies have proceeded on the theory that there is no law superior to theirs, and that their brutal methods are justified by their results.

The shame of our age is that men are committing the most shameless acts of immorality in the name of high morality. Methods which are abhorred and denounced in one's opponents are rationalized and justified as moral imperatives when employed by oneself. Men talk of justice and brotherhood, of a classless society and universal peace, but they act as if these ideals were demons out of hell, lashing them on to the most horrible acts of injustice, hatred, and violence.

It is clearly the part of sound method in our atomic age to look for a workable formula which will regulate the differences between the East and the West and discover a *modus vivendi* for the two sections of humanity which are now so dangerously riven and separated by seemingly irreconcilable ideologies.

It is clear that the rivalry between these ideologies cannot be decided on the battlefield. Both power blocs are in possession of the globe-destroying power of the A-bomb and the H-bomb. Neither will be intimidated by the preponderance of arms on the part of the other. It is inconceivable that the statesmen of the world will be so mad as to try to win a decision through atomic warfare. The alternatives confronting mankind today are coexistence or nonexistence. This being the case, it is clearly the part of patriotism, of enlightened self-interest, and of altruism to seek ways of living together on this earth in spite of conflicting ideologies.

In the field of religious controversy it was once thought that differing religious persuasions could not live on the same earth, let alone in the same country or city. During the seventeenth century Europe was drenched in blood by religious wars. The stakes then were even higher than in our day, for it was not only this world that was involved, but the next world as well. Yet after much bloodshed, it was found necessary at long last to work out ways of toleration and coexistence, leaving the ideologies to take care of themselves. No religion abandoned its position, its claims to being the sole repository of true religion, or its right to missionary activity. But somehow ways were found for all to live together. Today in many parts of Europe and America different religious groups have learned not only to live together but to work together in amity and friendship for the objectives common to them all.

There is no other solution to the political and economic differences which are now tearing our world apart. The dread alternative is universal destruction. For our civilization to survive, it is clearly necessary to revise the mood and thought pattern of our age, and to recharge our world culture with a new devotion to the sanctity of method in human progress.

With such a faith, built upon the reality of purpose in the universe, the significance of the individual, and the sanctity of method, we can spread wide our adventuring sails and plow resolutely into the surge and thunder of our unpredictable odyssey, confident that our high hopes will, from time to time, find their blessed anchorage in some harbor of our hearts' desire.

Dreams and Visions

VALEDICTORY ADDRESS
HEBREW UNION COLLEGE
JUNE 12, 1915

Age worships at the shrine of Memory, Youth in the temple of Hope. Age, no longer able to respond to the incessant demands of active life, retreats into the silent corridors of the past, wandering leisurely through them, reviewing the old familiar things and touching the scented fingertips of long-departed glories. But full-blooded and high-mettled youth, charged with hope and thrilled with ambition, beats impatiently upon the gates that bar the way to the promises of tomorrow and welcomes the new day with its struggles and its tasks and its wonderful possibilities. "Your old men shall dream dreams, your young men shall see visions." Age has dreams—dreams of the days that were. Youth has visions—visions of the days to come.

All great religions begin with a vision. That, in truth, is their moment of revelation and consecration. Then, indeed, all religions are true, for the holy fervor which is theirs purges them of all that is sordid and false. It is then that Judaism, Christianity, Buddhism, or Islam sweep through the world propelled by the power of inherent truth. It is then that all religions are creative, apostolic, and revolutionary. But time soon dampens the first flush of enthusiasm. Religion settles into well-defined grooves, institutional precedents, and traditions. And promptings of the innate spirit of man are no longer the sole arbiter of future action. Tradition, the past, is now the tyrant of the future. Religious thought is no longer evolving, self-expanding, and self-determining. It must now be cast in the narrow molds of dogma, with the result that catholicism gives way to sectarianism, ideals to creeds, religious fervor to stilted piety. Religion,

13

which means essentially the enlarging, the deepening, and the widening of life, becomes untrue to itself in endeavoring to enclose, confine, and circumscribe life. The supreme function of settled religion becomes the glorification of the past, the worship of history, and the conservation of the things that were.

In the dawn of its national life, Judaism caught a glimpse of a wonderful vision which transfigured its whole being. A people of tradesmen and herdsmen became prophets of the living God. Obedient to the beckoning of its vision, Israel discovered new realms for the human spirit, new worlds for the soul's activity. But a reaction soon set in. Phenomenal activity was followed by spiritual languor and fatigue. Age was claiming its due. Law and not life was apotheosized; the Book and not the spirit which produced it. The vital religious instinct of the people, which at all times struggled to express itself in newer and truer forms, became strait-laced in the narrow confines of hermeneutic laws. The past was encroaching upon the future; the dream was stifling the vision.

Such is the uniqueness and potency of Israel's vision that it is never wholly lost. It is a perpetual light that flickers in the vast gloom of life but ever and anon blazes forth in wondrous brightness, illuminating its world. When Israel is least original, least creative, most accommodative, its innate longing for the wider fields of the spirit, the higher levels and the purer air, asserts itself. Hence, a Platonized Judaism. Hence a Judaism beaten into the framework of Aristotelianism. Hence a Judaism acclimating itself to the many schools of present-day realism and idealism. These varied interpretations are the manifestations of the vital impulse of an inspired religion struggling to liberate itself, craving for life, movement, flexibility. Judaism must live and function. It must, therefore, always be fresh, virile, rational, in consonance with the highest truths of the age. Judaism culls truths from all fields of human experience, but it subjects them all to its own interpretation. It combines with them to the greater glory of all component parts.

It is, indeed, in this work of interpretation that the true originality of Judaism lies. Not so long ago the pre-eminence of Israel's religious genius was called into question. The Bible, it was claimed, was an echo of Babylonia. The Mosaic law was a revised copy of the older Code of Hammurabi. The religious festivals of Israel were Canaanitish in origin. The Jews were priests but not prophets; enthusiastic disciples but not masters. A more critical survey of primitive religions, however, soon convinced men that originality in religious thought lies not in the crude matter of laws or customs or festivals. These are the unconscious creations of all peoples, the spontaneous expressions of social activity. True originality consists in the conscious reinterpretations of habitual practices, in the re-evaluation of all social practices with an eye to human regeneration. It is to take the mean clay and mold it into a form of worth and beauty; it is to take the expressionless block of marble and chisel it into a statue bodying forth a divine truth; it is to take scattered words and thoughts and weld them into the glory of a lyric; it is to take mute chords and strike them into a heavenly harmony that calls for the originality of the creator, the vision of the poet, the fervor of the inspired one. Judaism found matter and gave it form. It took the superstitions of primitive man and transformed them. It turned the Sabbath from taboo into a holy day commemorating the covenant which exists between God and man. It gave to the nature festivals significance by investing them with an ethical-historical character. It elevated the Festival of Unleavened Bread by making it a festival of freedom, and the Feast of Weeks by making it a festival of revelation. It took divination and transformed it into prophecy. It seized upon the soul of sacrifice and called it prayer. It raised polytheism to henotheism, and henotheism to monotheism. Herein, then, is the originality of Judaism: in its being an ever-evolving moral form-principle, and an eternal alchemy by which all the verities and sincerities of life are transformed for the weal of the social order.

The Reform movement of the last century, in its radical reinterpretation of the past, in its re-evaluation of all traditional values, and in its adaptation to the demands of a new life, gave another inspiring proof of the originality and the creative genius of Israel. It proved, moreover, that the dream had not yet crushed the vision of the people, that the perpetual light could shine forth in splendor and brilliance if the breath of new ideas but strike it. The principle of reform is the *sine qua non* of Judaism's life and progress, and he who denies it is ignorant of the true essence of his faith. Nay, more: he who in an age such as ours, an age of "inspiration and impulses," of intense intellectual activity, of critical research and unparalleled individualism, would incarcerate the spirit of Judaism in the four ells of the past is an unconscious enemy of his faith and of humanity.

Unfortunate, indeed, would be the lot of us who have been granted the sacred privilege of being rabbis in Israel, were our future task but the preservation of the past, the guardianship of the law; were we to be mere channels through which the traditions of the past should flow. Such a task belongs to old men who have dreams and not to young men who see visions. But ours is the blessed lot and rare opportunity of functioning as active agents in a creative Judaism, of reforming, developing, and enriching our heritage. We enter our new lives inspired by that same vision which led our forefathers out of the mists of history, through the wide stretches of spiritual experience onto the mountain heights of moral achievement. We wish to be true to this vision of our fathers by dedicating ourselves to a Judaism which shall ever echo the highest ideals of the human soul, the loftiest truths of the human mind; a Judaism which shall be the implacable foe of all reaction, the friend of all progress.

The Undefeated Optimism of Our Faith

SERMON, THE TEMPLE
MARCH 7, 1943

There is a Midrash which says that there are ten Psalms recorded in the Bible which were sung by Israel in the course of its history, in the midst of a crisis or after the crisis—ten songs of faith. The first was sung when the Children of Israel were freed from Egypt. The second was the song of triumph by the Red Sea. The third was in the wilderness, when the well suddenly appeared and provided water. The fourth was the song which Moses sang before his death. The fifth was sung by Joshua after his victory over the five Amorite kings. The sixth was the song that Deborah and Barak sang when the Children of Israel had conquered Sisera. The seventh was the Psalm of David when he was delivered out of the hands of his enemies. The eighth was the song of Solomon sung at the dedication of the Temple. The ninth was the song of Jehoshaphat as he went to battle against the Moabites and Ammonites. The tenth is the grand and mighty Psalm which the Children of Israel sang and will sing to the end of days at their future, final, and everlasting deliverance.

It is a beautiful and significant Midrash, which calls attention not to one crisis in Jewish history, but to many. The history of Israel is a history of crises. But from all of them, Israel emerged triumphant and singing, and at the very end there will be a song of everlasting deliverance. This Midrash is but one of many of nigh numberless testimonials which we find in our sacred literature and in our history of the undefeated optimism of our faith and of our people. In every trial, and in every

17

severe national tribulation, there was manifest a remarkably unshakable confidence in the final outcome, in the triumph of the right and in national survival.

There is a famous chapter from the Book of Jeremiah, written just before the first exile—before the destruction of the First Temple. Disaster was in the offing. Jerusalem was besieged. The plight of the city was hopeless. The leaders were about to be led away in chains. The sanctuary of the Lord was about to be put to the fire. At that moment, a moment of dread anticipation, of impending tragedy, the prophet says to his people: "Yet again there shall be heard in this place whereof ye say: It is waste, without man or beast, even in the cities of Judah and in the streets of Jerusalem, that are desolate—the voice of joy and the voice of gladness, the voice of the bridegroom and the voice of the bride." The prophet Jeremiah was commanded by the Lord to buy a piece of land in this country which was soon to be conquered and to have the deed signed and sealed and put away in an earthen vessel, that it would last as a symbol of confidence that "houses and fields and vineyards shall yet again be bought in this land." Optimism in the face of doom.

Whence did this optimism spring? It sprang from the people's unshaken faith. The people had sinned. The people had provoked God. God had punished them severely, broken their national pride, cast them out in exile. But if a sin can bring on punishment, repentance can bring on forgiveness and restitution. There is a just God. There is a just law of providence and retribution. Jeremiah passed through the people speaking in the name of God: "Like as I have brought all this great evil upon this people, so I will bring upon them all the good that I have promised them."

Many centuries later, when the Second Temple was destroyed, and Jerusalem was again laid waste and the masses were led away as slaves to work in the salt mines, it again seemed that Israel was forever lost. At that dire moment of national calamity, the great teacher Jochanan ben Zakkai established a new school. For what had been destroyed? A building! A city! Many cities! An army! Israel was more than that. Israel was a people. Israel was an idea. Israel expressed itself in spiritual powers, in Torah, in a code of life, in a complex of ideals. Israel had projected the vision of a spiritual Jerusalem. Zion and the Holy of Holies were now in the hearts and minds of the faithful. Carthage was destroyed. The Carthaginians disappeared. Rome was destroyed. The Romans disappeared. Judea was destroyed. The Jews survived.

Eliezer, Joshua and Akiba, disciples of Jochanan ben Zakkai, saw the ruins. Eliezer and Joshua broke out into weeping and rent their garments. Akiba laughed. They turned to him: "Why do you laugh?" "Why do you weep?" they were in turn asked. "Behold," they said, "the sanctuary of the Lord, the Holy of Holies! Wild beasts prowl about it. The Temple is destroyed. Our people are in exile. The enemies have triumphed." Akiba turned to them and said: "The earlier prophecy has been fulfilled which said, 'Therefore shall Zion because of you be plowed as a field and Jerusalem shall become heaps and the mount of the Temple as a ruined forest.' Now the other prophecy will be fulfilled: 'I shall return unto Zion, and will dwell in the midst of Jerusalem. There shall yet old men and old women sit in the broad places of Jerusalem and the broad places of Jerusalem shall be full of boys and girls playing there.' If the earlier prophecy had not been fulfilled, this latter prophecy of redemption could not be fulfilled." This undefeated optimism prompted Eliezer and Joshua to proclaim: "Thou hast comforted us, O Akiba, thou hast comforted us!"

As you notice, this optimism of our people was not the result of easygoing lives or of a pleasant, untroubled existence. Out of disaster, suffering, and exile, it rose triumphantly to proclaim its unbroken faith in tomorrow.

The life of our people was never a calm and placid one. It was always a life of swords, of conflict, of strain. The very name Israel was given to our Father, Jacob, because he wrestled with angels and men, and was not defeated.

Our national existence began in slavery and revolution. We reached the Promised Land after forty years of wandering in the desert. A whole generation perished along the way. Our ancestors had to fight for every foot of soil in Palestine before they could settle there. The period of the Judges was the battle age of our early history. Spiritually we fought against the entire heathen world for nearly fifteen centuries—against the paganism of the Canaanites, the Egyptians, the Babylonians, the Greeks, and the Romans. The whole world was idolatrous. One little people alone resisted. From the days of Assyria to the days of the Third Reich, the empires which waged war on Israel were the most powerful empires in the world.

We were never relaxed! We were always braced against alien foes and alien influences. Frequently our people tasted defeat, degradation, slavery, exile, the fury and hatred of rulers and mobs. To have remained full of hope and faith in the future, after so many centuries of strife and frustration and suffering, is a tribute to the soul of the people, and points to deep springs whence the soul draws its sustaining strength.

What were those strengths? Ideas. Certain beliefs. In the first place, strength came from the belief in God. In their successive defeats our people beheld the triumph of their just God; in their rescue they beheld His mercy and everlasting goodness. It was God who explained for them the tangled web of their strange career and checkered experiences. They came to believe that they were singled out for high rewards and hard punishment because God had singled them out for a holy destiny.

Their suffering had one of two origins. Either they had sinned against the moral law and must atone for it, or they, being God's chosen servants, must atone by their suffering for the sins of the world. In either concept there was hope. On the one hand hope in repentance, on the other hope in the redemption of the world. Neither concept yields to despair. Both ennoble. A sinner who is aware of his sin is also aware of God against whom he has sinned; to that extent he is already halfway to repentance and return to God. A man who knows that he is off tune can recapture the true harmony of his life. Our people's faith in God, even when they knew themselves not to be righteous, sustained them in their darkest hour. "Art not Thou from everlasting, O Lord my God, my holy one? We shall not die."

This concept of suffering for the sins of the world—that is, for an ideal—gave a note of grandeur and sublimity to Jewish life in its darkest hours. There was world significance to their tribulation. A great cosmic drama was being enacted and they were the central figures in that drama. They were helping to fashion a new world, as God willed those new worlds to come about. They were helping to perfect a new world. They were the summoned ones to help in that cosmic cause. Being the leaders, the pioneers in the spiritual work, theirs was a crown of thorns. As the hammer of destiny was fashioning new worlds, Israel was the anvil which bore the strokes of the hammering. Suffering for a cause was a badge of honor. Therefore the prophet was able to say to his people: "The people who walk in darkness see great light."

Even the other kind of suffering—personal suffering for personal deficiencies and moral inadequacies—even that kind of suffering may purify a man and lift him to new levels of insight and sympathy. There is a challenging phrase in the Bible: "Moses was close to darkness when he sought God." Often it is in the darkness of our lives, in our misery and in our defeat that we discover God. It is in this confidence in God and in Israel's noble ministry of suffering that the undefeated optimism of our people is to be found.

There is one other thought that I would like to leave. Israel believed, because their religion taught them to believe, in the perfectibility of the world. There is evil in the world, but it can be overcome. Judaism was never a Pollyanna religion. Judaism faced reality; Judaism saw and acknowledged war and poverty, exploitation, lust and hate. These were realities, but they were capable of being overcome, and man has it within himself to overcome them.

The end of all creation is good. All that the Lord has created He created for the ultimate good. The human world was not created that it should run down ultimately into chaos and anarchy. God created it out of chaos. He formed it that man may dwell upon it. Our religion is a Messianic religion, a religion that believes in a nobler, a finer, a juster, more peaceful world when wars will cease and poverty will be abolished, where every man will sit under his vine and his fig tree and know war no more. It is within the power of man to hasten that day—to retard or advance it.

The evil of the world should not discourage man. It should challenge him to work for the golden day which is yet to come. The world can be made livable and men can help to make it so. The pessimistic philosopher Schopenhauer was quite correct when he declared that "optimism is as irreconcilable with Christianity as it is with Buddhism and Brahmanism. The fundamental characteristics of Judaism are optimism and realism."

Our people today face another crisis, perhaps their greatest in history—the crisis of mass slaughter, the crisis of extermination. This is the time to draw consciously and deliberately upon the undefeated optimism of our people, based upon confidence in a just God, based upon the conception of the noble ministry of suffering, and based upon faith in the perfectibility of human society. The world is suffering for its sins. It is atoning for its sins. God will accept the atonement. Even as He has smitten, so will He forgive. That is the law implicit in the history of our people. Men and nations are suffering today. Israel is suffering more than anyone. That has been our tragic noble privilege through the ages. We are again the anvils upon which history is being fashioned. Out of this evil, out of the evils of our day, out of the bitter conflict of our world, a new and better day will come. "The redeemed will yet sing a new song."

Slough Off the Dead Husks

SERMON, THE TEMPLE
ROSH HASHANAH, 1951

There is food for thought in the fact that the Jewish people celebrates its New Year in the autumn of the year and not in the spring. Although the Jewish calendar actually begins in the spring with the month of Nisan, the New Year is celebrated in the fall of the year, in the month of Tishri.

Normally autumn is a season for somber reflections. Of autumn the poet Shelley sang: "The warm sun is failing, the bleak wind is wailing, the bare boughs are sighing, the pale flowers dying, and the year, on the earth, her death-bed, in a shroud of leaves dead, is lying." In such a melancholy season man is inclined to think meditatively and rather sorrowfully of his past. He is inclined to recall rather than anticipate. It is a time for remembrance rather than for hopes. He is waiting, so to speak, not for the curtain to rise but for the curtain to fall.

It is precisely at such a time, when nature is sere and withered and the mood of man is correspondingly low and depressed, that the Jewish people celebrates Rosh Hashanah, its high festival of renewal, whose imperial message is one of challenge, of enterprise, and of aspiration. Against a background of approaching winter and death, our holiday summons men to new enterprise. It urges men to cast off their old, worn garments of weariness, defeat, and frustration, and to put on the new bright raiment of hope. Our Rosh Hashanah speaks of things new—a new hope, a new heart, a new world.

There have always been those who maintain that there is nothing basically new in the world, and those who find newness and revelation everywhere. There have always been those who see no miracles in life at all, and those who see nothing but miracles. The latter are the poets, the

22

saints, and the builders of new worlds. The cynic and the pessimist have
denied that there can be anything new or that life can renew itself, or that
society can rebuild itself after a nobler pattern, or that man can rebuild
a new life for himself on a higher plateau of living. "There is nothing
new under the sun . . . all things are full of weariness. That which hath
been done is that which shall be done. That which is crooked cannot be
made straight, and that which is wanting cannot be filled." On the other
hand, there have been men of faith in all ages who have maintained that
even as God renews His world every day, so can man fashion a new
heaven and a new earth for himself and that there are no limits to the
progress which he can achieve.

There are people who are discouraged or frustrated and who surrender themselves to defeat. They rationalize their surrender in one way
or another. "It is not worth the effort. Life is cheap and meaningless. Man
is caught in a hopeless trap."

There have been and still are religions which declare that man is
governed by fate, and that it is, therefore, hopeless or even impious to
try to change what has been decreed. Such doctrines of fatalism are found
in some of the religions of India, in Islam, in Calvinistic Christianity. It
is at the heart of the present-day philosophic vogue of existentialism. It was
a widespread tenet of the pagan faiths of antiquity.

"Pray not at all," chants the chorus in Sophocles' *Antigone,* "since
there is no release for mortals from predestined calamity." Man is caught
as is a fly in a spider's web. Zeus himself and all the other Olympian gods
are subject to the same blind, relentless force of fate, destiny, or necessity.

The Hindus believe in the rule of Karma. What a man did in his
former existence determines absolutely and inevitably his fate in his
present existence. There is no turning aside. What was done cannot be
undone.

These beliefs and philosophies make man subject either to the
compulsion of impersonal nature, or to the influence of the stars or
planets, or to his own past irrevocable acts or to the unaccountable will-
fulness of some divinity. Judaism denies and rejects all these beliefs.
They are all controverted by the message and the spirit of Rosh Hashanah.

The problem of human freedom was not unknown to the thinkers
of Judaism, and they were not unaware of the difficulty in reconciling
man's freedom of choice with God's omniscience and providence. But the
intellectual difficulty which they encountered in their effort to solve this

problem—one of the many unsolved problems and contradictions which abound not only in the field of religion but in the field of science as well—did not move them to commit the grave error of denying free will to man altogether. They realized that there were limitations to human freedom, but they also realized that there were vital areas in which man was free—in which man had a vivid intuition and an experience of freedom. Because the boundaries between what was free and what was determined were not clearly defined, man should act as if boundaries did not constrict him, insofar as his moral initiative was concerned. As the Jewish philosopher Bachya put it, "How much man is free, no one knows, but he should act as if he were free." In a profound sense, it is our duty to develop the freedom within us, just as we develop our mind and reason, although they too have their limitations.

Good and evil may befall man by accidents over which he has no control, but there is so much of evil that man himself brings about, and so much of good. It is part of recorded history that man has, by dint of his will and exertion, improved his lot upon earth, elevated his standard of living, increased his physical security and the amenities of life, diminished want and poverty, and improved health and education—and there are no visible limits to such improvements. Even though not absolutely free, man has within his limitations accomplished much which he never would have accomplished if he had accepted literally the idea that "that which is crooked cannot be made straight and that which is wanting cannot be filled, and there is nothing new under the sun."

Judaism proclaimed to the world the liberating doctrine of moral freedom, and therefore, also of responsibility. "See, I have set before thee this day life and good and death and evil. . . . I call heaven and earth to witness that I have set before you this day life and death, the blessing and the curse. Therefore, choose life that you may live, you and your seed. . . . Choose ye this day whom ye will serve."

Man is not subject to the influences of the stars and planets, declared our faith, or to external forces which consign him helplessly to the inevitable. He is not an astrological pawn. "Thus saith the Lord: Follow not the way of the heathen and be not dismayed at the signs of the heavens as the heathens are dismayed at them."

Nor is man forever doomed to the errors and the consequences of his past conduct. He is free to repent and through repentance to nullify the evil influences of his past over him. One of the noblest and most inspiring contributions which Judaism made to the spiritual development of mankind was the concept of *Teshuvah*, repentance. Repentance means the opportunity of a new start, the chance to correct what man had left crooked, to fill that which is wanting in one's life. Repentance is the central motif of this entire holy season. It is the luminous theme around which these heroic spiritual days revolve. "As I live, saith the Lord God, I do not desire the death of the sinner, but that he should return from his evil ways and live." "For Thou knowest our frame; Thou rememberest that we are dust."

There are few things that are irrevocable in the world. Death is one of them; but as long as there is life, there is always the promise and the possibility of the new. According to the liturgy of this day, even after God has decreed the fate of a man, even after it is written down on New Year's Day and sealed on Yom Kippur, man can nevertheless, by repentance, prayer, and charity, undo the evil decree.

In our tradition God Himself is represented as building worlds and destroying them—experimenting, as it were, with His own handiwork. God wiped out His first creation because He was not satisfied with it. "And God saw that the wickedness of man was great on the earth and it repented Him that He had made man and the earth, and God said, I will destroy man whom I have created from the face of the earth." He sent the flood which practically wiped out the race of man, and then the Lord God created His world anew.

Not only is man free and able to renew himself and to make a fresh start, but in this enterprise toward newness and regeneration lies the meaning and significance of his life. Concerning all the things which God created in the first days of the world, the Bible says, "And God saw that it was good." The creation of life, the firmament, and of all the beasts of the earth are characterized as good and very good. But of the creation of man, who was made in the very image of God, it is not said that it was good. Because, say the rabbis, man was not created perfect but perfectible. His destiny and the purpose of his life is to perfect himself and his world—regardless of the struggle, the strain, and the sacrifice.

The philosopher William James wrote:

> For my own part, I do not know what the sweat and blood and tragedy of this life mean, if they mean anything short of this. If this life be not a real fight, in which something is

eternally gained for the universe by success, it is no better than
a game of private theatricals from which one may withdraw
at will. But it feels like a real fight—as if there were something
really wild in the universe which we, with all our idealities and
faithfulnesses, are needed to redeem; and first of all to redeem
our own hearts from atheisms and fears. For such a half-wild,
half-saved universe our nature is adapted.

These then are my last words to you: Be not afraid of
life. Believe that life is worth living, and your belief will help
create the fact. The "scientific" proof that you are right, may
not be clear before the day of judgment (or some stage of being
which that expression may serve to symbolise) is reached. But
the faithful fighters of this hour, or the beings that then and
there will represent them, may turn to the faint-hearted, who
here decline to go on, with words like those with which Henry
IV greeted the tardy Crillon after a great battle had been
gained: "Hang yourself, brave Crillon! We fought at Arques,
and you were not there!"

Those who are engaged in creative work—the artist, the craftsman,
the builder, the reformer—experience in their work a sense of newness,
a refreshment and exhilaration, regardless of how humble their work may
be. They seem always to be drinking from the Fountain of Youth. "They
bring forth fruit in old age; they flourish and are verdant."

The great revolutionaries of history believed that they were ushering in a new world and that their achievement marked the beginning of
a new calendar in the history of mankind. Upon the seal of the Republic
of the United States of America the Founding Fathers placed the inscription, *Novus ordo seclorum*—a new order of the ages. They were convinced that what they had achieved was a landmark on the road of human
progress.

I am afraid that too many of us yield too soon to the habits or the
discouragements of our past, the routine of our present, or the sorrow
of some irremediable loss. We become frozen into passivity, resigned or
beaten into resentful capitulation. I am afraid that too many of us
accept too readily old slogans, old standards, and old prejudices. We fear
and resent and resist what is new.

The new is not always the true, but neither is the old. Scientific
textbooks are outdated and discarded every few years. What was universally accepted a decade ago has been found, upon further research
and experimentation, to be false or only partially true, and science has

been quick to abandon or correct. At this very moment science is going through a most revolutionary reorientation, and the most time-honored of its basic tenets and conceptions are being discarded. An altogether new set of principles concerning the nature of the universe, of time and space, and the origin of matter, energy, life, and consciousness is being propounded. The truly scientific mind is humble and is eager for new ideas which can help to explain more accurately the nature, the origin, or the relation of the things and forces in nature.

This is not the case when it comes to the social life of men, their personal lives, their economic arrangements, or to international relations. Here they cling tenaciously to old ways and outdated philosophies. They resent the prophet of new ideas. They seek to discredit or destroy the spokesman of unpopular new doctrines. Men denounce him as the disturber, the enemy. "The man of the spirit is mad."

It is for continuous newness in these realms of human life that our religion pleads. Our faith urges us to make new covenants with a better, juster, kindlier, and freer life, and not to be content with the past. For while there was much good in the past, there was also much evil in it. Our faith urges us not to be content with the present, for while there is much good in the present, there is also much evil in it.

Our present age is tired and afraid. There are no grand liberating ideals sweeping over our world today. On the one hand there is a fearful dictatorship which has been clamped down upon a large section of mankind. This dictatorship is certainly not new. It is a dark and savage tyranny, a throwback to ancient forms of bondage and to the most ruthless voodoo disciplines of primitive society. It is the dead hand of the past, but it is a deadlier hand today because it is veiled in science and technology. On the other hand, human freedom and democracy have lost their revolutionary fires, their crusading zeal. They are on the defensive. They are building a Maginot line around themselves, as a defense against an aggressive Communism. They are joining hands and seeking allies among their sworn and unreconciled enemies. They are not trying to build a world-wide fraternity of freedom-loving peoples, united by common needs and aspirations. They are attempting to cement with gold a military alliance of frightened governments. Democracy is no longer the mighty faith which in the golden prime of its youth shook the foundations of the world, toppled kingdoms and empires, and broke the chains of enslaved peoples everywhere. The democracies seem to have become old institutions which are fighting for survival, neglected shrines at which the fires of dedication and sacrifice are burning low unto extinction.

All this is sad to contemplate. For in essence democracy and freedom represent the newness and freshness of social life, the eternal springtime of humanity. Unfortunately, we have become so accustomed to them that they have lost their spell over us. Somewhere I read the phrase "the film of familiarity," which tragically screens today the great ideals and institutions of liberty, self-government, and the inalienable rights of man which in the past kindled the spirit of generations with high exaltation, with ardor and devotion.

We must begin to see them again with new eyes. Herein lies our salvation. There are times when our liberties are threatened by foreign foes, but most often they are undermined from within, by ourselves, because we lose our faith in them or because of fear, or panic, or impatience, or the disastrous lure of expediency.

Democracy will not be saved for mankind by destroying Communism, nor will we stop tyranny abroad by stifling freedom at home. Mankind will ultimately destroy Communism by living and practicing courageously the exacting mandates of political, social, and economic democracy. It is not in Korea that the issue of freedom versus dictatorship will be settled, but in every town, village, and city of our beloved country, and in the conduct and way of life of every individual citizen here and in every other democracy on earth. The global strategy of democracy begins at home. Our expeditionary forces will do nothing to save it, if it collapses at the base.

We must renew our faith and our dedication to our own ideals and set about rectifying all that we know to be wrong. We should slough off all the dead husks. We should dare to experiment with new forms of economic and social life while employing all the time the tried methods of democracy. Democracy is a permanent, peaceful revolution! It anticipates unrest by timely change and adjustment. Ours is not yet the perfect society. There is still too much poverty, exploitation, bigotry, crime, vice, and group and class hatred in our midst to justify any complacency. Read the record of broken homes, of juvenile delinquency, of gambling, of police and official bribery and corruption, and of influence-peddling. The road is still long, but it is an open and a promising road. "The real slavery of Israel in Egypt was that they had learned to endure it." The danger lies in our accepting as inevitable what is inadequate in ourselves, in our country, or in society.

The message of Rosh Hashanah comes to us with the full surge and thunder of William Blake's mighty challenge:

> I will not cease from mental fight,
> Nor shall my sword sleep in my hand
> Till I have built Jerusalem
> In England's green and pleasant land.

Not only in England, which was Blake's country, but in our own country and throughout the world.

The curtain may be falling upon a dying world. It may be rising upon a brighter and better world. What our God-given Holy Day is trying to tell us is that we alone can determine whether it shall rise or fall, even as we alone must devise the plot, write the words, and act the parts. The whole drama of social life is of our own composition.

It all depends upon our wisdom, our courage, our faith.

Opening Windows on Life

SERMON, THE TEMPLE
FEBRUARY 10, 1957

In recent years a system of thought has won adherence in secular as well as in religious circles, and it is called by a rather difficult name—existentialism. It is a difficult term to define. The system which it covers is rather elusive and lacks logical precision. The secular branch of this philosophy has had as its chief spokesman the French author Jean-Paul Sartre. This philosophy frequently verges on what might be called intellectual and moral nihilism. Existentialism has won a considerable number of adherents in Christian circles, for when that philosophy is translated into theological terms, its main doctrines differ very little from those of Paul, Augustine, or Calvin, except that they are now accoutered in modern livery and seem to possess the authority of the latest in philosophic terminology.

Basically this thought is grounded in deep pessimism, in disillusionment with life. Its mood is a mood of crisis, and its idiom is death. It maintains that man cannot ever escape the predicaments in which his existence is involved. His mind is entangled and caught up in irresolvable paradoxes. His efforts at social reform and ethical self-improvement will never bring about the good society, the Kingdom of God. It is even suggested that the very thought of men cooperating in the establishment of a good society is presumptuous, further evidence of man's besetting sin of pride; that man's only hope in the world does not lie within himself, his efforts, his aspirations, but in redemption by a power not himself—by God.

The founding exponent of what might be called religious existentialism was Søren Kierkegaard, a brilliant theologian who lived more than a hundred years ago. Kierkegaard rebelled violently against the humanistic trends which he found among his Protestant theological colleagues. He was contemptuous of all effort at social reform and at self-reform. His theology was dominated by a tormented sense of guilt and sin and dread and catastrophe, by a tragic view of life, of man's utter helplessness to improve himself.

This system of thought has appealed to quite a number of religiously minded people. The pessimism underlying it has been deepened in our day by disillusionment with those scientific, social, and political movements which promised so much and yielded such a large measure of anguish and human suffering.

Judaism rejects such an exaggerated pessimism toward man's nature and endowments and achievements. According to Judaism's basic thought, man can make, and to a large degree has made, his own world, and in spite of frequent and tragic setbacks it has been a progressing world. Man has moved forward, to more knowledge, higher standards of living, greater social justice, better health conditions, and more intensive efforts toward the eradication of poverty. Judaism takes a wide perspective. It sees man rising, by the power of will and struggle, aided by the grace of God, from the jungle of barbarism, slavery, poverty, and disease to the higher places of enlightenment, security, justice, and freedom. Judaism maintains that there is an ascending curve in the long evolutionary record of mankind.

In the eyes of our religion, pessimism is a form of atheism, for it ignores the creative spirit of God which is in man. It is true that man cannot see beyond the horizon of his times. What is ahead of him he does not know. But Judaism has constantly reminded men that beyond all horizons, and each horizon, is God.

The human cave dwellers certainly could not see the shape of things to come. Yet in their dark imprisoned minds there already lay, impounded as it were, all the marvelous achievements of men that were to come: inventions, discoveries, music, philosophy—things which those ancestors surely could not grasp and certainly could not anticipate. They would have been justified, if they could think at all of these things, in a total pessimism about the future of the race. But they would have been utterly and completely wrong. They did not realize the capacities of their own minds, the reaches of their own imagination. They could not see how the minds of their descendants would push out with an irrepressible urge

—push out like the flower in the seed—push out to see more, understand more, master more. They could not realize, those men who dwelt in caves, our ancestors, that they were but a stage in a long and heroic process of human existence; created beings and at the same time creators; fashioned, yet themselves fashioners. They could not grasp the full play and the full glory of human adventure, the epic of man on the rungs of aspiration and mounting achievements, ascending to breathless heights where they would be but a little lower than the angels. Had they been able to trace the amazing odyssey of their descendants, they would not have despaired of the future of their race.

The human story is the story of the opening of windows upon life. Man has had to remove the dark shutters of his existence—ignorance, superstition, fear. Man has had to open wide the casements, so that light and air might flood his habitations. If man had not done that, he would continue to dwell in darkness, in the dank gloom of littleness and ignorance and selfishness and unfulfillment.

The human story is that of the unconquerable men and women who are aware of, yet at the same time unreconciled to, their limitations, their handicaps, their confinements, and their defeats; men and women who beat and tear at the blinds and shutters of their lives, against the disabilities, till they let in the radiant sunlight of mastery, enlargement, and realization.

The human story is that of heroic men and women who, by their own sacrifices, either of self or of substance, by consenting to be despised and rejected for the sake of an ideal, by becoming acquainted with grief and sorrow for the sake of an ideal, succeed in breaking the chains of other men, lifting burdens from their shoulders and their hearts, and exorcising the evil spirits of fear and ignorance and superstition from the dwelling places of men.

The prophets of mankind, the seers, the poets, the scientists, the seekers of knowledge, the teacher and the social reformer—these are the men who open windows upon life and enlarge man's vision and man's world.

Judaism has always challenged man to open windows upon life—to reach out, to rise up, to go forth, to go beyond. God said to Abraham, "Get thee out from your country, from your kindred and from your father's house—to the land that I will show thee . . . and I will make of thee a great nation." By replying to that challenge, Abraham became the founder of a new faith and the builder of a new civilization. God said to Moses, "Come now and I will send thee unto Pharaoh and bring forth My people out of Egypt." By accepting the summons, instead of remaining where he was, in the comfort and the security of his dwelling place in the land of Midian, Moses became the first emancipator of mankind and the pioneer of human freedom. God said to Isaiah, "Whom shall I send and who will go for us?" And Isaiah said, "Here am I. Send me." By so doing, Isaiah became a prophet to his people and to humanity. Every prophet experienced the selfsame call and the selfsame summons. They were called away from what they were to what they were meant to be. And what were they meant to be? What did these prophets call upon their people to be and to do? "I the Lord have called upon you—I have taken you by the hand—I have given you for a light unto the nations—to open the eyes of the blind—to bring out the prisoner from the dungeon and those who sit in darkness into the light." Open windows upon life— that is the challenge!

The world recently celebrated the seventy-fifth birthday of a remarkable woman who at the age of nineteen months was stricken blind, deaf, and mute—Helen Keller. If ever a human being was consigned to tragic helplessness and hopelessness and uselessness, Helen Keller was that person. Her story is well known to you as it is now known to the whole of mankind. Her struggle upward to overcome her appalling, well-nigh insurmountable handicaps; her indomitable courage, which sustained her as she summoned every ounce of her spiritual energy and resources, trying to piece together an awareness of life about her, to link up through darkness and dread silence with the world of man and of nature about her, to recover speech while unable to hear sound, to educate herself, to go through school and college, to graduate with honors, to become a noted writer, to be able to found institutions for the care of others as disabled as she was—all this has become an inspiring symbol of courage for the human race. By the power of will and faith, by self-challenging and self-summoning, Helen Keller literally opened windows upon the world, for herself and for others.

She could have remained buried in her darkened world, a pitiful and self-pitying victim of fate, but instead she beat her hands against the doors and shutters of a prison house until she was able to step forth free and redeemed into the light of a purposeful and creative life.

Equally remarkable and equally heroic is the life of Helen Keller's teacher and companion, Anne Sullivan. If ever there was a human being who literally opened windows on life for another, it was this fine woman. Anne Sullivan herself was almost blind. Later an operation partially restored her sight. In the book *Teacher*, Helen Keller tells the story of this remarkable woman who led her out of darkness.

> It is interesting that this Anne Sullivan herself had forcibly and with heroic effort to open windows on her own life. She was the daughter of Irish immigrants. She was born in squalid poverty. As far back as she could remember she had had trouble with her eyes; her mother died when she was eight years old, leaving three children. Her father abandoned them two years later and Annie never learned what became of him. Her younger sister Mary was placed with relatives. Annie and her seven year old brother Jimmie were sent to the State Alms House. Jimmie died a few months later of tuberculosis. No one outside was interested in Annie. She had no friends but her fellow paupers. Finally after four years, she managed to escape by flinging herself at a group of visiting welfare workers, crying out, "I want to go to school." At the Perkins Institute for the Blind Annie learned Braille, and the manual alphabet. And she remained at Perkins for six years more, graduating as the valedictorian of her class.

This woman, who had painfully climbed the steep stairway of self-redemption, undertook the task of helping the blind to see and the deaf to hear and the mute to speak in the degree that nature and the resources of the human spirit would permit. Her story has been told— her almost superhuman patience with this child, Helen Keller, whose unconscious rebellion against the unexplained afflictions of her life had made her wild and temperamental; the long, weary hours and days spent in teaching her pupil the manual alphabet, to spell out words which meant nothing until she was able to reach the consciousness of her pupil. Helen Keller describes this moment of miracle which I summarize from her book, *The Story of My Life*:

> It happened at the well house, where I was holding a mug under the spout. Annie pumped water into it, and when the water gushed over onto my hand, she kept spelling w-a-t-e-r into my other hand with her fingers. Suddenly I understood. Caught up in the first joy I had known since my illness, I reached out eagerly to Annie's ever-ready hand, begging for new words to identify whatever objects I touched. Spark after spark of meaning flew from hand to hand and, miraculously,

affection was born. From the well house there walked two en-
raptured human beings, calling each other "Helen" and
"Teacher."

Anne Sullivan eventually taught Helen Keller to read Braille. She
taught her how words were uttered by having Helen place her fingers
on the throat and lips of her teacher; slowly Helen learned how to talk.

At the age of sixteen Helen wanted a college education. She en-
rolled at Radcliffe. Anne Sullivan helped her to prepare for entrance
examinations, sat with her in every class, and laboriously spelled into her
hand every lecture and classroom discussion until Helen graduated with
honors. She pays her teacher the following tribute:

> There was such a virtue and power of communication in
> Teacher's personality that after her death I was emboldened
> to persevere in seeking new ways to give life—life and yet more
> life to other men and women in darkness and silence. Teacher
> believed in me, and I resolved not to betray her faith.
> "No matter what happens," she used to say, "keep on be-
> ginning. Each time you fall, start again, and you will grow
> stronger until you find that you have accomplished a purpose.
> Not the one you began with, perhaps, but one that you will be
> glad to remember."
> And who shall count the innumerable times she tried,
> failed, then conquered?

Here is the full grandeur and the nobility of life! The opening
of windows on life—for yourself and for others.

Such people challenge all of us; such people make us ashamed of
our own all too ready excuses for failure, make us ashamed of our loud
complaining, of our succumbing to the first misfortune, or defeat, or
sorrow.

Every year the American people gratefully celebrate the birthday
of another human being who opened windows on life. Abraham Lincoln
set free not only the slaves, but set many free, really free, of their self-
imposed limitations, of their unwillingness to open windows upon life
because of self-pity or because of fear or because of pride. Men the world
over find in his life a vindication of their own hopes and possibilities.
He too was poor. Poor in a vast, lonely, and empty wilderness, poor in
the midst of a life that was harsh and crude and crushing. He was born
into ignorance and reared in the midst of ignorance—no schools, no
teachers, no guides—an awkward child, an ungainly and uncouth youth.

Yet this man rose out of his world of poverty and ignorance and super-stition and disability, by dint of effort, by dint of what must be called character—for character is the sum total of all that I have been saying this morning.

I chanced to glance at the newspaper this morning and I came across the following interesting chronicle of the failures of Abraham Lincoln:

> Abraham Lincoln lost his job in 1832—he was defeated for leg-islature in 1832—he failed in business in 1833—his sweetheart died in 1835—he had a nervous breakdown in 1836—he was de-feated for speaker in 1838—he was defeated for nomination for Congress in 1843—he lost for a renomination in 1848—he was rejected for land officer in 1849—he was defeated for the Senate in 1854—he was defeated for nomination for Vice-President in 1856—he was again defeated for the Senate in 1858—he was elected President of the United States in 1860.

Because of such men, who will not be reconciled to failure or dis-ability, who are not content to spend their lives in the mean circumstances in which they were born; because of such men and women, who open windows upon life for themselves and for others; because of such men and women, who are filled with what the Bible calls "the power of the spirit," "a people who walk in darkness have seen a great light and those who dwell in deep darkness have known that a light shines upon them."

Nothing Is Changeless

SERMON, THE TEMPLE
SUCCOTH, 1962

One major lesson which we may learn from nature is that nothing is static or changeless. In some phenomena of nature, change is sudden and dramatic, such as volcanic eruptions, earthquakes, tornadoes; in others, change is hardly perceptible, like the quiet action of winds and waves and the slow movement of glaciers. But change, nevertheless, goes on. In all organic life there is ceaseless adaptability, cycles of growth and decay. In plant life there is the bud, the blossoming, the fruit, and the withering. In man there is birth, growth, and death. Nothing remains indefinitely the same.

There is a lesson in all this. There are two forces which are constantly at work in human society—the instinct to conserve and the drive to change. The instinct to conserve, to keep things as they are, is strong. Men know that change is fraught with uncertainty, at times with danger. Why risk experimentation? Why not stay with tradition? Social habits are deep grooves. It is easier to stay in grooves than to get out of them. It is far simpler to do a thing because that is how it has been done right along, or because that is the way all other men do it. We feel ourselves safe and we like to think ourselves free within our customary routine of thought, attitude, and action. People find psychological security in conservatism, regardless of what else they find.

There has always been another force at work in society—a drive to change, to experiment, to probe into the unknown. Perhaps there is a better way of doing this thing. Perhaps there are lovelier and greener valleys across the mountains. Perhaps there are new lands beyond the seas. Perhaps there are hidden sources of power in nature which we should explore. Perhaps slavery and poverty and war and racial hate are not the last word and can be done away with. This is the spirit of inquiry which is at work in man, the pioneering spirit, the adventuring urge which is not afraid to strike out along new and unfamiliar roads.

These two forces have been at war, more or less, with each other since the beginning of time. They are still at war today—the struggle between what is and what ought to be or might be, between shelter and progress, between caution and enterprise.

In our day those who fear all change and who are convinced that social security is to be found only in conserving the old, in remaining entrenched in familiar ways, have resorted to desperate weapons to stop all political and economic change. They have been responsible for Fascism, Nazism, and racial violence. These men are blind to the inexorable law of change which governs all nature and all life—and they are doomed!

On the other hand, there are those in our day who welcome all change, regardless. These men also resort to desperate weapons, to bloody revolution and dictatorship, to force the change which they desire. But a blind idolatry of change, a pointless and unintelligent destruction of old ways and time-honored institutions just because they are old and not because they are false, leads to chaos, not to progress. These men, too, are doomed, but they, too, will not relinquish their hold before they cause much suffering in the world.

Somewhere in between is the golden mean. Our Festival of Succoth symbolically suggests this golden mean. A *succah* is a booth—a temporary dwelling place—which our forefathers built on their way to the Promised Land. A *succah* is not a permanent dwelling place. A settled community does not live in tents. Our ancestors were told to dwell in booths, to be always ready to move on, never to stay put until they reached their goal. They marched, they rested, and then they marched on again. This is the law of human progress!

But even in their wanderings and at the very outset of their wanderings, they were given a Torah, a set of guiding moral principles for progress. They were commanded to build and to carry along with them in their wanderings a sanctuary, a movable tabernacle, to remind them always of the presence of God in their midst. Their progress was to be disciplined by the consideration of moral laws, carried out in the sight of God, and directed toward the Promised Land.

Mere booth-building is nomadism, and nomadism never built a

civilization. Mere "going places," mere "change for its own sake," mere reckless adventure is aimless wandering. It leaves the heart weary and the mind exhausted, and frequently leaves the wanderer lost in a brutal wilderness of scorpions and fiery serpents. But where there is a definite objective and a valid ground for change, and where the methods to be employed are morally sound, then, most assuredly, men should move forward. Then it is wise to regard the present position as only a stage in a process, a stopping place on the way to something better and nobler.

"For I caused the children of Israel to dwell in booths, when I brought them out of the land of Egypt." On their way from slavery to freedom, from Egypt to the Promised Land, there was to be no permanent resting place, and no fixed abode. Nothing must deter the people—fear, danger, or the ensnaring memories of the security of serfdom and the fleshpots which they enjoyed in the land of the Pharaohs. When the Israelites faced death at the Red Sea, with the impassable waters before them and the avenging Egyptian hosts behind them, the divine command was given: "Speak unto the children of Israel and let them go forward!" Always go forward! This is the ordinance of human progress. This is the law of spiritual growth in man. And this is one of the beautiful lessons which the temporary *succah*, so quickly erected and so quickly dismantled, suggests. At no stage in life must we regard ourselves as having arrived. Never say: This is it. I am through struggling, striving, aspiring. This is the place which I have chosen as my permanent dwelling place.

The rabbis have declared: "The righteous have no ultimate rest, neither in this world, nor in the next." The righteous of the earth and the wise among men find their happiness not in complacency, "shut up in measureless content," completely satisfied with the fruition of their life's projects and purposes, but in carrying on, always grateful for what has been achieved, always eager for what might yet be achieved, never disquieted, but always ardent, expectant, forward-looking.

I THINK OF GOD AS of the creative energy of the human universe, the source of all that is and is to be, the substance and the form and the purpose of everything. I think of God as of the personality of the universe, whose wisdom integrates the world, holds it together, directs it to His own ultimate purposes. I think of God as of the omnipotent goodness, as of the ultimate and absolute truth, as of the moral ultimates, the best in the universe . . .

My conception of the universe is not dualistic nor pluralistic but monistic. It is one. God is omnipotent; God is omniscient. For God is all, and in all. It is I who am impotent in many things, and finite and weak and struggling; and God meant that I should be finite and weak and struggling, for without these things human life is unimportant. Infinite life, eternal life, divine life does not require struggle, but human life, finite life finds its whole meaning and significance in passing from the lower to the higher, from the bad to the good, from the good to the better . . .

At times my vision of Him is not clear. At times I feel like a man lost in a fog. At times when I behold about me great sorrow or the tragedies which come into the dwelling places of the children of man, I am full of doubts and fears; I am troubled and bewildered, and shadows fall athwart the broad path which leads to Him. Every man and every seeker after God will have these moments of doubt and fear and loneliness. But as he meditates, as he retraces his steps along the path which he has followed, as he reasons through the problem anew, his faith returns stronger and more healing than before. And on his lips come the words of the ancient Psalmist, beautiful words, healing words: "The Lord is my light and my salvation; what need I fear."

FROM "MY QUEST OF GOD,"
THE TEMPLE
DECEMBER 12, 1926

"The Lord Is My Shepherd"

Rabbi Silver felt that "the accent in Judaism is never on abstract speculation but on an ethical message and a program." There is an occasional talk or sermon which wrestles with the standard theological insolubles—the nature of God, the paradox of free will and determination, the problem of evil. But, on the whole, names like Barth, Heidegger, Sartre, or even Buber—so dear to many religious thinkers of our time—scarcely appear in Rabbi Silver's public discourses.

On the other hand, his faith in God was real. And though he avoided hair-splitting definitions of that faith, he knew when it encountered an enemy. Wherever he met the counsel of despair, or the call to base faith upon absurdity rather than reason, he knew that "Judaism differed." He did not see any point in substituting the concept of a "struggling God" for Judaism's monotheistic Deity in order to resolve the problem of evil. And whether or not evil was real and man was possessed of free will in an ultimate sense, man ought to act as if evil were real and he were free to battle with and overcome it.

One semi-theological issue did engross Rabbi Silver through all the years—the matter of science and religion. A sizable number of his talks and references are attempts to show that there is no conflict between them. On the contrary, belief in God is the most rational of hypotheses when one looks at nature, man, and history.

This is the way of Biblical and classical Judaism—both to deduce what we can about the nature of the Creator from the evidence of His creation, and to avoid overmuch speculation about that which is hidden from the grasp of the finite man. And Rabbi Silver was very much a Jew in the Biblical and classical tradition. Not that he was unfamiliar with or unattracted to the religious moods of Judaism's fringe elements. His doctoral thesis dealt with the speculations, often cabalistic and fantastic, of Messianic groups. His library was filled with well-thumbed and annotated books of the esoteric Jewish tradition. But personally he was a "mainstream" Jew, committed to the classical tenets of the Jewish faith.

Abba Hillel Silver's God is, then, the old Jewish God, who refuses to be caught in any theologian's definition. He is a Deity whose relationship to finite man can be expressed in changing ways and felt on many levels. He is the transcendent and mysterious God whose "thought is not our thought and whose ways are not our ways." But He is also the God who exhorts, weeps with, and comforts the individual. The Jew of old found no difficulty in having a relationship with God who was at one and the same time the mysterious "other" and the intimate "Thou." Neither did Rabbi Silver.

Why I Believe and
What I Believe

SERMON, THE TEMPLE
NOVEMBER 25, 1923

Every so often, one should take stock of his spiritual resources as of his material resources, else they will dwindle through neglect and disappear through poor husbandry. Especially should one try to re-examine the premises upon which the active convictions of his life are based; to weigh and revise, if necessary, his program for life.

Good acts, when they run to habit, create character. But intellectual ideas, when they run to habit, create opinionated men. The mind stagnates and intellectual growth ceases.

Most religious men inherit their religion. They accept their religious ideas without much ado, and pay them the homage of lip and knee. But even these men, from time to time, especially when life assaults the citadel of their tranquillity, oftentimes turn upon these comfortable ideas and begin to demand their credentials and their passports.

I have often asked myself why I believe and what it is that I believe in. One of the primary convictions of my life is my belief in belief. I believe that man has a right to believe, that man has a need for belief, and that man is justified in having beliefs. I do not have reference now to any particular belief. Of that I shall speak anon. I have reference to the privilege of the human soul to exercise faith in those domains which are beyond and perhaps above the ascertainable and the calculable.

Why do men believe? It is, of course, folly to assume that thousands of generations have been hoodwinked and preyed upon by priests and by religious mercenaries who have taught them to believe in things that are

42

not so. That is naive. Men believe for the same reason that they breathe: because they must. The life of man demands physical sustenance. Of course, not everything we believe is so. There are many false beliefs. But then not all the air we breathe is pure. The fault is not in the belief but in the object of such belief.

Belief is the outreaching of the human soul to grasp this confusing complex which we call the universe. Belief is the attempt of the human soul to bring order out of chaos, to piece together the bits of facts and phenomena which are presented to the human mind; to organize life so that man can live within the universe, can thrive and grow.

Here is a universe as it presents itself to man, a universe whose magnitude man's mind cannot grasp, which endures through eternities, unknowable to man. Here is a spark of this universe, the earth, hurtling through space at a fearsome pace, drawing its life from a sea of fire, inhabited by myriad forms of life, organic and inorganic. Life species are born and die, grow and decay, absorb and are absorbed. Here is a world full of beauty and ugliness, of warmth and satiety, of cruelty and pity—a vast vexing complexity. Man stands before it all and asks: Whence and whither and why? What hand fashioned it? What mind conceived it? What are we doing here? What is our relation to it all?

Surely the mind of man cannot be satisfied with the few facts which descriptive knowledge gives him. Man must postulate certain beliefs to make this universe intelligible; to organize it, to make it livable for him.

It is a mistake to assume that there is one world or realm of things that may be known objectively, scientifically, accurately, and another realm of vague, hazy, subjective notions which we call the realm of faith. Everything in life is predicated upon belief. Science, which we regard as objective and mathematically certain, is based upon certain postulates and conventions which cannot, in the very nature of things, be established scientifically. Science speaks in terms of time and space. Yet time and space have never been defined. Science speaks of a law of cause and effect, yet all that science can establish is the law of unbroken continuity.

Science will take a piece of matter, weigh it, measure it, analyze it, and describe it. We will think that here is objective reality; here is truth which cannot be disputed. Yet science in weighing and measuring objects uses the human mind, which is itself unweighed and unmeasured and unfathomable. Science uses the categories of the human mind, which are themselves abstract; and it uses our senses, which are themselves faulty and inadequate and only relative.

Science is now discovering that what we regarded as matter in reality must be reduced through particle and atom and electron to a stream of electric change, just a sea of energy, which is another word for that spiritual something which we call life. Life in motion and life in manifestation—that is all that matter is.

Science has come to realize what religion intuitively discovered long ago: that you cannot reduce life, organic life, your life and my life, to chemical and mechanical terms. You cannot weigh and measure and hope to arrive at the mystery and the explanation of life; and so science, too, has a large measure of convention and hypotheses and faith—all respectable ingredients of that which we call belief.

We believe, then, because we have to, because without belief we could not live intelligently. Now what do we believe in? What do I believe in? First of all, I believe in God. No machine creates itself, and no universe just happened. A world so involved, so intricate, and yet so delicately adjusted implies incontestably a design and a designer, a purpose and the mind that purposed it. We cannot know that spirit, that mind, as we know an object—by our senses; indeed there are many things much nearer to us that we do not know by sight or touch. There are things real and sure that the most delicate microscope cannot see. For example, a human thought. No eye has seen it, no sense has ascertained it. It is not of the things that can be seen; and yet there is nothing more real in your life than that spiritual something which you call a thought.

God created this universe not necessarily in time. There is a creation which is above time. There may never have been a time when the world did not exist, and yet we may rightfully say that the world is the creation, the emanation of God. Man creates a thought, and yet there was perhaps never a time when a living man did not create thoughts. The world is the photograph of the spirit; the world is the mirror, the reflection of God. It is, therefore, in a sense, less real, because it only represents the absolute reality, which is God. God dwells in this world, which is His reflection. The world represents Him, but He has not exhausted the full content of His being, and His reality is not exhausted by this reflection of Him which we call the universe.

I can cast my voice through a small instrument, the radio, and that voice of mine will travel through infinity; it will never be destroyed; it will always endure. Now that voice is part of me. I live in that voice. It carries my message. I create it, and yet I, the content, the full content of my being, am not exhausted by that voice.

I can send a thought through space that will reach a man ten thousand miles from here. I live in that thought; that thought carries part of my personality. It is I, and yet that thought is less than I because I am the creator of it.

I say that while God dwells in His universe, while the universe is the content of God, the fullness of God, God is not exhausted by His universe. The universe changes, grows, and decays, and grows again. It is subject to the accidents of time and place. God, who fashioned it, is changeless, perfect, and eternal.

That is my first belief. And my second belief is this: that the universe which God created is one, for everything has its origin in one, animate and inanimate, organic and inorganic. The unitary cell and man are all of the one. They differ in degree but not in kind. Everything that is, the stone and the plant and the beast and the Spinoza of the human race, may all be reduced to that one substratum, that basic sea of endless energy which is stirred and moved and guided by one omnipotent purpose.

Everything belongs in the universe; everything is linked to one basic purpose; nothing is strange or foreign, and nothing just happens. This purpose unfolds itself in the life of the plant, and the beast, and the individual man, and nations, and solar systems, and the universe. It is one, and everything within that universe is related. You cannot stir a flower without the troubling of a star; you cannot spin a top here but its vibrations will widen and reach out and touch the uttermost sphere of the universe.

That is my second belief. And my third belief is this: that this purpose which we call God is perfect; that the universe is the dwelling place of a perfect plan, which to us, because of our finitude, because of our frailties, oftentimes appears imperfect and inadequate. The soldier in an army of millions, sent upon an unpleasant mission, will sometimes say, "This mission is useless," and he will rebel against it; and oftentimes the captain will think that a certain maneuver is senseless and wasteful and meaningless, but only he who is at the head of that army, the general in whose mind the whole campaign has been planned, can know whether an individual act or movement or motion or maneuver has meaning or not.

There is evil in the world, but there is evil only in our world, in the world of men, and that evil is real. There is sin and suffering and war and cruelty, but all these things have a purpose and a meaning, and evil itself, in relation to the vaster scheme of God, is good.

How do we know this God? We do not know Him as we know a stone or a plant or a geometric formula. We know Him as we know when a thing is beautiful, when a thing is good, when a thing is true. We know Him, in other words, by the whole grasp of our being, by our complete personality. God reveals Himself to man most in moral values. God is truth, and God is goodness, and God is grace. It may not be our goodness and our beauty and our truth, but after all, our beauty and our truth and our goodness is a groping, an outreaching, a quest for the divine wisdom and goodness and grace, and that quest of the human soul is the most divine thing in us, and the most real thing in us. Truth and goodness and beauty in the world are more real than steel or concrete, which seem so dominant and controlling in our life.

If we reach up through these avenues of the good and the true and the beautiful, we reach the throne of God. No man has ever realized his life or ever found the meaning of life in food; no man has ever found the meaning of life in dress; and no man has ever found the meaning of life in passion. But some men, when they heard a perfect harmony, or when they saw a scene of unutterable beauty, or when they loved with a sacrificial love—some men have caught sight of the meaning of life.

When one sees beauty or performs an act of supreme goodness, or when one's mind reaches to a truth, there is a release within the human soul. There enters a glow and an illumination. There comes about an enrichment of personality, an emancipation of the human soul, which caused the seer and the prophet and the dreamer of old in his moment of ecstasy to fall upon his knees and worship, for he knew that God was then speaking to him. That is how men know and experience God.

Now, to this God I should like to pray. He does not need my prayers, but I need to pray. That is how I approach Him. That is the rhythm of my soul on its eternal pilgrimage. He will not answer all my prayers. Perhaps it is better so. But when I pray—and one does not always pray when he utters prayers—when I pray really, there are certain doors opened and certain veils held apart. I see more clearly, and my own will and my own purposes are purged and purified and strengthened, and I know that my prayers are answered.

I should like to attune my life to God's life; I should like to bring myself into harmony with His purpose, and the only way I know of doing that is by living on that high plane of moral values which are the reflection of God's true essence. I know, and you know, and every living man knows that when he is in the midst of a noble enterprise, whether it be in the pursuit of righteousness, or in the quest of beauty, or in the performance of an act of love or charity, he is approaching the ultimates of life, he is approaching a reality which cannot be doubted. He is approaching God. And I know, and you know, and all men know that when we pursue that which is unrighteous and not good and not true and not beautiful, we are being estranged and removed from that purpose which we call God. The one is reward, and the other is punishment—here and hereafter.

There is no other reward but nearness to God, and there is no other punishment but estrangement from God. God does not reward us with wealth; God does not punish us with sickness. The good have suffered sickness and the evil have enjoyed wealth. The reward of the good life is goodness, and the reward of an evil life is evil. Kinship with God, or estrangement from God—that is Providence.

I believe in accepting everything that has been alloted to me, humbly and in resignation. Happiness I accept as a gift; sorrow as a test. "Yea, even though He slay me, yet do I hope in Him." "Thy will be done," said a sage once, "even if it be my undoing."

He is my God in life; He is my God in death. It may be that my life is immortal. It may be that He has imparted to my frail being and to the frail being of all the children of man the gift of life eternal; but it may also be that I am only a spark out of the great fire, a spark which shines for a moment, then dies. But what matters that I die or men die? God lives, and as long as God lives my life and my death are not meaningless.

"In His hands I entrust my spirit, when I sleep and when I wake; and with my spirit my body, too. The Lord is by me. I shall not fear."

Science and Religion

SERMON, THE TEMPLE
MARCH 22, 1925

The conflict between religion and science is more apparent than real. There is no fundamental issue between them. While the conflict has been waged long and furiously, it has been on issues utterly unrelated either to religion or to science. The conflict has been largely one of trespassing, and has resulted from the attempt of the one to poach on the preserves of the other. As soon as religion and science discover their legitimate spheres, the conflict ceases.

Religion, of course, has been very slow and loath to surrender its claim to sovereignty in all departments of human life; and science, flushed with recent victories, has been quick to lay claim to a similar sovereignty. Hence the conflict.

There is, of course, some excuse for religion to entertain imperialistic pretensions, for in religion all the arts and sciences originated and under its aegis they flourished for a very long time.

The first architecture of mankind was religious architecture—the temple. The first poetry of mankind was religious poetry—the hymn. The first drama of mankind was religious drama—festival pageantry and ritual. The first science of mankind was religious science—magic, astrology, and priestly therapeutics. All government was originally theocratic. The ruler was either himself the high priest or was ruled by the high priest. All law was religious law. All social custom was religious custom. There was no separation between the sacred and the profane. Religion enswathed the whole life of man as with an element.

One can, therefore, readily understand the unwillingness of religion to yield up its hegemony in this realm to the steady secularization of life.

48

Such abdication was nevertheless inevitable. The wards of religion—the arts and the sciences—were not content to remain forever under the tutelage of religion, for in the course of time this tutelage became oppressive. As religion was institutionalized it became extremely conservative, set in its ways, and jealous of its prerogatives. The young, eager, and venturesome wards of religion fretted under this restraint. They began to strike out for themselves along independent ways to a freer life. With that the tendency towards secularism began.

Politically the struggle was a bitter one. The medieval church regarded itself as sovereign in all fields of human activity. It claimed supremacy in matters both temporal and spiritual. It inherited the imperial ideology of ancient Rome. The sovereignty of national monarchs was subordinated to the interests of the church-empire. The political self-consciousness of national rulers and peoples could not, however, be permanently repressed. The struggle set in between the secular state and the imperial church. The state triumphed, and its triumph spelt the ultimate secularization of government and the entire state apparatus.

The church lost, but religion gained. Political power inevitably corrupts religion. Politics is essentially a practical problem of administration and of adjusting the conflicting interests of individuals and groups within the state. It must, by its very nature, submit to expediency. To keep the political machinery going it is necessary to make compromises of all sorts. Religion, however, is not a matter of expediency. It represents the ultimate social idealism of the race. It must steadily hold aloft ideals toward which men should move. When religion becomes political it loses its prophetic voice. Similarly when politics becomes clerical it sinks into a morass of confusion and obscurantism.

Science, likewise, demanded manumission at the hands of religion. The medieval church had taken over the astronomy of Alexandria, the metaphysics of Aristotle, the psychology of Plotinus, and the cosmology of Genesis. It gave the obsolescent sciences of the ancient Greeks and Hebrews the imprimatur of orthodox religion. Within this dogmatic framework the newer experimental sciences could not expand.

The unquestioned authority of theological rubrics in scientific matters had to be challenged. The respective spheres of science and religion had to be sharply defined. The process was long and painful. But the work which was begun by Bruno, Copernicus, Galileo, and Kepler was continued with increasing zeal, and religion was constrained to retreat, time and again, before the victorious onslaught of scientific discovery. The church suffered major defeats, first in the realms of astronomy and geology, and latterly in biology and in other fields of human knowledge.

The church did not surrender without a struggle. Blindly it sought to quench the new enlightenment. By means of bulls and edicts, through inquisitions, anathemas, and excommunications, it attempted to prorogue and proscribe truth and to destroy the undeterred truth-seeker. It failed. Here again the church lost but religion gained.

For religion, tied to the dead body of antiquated scientific notions, was tragically handicapped. The authority of its spiritual and moral verities was vitiated by the pseudo-sciences with which they were intertwined. Men could not readily dissociate the two, and their rejection of the one entailed also the rejection of the other.

Obviously the issues over which religion and science, and religion and secular national sovereignty warred had nothing whatever to do with the essential principles or purposes of religion. The church was simply thwarting the processes of decentralization which had set in in the realm of human knowledge and political organization. The erstwhile wards of the church had attained their majority and were clamoring for independence, but the church would not relinquish its strict and jealous guardianship. But there was never any real conflict between religion and science as such.

There cannot be. Their respective worlds are different though not oppositive. Their methods are dissimilar and their immediate objectives are not the same. The method of science is observation, that of religion contemplation. Science investigates. Religion interprets. One seeks causes, the other ends. Science thinks in terms of history, religion in terms of teleology. One is a survey, the other an outlook.

There is no conflict between true religion and true science. The conflict is between superstition disguised as religion and materialism disguised as science, between pseudo-science and pseudo-religion. Religion and science are the two hemispheres of life; they are different although converging truths; they have two distinct areas of service and of investigation. Science concerns itself with the how and the what. What is this? What is its physical and chemical composition? How is this effect brought about? By what cause? Religion concerns itself with the why and the whither, with purposes and ultimates. The method of science is observation and exposition. The method of religion is interpretation and contemplation. Science has an historical interest: How did this thing come to be? What

stages of development did it pass through? Religion has a teleological interest: it concerns itself with the end, the purposes, the goal, the objectives of
reality, concerning which science has no interest. Science concerns itself
with mastery of the physical world, including man; the physical world
which concerns man; the physical world in which man lives: science wants
to discover its laws, its forces, its operation, its construction. Religion concerns itself with man's personality, with his spiritual world, and with man's
spiritual adjustments to this world in which he lives. Science is the response
to the human need for knowledge and power. Religion is the response to
the human need for hope and certitude.

Science and religion have a common source and a common goal.
But their realms are different; their avenues of approach are different;
their roads are different, although they start from the same place. Both
religion and science originate in human life; they are both called into
existence by the struggling, suffering, and advancing life of man. Both are
man-made, and like man himself hedged about with limitations. Neither
can claim superior authority as having come from a superior level. Man
was created out of dust; so was his religion; so was his ethics; so was his
wisdom; so was his science. But inspired dust; dust electrified with the
spirit of God; dust which is continually forming itself into increasingly
ascending loveliness.

Science was called into being by the life of the race, to give it
knowledge, organization, control over the world. Religion was called into
being by the race to give it hope and confidence and buoyancy, to lift it,
to transfigure itself ever and anon. It is not right for science, because it has
been blessed with marvelous achievements in the last few generations, to
assume that it is truer than religion; that somehow it discovers more
objective truth than religion; that somehow it deals with reality, while religion concerns itself with rather vapory, intangible emotions, which, if
you will, you can just brush aside. That is fallacious reasoning. Science has
just as many limitations as religion has, because science is just as human.
Scientific truth is, after all, human truth, and what the eye of the scientist
sees is what a man sees. Absolute reality is beyond the ken of any man—
even beyond the ken of the most powerful telescope and microscope.
Science labors under the same restrictions—senses which are faulty and
inadequate, and intellect which has a definite construction beyond which
the mind cannot go; postulates and axioms which the intellect is compelled to assume, being unable to prove, and interests which the organism

gives to the mind, which the mind cannot escape. In other words, the scientific man is just as bound and shackled by the inevitable human bonds, the needs of the organism, as the religious man. There is no such thing as abstract, transcendental, absolute scientific truth.

Let science continue to discover fact after fact and truth after truth. Let it by all means advance the human mind, expand it, stretch it. Let it give man mastery over the earth, and let religion bestow upon these new discoveries its apostolic benediction, for the true spiritual life does not need clay buttresses and pillars built of sand to support it. Let religion speak of the things which concern the spirit of man. Let religion speak of human personality, where science is utterly lost. Let religion speak in terms of faith, of the origin of human life and the destiny of human life.

Science can discover the laws operating in human life, science can describe; but science cannot account for the vital urge or impulse in the universe, nor can it tell us whither all this stupendous vital force is moving. Chemistry, physics, and biology have never been able to explain providence and genius and the human hankering after perfection, and love and the sentiments of human affection. The scientist can tell you everything about the physics of sound; he can tell you the vibrations of each note; he can tell you about the tones and the overtones of each chord. But that knowledge will not build you a symphony. The scientist is not a Beethoven. Beethoven derived his inspiration not from scientific knowledge concerning sound, but from the deepmost depths of his soul. The scientist of language can tell you everything about words, their origin, their composition, their history, their grammar, their syntax; but the scientist does not write *Hamlet*. The poet derives his inspiration for his creative spirit not from scientific knowledge about things but from the soul of things themselves—from the heart of the universe, the essence of the universe, the will of the universe, the thought of the universe. Religion concerns itself with the heart of things, with the essence of things. Religion is in its own domain when it speaks about God; when it tells men of a benign and intelligent purpose underlying all reality at its beginning and at its ultimate end. Religion is in its own legitimate domain when it speaks to men of the possibility of establishing communion and fellowship with this all-spirit of the universe. Religion speaks its own voice when it speaks of human destiny, of the goal of life, of the things in the golden future concerning which science can tell you nothing but faith can tell you much.

I sometimes think of religion as borrowing credit from the infinite in order to increase the traffic and commerce of human life, which the ready cash of scientific truth would not justify. Religion is anticipatory. Religion projects programs, schemes, and ultimates for the human soul. When religion speaks to man of the endlessness of his life and the eternal quality of his every act, it is in its own sphere. When religion concerns itself with the wish, the wish which is the unit of conduct—for we live not by the things we know but by the things we want; when religion attempts to direct our will, our desire, our longings, our cravings, towards a social end, religion is within its sphere. When religion seeks to unify life by giving it a central motif, to consecrate life by giving it an ultimate goal, religion is doing its work. When religion rediscovers its prophetic voice and speaks to men of justice and righteousness as demanded by the universal spirit, and as demanded by the possibilities of human life; when religion calls men to holiness and to brotherliness and to the augmentation of personality, then religion is itself imperial and queen on its alabaster throne, with none to make it afraid.

Science or religion—which will survive? Why, both—if man is to survive. Without religion, science is a dreadful destroyer, a machine that will crush the very man who invented it; for the mind let loose in the world, unrestrained by ethical and moral consideration, uninspired by purpose, is so much dynamite in the hands of a child. Religion without science is a helpless thing, subject to all the dangers of superstition, subject to constant degeneration, because with the mind atrophied and the intellect left untrained, a man remains permanently incomplete. Science and religion are friends.

God created His world by wisdom, and the beginning of wisdom is the fear of the Lord.

Do Not Be Ashamed to Speak of God

The Development of Human Personality Through Religious Experience

ADDRESS, NATIONAL CONFERENCE OF
SOCIAL WORK
MAY 28, 1926

Perhaps it would be well to begin by defining our terms. What do we mean by personality, and what do we mean by religious experience? I shall not attempt to give you technical definitions, for the simple reason that they are not to be had. We may accept as a working definition the concept of personality as the organized self of man functioning as a unit in social life; and religious experience as participation in beliefs touching the ultimate spiritual realities of life and in the mood and activity which derive from them.

The question presented to us, then, is how such beliefs in the essential spirituality of the universe and the participation in those characteristic acts and words which we call religious help man to function more effectively as a creative unit in society. I maintain that such a faith will, in the first place, help man to surmount the intellectual difficulties which he is likely to encounter, and which, if not overcome, may overwhelm and defeat him; and, in the second place, that such a faith will make possible abiding ideals which will stimulate his will and give direction and unity to his life's purposes.

Not all the tribulations of man are physical or psychic in their nature. We are too prone in our day to reduce all human unhappiness to economic want, to physical handicaps, or to mental maladies. There are other causes which may contribute to the destruction of a man's efficient self, not the least of which is intellectual confusion. There are men who take ideas seriously and who react to them more sharply than to external forces. There are men whose peace of mind depends upon the finding of a satisfying philosophy of life which will master their doubts, strengthen their hearts, and give them confidence and hope to face the disillusionments of life.

Not so long ago an eminent psychologist sent out a questionnaire to a group of men and women, asking them to answer this question: "If you became convinced that God did not exist, would it make any difference in your life?" The replies, as you may well imagine, were varied. Some said that it would make no difference whatsoever. One said that it would make him feel terribly lonely. Another said that it would make him afraid to face either life or death. And still another said: "If I became convinced that God did not exist, I would destroy myself." The last reply seems extreme. But those who are acquainted with the dynamics of ideas, with their powers of disruption and integration, will not question the sincerity of the reply. An idea may destroy and may give life. It may wound mortally and may heal miraculously.

You will recall that shortly after the theory of evolution was launched in the world, a wave of suicide swept through England and Western Europe. The doctrine was new, as yet unanalyzed and uncorrected. There were people who drew some headlong and disastrous conclusions from it. The universe, they reasoned, must be without purpose or intelligence—a blind mechanism moved by equally blind forces. The world of the living is a bloody arena wherein plants, beasts, and men struggle terribly and ruthlessly for survival. Within this fearful world they saw room neither for ideals nor hopes nor spiritual aspirations. Among these people there were those whom life had sorely tried and heavily burdened, and who quite naturally asked themselves: "Why then should we persist in this unequal struggle? Why endure the vicissitudes of fortune? Our sacrifices are of no avail. Why travel the hard road, seeing that at the end of it there is nothing but defeat and annihilation? Therefore death is a welcome release."

Tolstoi, in *My Confession*, writes: "There was a period of my life when everything seemed to be crumbling, the foundations of my convictions were beginning to give way, and I felt myself going to pieces. There was no sustaining influence in my life and there was no God there, so that every night before I went to sleep, I made sure that there was no rope in my room lest I be tempted during the night to hang myself from the rafters; and I stopped from going out shooting lest I be tempted to put a quick end to my life and my misery."

Now, Tolstoi lived a full life. His vital energies were not thwarted or driven into a cul-de-sac. His biological needs, his aesthetic needs, his scientific needs were to a great degree satisfied. Yet one unfulfilled need was threatening to overthrow his whole world. He lacked the sustaining influence which comes from a realization that the universe is not a thing but a personality, the manifestation and the dwelling place of a creative and benevolent intelligence, and that man in his finite way may partake of it, and in his creative efforts is its co-worker.

I know that not all men are as sensitive to the influence of ideas as Tolstoi, but I also know that few men who think at all about those eternal problems of life, the whence and whither and why of things, would not be helped to a sweeter and freer life once this heroic postulate of faith is made the driving motif of their life.

The need of God is as real a need in human life as the need of food. It may not be as immediate, but for the realization of life's highest possibilities and for the encompassing of life's noblest program it is as indispensable. It has sometimes been said irreverently that man created God. Beneath this surface cynicism is a profounder truth, which often escapes those who utter it. The profounder truth is that man is so constituted that the desperate needs and emergencies of his life compel him to create a God idea. Was it not the skeptic of the eighteenth century, Voltaire, who said that if there were no God, the human race would be compelled to invent one? Why? Because man needs the assurance that the great hunger for self-perfection, which is his goad and his goal, may someday be satisfied.

There is one fundamental hunger in human life, and that is the hunger for completion. "There is no motive in life," Professor Hadfield once said, "so persistent as this hunger for fulfillment, whether for the needs of our body or for the deepest spiritual satisfaction of our souls. . . . As nature abhors a vacuum, so every organism abhors incompleteness." In his mental and spiritual life man too seeks completion. He struggles to develop his mind, he strives to improve himself, he reaches into the unknown for new truth and new beauty and new resolutions. There is in each of us an inarticulate yearning for undiscovered continents. We hunger for the limitless horizons, the distant fields of splendor. This spiritual restlessness is man's most precious legacy, his cross and his crown and his immortality. He knows that he is incomplete, but he has a vision of perfection and completion.

In a Godless world man's hunger for completion is doomed to disappointment and must turn to bitterness and gall. There is no room for it there. In a universe wherein there is neither purpose, nor reason, nor intelligence, this hope of man is a tragic, mocking futility. And the hope thus denied, like all frustrated desires of man, will turn upon him and devastate him.

But give that man the faith that he dwells in a universe where God is, where personality reigns, in which all things are linked together by one divine purpose, whose attributes are justice and goodness, and that he, frail and finite though he may be, is yet cooperating in the glorious unfolding of that purpose, and behold, what a current of hope and confidence you send into his life. With such a faith no man can be utterly lonely or lost. The consciousness of God will be like the presence of a mighty kinsman, a friend by his side. Misfortune will not crush him. For is he not always in the safekeeping of One who planned all things well? He will fare forth on the greatest adventure of life in high hope and will seek the undiscovered lands of the spirit, confirmed in the faith that such lands do exist, and that he may someday be privileged to enter them.

There is yet another way in which the experience of faith contributes to the development of human personality. The human soul is frequently a battlefield. The traditional moralist calls it the struggle between the higher and lower self. The modern psychologist calls it the conflict between will and impulse, between the social self and the suppressed instincts, the antisocial self. Man's hope lies in the victory of the social self, and his well-being depends upon the emancipation of the inhibited self through moral sublimation. Man can win this victory only through the exercise of his will continuously, and especially in the great crises of life. And, as Professor Hadfield correctly observes, "Nothing can stimulate the will as potently as an ideal." But the abiding ideals of life must find their source and origin in faith.

If the world is impersonal and mechanical, and man the plaything of heredity and environment, there can be no meaning to human ideals. Why have ideals at all; or, having been beguiled into them, whence will come the courage to endure for their sake, to traverse the dolorous road of frustration before we can reach the goal of consummation? Whence will

come the consoling faith that if we fail, someone will take up the torch
which our tired hands have let fall and carry it on? Whence will come
the great assurance that some day some one will make real the ideals for
which we have given the blood of our souls?

Could you as social workers face the drabness of that world into
which your calling daily takes you, the want, the misery, the stunted
growths, the tangled lives, the sins, the tragedies, if you believed that all
that is, is inevitable; that "that which is crooked cannot be made straight,
and that which is wanting cannot be filled, and there is nothing new under
the sun"? Could you bring to your ministry or could you derive from it
the lift and enthusiasm and the consecration, unless you felt that life is
perfectible, and that men can be renewed and remodeled according to a
higher pattern of goodness and justice and beauty? These are ideals,
grounded not in knowledge, but in faith, faith in the reality of a spiritual
order of goodness and truth and beauty in the universe—faith in God.

The realization of this spiritual order underlying all things makes
ideals possible. And these ideals galvanize the will of man and integrate
his personality. These ideals will redirect into socially beneficent channels
those instincts which he has been compelled to suppress because of their
antisocial tendencies. He will experience a release from conflict, a freedom from bondage which will bring him peace and happiness.

Just as the individual man or woman who is sincerely religious is
better equipped to face the trials of life, so, of course, is the family better
able to meet problems and crises if it is pervaded by a religious sentiment.
The quality of reverence, which all great faith inspires, will dwell in its
midst, and reverence is a congenial soil for the growth of other moral qualities. The home suffers an irreparable loss when it is secularized. The home
needs the spirit of sanctity, the atmosphere which the Psalmist describes
as "the beauty of holiness," in order to preserve itself amidst the disruptive
influences of modern life. A broken home is first and foremost evidence of
a lost reverence, of a broken faith. To conserve the home for civilization
we must have recourse not to legislation but to religion. "Holy, Holy,
Holy" must be inscribed above the portals of our home. God dwells here!
In His presence all of the relations of parents and children, of husband
and wife are determined and sanctified. In such a home the personality
of the parent will be magnificently enriched through the many sacred
relationships of family life, and in such a home children grow up with a
deep-rooted reverence for life's sanctities and sincerities.

If in your daily ministry, then, you can communicate this faith to a fellow human being in need of light and a new source of power, you will be bestowing upon him life's greatest boon, even as you will be enjoying life's rarest privilege. Do not be afraid to speak of God. Do not speak of creed, or dogma, or formula. Do not attempt to proselytize. That is not your task. But suggest to the groping mind or the tired heart the thought of God: Helper, Kinsman, Friend.

Do not be afraid to speak of God because you are a layman. What you require is not ordination, but consecration. All the prophets were laymen, shepherds and herdsmen and carpenters and dressers of sycamore trees . . . Speak of Him not as a professional man. Speak as a fellow human being, a traveler upon the same road, a pilgrim to the same shrine. Speak when life's flood is at its lowest ebb, when all else has failed, and darkness settles on the soul; speak in a still, small, confident voice, of God. Speak, and men will listen and men will understand.

Our Responsibility for Evil

SERMON, THE TEMPLE
ROSH HASHANAH, 1940

Frequently during the past few years, and more especially during the last few months, I have heard men ask: "Where is God?" Men of faith everywhere are being accosted by the same petulant query with which the Psalmist of old was confronted: "Where is thy God?"

Logically, of course, one had the right to assume that now, least of all, would men ask such a question. Witnessing the violent tragedy of death and destruction which mankind has brought upon itself, one had the right to assume that man would turn to God with increased faith and fervor, and acknowledge the complete vindication of Him and of His moral law. But men are seldom logical when they are hurt, baffled, and unhappy.

When men are prosperous they do not worry much about God or His existence. They do not say, to quote Jeremiah, "Where is the Lord that brought us up out of the land of Egypt and that led us through the wilderness . . . that brought us into a land of fruitful fields?" Prosperity and well-being are taken for granted, as man's just meed and due. What we possess and enjoy, singly or collectively, we tacitly assume to be the result of our achievements and entirely due to our merit. "My power and the might of my hand have gotten me this wealth. . . ."

It is when men are hurt, bereaved, or helpless that many people become rebellious and caviling and demand: "Where is God? Why does He allow this? Why does He not intervene?" The power which they did not invoke gratefully in times of prosperity they cavil at fretfully in their adversity.

The truth is, of course, not that God has forsaken the world, but that the world has forsaken God. The ancient admonition has again come true: "And it shall be if thou forget the Lord thy God and walk after other gods, and serve them, I forewarn ye this day that ye shall surely perish. . . ." Never has the law of divine compensation been so completely and dramatically vindicated.

If our days are shot through with agony and despair, if war stalks through the fair cities and lands of the earth, if death rains from the skies and if the four dread, gaunt Horsemen of the Apocalypse again ride through the world, is it not due to the gross and unpardonable sins of our age, to the acts of betrayal, perfidy, and selfishness of governments, leaders, parties, and masses?

The last war was a bloody atonement for wide and universal crimes. After more than four years of massacre and horror, nations resolved upon repentance. They pledged themselves to put an end to the era of political intrigue and national rivalry and to establish a new order, one that would be built upon righteousness and upon respect for the rights of all nations and of all minorities. In their chastened mood they set up institutions and agencies for the peaceful solution of international conflicts and for collective punishment of any aggressor. A new day had dawned for mankind. Like slavery, international aggression and war were to be things of the past. Hopes ran high. Bright trumpets sounded on new horizons.

But it was not long before the new altars which had been erected by a repentant world were defiled by the very hands which had erected them. As the nations moved away from the battlefields where they had known agony, soul-searching, and repentance, they returned to former rivalries and shameless schemes of conquest. The promising new world order was destroyed by the nations which had created it. They scuttled the League of Nations. They undermined collective security. They refused to obey the behest of their own pledges and covenants to protect the weaker nations against aggression and minorities against persecution. The long sordid record of twenty years of moral evasion and hypocrisy culminating in the Second World War need not be rehearsed here. It is all too well known. The statesmen of the victorious nations failed to see, because they were spiritually blind, that the same unchecked and unpunished lawlessness which could bomb cities and civilians in China or Ethiopia could someday bomb their own cities and kill their own citizens. They did not see, because they would not see, that the same unchallenged and uncurbed barbarism which crushed and robbed the Jews of Germany and drove them forth as helpless refugees could someday loot and rob their own citizens and drive out millions of their own people, Christians and so-called Aryans, as homeless refugees. The Poles, in the stupidity of their national arrogance and intolerance, thought that only Jews could be declared subhuman, branded as pariahs and forced to wear the yellow badge of serfdom. Frenchmen thought that only Czechoslovakia could be overrun and conquered. Englishmen never dreamed that their children might someday have to seek asylum in far distant places nor that the ships carrying their children to refuge would someday be sunk by the same Nazis whose fury and madness was scattering helpless Jewish children over the face of the earth. Each thought only of himself. And the God of nations, the God of universal law and justice, meted out to all of them a common cup of staggering confusion from which they must now drink.

Similarly the nations which had lost in the last war were not content to seek merely redress and restitution; nor were they prepared to repent of their share in the crimes which had hurled them and others into conflict. When circumstances came to favor them, their old and for a time thwarted lust for conquest and domination and military glory reasserted itself. Like the dervishes of old, like hysterical shamans, they whipped themselves into an orgy of emotional patriotism and stripped themselves of all the decencies of civilized life. They danced the wild, unrestrained dance of folk pride, of chauvinism and racism. Blindly they cast aside their liberties and their humanities and rushed out, in a berserk rage, upon the world, to trample, to conquer, and to subdue. Madrid, Warsaw, and London could be bombed, never Berlin, Munich, or Frankfurt.

If these peoples are suffering today, and have begun to count their wounded and slain in the tens of thousands, if they know want and scarcity and the biting chill of the chains of serfdom which have been riveted upon them, if they experience mounting physical and spiritual deprivations for which the trumped-up glories of battlefield victories are no adequate compensation, is it because there is no God in the world? Or is it because these peoples have set up in their midst false gods, whose altars clamor for human sacrifice, and whose shrines, like that of ancient Diana of Nemi, call for High Priests who are runaway slaves, who murder their predecessors and must in turn be murdered by their successors? "They chose new gods; then there was war in the gates." When men forsake the God of truth and peace and worship the gods of lies and war, shall they not suffer the consequences? Shall God be held unjust or, indeed, nonexistent, because He avenges His moral law?

There is a relentless exclusiveness to the loyalty which is demanded by God. One cannot worship God and at the same time also worship Mammon, Mars, Moloch, or Pan, tribal and chthonian deities, whose essence is but the magnified frailties of mortal man. "Thou shalt have no other gods beside Me." One must be either for God or for Baal. Our own age has been for Baal—for many cruel and deformed Baalim. And now our earth resounds with the death cries of a perishing generation whose false gods have brought their worshipers to the brink of self-annihilation.

Shall we now blame God, who has warned men, betimes and often, to abhor and to turn away from such false gods, not to covet the silver and gold that is upon them, and not to be ensnared by them? Shall we now blame God, who has commanded man to worship only Him, the God of justice, love, and peace, the Father of all, who loves all men, strong and weak alike, as His children, and who has commanded men and nations to take pity on the weak, to shelter the stranger, and to regard all men as brothers?

Where is God? Where indeed! Men have torn Him from their hearts. They have banished Him from their habitations, from their chancelleries, their academies and from their marts of trade. And now God has returned in the consuming wrath and fire of retribution. He is chastising our age and purging it again. Perhaps this time the nations will learn not to contemn His law or deal lightly with His divine commandments. Perhaps in their common fellowship of suffering they will discover a common comradeship of purpose to defend those common ethical and spiritual ends which are their common safety and which tolerate no exceptions. Then God will assuredly forgive and pardon, and He will return as dew to a parched land, as a healing and a balm. "For God does not desire the death of the sinner, but that he should return and live . . ."

Religion never assumed that God had created a perfect world for man to dwell in. If that were so, creation would be altogether meaningless. Creation would have no history, and human life would be denied all struggle and therefore all achievement. Religious mythology did conceive of a paradise, but it placed it at the two extremes of human existence —at the beginning and at the very end. In the Garden of Eden, before man's fall, there was perfection; and at the "end of days," in the golden millennium of Messianic times, there will again be perfection. In between these points, which are on the distant horizons, there stretches the long, hard road of man's slow evolution, the broken road which winds through a wilderness of disappointments and heartbreaks, but which alone leads man to experience, knowledge, wisdom, freedom, and peace.

God did not create man or society perfect, but perfectible. He gave men a law by which to attain perfection, and a way of life by which to achieve happiness. As an antidote to the selfish inclinations which He has placed in the hearts of men, none altogether purposeless, God gave man the Law. If man chooses to ignore that Law, it is not God who fails man, but man who fails himself and God. It is not for God to make man's world perfect, but for man to perfect his own world according to the Law revealed to him by God. God has left man largely free to fashion his destiny and has dowered him with the necessary measure of will and freedom to carve out a blessed destiny for himself. If man resolves to strive mightily and labor earnestly, he can achieve, so we have learned from experience, high levels of intellectual and spiritual perfection and reach new peaks of nobility and happiness.

But man must be willing to enter the struggle for perfection and to suffer and to sacrifice for righteousness. There is no other way to attain the Kingdom of God, which is the kingdom of man's own blessedness. This is the condition of man's advancing life. This is the law of human progress. Leaders of men, especially, must be prepared to set the example of sacrifice and fortitude. Jeremiah must be prepared to be stoned to death, Jesus to die upon the cross, and Socrates to drain the beaker of death. Such suffering is not punishment, but purification, not merely of those who suffer but of those for whom they suffer. It is in this sense that the rabbis declared: "Blessed are sufferings, for they atone like sacrificial offerings."

Wise men learn from suffering and are improved by it, like malleable iron which is hammered into greater strength by each falling blow. When Akiba was asked to explain his dictum, "Blessed are sufferings," he said: "Menasseh did that which was evil in the sight of God, although his royal and pious father, Hezekiah, had taught him the whole Torah and all the mandates of the good life. All the teaching which he received did not influence him for good, but suffering did. As it is written: 'Menasseh was bound in chains and carried into exile to Babylon and when he was in distress, he besought the Lord, and humbled himself greatly before God, and prayed unto God.' "

Many trials await our generation and much suffering. We may not be at the end of this world war, but at its beginning. The areas of conflict may widen. The tides of death and destruction are sweeping on and may engulf other nations before they finally recede. We will do well to regard this universal calamity as God's visitation for the sins of our age. We will do well to think humbly of repentance and contrition. We will do well to be of strong faith and cling to the conviction of the faithful men of all times that "while the Lord has chastened them sore He will not give them over unto death." We will be wise to gird ourselves morally for the great and long struggle ahead and be prepared to play a manly part in it, for it is better to die as free men for the Law of God than to live as slaves under the law of tyrants.

This hour calls not for fear or doubt or despair, but for faith and valor and the buckling on of armor, both physical and spiritual. We are met in the Valley of Decision, and the hour is the hour of destiny. It is an eternal moment, when epochal decisions are being made which will affect the lives of generations yet unborn. The remaining free peoples of the earth must rally as one to slay the evil which threatens all mankind, the evil which they tolerated all too long and which they permitted to wax and grow mighty and menacing because they were blind, because they had grown thick and gross, had forgotten the covenant of God, and had worshipped "new gods that came up of late, and sacrificed unto demons and no-gods."

We Jews who fought all the savage and brutal gods of ancient days, in the name of a God of justice and love; we Jews who have suffered throughout the ages as we are suffering today, because we were called by His name, must again find our places in the vanguard of the free armies of mankind, and fight, with invincible courage, the bloody priests of the Baalim, all those who breathe hate and war, who would deny man his divine patrimony of freedom and dignity, who would divide the human race into men and mongrels, and who would wield the whips of the taskmasters over an enslaved world.

Because our age has been cynical, so-called realistic and practical, but actually afraid and commonplace, because it has had neither lift nor vision nor aspiring faith, it has gone stumbling from one disaster to another and has finally ended up on the edge of a wilderness. It is only through faith in God, a living nourishing faith, that we can win through.

Democracy without a conquering faith in a living God of justice and freedom cannot win against the powerful forces which are arrayed against it. It must confront Baal with Yahveh. Democracy was born in faith, grew strong in faith, and must die when it loses that faith. Democracy without faith has no spiritual resources upon which to draw, no enkindling loyalty, no vision; and without vision a free people must perish.

If our faith in God and in His moral law can be revived, a faith in and allegiance to a Power that is greater than the state, greater than any or all forms of human organization and authority, then we shall come to know beyond the peradventure of doubt that human despotism and cruelty and hate and the destruction of the weak cannot triumph in the end, and we shall find the courage to challenge evil, the means wherewith to destroy evil, and the strength to endure until the victory is won.

Return Unto Your Rest, O My Soul

SERMON, THE TEMPLE
NOVEMBER 20, 1960

There are times when all of us are inclined to utter that prayer which is found in the beautiful 116th Psalm: "Return unto your rest, O my soul." For we are all human, and therefore subject to all the predicaments of humanity. We are all hedged in and constrained by the inevitable limitations of life. We all experience at one time or another failure and frustration. We are exposed to accidents, sickness, loss and bereavement, to all the scourges and the scars of life. "Man is born into trouble," said Job, "as the sparks fly upward." No man moves steadily through a lifetime of unbroken serenity. Not all of life is banqueting and minstrelsy. There are some whose tears are their food day and night, as the Psalmist said. There are those over whom all the waves and billows of misfortune have swept. There are those who walk the lonely road, who feel themselves forsaken and forgotten in a night without stars. Is there any wonder, then, that a prayer sometimes comes to the lips of such men and women, to all of us: "Return, O my soul, to your rest."

This disquietude of the soul, this dejection of spirit, is a constant in human experience and was known, of course, to the ancients as well as to the modern man. How did the wisest and noblest of them react to it? How did they surmount it? How did our forefathers confront these common, ever-present, ever-recurring situations which brought fear and distress and oftentimes desolation to their hearts? Our forefathers knew the human soul, although they had not developed any science of psychology and were not acquainted with the solemn ritual of the confessional

67

couch. They knew that it was good for man to unburden himself when the load upon his heart was too heavy for him. And so they turned, not to a psychiatrist, but to the invisible God and His invisible presence, and poured out their hearts to Him, whose ear is always attentive: "O God, incline Thine ear to me, and hear my speech." They felt confident that they could always call upon Him. God would be waiting for them. One need never make an appointment with God: "Thou art unto me as a dependable refuge, to whom I can always come." Our ancestors felt relief from despair; they felt refreshed and glad of heart when they could unburden themselves to their God. "I loved it when the Lord listened to my voice, when He inclined His ear to me whenever I called."

They confided to the listening ear of God all that was troubling them, all their dark and dread fears and anxieties, all their heartaches, all their sorrows. "The snares of death have encompassed me, the straits of the nether world have taken hold of me, I suffer distress and anguish. O Lord, I beseech Thee, deliver my soul! Return my soul unto its rest! I am greatly afflicted and men are all a vain hope. I cannot turn to them but Thou canst deliver my soul from death, mine eyes from tears, and my feet from stumbling. With Thee I can walk confidently in the lands of the living."

All this is found in one beautiful Psalm, Psalm 116. Having confided the troubles and the secret burdens of his heart to God, and having reasserted and, in a sense, rediscovered his faith in Him who is gracious, righteous, and merciful and who is near unto all who call upon Him; having confided to Him, this sorely tried, confused, and frightened man then was able to arise from the invisible presence of God, the great comforter, reassured, strengthened, his troubled soul at rest, saying, "O Lord, I am Thy servant, Thou hast loosed my bonds."

Faith in God is the great loosener of bonds. It frees us of all that binds, fetters, and shackles, whether it be the fear of life or the fear of death, whether it be fear of the power of others over us or fear of the lack of power within ourselves. Faith in God tends to cleanse and to clear our hearts, our overburdened and sorely tried hearts, of pride and anger, of envy and lust, of power and pride of possessions, of all which feeds the consuming fires and destroys our tranquillity as well as our integrity. Faith in God brings the balm of life, the balm of resignation and of reconciliation to all human suffering. It was the poet Solomon Ibn Gabirol who said: "Poverty, sickness, and terror are easier to bear with faith." It was the

Psalmist who declared: "I drink the cup of salvation when I call upon the name of the Lord."

Hasidism was a seventeenth-century movement among our people which summoned men to a resurgence of faith and hope, of song and ecstasy, at the very time when the Jewish communities of eastern Europe lay bleeding and broken as a result of the terrible Cossack uprisings, and when those communities had been spiritually desolated by the appalling Messianic fiasco of Shabbethai Zevi. The founder of Hasidism, Israel Baal Shem Tov, called upon the people to rekindle their spirit of hope and faith, to begin singing in the midst of their terrible afflictions. "When God wants to punish a man, He deprives him of his faith." Not of his wealth, not of his health, but of his faith.

I am afraid that many today have been punishing themselves by emptying their lives of a real faith in God. Disinterest does create a vacuum which they fill with something else, with other categories of faith—for example, faith in the satisfaction which material possessions might bring them; faith in the idols of wealth or power or position, idols which simply crumble when evil befalls them. There are those who have lost their faith in God because things have not turned out as they had hoped. I think it was the Austrian, Arthur Schnitzler, who once wrote: "We know of some very religious people who came to doubt God when a great misfortune befell them, even though they themselves were to blame for it, but we have never yet seen anyone who lost his faith because an undeserved fortune fell to his lot." These are the men and women whom the rabbis called men of little faith. "He who has a piece of bread in his basket and asks, 'What will I eat tomorrow?' belongs to them who are of little faith." How many are there in our midst who have more, far more, than a piece of bread in their basket, who have cake and frosting for themselves and their families, who nevertheless burn themselves out before they are forty or fifty years old, trying to make sure that there will be not another piece of bread, but perhaps another million dollars in their basket? What is really the faith of such people? What are they trying to prove to themselves and others? What kind of god are they worshiping?

There are some who believe they have lost faith in God on intellectual grounds. Science has not proved the existence of God! Therefore, faith in God is unreal, unnecessary. But faith is not a matter of knowledge. We are justified in believing even when our knowledge is incomplete. The truly religious man has never maintaind that he knew God—quite the contrary. The most profound religious minds of all times have always insisted that God is unknown, the hidden God, beyond man's grasp and comprehension. Let it be remembered that science has not yet disproved or undermined a single religious truth. Science has not demonstrated scientifically that all life is at bottom physical. It has not explained life and consciousness and mind and will in terms of matter in motion. It has not proved that man is mere clay, worked upon by external forces, a mere automaton reacting to external stimuli. Science has not proved that nothing of a qualitative nature distinguishes man from other living animals. Quite the contrary! It is becoming increasingly evident to the scientific seeker after truth that the hypothesis of a creative intelligence is the only hypothesis which accounts for the facts of existence. Science and religion are not in contradiction. They complement each other. Science is the response to the human need for hope and security and dignity. The responsible scientist will not make any religious pronouncements on the basis of facts gathered in his scientific laboratory. He will not make any pronouncements on the origin and destiny of human life or on the purposes of creation and man's place in the scheme of things. Science offers no philosophy of life, but mankind needs a philosophy of life which is congenial to man's existence on earth and to his striving to perfect life. Man is so constituted that the demands and the emergencies of his life compel him to a belief in a God—creator, ruler, friend, architect of justice and love, and their sure and ultimate defense. This faith, uncontradicted by science, yet responsive to fundamental human needs; this faith, when active and vital, masters man's doubts, strengthens his heart, and gives him confidence to face all the possible sorrows and disillusionments of a lifetime. A true man of faith believes even when he cannot see all things clearly—which man will never see. On the wall of a cellar in the city of Cologne where Jews had hid from the Nazis, the following inscription was discovered after the war:

> I believe in the sun even when it is not shining . . .
> I believe in love even when not feeling it . . .
> I believe in God even when He is silent . . .

This is faith! This is a song in the night! This is the immortal hope, the resurgent hope, the undefeated hope of man. I am fond of repeating the anecdote which is recorded by Solomon Ibn Verga in his account of the expulsion of the Jews from Spain. He tells the story of the refugees who fled. Those who lost their faith remained in Spain and abandoned

their faith; those who had faith fled the country. A shipload of these refugees was swept by a plague, and the captain of the ship cast everybody
upon a barren and uninhabited coast. Most of the unfortunate perished
from hunger and exposure. Some of them pressed on desperately to find
some human habitation. Among them were a man, his wife, and their
two children. They struggled on through the barren wastes until the
mother, exhausted, fainted and died. The man then carried his children
in his arms and upon his shoulders until he, too, fell down and fainted
from hunger and exhaustion. When he came to, he discovered that his two
children had died. He then arose and said: "Master of the universe, much
hast Thou done to make me forsake my faith; know, however, that in
spite of all I am a Jew and I shall remain a Jew, and nothing that Thou
hast brought upon me, or art likely to bring upon me, will make any difference." He then covered the bodies of his dead children with earth and
scrub and walked on into the wilderness to find a human abode. This is
faith! Here in the bitter cry of this tortured Spanish Jewish refugee you
may find a key to the mystery of Jewish survival.

When Job, the utterly righteous man, honored by all and prosperous, is suddenly bereft of family and possessions, and is broken in body by
a loathsome disease and cast out as a leper beyond the city walls, there to
scrape his tortured body with a potsherd; when Job, in the darkness and
the chaos and the bitterness of his soul, nevertheless persists in his faith,
and cries out, "Even though He slay me, yet will I hope," there, my
friends, is faith!

There are not many who are capable of such faith when they are
supremely tested in the crucible of suffering and tribulation. But all may
find what you may call preventive medicine for the unexpected hurts and
aches of their spirits. All men may find a measure of peace and rest of soul
in the midst of the tumult, the turmoil, and the changing fortunes and the
shifting tides of life—in faith. "Why art thou cast down, O my soul, and
why art thou disquieted within me? Hope in the Lord!" The silent stream
of God is always there, all around us. Drink of it! This is how God helps
you. Drink of the stream of faith. Drink of it and your soul will be refreshed and your soul will find peace.

II. THE WAY

B EING by temperament a radical, trying to cling to "root" values and basic principles, I have endeavored not to lose my course in the turbulent but surface crosscurrents of my day but to steer steadily down the sure and deep channels of human progress. I am convinced that there are certain human ideals which are indispensable to any age, regardless of its intellectual, political, or economic complexion.

These abiding social values are quite old-fashioned. They are not new or clever or smart or heady like a new wine. They are as unsensational as a mathematical formula, quite like the mathematical formulae to which physicists are now attempting to reduce this whole complex and exciting universe of ours.

It is with these social tasks that I have linked my ministry. My loyalty to them derives from an overmastering faith in a universe that is not a blind mechanism but a divine personality manifesting itself eternally in wisdom, beauty and goodness.

STATEMENT, *THE CLEVELAND PRESS*
JANUARY 8, 1934

"What Does the Lord Demand of You . . ."

There was never any question in Abba Hillel Silver's mind about where our civilization could find firm ground for its values, where his own people could find their "elixir of life," and where the individual could find steady inspiration and guidance. Torah, the word which in its narrow sense means the Five Books of Moses, in a broader sense all of Jewish sacred literature, and in an even broader sense all learning and wisdom—this was the fundamental ingredient of the Jewish way of life.

Rabbi Silver's scholarly pursuits amazed his colleagues, who knew how congregational life could weaken a rabbi's commitment to study. And, in fact, it must have been very difficult. But every spare hour found him with a book. He even insisted on pursuing studies which carried him into realms of scholarship usually reserved for those who are well protected by high academic walls from the energy-sapping demands of public life. His books, like *Messianic Speculation in Israel* and *Moses and the Original Torah,* or articles like "The Lunar Calendar in Ancient Israel," or the careful research and breadth of quotation which accompanied every address and sermon all give testimony to serious and continuous intellectual discipline.

Even as Rabbi Silver remembered that a rabbi had to "learn" all his life, he never forgot that the central connotation of the title *rabbi* was "teacher." Some rabbis will be surprised to learn that even when he was caught up in the maelstrom of Zionist activities during the crisis years and had to commute hundreds of miles each week, he returned to Cleveland every week to teach classes of children in his temple.

His prime vehicle for instruction was the pulpit. The Temple in Cleveland is still one of the few synagogues in the United States that conduct a major worship service on Sunday morning. One reason for insisting on this Sunday service is the fact that it lends itself to full-bodied presentation of a subject in a way not possible at a Friday-evening or Saturday-morning service. On Sunday the sermon did not have to justify its subject by the kind of linkage with the Biblical portion of the week that is traditional on the Sabbath. The presentation did not have to be squeezed in between a full evening or morning of prayer and Torah readings.

Dr. Abba Hillel Silver used the flexibility of the Sunday morning service to present discourses with a wide variety of both subject and style. There were "inspirational" talks linked to the Jewish holiday calendar and homiletical discourses in traditional rabbinic style. There were discussions of important current events, civic issues, noteworthy books or plays. There were sermons dealing with the problems of personal and family life. And there were discourses whose aim was primarily to impart carefully organized information about Judaism, history, the Bible, ethics, etc. A favorite form of this latter category of presentation was a sermon series which could at times stretch into five or six sections. "The great religions of the world," "A thousand years of Jewish history," "Great women of the Bible"—these were the kind of themes he treated in the series form.

The section which follows offers a sampling of sermons and discourses illustrating the "root" values which Rabbi Silver derived from his religious tradition and which helped him to "steer steadily" through the "turbulent cross-currents" of his day.

How Shall We Measure Life?

SERMON, THE TEMPLE
ROSH HASHANAH, 1928

Each year marks the passing of time and the passing of time brings to us reflections, somber and earnest, touching life, its meaning, its goal, and all its strange vicissitudes. One question among many emerges from these reflections. How shall we measure life? By what rule shall we gauge it? Shall we measure life by time? Shall we say that he who lives longest lives best? Assuredly, there are few people who really believe that length of days is life's highest prize. We all wish to live long enough to carry through our life's program, and to see, if only in part, the fruits of our labor. But we would never conceive of ourselves as having lived splendidly simply because we had lived to be seventy or eighty years old. The size of the canvas does not determine the value of the painting, nor does the number of our years determine the worth of our life. "It is possible," said the Roman sage Seneca, "or rather usual, for a man who has lived long to have lived too little."

If we are to think of life only in terms of time, we are likely to be saddened by the prospect as we grow older. For on the sunny side of the hill of life, on the upgrade, time brings with it joy and eager anticipation, but on the shadowy side of the hill, on the downgrade, time brings with it, as often as not, sadness and disillusionment and the thought of the certain and ineluctable end. In our youthful years time means the burgeoning of our hopes, the relish of novel experiences, the glow of ambition. In our aging years time means the ripening of all things unto harvest, the ingathering, the retarded tempo, the reduced powers and hopes bounded by ever narrowing rings.

It is true that time teaches us wisdom. Time softens sorrows, subdues passions and oftentimes brings peace to the restless soul. But time also wears all things down, robs us of the rich zest of living, teaches us what we cannot do, and brings us at last, spent and wearied, to the gates of death.

What does human life amount to after all, when taken as time? It is amazingly insignificant. The whole life of man is less than a second in the cosmic calendar, less than a point on the chart of time. Our life is just a moment's continuation of that life which was in our ancestors and further back through unnumbered generations in the animal, in the protoplasm, in the unicellular organism, in the sun-heat and the flaming, leaping seas of hydrogen. Our individual life is but an imperceptible vibration in that infinite throb of cosmic life. How can it be measured at all? It is so infinitesimal. What meaning has the flurried eddy of a man's three-score years and ten, when one comprehends the immeasurable sweep of the tides of time? "A thousand years are in Thy sight but as yesterday, and as a watch in the night." Nay, ten thousand thousand years are in Thy sight but as yesterday! Perhaps a thousand million years passed before the first invertebrate evolved out of the lowest form of life. Another five hundred thousand years possibly elapsed before the first vertebrate and the first mammal appeared, and incalculably long cycles of time before man emerged from the man-ape. Against this background of stupendous epochs —eras which even our imagination cannot encompass—what is man's puny life of three-score years and ten?

How then shall we measure human life? Shall we measure it in terms of possessions? Is that man to be credited with having lived most who has accumulated most? Shall we say: "Behold, this man got the most out of life. Witness his wealth. This man got the least out of life. Witness his poverty." Is this the true gauge of life? Few of us would really consent to this. When we wish to speak kindly of someone who has departed from the world of the living, do we say of him: "He lived superbly as proved by the money which he accumulated?" If we were to write our own epitaph, I dare say that this would be the last thing we would think of for our final eulogy.

For few of us are really beguiled in our judgments touching the relationship between wealth and life's real values. Most of us who strive after material success do so not because we regard it as life's highest good and the true criterion of life's worth. Rather do we seek it in order to acquire by means of it other, and to us more valuble, ends—security, independence, power, the respect of our fellow men, and a chance to play a role in the world.

Some people, to be sure, do think of wealth as life's greatest good. In their estimation, life is summed up in beautiful houses and rich appointments, in costly raiment and glittering jewels, in many servants, in much luxury and ease. The wise man only pities them. The wise man does not underestimate the need for material things in providing himself and his family with the indispensable requirements of civilized living. He is not an ascetic and he does not make a virtue of want and privation. But he does not confuse that which is necessary with that which is ultimate. He sees things in their proper perspective—as means to an end, as aids in removing some of the obstacles in the way of life's advancement. He knows too, as Socrates knew, "how many things there are in the world for which he has no use"—how many are the things he can get along without, how frequently the superabundance of things becomes a burden and a drag, and how often wealth makes us slaves more abject than ever poverty makes us. Man does not require much to be happy. It is in his passionate striving after the excessive that the root of his unhappiness lies.

The great Russian, Tolstoi, illustrates this truth in one of his legends called: "How Much Land Does a Man Need?"

Pakhom was a muzhik—a peasant who was not rich but who had enough. He was satisfied. But one day he visited a richer relative in the city, and envy made him dissatisfied. His few acres were no longer enough. He wanted more. So with his savings of a hundred rubles, with selling a colt and half his bees, with putting his son out as a laborer, and with borrowing, he succeeded in buying some more acres. He sowed his land and prospered. He was happy. He thought he knew now how much land a man needs.

But soon the rumor spread that people were moving to new places—down the Volga—where there were rich, fertile acres free for the asking. Pakhom reasoned: "Why remain here in straitened circumstances? I can sell my house and land, and with the money I can buy many more acres down there in the Volga region, and together with the free land which I will obtain there I would have a real establishment." And so he did. He settled in the new place and again he prospered—on an even larger scale. Now he knew how much land a man needs.

But again glamorous rumors reached him of land most good and nourishing in the territory of the wandering Bashkirs which could be had for a song—thousands of acres of it. Pakhom was fascinated by the prospect. So he again gathered up all of his available capital and traveled five hundred versts to the land of the Bashkirs. He was well received and he was told that he could have all the land he wanted. The price was one thousand rubles a day—all the land that a man could go around in a day was his for one thousand rubles. There was but one stipulation. If he did not come back within the day to the place from which he started, his money was lost.

Pakhom was delighted. He knew that with his sturdy peasant legs he could cover a good deal of land in a day—in fact all the land a man needed.

Early at dawn he arose, and with the Bashkirs watching him, he set out upon the steppes. He walked about a mile, halted, and dug a little pit and piled turf in it to show where he had passed, and then went on. He quickened his pace. He stopped and dug other pits. It began to grow warm but still he kept on in a straight line. It was too early as yet to turn around. He saw in front of him beautiful black soil covered with lush, green grass. No, he could not forego that. So he continued in a straight line. The farther he went, the better the land became. He began to feel weary. He thought of turning—but no, he must not miss this land. "Endure it for an hour," he said to himself, "and you have a whole lifetime to live." But the sun was now high in the heaven. And so he turned sharply to the left and went on a long distance again in a straight line. He knew that he should be turning again to the left—but the land was so rich and the soil so moist and fertile. He walked on and then he turned the second corner. When he started on the third side he knew that he must hasten his pace. The sun was already far down in the west. He must now hurry back to the starting point, which was now a full ten miles away. But his legs began to fail him. He felt a desire to rest, but he dared not. His money was at stake. The sun was sinking lower and lower. He took to the double-quick. He threw away his blouse, his boots, his flask. He hurried on, weary and staggering. His breath began to fail him. His mouth was parched. His heart was like a mill beating. He was afraid of dropping dead, and yet he could not stop. He ran and ran. He was getting nearer. Now he could see the starting point. The Bashkirs were waiting. Pakhom exerted his last energies. He threw himself forward with his body, reached out his arms to the starting point, and collapsed. A stream of blood poured out of his mouth and he lay—dead. A Bashkir took a hoe, dug a grave, made it just long enough, from head to foot—seven feet—and buried him.

And this was all the land the man needed . . .

What then is the true measure of life? Not time. Not things. Is it happiness? Shall we say that the man who has been most happy is the one who has gotten most out of life? But then what do we understand by happiness? Shall we say that it is contentment, ease of mind, a sense of general satisfaction with one's self and with life? Then the least enterprising among men, the most stolid and unimaginative, the vegetative temperaments, the meagre souls would have to be accounted the most happy. For these, as a rule, are the most complacent and satisfied. But are we truly inclined to concede this? Shall we say that those whose souls are tuned to a higher pitch, more vibrant and sensitive, the pendulum of whose life swings to greater heights and to lower depths—the artist, the prophet, the dreamer, the thinker, the leader of men—shall we say that their lives are less blessed, and weigh less in the scale of being? Do we not rather see in these lives, shot through as they frequently are with fury and despair, flung into revolt, hurled against the brute might of circumstance, and yet reaching up, tortured and bleeding, for the divine gift of truth and beauty, do we not see in them the very acme and perfection of human existence? When you think of the great men of the earth, "when you call to remembrance the great and the good through whom God hath wrought great glory"—Moses, Jeremiah, Jesus, Michelangelo, Dante, Spinoza, Shelley, Lincoln—do you think of them as happy? Clearly there is no visible relationship between magnificent living and happiness.

The ancient Stoics drew a sharp line of distinction between pleasure, which they called *voluptas,* and happiness, which they called *gaudium.* The distinction is readily apparent. Pleasure is a physical, bodily enjoyment borrowed from without, induced by physical things, by food or drink or play or passion. It is a moment's or an hour's stimulation, followed by sharp reactions. The more it is indulged in, the longer are the periods of reaction, ennui, and depression. Happiness, they held, is an intellectual enjoyment, rising from within, "from our own store." It springs "from the knowledge that we possess the virtues—that we are brave and just and true." Such happiness, which to us seems to be a rather stern and cheerless happiness, they held to be unbroken and continuous. But this Stoic definition makes no allowance for the accidents of fortune, for the sorrows which crowd in even upon the brave and the just and the true —"for the arrow that flieth by day and the pestilence that walketh in darkness," for the evils which come unsought, unheralded, and unwelcome, and which turn even the *gaudium,* the justly merited serenity of men, into bitterness and despair. It is not ours to order "tomorrow's bloom or blight." It is not ours to decree that among the wheat there shall be no tares. Nor does this definition take into account the fact that the very men who most aspire to be brave in a world of moral fear, to be just in a world of oppression and exploitation, to be true in a world of deception and falsehood are the very ones who most often taste the bitter dregs of defeat and disillusion, and who most often experience the feeling of the utter emptiness and uselessness of all their efforts.

No, happiness is not always within our ordering, nor is it ever continuous, nor can it summarize the profoundest meaning of life.

How then are we to measure life? By success? Shall we say that he who has achieved what he set out to achieve has derived the most out of life? Then those with the lowliest ambitions, whose life aims are the most ordinary and commonplace, would have to be adjudged victors by this test. For it is they who succeed most. The man whose ambition is high, who links his destiny to a soaring vision, who brushes aside the petty gains near at hand for the distant goal is not likely to succeed. His hope outdistances him. His arms cannot embrace what his soul descries. Ofttimes such men have nothing to show for their labor but the labor itself, nothing to show for their sacrifices but the sacrifices themselves—and the heartaches.

There is an Indian fable which bears out this thought of ours. An Indian chieftain once commanded his three sons to climb a certain steep and difficult mountain and to bring back some object from the highest point which they reached in their climb. Toward sundown the three sons returned. One had climbed halfway up the hard and dangerous slope and brought back a cluster of rare flowers which he had found there. The second had gone farther and brought back specimens of rare stones which he had discovered there. The third, the youngest and the bravest of the three, had by his pluck and daring climbed to the very top, but he had found nothing there to bring back with him. The crest of the mountain was above the timber line so that nothing grew there, and it was one solid rock from which he could abstract nothing. "Father," he said, "I have brought nothing back. I have nothing to show for my labors. But from the heights which I reached I caught sight of the sea! . . . I caught sight of the sea! . . ."

No, success is no more a true measure of life than it is a true index of character. There are men who are great in the arena of thought and character and helpless in the arena of action.

How then, shall we measure life—our life? Not by time, not by things, not by happiness, not by success. By what? Why, by growth! Growth! Mind and soul growth! How much have we grown since yesterday, since yestermonth, since yesteryear? By how much have we bettered our yesterday's best? Are we able to find beauty today where a while ago we could see none? Are we more reverent of truth today than yesterday? Do we love more truly now because we have learned to understand more profoundly? Do human sorrow and human joy and all the sweet, sad music of humanity stir us more deeply now because we have attuned our souls more accurately? Were there any fears which darkened our days in the past, any hates or bitterness, any selfishness or self-deceptions which we have now sloughed off and cast aside? If so, we have grown and we have lived.

Man's true life does not take place in time or space but in the secret processes of growth. All life is growth. The splendor and miracle of the universe are growth, unfoldment, becoming—the life-seed passing through the dark mysterious stations of death and resurrection until it breaks forth into the breathless glory of flower and fruit. "And the earth brought forth grass, herb yielding seed after its kind, and tree bearing fruit, wherein is the seed thereof, after its kind; and God saw that it was good." This was the supreme miracle of creation. Everything is a growing and a becoming. Nothing is done. Nothing is ended. Stars grow. Planets grow. Worlds grow. Throughout all creation is an unceasing, throbbing life which manifests itself endlessly in endless variety.

To live is to feel continuously the teem and thrust of expanding life within one's soul, the thrill of new ideas, the throb of new purposes, the stir of revelation and new insight. Some plants live longer than others, some are hardier than others, some are more colorful and fragrant than others, some bear fruit while others do not, but there is one ineffable glory which they all share—they grow. They fulfill their destiny. Some men live longer than others, are richer, happier, more successful. That is interesting but not important—not the crucial test. The real test is growth. Do they grow? Are they fulfilling their heroic destiny of endless spiritual and mental inflorescence?

This measure of life is a hard measure, for it does not preclude pain and suffering. All birth and all growth in sentient creatures are attended by pain. This is the law of the physical world. It is also the law of the spiritual world. No one can attain to the compensations of maturity, to the satisfactions of abundant life, physical or spiritual, without these growing pains. We must be ready to pay the price.

If, then, my friend, you have made of your life a developing romance, a legend of budding and blossoms, if you have made your past fruitful and your present a seedbed for future growth; if you are striving sunward even though it be through pain and struggle, if every year an added measure of mind- and soul-ripening comes to you—keener perceptions, finer discriminations, sounder judgments, deeper loyalties; if you feel that you are growing, then you are alive, and the greatness and the glory of life are yours, and you are to be called blessed among the children of men.

The Law of the Golden Mean

SERMON, THE TEMPLE
JANUARY 23, 1949

The chief contributions of Judaism to the civilization of the world are two: the Jewish concept of the one spiritual God, and the Jewish code of ethics known by the general term of Torah. Both of these were evolutions and refinements of beliefs and ways of life which were common in pre-Israelitic times. The originality of Judaism consists not in creating something out of nothing, any more than the originality of a scientist or philosopher consists in creating something out of nothing. Rather does the genius of Judaism and the originality of its contributions consist in having taken the common clay of the primordial and unreflective folkways and molding it into something finer and nobler, thereby enabling mankind to advance to higher terrains of faith and conduct, of freedom and truth.

Judaism was a revolutionary set of moral and spiritual ideas, not a system, necessarily, but a complex of revolutionary ideas which shook the ancient world. Judaism challenged and defied a long-existing and indurate religious culture to which the whole of mankind had been habituated by countless thousands of years. Judaism disputed that religious culture—not the religious culture which was common to primitive and backward people alone, but the religious culture of the great civilizations which had developed along the Nile, the Tiber, and the Euphrates, and on the isles of the Aegean. For a thousand years a stiff-necked, undaunted little people inhabited a narrow strip along the Mediterranean and some hillsides overlooking that ancient sea. For a thousand years that little people clung to its own challenging vision of God and human destiny. It lived there as on some fortress island besieged by circumambient heathen, and it repulsed all assaults which tried to destroy its vision of God and men. After a thousand years of clinging to its own vision and defying the world, this vision finally triumphed.

While Jewish ethics are not a philosophic system, it is not difficult to discover in these principles and teachings certain definite attitudes, certain predilections, certain perspectives, and definite trends which run through the whole pattern of what we call Judaism. This morning I shall refer to one of these characteristic features—namely, the practical soundness, the remarkable sanity, the fine moderation, the utter sobriety of Jewish morals. Judaism is a code of conduct within the reach of man. It is intended for man as he is: a mortal, finite, imperfect, groping, aspiring human being. Judaism is a code of conduct intended for this rough-and-tumble world of struggle, conflict, and frustration—not for some romantic Arcadia. It is a livable code of ethics.

Judaism does not begin by burdening man with the load of an original sin, brought about, according to legend or belief, by the disobedience of the first man. Judaism does not discourage man by proposing unattainable objectives beyond human reach. In the thirtieth chapter of the Book of Deuteronomy we read: "This commandment which I command thee this day is not too hard for thee; neither is it far off." That is the significant quality of this way of life. Nor does Judaism assert that man can never obtain salvation by his own good works, that only God's grace can redeem a man. Again, I refer you to the Deuteronomic text: "Behold I have set before thee this day life and good; death and evil . . . choose thou life." It is for man to determine his own ethical destiny! God is merciful and compassionate. God will help, God will receive the repentant sinner, but it is man who must find the way to God.

This fine moderation of Jewish ethics was something more than the Greek idea of the golden mean. The Greeks, one of the most marvelous people of all times, also a small people, were artists by nature, and they favored in all things proportion, order, symmetry, balance. On the portals of the Temple of Apollo at Delphi were inscribed the words "Nothing in excess." Virtuous conduct is balanced conduct. Evil is excess. Evil is deficiency.

This concept is not quite adequate as an ethical formula for human conduct. It does not provide for the practices of self-sacrifice, martyrdom, and humility. It does not provide for the qualities which occupy such an important place both in Jewish and Christian ethical thinking—resignation and compassion and forgiveness. Judaism taught men to aspire, to strive after perfection, not necessarily to seek a golden mean. "After the Lord thy God shall ye walk."

God is infinite. How can man presume to walk after God? This means to try in your human way to copy the attributes which Torah ascribes to God. Just as God visits the sick and comforts the mourners, so do you in your life seek to imitate these qualities. Judaism urged that a man should sanctify himself in matters permitted to him, and above all, Judaism challenged a man to help establish the Kingdom of God upon earth, to fight for justice, to war against wrong. The ideal man was not the imperturbable aristocrat, but the man who stepped into the bloody arena of life. The Greeks produced marvelous philosophers and artists, but no prophets. Judaism produced the prophets of mankind.

Jewish ethics cannot quite accept the Greek idea of the golden mean as the complete and comprehensive ethical formula. Judaism demands more of man than the finding of a balance between two extremes. However, Judaism also tells man: "Thine is not the duty to complete the task, neither art thou free to desist from it." The road is long and hard. The goals of mankind are far distant. Strive to reach them, but do not break your heart. If you have advanced one step in the right direction, if you have helped your community, your family, or one human being to advance one step toward the Kingdom of God, be satisfied.

Balance, but never indifference. Balance, but never inactivity. Let me point to a few ethical judgments and ordinances which illustrate this quality of temperateness. Take the question of property. Private property or possession of wealth are subjects which have agitated society since the beginning of time and remain today the great foci of conflict and international struggle. Some schools of thought declare that the possession of private property is morally wrong, and that the possession of wealth is an unmitigated evil. Famous religious orders have been founded on the principle of voluntary poverty along with the rules of chastity and obedience. Poverty is one of the three principles of monastic life. "If thou wilt be perfect, go and sell what thou hast and give it to the poor. And thou shalt have treasure in heaven, and then come and follow me."

Judaism makes no such demands. Possession is not looked upon as evil. We are admonished to respect the property of our neighbor just as we do our own. We are admonished to share what we have and to help the less fortunate. We are not admonished to help others by becoming poor ourselves. We are called on to abolish poverty by assisting justice in society. The desirable norm is expressed in the prayer of a pious man who turns to God and says: "O God, give me neither poverty nor riches. Give me my daily bread lest I be rich and deny God, or lest I be poor and profane the name of God."

In the New Testament Jesus outrages the ethics of the Judaism of his day. He says, "Ye have heard that it hath been said: Thou shalt love thy neighbor and hate thine enemy. But I say unto you, love your enemies." Nowhere in the Hebrew Bible is anyone taught to hate his enemy; nor, on the other hand, do we find "love thine enemy," because to do so is psychologically impossible. We are admonished in Leviticus: "Thou shalt not hate thy brother. Thou shalt not take vengeance." We are urged to forgive our enemies, but we are not admonished to love our enemies. We are told to love our neighbors, and to welcome the stranger. In interpreting the concept "love thy neighbor as thyself," the rabbis pointed out that, if exaggerated, the maxim suggests an impossible standard. Properly interpreted, it means that all that one expects his friends to do for him he should be prepared to do for them. One does not expect his neighbor to sacrifice his life for him. "Love thy neighbor as thyself" is fittingly interpreted by Hillel: "If I am not for myself, who will be? But if I am only for myself, what am I?"

Life is possible only through cooperation between men, and no more is really necessary to keep this a decent world in which to live. There are times when a man must endanger his life to save his neighbor. If your neighbor is drowning, for example, it is your duty to rush to his rescue even if you endanger your own life in so doing. But in the ordinary run of things such sacrifices are not demanded of a man.

An interesting problem is posed by the rabbis. Two men are lost in the wilderness and in danger of dying of thirst. There is not enough water in the flask for two. If they share, both will die. What is proper? One teacher says both should share, that neither should see the death of his friend. Akiba pronounced the ethical decree: "The one who holds the flask shall drink and live." Let one life at least be saved. How can you know your life is less than your neighbor's? A man is obligated to fulfill all the commandments, but not to sacrifice his life for them, except for three—idolatry, incest, and murder. All the other commandments are pushed aside when it is a question of life and death. All the laws of the Sabbath can be abrogated to save a human life. When a man willingly sacrifices his life in the observance of a commandment, he is guilty of destroying a human life.

An instance of the committed rationality of Jewish ethical ideas involves the question of divorce. In early Christianity, divorce was looked upon as immoral and remarriage was termed adultery. Orthodox Christianity still holds this view. On the other hand, in pagan society, especially in the Roman world, divorce was so frequent that the family unit disintegrated. What was the Jewish attitude toward divorce? Jewish laws did not make divorce difficult. Legally, the right to divorce remained undisputed. But the ethical sense of the people drew safeguards around the law in order to reduce the incidence of divorce. It was not prohibited, but the moral sense of the people created a public opinion so powerful as to discourage its practice. In the Book of Malachi, we have the statement: "And this further ye do: ye cover the altar of the Lord with tears. With weeping and with sighing, insomuch that He regardeth not the offering any more, neither receiveth it with goodwill at your hand. Yet ye say: wherefore? Because the Lord hath been witness between thee and the wife of thy youth, against whom thou hast dealt treacherously though she is thy companion and the wife of thy covenant . . . for I hate 'putting away,' saith the Lord, the God of Israel." In the Talmud we find such dicta as this: "Whoever divorces his wife, the altar sheds tears on his account." Judaism did not set up any inflexible laws prohibiting divorce. Judaism did not force people who could not live together to continue their unwilling bonds. On the other hand, it gave no encouragement to the practice of cheap and easy divorce.

On the whole subject of sex Jewish ethics were sound and sane. In ancient times and to this day religious sanction is often given to celibacy, especially among priests and holy men. Celibacy was based upon the dualistic view that the world consists of matter and spirit. Matter is the source of evil, and therefore sex impulses are hostile to man's development. In Buddhism and Christianity the idea is developed that the perfect spiritual life is one of celibacy. There is no monkery in Judaism. Judaism never accepted the philosophy that the body is evil. "The spirit is thine and so is the body." "Marriage is holy and numerous offspring are a blessing from God." "Be ye fruitful and multiply and replenish the earth." Paul granted the necessity of marriage only to curtail immorality, but the unmarried state was preferable. Judaism consecrated marriage: "He who has no wife remains without joy, without blessing, without a helper.

He is not a whole and completed man." It is overindulgence, lust and not love, which is deprecated by Judaism. Similarly Judaism never accepted asceticism as a way of life. Judaism wanted men and women to enjoy all that was put on earth for the enjoyment of man.

Take the matter of war and peace. Some religions preach pacifism as an ethical ideal. And, of course, there is the teaching of the founder of Christianity, "turn the other cheek." Judaism was the first great religion to teach peace. "Beat thy swords into plowshares, thy spears into pruning hooks. . . ." On the other hand Judaism never taught that men should not resist evil and that wars were always wrong. The most peace-loving man of the Bible was Abraham. When his herdsmen and those of his cousin, Lot, began to quarrel among themselves because the cattle of each had multiplied to the extent where the land could not feed them all, Abraham went to Lot and said, "Why should we fight one another? The earth lies open before us. Choose what you want. If you wish to go with your herds to the north, I will go to the south; if you go to the east, I will go to the west. Let us not fight with one another." But this same Abraham, when Lot was attacked by marauders, marshaled his entire household, pursued the rebels, slew them and recovered Lot's possessions. Wrong must frequently be resisted, but the goal of life is the peaceful adjustment of differences and disputes among men and nations.

Balance, but never indifference. Balance, but never inactivity. A man should do that which he owes to himself, to society, to God. He should not sacrifice one for the other. And within this system Judaism taught man that he can live a happy, wholesome, and harmonious life.

The Vision of the One World

SERMON, THE TEMPLE
JANUARY 30, 1949

When Israel proclaimed the ideal of the one God, it also proclaimed the ideal of the one world. The concept of one Creator means not only that the whole physical universe is one, but that the whole of humanity is one. The physical universe is one, and that means not only the earth and the planets and the solar system, but all the vast galaxies and oceans of suns and star fields—all that is in the infinite reaches of space has been created by one God and is governed by the laws fixed by the one Creator. "He commanded the sun and sealeth up the stars. He alone stretcheth out the heavens," we read in Job; "he alone made the Bear, Orion, the Pleiades, and the Chambers of the South."

Polytheism posited a pluralistic universe, a universe of separate spheres, each one governed by its own deity. Polytheism therefore also posited a world of men that was broken up into separate races, nations, peoples, and tribes, each one governed by its own deity and by numerous minor subsidiary deities. Judaism, on the other hand, in positing one universe, also posited one human race created and governed by the one universal God. Judaism rejected polytheism; it rejected henotheism, which is the belief in one God for each nation or race or tribe. Judaism rejected trinitarianism; it rejected dualism; it rejected every doctrine which tended to attenuate, lessen, or qualify the absolute unity of God. For each such attenuation meant not only the lessening of God's omnipotence, but also introduced the idea of division in the universe. This same concept, when it came to be reflected in ethics, meant a division in humanity, and that Judaism would not accept.

One God, therefore, meant one humanity, one common faith, one father, one family. Monotheism spelt brotherhood. And not only this—it meant something else. Just as the one God decreed one law for the physical universe, so He decreed one law for the spiritual world of man, binding upon all men, applicable to all men, sovereign over all men. Not only is there one humanity, but all races within that humanity are subject to the same moral law: none is a favorite, none is beyond it.

There is unity in nature; there is unity in mankind. Of course, there is infinite variety in nature. We do not understand ultimate reality; we cannot explain the how and why of physical phenomena. We can only plot the laws which govern the relationship between phenomena and nature; nevertheless science has made us realize that beyond all the surface variety in nature, there is a fundamental oneness. Even matter and energy are one and interchangeable. In the selfsame sense, there is infinite diversity in mankind; men are differently endowed, no two people are alike, nations differ, races differ, masses differ, men differ, but underlying all this diversity there is a basic unity, so that one moral way of life is binding upon all. King and subject alike, white and black alike, young and old alike are under the same law—this is what Judaism taught.

Our religion did not wish to wash out these differences between men. In fact, Judaism placed considerable value and importance upon individuality both in man and in men collectively. Judaism had no quarrel with the fact that the garden of humanity is planted with a vast variety of flowers. Rather, it welcomed this variety and multiplicity and colorfulness in the life of mankind. "Men differ," say the rabbis, "in voice, in appearance, in intelligence, in opinion. Blessed is God who would not make all men alike."

But Judaism simultaneously proclaimed that however much men differ, all are made in the image of God. Adam, the first man, was created out of the dust which God had gathered from the four corners of the earth, and of dust possessed of all the colors of the earth, so that wherever man is, he is the creation of God and made in the image of God. Each human being, however much he differs from his neighbor—from all his neighbors—is worthy of dignity and respect. The rabbis say that wherever a man walks, a troop of angels precede him, proclaiming: "Make way for the image of the Holy One, blessed be He."

Every man is worthy of respect and has a rightful claim to social equality. God created only one man, although he could have created a half dozen or an infinite number, so that no one has the right to say, "I come from better stock than you do." Similarly, as regards national entities, Judaism never advocated international amalgam. Quite the contrary. All nations were created by God, and each has its function to perform. Each is distinctive and is worthy of that distinction, and each can use that distinction for the common good. But simultaneously Judaism urged that all nations harmonize their interests and live in peace, cooperate internationally for the common good so that all might become one society, "to do Thy will with a whole heart." The ideal of the one world as preached by our historic faith does not call for an amorphous cosmopolitanism, or for one universal language, or for standardized religion. It does call for peaceful coordination and adjustment among nations and peoples, making full allowances for those individual forms of life which, because of historic associations, nations and peoples cherish and desire to perpetuate.

The idea of the One Father or the one family is not just an attractive idea. It imposes a tremendous moral obligation upon a human being. In the pagan world, for example, if one member in a community waxed poor, he was rejected and thrust aside. Impoverished, he had forfeited his claim to be a respected member of society. Judaism proclaimed his dignity. A poor man is still a man. He is your brother even though he be poor. Therefore the Bible says, "If your brother become poor, you must help him so that your brother may live with you and in your midst." Judaism was the first great religion to legislate for the protection of the poor. When a man harvested, he was required to leave certain portions of his field for the poor. A special tithe was set aside for the poor, and the matter of defending the poor was a chief concern. There was a fierce sense of fraternity, of brotherly responsibility in the preachments of the prophets. One society—rich and poor alike, native or stranger. Judaism rejected that conception of iron curtains between peoples and nations. God was God of all mankind, of the native and the stranger. So we read in the Bible: "Thou shalt not oppress the stranger, for ye were strangers in the land of Egypt."

In none of the other literature of mankind in ancient days do we find such a mandate. To other peoples the stranger was a barbarian. To the Jew he was a brother. One society, rich and poor, citizen or stranger, wise or simple. "A man should not say," declared the rabbis, "I will love the wise, but I will despise the ignorant. Rather should a man say, I will love all of them." No snobbery, no false pride, no hierarchies in human relationships. All belong to one family. Furthermore, this is one world not only for the Jew, but also for the non-Jew. The Jewish people in olden days was a small people surrounded by nations who were their enemies. In a sense, that was true of all peoples of antiquity. But this little people of Judea was particularly harassed, because it differed from the rest of the world in rejecting polytheism and idolatry, and in maintaining a revolutionary faith in one God. This faith incurred the hostility of all the people about. Judaism taught that the God of Israel is also the God of all the gentiles and that the Jews have no special claim upon God. "Are ye not like the Ethiopians in my sight, O children of Israel? Did I not bring up Israel from the land of Egypt, but also the Philistines from Caphtor and the Syrians from Kir?"

God intervened in the history of all peoples. Israel was a chosen people only because it was within Israel that the idea of the one spiritual God first was manifest. Israel was chosen not for special favors, but for religious leadership to become, according to Isaiah, "a light unto the gentiles." What was given to Israel by the peculiar circumstance of having been the first to conceive of the one world was not a diadem of jewels, but a crown of thorns, for leadership means suffering and a double measure of moral responsibility.

In all else all nations are alike in the sight of God. There was a wicked people in ancient days in the city of Nineveh. Nineveh was the enemy of Israel, and God had directed that that city should perish for its sins. Jonah went to that city and admonished the people for their sins. Jonah did not want to go, but if you recall, God said unto Jonah, "You have great pity upon a little blade which grew up overnight and perished in a day because it gave you a measure of protection from the heat of the sun. Should I not have pity over the great city of Nineveh? They are my children just as much as the children of Israel. Even when a wicked people must pay for its wickedness, they are still God's children." When the Egyptians were drowning, according to legend the angels broke into song. God rebuked them: "My handiwork is drowning in the sea and ye sing songs."

Here is an amazing attitude toward other peoples and especially toward one's enemies. You will recall that perfectly astounding colloquy between God and Abraham concerning Sodom and Gomorrah. God decided to destroy the cities of Sodom and Gomorrah. And this Jew, Abraham, who had no particular interest in these cities, pleads with God:

"Great God, will you not save the city of Sodom if you find in her fifty or forty or thirty or twenty or ten righteous people?" He begs of God to save a wicked people, an enemy. That is the spirit of Judaism. You will recall that magnificent prayer of Solomon on the occasion of the dedication of the new Temple in Jerusalem, and the verse: "Moreover concerning the stranger that is not of thy people Israel. If a stranger of a far country for Thy name's sake shall come and pray towards this house, hear Thou in heaven thy dwelling place and do according to all that the stranger calleth Thee for." At the time that Solomon and his father build a central sanctuary to the God of Israel, Solomon thinks of the stranger who may have needs of his own for which he should like to pray to the unknown God of Israel, and Solomon begs of God that He should do according to all that the stranger "calleth Thee for." "For my house is a house of prayer for all people." That is Judaism. No superior races or inferior races. No superiority or inferiority in the sight of God. Judaism welcomed any man, regardless of race, who sought to be admitted as a proselyte into the house of Israel.

Some of the foremost leaders of our people, even David and Akiba, were descendants of men and women who were not of the house of Israel. R. Jeremiah said: "A gentile who lives a Godly life is like a High Priest. Whence can you know that a gentile who practices the Law is equal to the High Priest? Because it says, 'Which if a man do, he shall live through them.' And it says, 'This is the Law of man.' It does not say: 'the Law of Priests, Levites, Israelites,' but 'This is the law of man, O Lord God.' It does not say, 'Open the gates and let the Priests, Levites and Israelites enter,' but 'Open the gates that a righteous people may enter,' and 'This is the gate of the Lord, the righteous shall enter it.' It does not say, 'The Priests and the Levites and Israel shall enter it,' but it says 'The righteous shall enter it.' And it does not say, 'Rejoice ye, Priests and Levites and Israelites,' but it says, 'Rejoice ye righteous.' And it does not say, 'Do good, O Lord, to the Priests and the Levites and the Israelites,' but 'Do good, O Lord, to the good.' So even a gentile, if he practices the Law, is equal to the High Priest." "I call heaven and earth to witness that whether it be gentile or Israelite, man or woman, slave or handmaid, according to the deeds which he does will the spirit of God rest on him." One world, one family, one moral law—Judaism was the first religion of mankind to preach the universal peace. Where else do you find this passionate call for men to lay down their arms, put an end to war, to unite in one international organization under the sovereignty of God? That is exactly what Isaiah and Micah taught. They were the first to give to mankind the conception of a United Nations. It all stems from this conception of one God, one humanity.

Well, we are far from having even approximated this tremendous ethical concept of Judaism. Never has the world been so divided as it is today, not only in two hostile camps, but in several, divided as though in the East there were one God and here a different God, two irreconcilable worlds, gods fighting one another. Time and again the world has been divided because men forgot the concept of one God. In our own country the North and the South forgot, and the nation was plunged into blood to solve a problem which never would have been created if the law of Judaism had been observed. How foolish are those who believe that the divisions between capital and labor, between private ownership and communism, represent differences between men which can only be solved by war. War never solves anything; war only divides mankind still further.

Today we are of the two worlds, the East and the West, the Soviet Union and the United States, and we hardly hear the voice of this ethical ideal which can alone bring salvation and healing to mankind! "How beautiful and how pleasant it is for brethren to dwell together in unity." That is Judaism.

The Mandate of Love and Justice

SERMON, THE TEMPLE
FEBRUARY 6, 1949

Two of the most precious jewels in the ethical crown of our faith are the concepts of justice and love. Pre-eminently in our faith, God is thought of as the God of justice. "And the Lord shall be exalted in justice, and the Holy One shall be sanctified in righteousness." In whatever terms or with whatever attributes our ancestors conceived of God, they could not disassociate His being from the idea of justice. Job, suffering all the torments of Hell, confused in his philosophy of life as a result of the unmerited suffering which came upon him, still proclaims, by way of holding on to something unbreakable, "Can God pervert justice?" That was inconceivable. And the fact that it was inconceivable gave Job the strength to live through the torments of his life. Similarly, the father of our race, Abraham, when he saw a wicked city being destroyed, and feeling that there might be righteous people among the inhabitants who might suffer undeservedly, turned to God: "Can the judge of the whole world not do justice?" To Abraham, too, it was inconceivable that God would be aught else but the God of absolute justice.

God's justice was the immovable rock upon which our ancestors built their entire ethical system. There is justice in the world, building itself slowly into the perfectly just society; and the true way to God is through acts of justice. The just man will be rewarded even though his reward may not come immediately. The unjust and the wicked will be punished. And yet, fundamental as is this doctrine of justice, our forefathers understood that there is much else needed to supplement and complement this concept. And so, in their characteristic manner, they said, "When God came to create the world, He first thought of creating the world exclusively on the principle of rigid and absolute justice; but

God realized that the world could not endure if it were built exclusively on justice; God considered building His world exclusively on the principle of love and mercy; but God realized that evil would then go unchecked." It was like pouring hot water into a glass, causing it to crack, or of pouring cold water into a hot glass, causing it to break; and so they said that God mixed the hot and the cold, merged the principles of love and justice, and, through the combination of the two, He built the world. This, the rabbis said, is the meaning of the Biblical phrase: "On the day when the Lord God (*Adonai Elohenu*) created heaven and earth." The appellation of God as *Adonai* meant mercy and love, *Elohenu* meant justice. It was the combination *Adonai Elohenu* that ultimately became the foundation of the world.

Now it is a favorite polemical pastime of some Christian apologists to speak of the God of Judaism as the God of relentless justice, a vengeful deity, and the God of the new faith as the God of love. It is simple enough, through a process of contrived selection, to build up any notion you want to based on Biblical texts, but the truth never lies in tendentious partisanship. And the truth is that in Judaism God is the God of justice *and* love; and therefore human society must be grounded in the dual principle of justice and love.

One can argue which should have priority, love or justice. Some have maintained that love is all too clannish, partial, and unreflective to be the basis upon which to build society; that justice is a more universal and more reflective and therefore more independent principle for social progress and organization. I say this is a subject for interesting speculation. What is not arguable is that as far as Judaism is concerned, the guiding ethical principles must combine the twin ideals of justice and of love. "The Lord, thy God, He is a God of righteousness and of mercy, and long-suffering, and full of mercy and of truth. He grants kindness unto the thousandth generation. He forgives iniquity and transgression and sin. But He will by no means clear the guilty." For the guilty disallow repentance, the possibility of turning away from an evil way. God is always there to receive the repentant sinner, because God is abundant in forgiveness; but for the obstinate sinner there must be condemnation and punishment. God does punish, not in order to destroy, but in order to correct.

This summary of the Jewish conception of God can be found in one of the great Psalms. "Judgment and justice are the foundations of Thy throne. But mercy and compassion go before Thy countenance." The passion for social justice dominates the ethical literature of our people. Justice is the heart of prophecy, which is the heart of our religion; and because the prophets of Israel conceived of God as the God of justice and of love—of justice tempered with love—they had the courage to confront kings and nobility with the challenge to do justice to those over whom they ruled and whose destinies they could affect. A humble prophet like Nathan could confront the mighty King David, who had sinned, and say unto him: "Thou art the man." A prophet like Elijah, a poor man and defenseless, could confront King Ahab, who had committed murder because of greed, and in the name of the God of justice denounce him: "I have not troubled Israel but thou and thy father's house." It was in the name of the God of justice that Jeremiah could stand at the gates of the Temple and say to those who thronged to the sacrifices: "Will you rob and steal and defy every just principle and then come into this house and say, 'We are saved'?" The prophets denounced all forms of exploitation because of their faith in the God of justice. They denounced all those who dwelt at ease in Zion, who lay stretched on beds of ivory and crushed the faces of the poor into the dust. I have repeated more than once in our discussions that Judaism was a revolutionary faith. It came to mankind and said: "Religion is not ritual, nor sacrifice. It is to do justice and to love mercy and to walk humbly with thy God." "Justice, justice shalt thou pursue." Justice was the cry of the prophets and of Judaism.

What is justice? What did our fathers conceive justice to be? They did not mean simply legal or formal justice. They meant far more, although they had much to say about these two elementary concepts. A man should not rob his neighbor, nor should he deceive, nor oppress, Jew or gentile. "Thou shalt not oppress a hired servant that is poor and needy, whether he be of thy brethren or of the strangers that are in thy land." Judaism has much to say about the law and the law courts. Justice must be even-handed. "Ye shall not respect the person of the poor nor favor the person of the rich, but in justice shalt thou decree the law." There shall be one law for the native-born and the stranger. When you think of what has happened in the last ten to fifteen years, of how governments arose which proclaimed two laws contradictory and mutually exclusive—one for one's own race and another for the people of another race—you can realize how far-visioned was this ethical concept proclaimed by Judaism twenty-eight hundred years ago. **One law for the native-born and for the stranger.**

Justice meant still more than that. To be a just man meant to work for the just society, to work for a condition of life where all handicaps would be removed from all men, where the shackles of poverty and ignorance would be loosed so that all could share in the good on earth, for all are God's children alike. To work for the Kingdom of God was the mandate of justice, "and the work of justice shall be peace and the effect of it, quietness and confidence forever." But while working for this perfect society, while identifying oneself with great social movements, a human being is not absolved of the responsibility of looking after the immediate needs of the man next door to him. Justice demands that you do whatever you are able to do immediately for those near to you, the members of your own community.

The same term used for justice is used for charity, for charity is a subordinate derivative of the concept of justice. Among our people laws were enacted to provide for the needy. Relief organizations were set up in every community, millennia before our community chests were organized, to see to it that no member of the household would go hungry or be in want. You will recall that famous definition of charity by Maimonides. He listed eight degrees of giving. The seventh is the charity given where the giver and the recipient are unknown to each other, given without humiliating the recipient and without taking pride for one's self. And the eighth is the charity where you help a man to help himself. That is the highest degree of charity and is derived from this basic concept of justice.

But justice is not love. To justice must be added love. One must be just beyond the requirements of law, beyond the strict social obligations society imposes upon men. One must add to his justice the gracious overtones of love. "Love thy neighbor as thyself." We could not live if men were only just to us. It is because some men love us and aid us when we do not deserve their love and their aid that we are able to live. "Love the stranger as thyself." This phrase, Akiba said, was the highest principle of the Torah. And this is what God said to Isaiah: "My children, what is it that I am asking of you? Is it not that you love one another and honor one another?" To train ourselves so that we will respect and love one another; not to hate, not to bear a grudge, not to be harsh in judgments of our fellow men. Never judge your neighbor until you have put yourself in his place. Do things for others, for God, not for the sake of receiving a reward, but out of love. Be rather among those who are persecuted than among those who persecute. There are values greater than charity. Here is *Gemilut Hasadim,* which we translate as loving-kindness. Charity is concerned only with money. Loving-kindness, *Gemilut Hasadim,* is a giving of one's self, service with one's whole body. Charity is only for the poor. Loving-kindness is to those who need what money cannot buy. The rich man, too, frequently stands in need of loving-kindness. Charity is only for the living. Loving-kindness is for the living and the dead. To speak kindly of the dead is a form of loving-kindness.

We find in our literature expressions which may startle at first, until one reflects on them. "Anyone who denies the principle of loving-kindness (*Gemilut Hasadim*) is as if he denied the existence of God." If you really believe in God, then you must believe in compassion and love, sympathy and human understanding, mutual helpfulness. There is a beautiful phrase of Hosea's which runs through my mind whenever I speak of Judaism: "Life is a covenant of brothers." That is what society is—one family, one God. Another prophet in speaking of God's relationship to Israel expressed the same idea this way: "And I will betroth thee unto me in righteousness and in justice, in loving-kindness and in compassion, and I will betroth thee unto me in faithfulness." God's relationship to His people is one of love as intense as the exquisite love of youth. But God also betroths the people unto Him in justice and righteousness. Yes, and in loving-kindness and in compassion and in faithfulness. Such is the relationship between man and his fellow man which alone can make for the perfect society. Justice, righteousness, loving-kindness, compassion, faithfulness. Justice and love are the great principles of Jewish ethics. These are the two brilliant jewels in the diadem of Jewish morality.

The Democratic Society

SERMON, THE TEMPLE
FEBRUARY 20, 1949

Hitler declared that democracy is fundamentally Jewish, not Germanic, and he was absolutely right—one of the few instances in which he was right. Democracy is fundamentally Jewish, not Germanic. In the Western world the roots of democracy lie deep in the Hebraic tradition. The so-called Aryan must trace back his political traditions to the Oriental despotism of ancient Aryan Persia and the caste system of Aryan India. The Greeks, that alertly progressive people, had no strong, consistent democratic tradition, and certainly Rome did not. Thucydides, Plato, and Aristotle opposed democratic forms of government. The favorite political form for Plato was the monarchy, and the ideal ruler of his republic was the philosopher-king. Plato's republic was not a representative democracy but a government at the head of which stood a philosopher-king with unlimited powers. Aristotle regarded kingship as the primary form of government, aristocracy as the next best form, and democracy as the lowest form. And Aristotle, of course, defended the institution of human slavery. Our Torah virtually abolished Hebrew slavery, which was the first step in the abolition of slavery everywhere.

The spirit of ancient Israel was hostile to all forms of political absolutism. Our forefathers were Semitic nomads for untold centuries, and theirs was the desert tradition which they took with them later on when they settled in Canaan. The desert tradition does not favor despotism or royalty. The leader of a tribe is only the first among equals; and that attitude, by the way, has persisted to this very day among the Bedouin.

T. E. Lawrence writes in his book *Revolt in the Desert:*

102

Among the Arabs there were no distinctions, traditional or natural, except the unconscious power given a famous sheik by virtue of his accomplishment; and they taught me that no man could be their leader except he ate the ranks' food, wore their clothes, lived level with them, and yet appeared better in himself.

This was the tradition which prevailed among our ancestors and became part of the pattern of the people. Centuries later, as a result of the warring with the Philistines in Canaan, Israel turned to the prophet Samuel, and asked that a king be set over them. Samuel resisted that demand. The demand for a king was looked upon by Samuel as a mimicry of heathen nations. The call for the rule of one man was interpreted as being an act which despised the rule of the one God. It was rebellion against God. Samuel warned the people against the choosing of a king. He told them what monarchy would do to them—forced service, the expropriation of their possessions. Tyranny would be hard on them. But the people said: "Lo, we want a king to rule over us so that we may be like all the other nations who have kings to rule and lead them into war." Samuel finally yielded under pressure. But the law in ancient Israel, when kings were finally appointed, closely proscribed and curbed their power.

And all the people shall hear, and fear, and do no more presumptuously. When thou art come into the land which the Lord thy God giveth thee, and shalt possess it, and shalt dwell therein, and shalt say: "I will set a king over me, like all the nations that are round about me"; thou shalt in any wise set him king over thee, whom the Lord thy God shall choose; one from among thy brethren shalt thou set king over thee; thou mayest not put a foreigner over thee, who is not thy brother. Only he shall not multiply horses to himself, nor cause the people to return to Egypt, to the end that he should multiply horses; forasmuch as the Lord hath said unto you: "Ye shall henceforth return no more that way." Neither shall he multiply wives to himself, that his heart turn not away; neither shall he greatly multiply to himself silver and gold.

When one contrasts this royal prerogative with those in other nations, one realizes how much the spirit of democracy prevailed among our ancestors. Israel's kings were under the surveillance of the prophets. There was a higher law which the king had to observe, as in the case of King David and Nathan, King Ahab and Elijah, and King Zedekiah and Jeremiah. In each instance the king had done wrong and abused his power, and the prophetic voice of the people faced the king and denounced him. The principle was early established that if the king sets about to violate a law of the Torah, the people are not obligated to follow him. The right of rebellion against a king is proclaimed in the law of Israel. From the records it is clear that the kings of ancient Israel did not have an easy time of it. Whenever there was any outcropping of royal oppressions, this freedom-loving people rose in rebellion. There are at least five instances in the Bible where the people dethroned a king. "All Jews were sons of kings." Every member of the people had status and dignity, and in the name of that status and dignity they challenged the king who usurped powers which did not belong to him.

The ideal form of government was theocracy. Theocracy—the rule of the state by God. But even in this instance, Israel was different from other peoples. There were other theocratic societies, but only in Israel were the priests, too, subject to curbs and controls by prophets who themselves had no legal prerogative. A student of theocracy, C. Ryder Smith, makes this interesting observation:

> The typically theocratic state is that of the Jews. Founded by God and directly governed by Him, its kings were no more than His servants, who, being guided by His prophets, enjoyed no personal right of initiative. In this attitude, to their Creator, and in respect of the covenant which they had made with Him, the Hebrew people stand practically alone in history so that theirs may be looked upon as a state of a unique kind.

It is true that Israel fashioned a state of a unique kind in which the king was curbed by the basic moral law and the priest was similarly confined within definite functions and authorities. There ensued among our people a long struggle to universalize the preachings of the priest, and to grant full participation to the laity in the religious heritage of Israel, and to establish a democratic leadership among the people. That was true of the functions of the priest; that was true even of prophecy.

You may recall the Biblical story wherein two laymen suddenly begin to prophesy in the camp. The people protest: "Moses, lock those people up. They dare to prophesy." Moses responds: "Art thou jealous for my sake? Would that all the Lord's people were prophets that the Lord would put His spirit upon them."

The greatest democratic victory in this struggle in Israel against the assumption of religious privilege by caste took place after the destruction of the First Temple, when our forefathers were exiled into Babylon. There they built that unique religious institution we call the synagogue. It was built by laymen. It required no ordained rabbi. Laymen would meet and their leaders would arise and lead the congregation in prayer. This synagogue outlived the Temple when it was rebuilt, and this synagogue has remained the characteristic religious institution in Judaism. To this day any ten Jews can organize a congregation, and anyone can worship and teach the law. The struggle which raged for centuries in ancient Israel was a struggle about who had the right to teach the law and to interpret the word of God; the democrats, the Pharisees, won the day. So we read in the Talmud: "Sanctity was not given to the priest alone." Priests and Levites and everyone shared the religious privileges.

Now where did the democratic ideal have its roots? Clearly in the concept that all men are created equal because all are created in the image of God. All are equal in the sight of God's law—rich and poor, native-born and stranger—because there is no superior ruler, people, or class. The ultimate appeal of a man who is denied his rights is not to the will of the ruler, but is to God and God's moral law.

I should like to quote several paragraphs from my book *The World Crisis and Jewish Survival,* in which I discuss the roots of modern democracy in the Western world:

> Modern democracy was born in the struggle for religious freedom in the sixteenth and seventeenth centuries. The Protestant Reformation was not merely a reformation in the realm of doctrine and ritual and a repudiation of the authority of Papacy and the hierarchical system of the Church. It was much more than that. The early leaders of the Protestant Movement did not themselves fully appreciate the forces which they represented. They were confused, and at times were inconsistent. They did not grasp fully what was happening in the mind and heart of the world. What actually was happening was a new determined upreaching on the part of men in the Western world for spiritual liberty, for the emancipation of man from the strait jacket of Tradition and System.
>
> The demand for spiritual liberty soon expressed itself in demands for other forms of liberty. Peasant revolts followed. Political and economic rights were demanded by humble people. By what authority? They had no authority. They had no

human law to which they could appeal. In whose name did they speak? In the same name and by the same authority as the ancient prophets of Israel presumed to challenge the kings, the noblemen and the powerfully rich of their day. They spoke in the name of God, in the name of a revelation from God. All men were equal because God made all men equal. The things which they demanded were the things which the Bible, the revealed Word of God, conceded to them, and to all men. The social revolutions of the sixteenth century which were quenched in the blood of a hundred thousand peasants received their inspiration from religions and revelation.

"The full thunder-cloud of the Hebrew prophets," writes James Martineau in his *Studies of Christianity*, "stealing over a world in negative stagnation, waked the sleeping lightnings of the soul, and for a while streaked the atmosphere of history with fearful portents. . . . The downtrodden serfs of Franconia had not long heard the glad tidings from Wittenberg, ere they began to draw parallels between themselves and the old Israel when the desert had been passed. . . . The earth was the Lord's, and the army of the saints was come to take it. . . . The time of jubilee was come, when every believer should have his field of heritage. . . . Throughout the great movement which in the third decade of the sixteenth century spread insurrection from the Breisgau to Saxony, the peasants were animated with the belief that the Gospel, armed with the sword of Joshua, was to subjugate the world, and that all the conditions of property, of law, of civil administration, under which secular communities exist, were to be superseded by institutions conformed to a divine model."

The quintessence of the spiritual idealism of the Protestant Reformation, which later on affected the life of the American people, lay with the various Anabaptist sects which sprang up in the wake of the Reformation. Some of these sects were hundreds of years ahead of their time. They believed in the absolute moral responsibility of the individual, in his inherent spiritual sovereignty, and in the right of private judgment in matters of religion. They held that the duty of the state was only to protect the good and to punish the evil, and beyond that the state itself was evil. The state had no right to circumscribe the freedom of the individual. These sects were the first to demand absolute disestablishment—the separation of church and state. They were the first to preach universal toleration and freedom of worship. They maintained that all property belonged to God. Some of them like the early Christians practiced

voluntary communism, which is a very different thing from the
secular, involuntary communism of our day—in fact, its violent
negation in everything but surface similarity.

Thus, out of victories won for religious freedom on the battlefields of the spirit, there stemmed other victories for man's political, economic and social freedom. The absolutism of king and
state was first curbed by the religious spirit of man demanding
at the point of revolution the right, not of universal suffrage
or of better living conditions, but the right to worship God as
it saw fit.

These doctrines of the Anabaptists were carried over to Hol-
land and England, and then to the American Colonies. The
Founding Fathers of our country adopted many of the doctrines
of these religious "fanatics." When they wrote into the Declaration of Independence: "We hold these truths to be self-evident—
that all men are created equal, that they are endowed by their
Creator with certain inalienable rights, that among these are
Life, Liberty and the pursuit of Happiness," they were giving
political expression to seminal religious Anabaptist doctrines.
When they countered the claim of the Divine Right of Kings
with the claim of the Divine Right of People to resist the tyranny of kings, when they proclaimed that resistance to tyrants
is obedience to God, when they engraved upon the Liberty Bell
the Biblical proclamation: "And Thou shalt proclaim freedom
throughout the land unto all the inhabitants thereof," or when
they placed on the first seal of the newborn republic of the
United States the figure of Moses leading the children of Israel
out of Egypt, they were marshalling religious truth, religious
authority and religious tradition to underwrite and sanction
their political freedom.

That is a chapter in the political history of our own country and
in the history of democracy that is frequently not recalled. One of the
grandest and noblest contributions of our immortal faith to the progress
of mankind was the concept of democracy, the vision of a society of free
men living in voluntary political association under the divine laws of
justice and brotherhood; and not only did Judaism give mankind the
vision but it provided that spiritual thrust and impetus to challenge
entrenched privilege and dare upheaval and revolution.

I was personally deeply gratified when, addressing the very first
session of the new government of Israel, the newly elected president, Dr.
Chaim Weizmann, took especial pains to call attention to this fundamental democratic thesis in Jewish life:

In the ancient world this tiny country of ours raised the standard of spiritual revolt against the rights of tyranny and brute force. The law of Israel and the vision of her prophets sounded a new epoch of relations between man and man, a new ordering of human society. The authority of the King of Israel was limited by law and tradition. The prophets of Israel did not fear to utter rebuke and reproof to kings and princes and with inspired words forged weapons to defend the poor and the oppressed, strangers and slaves, and the orphan and the widow.

The very principle of the institution of kingship was hateful to the spiritual leaders of the people. "I will not rule over you nor shall my son rule over you. The Lord shall rule over us," declared the judge to the assembled people. The warnings of the prophets against the dangers of tyranny thunder from on high to the ears of our people to our last generation.

In Israel this authority of one man was derived from the noble conception that people are naturally free and are freely accepting the rule that law and just judgment do not need compulsion from above to live as ordered by society. The root of the principle of the constitution of that novel state was the limit set for the authority of the king, and in this sense the ancient Hebrew policy was the mother of constitutional government in the modern age.

Democracy is fundamentally Jewish, and in the great struggle which is raging throughout the Western world between various forms of dictatorship and democracy, it is really the spirit of Israel and of Judaism which is struggling for survival. It is the Biblical tradition which has been assaulted and which is fighting to survive. It is Judaism, vigorous, alive, challenging; and human beings and institutions which had their origin in Judaism which are the forces still fighting in the world to establish the Kingdom of God, which is the kingdom of free men banded together in human brotherhood doing the will of God in the world.

The Challenge to the Individual

SERMON, THE TEMPLE
FEBRUARY 27, 1949

When Nathan, the prophet, pointed his accusing finger at David and said to him: "Thou art the man," he not only placed the responsibility where it belonged—at the door of the perpetrator of the crime, even though this perpetrator was the king—but he also indicated for all time Judaism's position as regards ethical responsibility. It rests squarely with the individual: "Thou art the man."

The Ten Commandments are in the second person singular. "Thou shalt . . ." "Thou shalt not . . ." "I am the Lord, thy God, who brought *thee* out of the land of Egypt"; "Thou shalt . . ." "Thou shalt not . . ." The individual stands in a direct and immediate moral relationship to his God. Man's relationship to God is direct and personal. When man sins, he sins not only against himself and against society, but most especially he sins against his God. "Against Thee, Thee alone have I sinned."

Man is, of course, a member of society. He lives out his life within a group or a class or a family. There is constant interaction between himself and others. And to that extent there is collective responsibility. We cannot altogether escape the rewards and punishments of the good and evil in the world about us. Our personal history is part of the history of the encompassing group. There are individual mitigating circumstances for the conduct of the individual, and our religion is fully aware of these extenuating circumstances. But when all is said and done, "Thou art the man." The moral imperatives are yours. The challenge is directed to you, and there is no escape. One cannot seek self-exculpation by blaming the society or class or family or the environment in which he finds himself.

One cannot hide behind others. When the first man, Adam, sinned, he hid from the Lord, but the voice of the Lord searched him out. There is no escape. For there is no ethical life possible for mankind unless the individual is made to assume his full share of moral responsibility. Our religion exalts the individual in order to make him a free moral agent. The individual is very, very important in the philosophy of Judaism. He is not just an insignificant ant in a heap. Every single human being is important because every single human being is made in the image of God and possesses his own authentic status and dignity and worth.

The rabbis say that every human being has the right to declare: "For my sake was the whole world created." This concept was not universally accepted in olden times, and certainly is not in modern times. The noted French philosopher, Auguste Comte, declared that humanity alone is real. The individual is only an abstraction. Judaism rejects that point of view. Totalitarianism states that the individual is an impersonal unit within the state or class. Judaism does not accept that point of view. Judaism maintains that the individual is possessed of rights which are bestowed upon him by God, and therefore they are irrevocable. States and governments have no right to take them away from the individual.

According to our religion, every man has a free road to God, and God finds His way to every man, however humble. In God's scheme of things no man is dispensable. Walt Whitman knew this when he wrote: "An individual is as superb as a nation when he has the qualities which make for a superb nation." One man is equal to a whole society if that man has in him the qualities which make for a great society. Therefore, every man has the right to be judged on his own merits. Therefore, every man is responsible for his own conduct.

This profound ethical concept developed slowly in ancient Israel. Originally the sense of group or race or national solidarity was so strong that the moral responsibility of the group submerged the moral individual. Society was a monolithic structure. For example, if a generation sinned, and merited God's punishment, it was assumed that this punishment would be visited upon the entire generation, on all men alike without distinction between the righteous and the wicked. Thus, in the generation of the Flood, everyone died, good and evil alike. God blotted out the whole of mankind. Again, in the generation of the Tower, the insolence of men had become so overbearing that they sought to build a tower to heaven; God scattered the whole race of men and confused their speech; and good and bad alike suffered the consequences of the collective guilt of their generation.

The rabbis, sensing the moral impropriety of such collective punishment, declared that up to the giving of the Torah at Mount Sinai, the law of collective responsibility prevailed, but after the giving of the Torah, the individual was judged by his own record. Historically this change in the moral thinking of our people did not take place at the time of the giving of the Law, but much later—at the time of the breakup and the extinction of the national state and the destruction of the Temple in the sixth century before the Common Era. Something revolutionary happened then in the spiritual life of the people. The strong bond of community was relinquished. The nation had disintegrated. The individual Jew would now adhere to his Judaism not as a matter of course, but as a matter of choice. His moral and religious responsibility were now personal and individualized. It was a matter of his own determination whether he would adhere to the faith of Israel. Furthermore, that individual could not survive and did not wish to survive as a member of a Jewish community unless the collective burden of national guilt which was believed to have brought about the destruction and the exile were first removed from him. There was no sense in going on if the children were to suffer forever for the sins of their parents. The individual reached out for moral freedom and a personal, individual relationship to his God.

A great searching of heart took place among the people. The Temple, which was the symbol of the survival of the Jewish state, was destroyed. Not only were the people in danger of extinction, but so was the faith of Israel. A new set of ideas was required to save Judaism. In the fires of that profound national tribulation a new ethical thought was proclaimed—man's personal responsibility—and accepted.

There is an amazing chapter in the Book of Ezekiel, Chapter 18, which discusses this problem of group versus individual responsibility.

> And the word of the Lord came unto me, saying: What mean
> ye, that ye use this proverb in the land of Israel, saying:
>> The fathers have eaten sour grapes,
>> And the children's teeth are set on edge?
> As I live, saith the Lord God, ye shall not have occasion
> any more to use this proverb in Israel. Behold, all souls
> are Mine; as the soul of the father, so also the soul of
> the son is mine; the soul that sinneth, it shall die.

> The soul that sinneth, it shall die; the son shall not bear
> the iniquity of the father with him, neither shall
> the father bear the iniquity of the son with him; the
> righteousness of the righteous shall be upon him, and the
> wickedness of the wicked shall be upon him.

> Therefore I will judge you, O house of Israel, every one
> according to his way, saith the Lord God.

Now the ethical responsibility was placed squarely where it belonged, and only to the extent that it belonged, upon the individual. Thus the individual man emerged unencumbered from the guilt of others, free and autonomous within his own ethical world, but within that independence and freedom a responsible moral agent. Does this mean that when the individual sins, punishment is inevitable? Not at all. God has opened wide the gates of repentance to enable man to free himself from the burden of his misdeeds.

> But if the wicked turn from all his sins that he hath committed,
> and keep all My statutes, and do that which is lawful and right,
> he shall surely live, he shall not die. None of his transgressions
> that he hath committed shall be remembered against him; for
> his righteousness that he hath done he shall live. Have I any
> pleasure at all that the wicked should die? saith the Lord God;
> and not rather that he should return from his ways, and live?

The task of building the good society is the direct responsibility of every man and woman, regardless of his or her capacities or station in life. Of everyone God demands according to the capacity of his person. In Deuteronomy we read that the covenant which God made with Israel was made with every individual. Of each the most is expected, according to the measure of his strength, and no one but God can evaluate the true worth of a man's contribution to society. The stone which the builders reject oftentimes becomes the chief cornerstone. Who can measure the impact of one single human life? Who can measure the importance of a single human act? When a pebble is dropped into the water, who knows how far the circles extend? Who but God? According to our sacred literature, it is the humble who inherit the earth.

Moral responsibility is direct and immediate. Do not say that some day when I become rich and have a lot of money, I will become a philanthropist. Do it now, even if it means sharing a crust of bread. And you are the man! Moral responsibility is direct and immediate. That is the

Jewish ethical concept. There are some who give generously to others, but neglect their own kith and kin, who ignore the responsibilities close at home. That is not the morality of Judaism. Here—now—you do it. *You do it!* And where there are people around you who are unconcerned with the rights of others, that is not an excuse for you not to be concerned. The salvation of mankind rests with the exercise of the moral initiative of individual men and women who come to move masses to emulation. "Thou art the man."

Many of us are prone to accept these doctrines. We think they are true, but we do not think that they apply to us. They apply to the other fellow. The ethical challenge of Judaism seeks to wake up the right people. And the right man is you, and the right man is I. You can be a builder of the good society regardless of your station or profession. And helping to build the good society makes life worth while and significant.

Ethics—by God or Man?

ADDRESS, UNIVERSITY OF MICHIGAN
NOVEMBER 11, 1954

I was asked to speak on the subject "Ethics—by God or Man?" As a rabbi, I shall try to give you the answer of Judaism to this question. I have no other. I am also persuaded that when all is said and done, there is no other answer which any God-centered religion can give.

There arose in Israel in ancient times, in a small country which was the crossroads of great empires and cultures, a group of men who had a unique and challenging message for their people and for mankind. By this message the world came to be profoundly agitated, and the spirit of man was quickened to new adventures in faith and social aspirations.

These men, the prophets of Israel, were the founders of Judaism. In later times and in other settings, their basic ideas gave impulse and substance to Christianity and Islam. They projected a way of life for men and nations, which, like some strong gulf stream, has flowed steadily and discernibly through the great waters of humanity for centuries.

They were not specifically theologians, these men who fashioned Judaism, nor did the faith which they founded ever boast of a systematic theology or an ethical science. There is no work on systematic Jewish theology until the early Middle Ages, a thousand years after the final canonization of the books of the Bible, two thousand years after Moses. There were many theologians and philosophers among the Jewish people, especially in later times, and some of these were not wanting in speculative power, but Judaism is not based upon their theology or philosophy. These religious philosophers, in successive generations, employed whatever philosophic thought was current in their day, from Platonism to existentialism, to defend or to corroborate the basic tenets of their faith, "to prove the ideas of the Torah by correct reasoning."

Judaism welcomed the light of reason to illumine for man the truths which it proclaimed. It never sought refuge in obscurantism. It never justified itself by anti-rationalism. It revered the human intellect as a divine endowment. "It is the Lord who gives wisdom; from His mouth come knowledge and understanding." It taught men to pray daily: "O, favor us with knowledge, understanding, and intelligence," but it was not impressed with intellectualism. It knew the limits of discursive reasoning and was not finally impeded by logical contradictions. Jewish philosophers never sought to accommodate Judaism to any system of philosophy but to re-enforce its basic tenets by the best speculative thought available. Their object was to explain and verify, not to equate.

That was wise, for the best philosophy of the day, like the best science of the day, like Aristotelian physics and Ptolemaic astronomy in their day, like Newtonian physics and Euclidian mathematics in our day, proved not to be the last word after all. The spirit of each age was allowed to have its say in Judaism, but never the last say, and nothing was permitted to endanger the quintessence of the faith.

Judaism is not as tidy and precise a system of religious thought as some men enamoured of systems might wish, any more than history is, but just as history, in spite of its troughs and crests and its patent incongruities, manifests a clear upward movement in human development, so does Judaism reveal in its development the progress and perseverance of a group of cardinal spiritual and ethical ideas. Judaism held high a light in the darkness of the world. Not all the darkness is dispelled, but there is enough light there to guide man along his way and society to a fuller and happier life. A clear knowledge of God is possible to no one, but a true worship of God is possible to everyone. This profound truth was made known to the foremost among the prophets, Moses, who when seeking to discover the nature of God was told that the face of God was forever hidden from mortal man, but that he might learn much about "all the goodness" of God. This was revealed to him in thirteen moral attributes. Judaism taught man a true worship of God through a way of life informed by ethical aspiration. "The beginning of wisdom is reverence for God." Reverence for God is made manifest through human conduct and action. The emphasis is never on abstract speculation or on theology. "He judged the poor and needy, then it was well. Is not this to know Me? says the Lord." It is in this sense that the phrase "to know God," which occurs frequently in the Bible, is to be understood. The knowledge of God means the worship of God, not an intellectual fathoming of His nature. All speculative ways of knowing God lead from one darkness to another. "A man, when he has made an end [of probing the mysteries of God], has hardly begun, and, when he ceases, abides in deep confusion." A modern philosopher, A. N. Whitehead, makes a similar confession for philosophy. "Philosophy begins in wonder. And, at the end, when philosophic thought has done its best, the wonder remains." However profound our insights, we must still resort to human categories to describe God, and we cannot escape the limitations which condition all human knowledge.

Judaism has no special metaphysics, no mythology, no unique "knowledge" or secret gnosis requisite for salvation, no evangel of a miraculous scheme of redemption. Judaism is Torah—a compendium of moral instructions and imperatives, a rule of life, a pattern of behavior, a "way" revealed in the life of a people through prophets and sages, which, if faithfully carried out, will build the good society on earth. "You shall teach them the statutes and the decisions and make them know the way in which they must walk and what they must do."

Judaism's chief concern is with man's life on earth and with social ideals working themselves out in history. The vision is of a day when "steadfast love and faithfulness will meet; righteousness and peace will kiss each other. Faithfulness will spring from the ground, and righteousness will look down from the sky."

Judaism's source of authority is God. The motive is the love of God and man. The confidence is derived not alone from revelation, as unaccountably mysterious as the origin of intelligence itself, but also from history and from the empirical experiences of the people of Israel and of humanity. The reward for man and mankind is now and in the future.

Judaism sees in human history and in the history of Israel no mere succession of events but the articulation in time of an immanent divine plan as well as divine judgment and purpose, glimpsed by man in retrospect and then only dimly, but known to God in its completeness, a knowledge which, paradoxically, does not preclude man's moral freedom. Man has been given an assignment in the over-all scheme of things which calls for the inexhaustible inventiveness of his mind and spirit with which he has been endowed by his Creator. The Creator of man is not uninterested in man's assignment.

The Jews were the first to interpret history. There is a pattern in all that transpires, and the pattern is a spiritual one. The good will triumph, for God has willed it so, but the triumph may be hastened by humanity's efforts. Climaxing Deutero-Isaiah's superb vision of the New Jerusalem and the Great Restoration is the verse: "I, the Lord, will hasten it in its time," which contains an apparent contradiction. If God has set a fixed time for the event, what is meant by His hastening it? A rabbi comments: "If Israel will merit it, God will hasten its coming; if not, it will come to pass in its appointed time." God's ultimate purpose does not dispense with man's participation in it nor absolve him of his duty and mission. This is a basic concept of Judaism. There have been those who have denied the very possibility of any philosophy of history. There have been others who, like Marx in modern times, built a philosophy of history on economic determinism and on a dialectic of materialism. Proof is as inconclusive for one point of view as for another, and one view is no more "scientific" or plausible than the other. Judaism postulated a Providential version of history based on faith in a God of history "who rules over all the kingdoms of the nations," who "makes nations great and He destroys them; He enlarges nations, and leads them away."

I referred at the outset to the prophets of Israel, the founders of Judaism. In Judaism, prophecy rose to the highest levels of spiritual revelation, and the prophet became a fearless spokesman of God's moral law to men. The passionate ethical earnestness of Judaism is best reflected in the life, labor, struggles, and sufferings of these amazing spiritual pioneers of mankind—"eagles soaring above the tombs" of the ancient faiths, to use a Shelley metaphor—who gave the basic stamp to Judaism for all times. Here, as in so many other cultural experiences of the human race, the peaks thrust up suddenly and sharply, at the very beginning, and were never thereafter surmounted.

The message of these trumpeteers of a new dawn for mankind remained forever the developing theme of Judaism: "Thus says the Lord: Stand by the roads and look, and ask for the ancient paths, where the good way is; and walk in it, and find rest for your souls." In the concord of their many voices, one strong dominant note is unmistakable—the good way! The good way is not to throng the courts of a temple and bring a multitude of vain offerings to God. It is not to listen to the voice of priest or prophet as if they were singing a love song with "a beautiful voice, playing well on an instrument," listening to what they say but doing nothing about it. The good way leads directly and humbly to where men penitently and prayerfully wash the blood of sin, cruelty, and oppression from their hands, search and make themselves inwardly clean, cease to do evil and learn to do good. The good way leads to where men, in struggle and in joy, build the good society through unity, freedom, and compassion. The good way is the way of the unwearied moral effort and unremitting action. At the heart of the message of Hebraic prophecy and subsequently of Judaism itself is a summons to men not to rest content with the evils of society or with their own personal shortcomings, but to set to work to correct them.

The prophets were never divorced from the contemporary scene. They were interested primarily in the moral tone of their nation and of society generally, in social righteousness, human brotherhood, and peace. They had spiritual kinsmen in the Psalmists, but these men were interested primarily in personal piety and in the individual's quest for the light and nearness of God. They supplemented each other, and historic Judaism is a blend of their vision, their passion, their piety, and their profundity.

In the eyes of the wisest among the philosophers of Greece, religion was a part of a system of ethics in which there was as little of the social passion of the prophets as there was of the lyric piety of the Psalmist. In the eyes of the teachers of Judaism, religion was the fountainhead of all ethics. Josephus, the cultured Pharisaic historian of the first century, draws attention to this vital distinction. "The reason why the constitution of this legislation was even better directed to the utility of all than other legislations were is this, that Moses did not make religion a part of virtue, but he saw and ordained other virtues to be parts of religion; I mean justice and fortitude and temperance (the cardinal virtues) and a universal agreement of the members of the community with one another; for all our actions and studies and all our words have a reference to piety towards God, for he has left none of these in suspense or undetermined."

There have been writers who, since the days of Heinrich Heine and Matthew Arnold, have drawn sharp contrasts between Hellenism and Hebraism, the two main influences in Western civilization. They discern a wide chasm between the Greek *Weltanschauung* and the Hebraic *Lebensanschauung*. The Greek mind, it is maintained, was engrossed in science, art, and philosophy; the Hebraic in religion and morality. Hebrew thought is dynamic, Greek thought is static and harmonious. "Repose, harmony, composure, and self-control, they were the Greek way; movement, life, passion, and strength mark the Hebrew way."

The Greeks went far in religion and ethics, but not far enough, not as far as the deep spiritual insights of the Jews, and the Jews fell far short of the Greeks in those areas where the latter excelled. That is why the peoples of the Western world at the close of the classical age turned for their scientific and artistic needs to Greece, and for their spiritual and ethical needs to Judea.

Plato speculated long about the nature of the Good, and having found a satisfactory definition in terms of the four cardinal virtues whose prototype was a heavenly Form, he did nothing about this Good. It remained an aristocratic intellectual truth. It was not converted into a prophetic compulsion so as to make the Good triumph in the world. He did not rush out into the agora and, lifting his voice like a trumpet, declare unto the Athenians their transgressions and to the House of the Achaeans their sins, summoning them to repentance and reformation. Nor can one conceive of Plato, or Aristotle, or Epictetus passionately pleading with the Almighty, in the name of Justice, to save the wicked city of Sodom for the sake of the few righteous men in it. Judaism did not speculate much on the nature of the Good, but it told man what is good and what the Lord requires of him "to do justly, to love mercy, and to walk humbly with God." All who heard Micah knew full well wherein they had individually and collectively failed to measure up to these requirements, and they knew, too, that what was indicated was not a continuous dialogue concerning these ethical concepts, but a beating of the breasts and a thoroughgoing amendment of their way of life. What was stressed in Judaism and what all God-centered religions must stress was that "the end of the matter, all having been heard: revere God, and keep His commandments; for this is the whole duty of man."

Basing his ethical life on God, on the will of God and the service of God, the religious man finds himself confronted with intellectual difficulties and grave paradoxes. Is man free to originate moral decisions and determine by his own action his spiritual destiny? If so, how do you reconcile this with God's foreknowledge and omnipotence? There have been and there are religions which maintain that man is not free, that he is in the grip of a universal causal law, that his status, actions, and decisions are foreordained and inevitable, that some men are elected and predestined by grace to eternal life and others are not. Man's merit does not exert any influence upon his destiny.

Judaism denied and rejected all these ideas. It gave men the assurance of a God who desires freedom and who granted man a capacity for freedom as part of his endowment as a human being made in the image of God.

Judaism proclaimed the liberating doctrine of moral self-determination and therefore also of moral responsibility. "See, I have set before you this day life and good, death and evil . . . therefore choose life!" God did not fashion man to be a helpless creature of passive receptivity but one capable of selection, decision, and origination. In his spiritual life he has been granted the artist's gift and privilege of dominating the material before him, and the more trained and skilled he becomes, the greater his freedom of execution.

The theological and philosophic problems involved in human freedom were not unknown to the teachers of Judaism, and they were not unaware of the difficulties in reconciling man's freedom of choice with God's omniscience or man's lot on earth with his just deserts. But the intellectual difficulties which they encountered in their efforts to solve these problems, a few of the many unsolved problems and contradictions which abound not only in the field of religion but elsewhere as well, did not move them to commit the error of denying free will altogether.

They were faced with a paradox, but the paradox did not faze them. They acknowledged it as one of the mysteries of the religious life—not, however, to vindicate God's omnipotence but to safeguard man's moral competency. They resigned themselves to the impossibility of solving what appeared to them an inherent contradiction. The great teacher Akiba declared: "Everything is foreseen yet free will is given to man." God's fore-knowledge cannot contradict man's freedom. God is aware of all possibilities, and yet man is free to determine his moral conduct.

God cooperates with man in his moral life, but does not coerce him. God created a moral universe and man's freedom is its hallmark. As a created being, man is determined; as a creative being, he is free. Human action affects history and God intended that it should, as part of a design not grasped by man.

The teachers of Judaism realized that while there are limitations to human freedom, there exist vital areas in which man is free, in which man has a vivid intuition and experience of freedom, and that man could grow into freedom and the proper choice of action through training himself in moral habits, through wider knowledge and maturer judgments.

Because the boundaries between what is free and what is determined are not clearly defined, Judaism urged man to act as if these boundaries did not exist at all as far as his moral initiative was concerned, "to cleave to the sunnier side of doubt," and not to proceed on the assumption that his actions are foreknown and his future foredoomed. It is man's duty to develop his freedom just as it is his duty to develop his mind and reason, although they too have their limitations.

In non-theological terms modern man finds this issue restated for him, as one between cultural determinism and free will. How can man exercise any choice or moral initiative whatsoever, seeing that his conduct and way of life are coercively conditioned by the society in which he is born and reared and by its economic, political, social, and legal requirements and mores? Within such a strait jacket of social repressions and traditions, how can the individual be sufficiently autonomous to master his own moral career and to be accountable for it?

The best thought of our day has veered away from the doctrine of cultural-social determinism towards a more dynamic conception. Man is able to fashion his own private world within the larger social framework, which in itself is not static but subject to change and redirection by man himself.

Judaism rejects an exaggerated pessimism with regard to man's nature and man's endowments. Man can, to a large degree, make his own world; and man has, to a large degree, made his own world. And by and large, in spite of setbacks and throwbacks, it has been a progressive world. Man has moved forward to more knowledge, to higher standards of living, to greater justice, to better health conditions, to greater and more energetic efforts in the eradication of poverty. Judaism takes a wide perspective on human history and sees definite progress, and though the pace is frequently slow and occasionally reversed, it sees man rising from lower to higher levels, from the jungles of barbarism, slavery, poverty, and disease to higher levels of enlightenment, of mastery over his environment, of health, justice, and freedom. There is an ascending curve in the evolution of mankind.

Judaism maintains that man is finite and yet not helpless. Man is conditioned, yet he is free to a significant degree. Man cannot think as God but man can think about God. Man does not know the ultimate answers, but in faith he can work with relative truth and find satisfaction and happiness in his work, provided it is sincere work and well intentioned and directed toward God and toward man.

Man cannot wait and should not wait until he can see the road clearly ahead to do the things which need to be done. Sometimes he must act on faith, even when he does not know what lies ahead. Sometimes he must move forward through mist and fog. He must do what has to be done with the material and opportunities which are at hand, trusting that what he is sincerely striving to do will prove to be within the pattern of the abiding design of human progress and God's purpose.

"Yours is not the duty to complete the task, neither are you free to desist from it." "Share your burden with God and He will sustain you." "He will never suffer the righteous to be moved."

Pessimism is a form of atheism, for it omits God from man's calculations, and ignores the spirit of God that is in man. Man should continue to strive and aspire and build again and yet again upon the ruins of his many broken hopes and dreams.

Men cannot see beyond the horizon of their own times. What lies ahead, no one knows. But Judaism constantly reminded man that beyond all horizons there is God.

The stars and planets were there and all the moving constellations before man ever recognized them. In the dark imprisoned mind of the cave dweller in the dawn of time, there already lay impounded all the marvelous achievements of man that were to come, all that he could not see, or grasp, or understand, all that he would have refused to believe—the inventions and discoveries, the power and the mastery, the worlds of music, song and poetry, philosophy, and science. In the mind of the primitive cave dweller there was already contained, as in a seed, all the blossoming and flowering civilizations that were to come, but he could not see the shape of things to come. He could not penetrate the curtains which enshrouded his visible and empirical world. He would have been justified in a total pessimism about the future of mankind, far more than men of later generations. For these already had a long recorded past to contemplate, a past which, in spite of all its turns and windings, did lead mankind forward to amazing progress and brighter prospects.

Judaism admonished men not to despair of the future, nor of their own strength, nor of mankind's inexhaustible spiritual resources, nor of God's cooperation. Long and hard is the way, but there is a way, and there is a goal, and the faithful children of light will follow it and will not grow weary.

The Mark of the Superior Man

SERMON, THE TEMPLE
JANUARY 30, 1938

Hillel said: "In the place where there are no men, strive thou to be a man." One wonders what he had in mind when he spoke of "man." A man is not easy to define. He is a compound of heaven and earth, of dust and star dust. Man, to use the phrase of the Psalmist, is fearfully and wonderfully made. He is clay, stamped in the image of God. Man is a bundle of contradictions, a tangled skein of emotion, a knot of instincts. Man is fashioned by innumerable and invisible hands of the past. Man is plastic to the mold of circumstances. Man is dynamic in the passions of his own creative realities. Man has been called a shadow, a bubble, a flitting dream, a withered grass. Man has also been called the crown of creation, a little lower than the angels.

You may recall that beautiful chorus in Swinburne's "Atalanta in Calydon":

> Before the beginning of years,
> There came to the making of man
> Time, with a gift of tears;
> Grief, with a glass that ran;
> Pleasure, with pain for leaven;
> Summer, with flowers that fell;
> Remembrance fallen from heaven,
> And madness risen from hell;
> Strength without hands to smite;
> Love that endures for a breath;
> Night, the shadow of light,
> And Life, the shadow of death.

All these things have gone into the character of man. Out of such complexities and incongruities, the seers and visioners of mankind have

sought to suggest such an organization of the inner life of man as would
result in the noblest and happiest type of human existence—in the superior man.

Numerous suggestions have been made as to the qualities which
go into the making of the superior man—the marks of the superior man.
Such attempts are frequently made in our Bible.

> Lord, who shall sojourn in Thy Tabernacle?
> Who shall dwell upon Thy holy mountain?
> He that walketh uprightly, and worketh righteousness,
> And speaketh truth in his heart;
> That hath no slander upon his tongue,
> Nor taketh up a reproach against his neighbour;
> In whose eyes a vile person is despised,
> But he honoureth them that fear the Lord;
> He that sweareth to his own hurt, and changeth not;
> He that putteth not out his money on interest,
> Nor taketh a bribe against the innocent.
> He that doeth these things shall never be moved.

That is the way a Judean poet who lived perhaps twenty-five hundred years ago defined his ideal of the superior man.

You may recall the popular poem written by one who is almost a
contemporary of ours, Rudyard Kipling, who also attempted to define
what in his judgment was the superior man:

> If you can keep your head when all about you
>   Are losing theirs and blaming it on you;
> If you can trust yourself when all men doubt you,
>   But make allowance for their doubting too:
> If you can wait and not be tired by waiting,
>   Or being lied about, don't deal in lies,
> Or being hated don't give way to hating,
>   And yet don't look too good, nor talk too wise;
>
> If you can dream—and not make dreams your master;
>   If you can think—and not make thoughts your aim,
> If you can meet with Triumph and Disaster
>   And treat those two impostors just the same;
> If you can bear to hear the truth you've spoken
>   Twisted by knaves to make a trap for fools,
> Or watch the things you gave your life to, broken,
>   And stop and build 'em up with worn-out tools;
>
> If you can make one heap of all your winnings
>   And risk it in one turn of pitch-and-toss,

And lose, and start again at your beginnings
    And never breathe a word about your loss;
If you can force your heart and nerve and sinew
    To serve your turn long after they are gone,
And so hold on when there is nothing in you
    Except the Will which says to them: "Hold on!"

If you can talk with crowds and keep your virtue,
    Or walk with Kings—nor lose the common touch,
If neither foes nor loving friends can hurt you,
    If all men count with you, but none too much:
If you can fill the unforgiving minute
    With sixty seconds' worth of distance run,
Yours is the Earth and everything that's in it,
    And—which is more—you'll be a Man, my son!

Now the Judean poet and this English poet were separated by continents and by centuries. The English poet had twenty-five hundred years more of human experience to draw on, yet there is a remarkable similarity in the marks of the superior man as described by these two men. The surface phrase and local idiom vary, but the essential meaning is frequently the same.

The Psalmist says: "Who shall ascend the mountain of the Lord? The man who walketh uprightly and worketh righteousness, the man who is wholesome, who is one, the man who has singleness of heart, singleness of spirit." The English poet says: "If you can talk with crowds and keep your virtue, or walk with Kings—nor lose the common touch." In both of these poems, the superior man is the one who is the same in all situations. The superior man is not a chameleon. You can anticipate the reaction of the superior man to every possible moral situation. He is not all things to all men. He has not one voice for those below him and another for his superiors. He is not dissolved or absorbed or neutralized by his environment. He walks through the world a defined, dependable, stable moral person. In other words, the superior man is wholehearted, integrated, one, and therefore is always a man of utmost simplicity. His thoughts are direct, straightforward, clear. His words are meant to convey thought, not to disguise thought.

The superior man always loves the straightforward and simple things of life, not because he is naive, but because he wants intelligently to understand the greatness of little things. The superior man has natural curiosity about everything in the world. For the zest of wonderment and mystery, he does not require excitement, the grotesque or the extraordinary. He is without affectation but is profoundly affected by the world of man and nature. To the simple man, the whole world about him is filled with friends, both great and small. His world is peopled.

One of the marks of the superior man is wholeheartedness and simplicity. Do not deal in lies, for lying means spiritual disintegration, spiritual chaos. A liar is a shattered and broken personality. He has desperately tried to adjust himself to all new situations not by holding himself intact but by breaking himself up in the attempt to meet a situation which suddenly confronts him. One's life can be held together by truth and only by truth. The rabbis said that the seal of God and of His universe is truth, and the seal of the superior man is truth.

The superior man will make a pledge to his own destiny and will link his life up with some cause, some ideal, some purpose even if the pursuit of that goal involves suffering and sacrifice. Kipling weights his ideal man with the quality of courage; the Psalmist, as may well be imagined, with that of justice.

To the Psalmist, the superior man is one who does justice, a man who does no evil to his neighbor, who takes no bribe. These are the qualities of justice which in the eyes of the Hebrew poet quite naturally stand out.

To the English poet whose tradition is one of courage and chivalry the ideal man is a man of courage ennobled by chivalry and self-confidence ennobled by modesty.

> If you can keep your head when all about you
>   Are losing theirs
>
> If you can trust yourself when all men doubt you
>
> If you can force your heart and nerve and sinew
>   To serve your turn long after they are gone
> And so hold on when there is nothing in you
>   Except the Will which says to them: "Hold on!"

Supreme confidence is the mark of the superior man. The Psalmist, too, knows of confidence, but not so much self-confidence as confidence in God. Strength pours into the life of the human being, not from the wellsprings of his own will, not out of the inner reverence of his own life, but because a faith and confidence in God whose will and purpose man obeys:

> I will lift up mine eyes unto the mountains;
> From whence shall my help come?
> My help cometh from the Lord,
> Who made heaven and earth.

He will not suffer thy foot to be moved;
He that keepeth thee will not slumber.
Behold, He that keepeth Israel
Doth neither slumber nor sleep.

The Lord is thy keeper;
The Lord is thy shade upon thy right hand.
The sun shall not smite thee by day,
Nor the moon by night.

The Lord shall keep thee from all evil;
He shall keep thy soul.
The Lord shall guard thy going out and thy coming in,
From this time forth and forever.

There comes a time in the life of a man when even his will can no longer tell him to "Hold on!"—when he is broken and beaten by life. It is then that God whispers to the man of faith: "Do not be afraid, for I am with you."

Another mark of the superior man is the avoidance of extremes. The man who is extreme is usually overzealous, fanatic, impetuous. If such a man is without ideals he will be acquisitive, a beast of a man. Even if he is a man of ideals, this extremism, this overzealousness will probably move him to become a fanatic, a crank, a bigot. If he has ideals he will probably count no cost too great to achieve his ideals. He will sacrifice means to ends. He will bring misery to men in his overzealousness to help and save them. It is this kind of person who tortures another person in order to make him happy. Such people burn people at the stake to save their souls or carry on bloody purges to establish the Kingdom of God.

Confucius, one of the wisest men of all times, said this to a favorite disciple:

> Have you ever heard, Lu, of the six shadows which attend the six virtues? No, he replied. Sit down, then, and I will tell you. Love of goodness without the will to learn casts the shadow called foolishness. Love of knowledge without the will to learn casts the shadow called instability. Love of truth without the will to learn casts the shadow called insensibility. Love of candour without the will to learn casts the shadow called rudeness. Love of daring without the will to learn casts the shadow called turbulence. Love of firmness without the will to learn casts the shadow called eccentricity.

All six qualities are virtues, but in their extreme, unharnessed and uncurbed, they become shadows which darken man's way through life.

The mark of the superior man is that he is neither hasty nor a laggard, neither forward nor shy, neither proud nor humble, neither hard nor soft, neither materialistic nor impractical, neither visionary nor yet without ideals. Now, it is terrifically difficult to hold this balance. But that is the mark of the superior man. This balance gives point to life, a sense of serenity. The superior man does not try to play safe. He only wants to be human, fair. He does not straddle an issue. He works and fights for his convictions. But he always tries to be understanding of the other's point of view and always remembers that he is a human being dealing with human beings, and that the Torah was given to human beings.

Another mark of the superior man on which poet and Psalmist agree is that the superior man reveres work and honest craftsmanship. He himself tries to be an honest craftsman and utilizes each hour and day of life in purposeful achievement to "fill the unforgiving minute with sixty seconds' worth of distance run." "Teach us, O Lord, to number our days!" says the Psalmist in prayer. This is the mark of the superior man— to do things, to do them well, to respect honest labor, whether it be work of the mind or of the hand.

Thomas Carlyle said:

> Two men I honor, and no third. First, the toilworn Craftsman that with earth-made Implement laboriously conquers the Earth, and makes her man's. Venerable to me is the hard Hand; crooked, coarse, wherein notwithstanding lies a cunning virtue, indefeasibly royal, as of the scepter of this Planet. . . .
>
> A second man I honor, and still more highly; Him who is seen toiling for the spiritually indispensable; not daily bread, but the bread of Life. . . . If the poor and humble toil that we have Food, must not the high and glorious toil for him in return, that he have Light, have Guidance, have Freedom, Immortality? . . . These two, in all their degrees, I honor: all else is chaff and dust, which let the wind blow whither it listeth.

Carlyle was a superior man. And the mark of his distinction was this mark, this regard for honest labor, whether of the hand or of the heart. The superior man is not just a man of culture and learning who can quote many books or who has at his command a number of languages or who can engage in charming conversations. These are valuable accomplishments, but culture in idleness which does not express itself in work, service, achievement, in acts does not create the superior man. In fact, our rabbis said: "All culture which does not have alongside it 'work' is in the end wasted, nullified, and not only that. It causes sin, spiritual degeneration."

Finally, the superior man, everyone seems to agree, is the man who masters his fortune and his misfortune.

> If you can meet with Triumph and Disaster,
> And treat these two impostors just the same

I do not know whether they are impostors, but I do know it is the superior man who masters them both. He does not permit sorrow to break his spirit or joy to destroy his sympathy. He bends triumph and disaster to his own spiritual ends, disaster for cleansing and purification, triumph for generosity, good will, and reconciliation.

The inferior man complains when trials, tribulations, and sorrow come into his life. He allows his spirit to go down to utter defeat. The superior man is just as sensitive to grief and sorrow, but he uses that sorrow to cleanse, to purge, to ennoble. "Our eyes see clearly only after they have been washed with tears."

There is a great phrase of one of the rabbis of our people: "What way brings a man to immortality? What way gives to human life an element of the eternal? It is the quality of suffering." The Psalmist cries out in one of his moments of understanding: "I thank you, O Lord, that thou hast chastised me, for making me drink deep of the waters of salvation." This is the mark of the superior man.

I might add this one other characteristic of the superior man—he is open-minded; he appreciates and seeks intellectual freedom. The superior man is never a dogmatist, never a doctrinaire, never a reactionary. He knows that life is an advancing experience, an unfolding realization. He is a seeker. The adventure of the human intellect in the undiscovered continents intrigues him. He hails every new vista which opens up before him. He does not scoff at the old because it is old nor does he resist the new just because it is new.

So, if you want to summarize what these poets of ancient and modern days regard as the marks of the superior man, it would be first and foremost wholeheartedness and simplicity; second, courage and confidence; third, moderation; fourth, artistry, craftsmanship, and reverence for man's handiwork; fifth, mastery of his fate; and finally, the free, open, and sympathetic seeking mind.

This is a man who will always dwell in the Tabernacle of the Lord and stand in the presence of his fellow men as a light and an inspiration.

I N ONE OF HIS LETTERS, the English poet John Keats wrote: "I feel more and more every day, as my imagination strengthens, that I do not live in this world alone, but in a thousand worlds." That, to a lesser degree, is true of all men, even those who are not poets. As their imagination strengthens, they come to live not in this world alone, but also in many other worlds. In fact, the whole purpose of education is to introduce us to new worlds, and, when you come to think of it, the whole purpose of religion is to extend and widen the boundaries of our individual lives to a point where we come to embrace in sympathy and in service other lives— our families, our neighbors, our countries, and the life of mankind . . .

FROM A SERMON
"THE IMPORTANCE OF MY WORLD,"
JANUARY 20, 1952

"If I Am Not for Myself, Who Will Be for Me?"

A man caught up in the sweep of historic movements, a leader in these movements—such a man is not usually expected to be interested in personal counseling or in the small and petty concern. of the ordinary individual life. It is no surprising, therefore, that most people do not think of Abba Hillel Silver in term of personal guidance for the daily and often trivial problems of existence. Members of his congregation knew otherwise They knew that most of his utterance from the pulpit were directed to the individual with his hopes and fears, his yearnings for love, companionship, security.

As in all of his teachings, Rabbi Silver's "counseling" is drawn from classic Jewish attitudes as expressed by the Bible, by the rabbinic sages, and also by modern "sages of the soul." There is nothing dogmatic or simplistic about his views. He observed the many sides of an issue, shunned easy formulae, and always drove to the heart of the matter even when the result of the analysis was only the restoration of a well-worn truth. He did not strain for originality. But again, the tenor of advice which Rabbi Silver offers has the flavor of his own positive personality. Rabbi Silver did not believe in pampering the individual who persisted in remaining "sick-

lied o'er with the pale cast of thought." Personally, he never came to conclusions or expressed his opinion without a great deal of thought. But he did insist that one must come to conclusions and express those conclusions in words and actions. Of course, he recognized the tragedy and heartbreak associated with genuine physical and mental disability. What society or the individual could cure by medicine, by economic reform, by social progress, he wanted cured. But he felt it was important to recognize that perfection was not possible in this world—"perfection is synonymous with death." Meanwhile a man must not indulge himself in self-pity. Within the limitations of his fate, he could build a great deal which was true, strong, and beautiful. He should use his will and clarity of mind to remedy those defects in his personal and family life which could be remedied. In this effort he would be helped by the example of those who have overcome handicaps, and by God.

It is, perhaps, an "old-fashioned" message. But when heard in an environment which tends to blame heredity, environment, or a mysterious "subconscious" for its troubles, it has remarkable freshness.

The Importance of Myself

SERMON, THE TEMPLE
DECEMBER 2, 1951

Principles are important. Institutions are important. Systems are important. But most important of all is man himself. All principles, institutions, and systems exist for man, and are determined by him. If man is regarded as insignificant and unimportant, then all these principles and institutions and systems have no point of reference. They become social aberrations, agencies of human degradation. On the other hand, if man himself is base and inferior, then his principles and his institutions and his systems will share in that baseness and inferiority.

The rabbis say that only one single man was created in the beginning of the world so that everyone will have the right to say, "For my sake was the whole world created." One human life is as important as the whole world. "He who preserves one human life, it is accounted unto him as if he preserved the whole world. He who destroys one human life, it is charged to him as if he destroyed the whole world." Man is equated with the whole world.

According to our tradition, Adam and every one of his descendants were created in the image of God. Man is preferred from among all created things because he was created in the image of God. And the rabbis say that creation conferred upon man not only distinction and importance, but uniqueness. "Men stamp many coins with one die, and they are all like to one another. But God has stamped every man with the die of the first man, and yet not one of them is like his fellow man." There is difference, there is distinctiveness to every human being. Nevertheless, men must all be united in divine kinship, one with another. Man is important and man is unique. "When a man goes on his way," say the sages, "a troop of angels precedes him, and they proclaim, 'Make way for the image of the Holy One, blessed be He.'"

Emerson said the very same thing in another way. "There is a great responsible thinker and actor moving wherever moves a man." "A true man is the center of things." Now, man does not derive his importance from the fact that he is perfect. Man is not perfect. Man is limited in many ways. His days upon earth are few. He is born unto trouble. He is given to sin and backsliding. His importance does not rest on the fact that he is a perfect being; in fact he is full of imperfections. "What is man that Thou art mindful of him, and the son of man that Thou takest cognizance of him?" Nevertheless, "Thou hast made him a little lower than the angels, and hast crowned him with glory and honor."

In our sacred literature, God always addressed Himself to the single individual, the man. Revelation is always personal, except the one revelation at Mount Sinai, when it appeared to all those who stood at the foot of the mountain; God spoke directly to every one of them. The Ten Commandments were given by the One to the one. "I am the Lord, thy God . . ." "Thou shalt . . ." "Thou shalt not . . ." "Thou shalt love thy neighbor as thyself." Second person singular.

Similarly, the true believer saw himself in a direct, personal, and unmediated relationship to his God. "The Lord is my shepherd. I shall not want . . ." "The Lord is my light and my salvation . . ." "I sought the Lord and He heard me and delivered me from all my fears." It is amazing when you read through the Book of Psalms, the outpouring of the religious soul of man, how much of it is written in the first person singular, and directed towards God.

Every man is important, and not only the mind of man, not only the spirit of man, but the body of man, too, is important. Once, as Hillel was taking leave of his disciples, they asked him why he was leaving them, and he said, "I am going to bathe. I am going to perform a pious deed." And they asked him, "Is bathing a pious deed?" "Why," he said, "certainly. Have you ever seen the temples and the circuses of the pagans? They have there the images of their kings and their rulers, and they charge a man to wash those images, and polish them out of respect for their subject. How much more so must I, who am made in the image of God, polish and wash my body, in which the spirit of God resides."

All that is normal in man, his unabused and unperverted desires and pleasures, are important. They help to bring happiness and satisfactions to his life, and these enjoyments and satisfactions are important. They help to keep his life normal and to preserve the order of things. Man is, of course, not an island unto himself. He is born into a family, becomes a member of a community, and is subject to the influence of environment and heredity. He is inextricably linked to numerous relationships as son or daughter, brother or sister, husband or wife, father or mother, neighbor, friend, citizen. As a man develops and grows, the number and the variety of his associations and his identifications, his fellowships in his business, in his profession, in his vocation multiply and extend. The more interests which a man develops, cultural or social, the more contacts he makes, the more bonds he establishes, the more involvements and commitments ensue. A man becomes part of a veritable network of associations in which he must find fulfillment for himself as well as balance and harmony between the obligations demanded of each relationship.

But always, in the midst of all these numerous connections and associations, always at the core of all things, remains the man himself and his undissolved, inviolate personality. Society is made up of individuals. The community is a fellowship of individuals. Governments exist to make secure the lives of individuals, to adjust their conflicting differences and to advance their common good.

This has not always been the accepted doctrine. In our day it has been most violently, and I am afraid, to a large degree successfully, challenged. Behind the totalitarian systems of Fascism and Nazism and Communism are doctrines and philosophies which either negate altogether or depreciate the importance of the individual, which exalt the all-importance of the state, the community, the collective. In varying degrees and emphases these systems all share this concept of the unconditional supremacy of the community over the individual, of the monolithic society, of the thorough coordination, of the *Gleichschaltung* of all men.

It is not just that these new systems give society or the community priority over the interests of the individual. That, even democracies have to do. After all, the welfare and progress of the individual is contingent upon the progress and the preservation of the community as a whole. Rather, these new philosophies, these pseudo-philosophies, claim for the community and for the group, for the collective—whatever it may be— supreme independence and sovereignty. They claim for them inherent rights, inherent authority, which they regard as prior to the rights not only of a given individual, but of all individuals. The individual to them is only an expression of the group. His life has meaning only as it is related to the all-dominant and overwhelming group. His rights derive from his group. He has no inalienable rights of his own. There is no primary and independent spiritual franchise for man in this system of thought. Man fulfills himself not through the development of his unique personality or his special endowments, or through cooperative effort with fellow human beings; man fulfills himself, according to this philosophy, through complete self-surrender, self-effacement, and total immersion in some kind of tribalism, whether it be the tribalism of the "folk," of a blood cult, of a proletarian class, or of some other closed group.

As a corollary to the exaltation of the collective and the subordination of the individual, there follows the doctrine of the omnipotent leader, *Fuehrer, duce,* who becomes the embodiment of the omnipotent state or society, demanding the unconditional obedience of everyone else. This theory is the basis of all concepts of dictatorship. And dictatorship spells death to all the ideals of human equality and human freedom.

These aberrations have had a great vogue in our generation. They are responsible for many disastrous political experiences in the world, including a tragic world war. Judaism has always waged war upon the concept of the absolutist ruler and of the transcendent and impeccable state. Judaism has always emphasized the importance of the individual, of man himself. Man possesses certain rights which are his inalienably, which have been given him not by the state or by society or by the class, but by God, his creator. All men and all races are equal in the sight of God, and are distinguished only by the merit which they achieve, by the worth which they acquire personally, by the service which they render to God and to mankind. Every man, whatever his race or color, every man, whatever his position in life, is precious in the sight of God. Every human being, however humble, is to be made secure within a Law, within an inviolable moral law which is binding upon every one, whether he be a king or a nobleman or a commoner, whether he be an individual or the collective. The state can err. The collective can do wrong. The king can sin and the nobleman and the priest and the rich and the poor and the employer and the employee—they all can, and all do, sin. They are all accountable to a supreme, impartial, universal, eternal moral law. And every sinner is free to repent, to return, to be saved.

This new conception of the supremacy of the state, which is endangering our world and is in defiance of the whole Biblical tradition, is properly characterized in this paragraph from Bertrand Russell's little volume *Authority and the Individual:*

> There are some philosophers and statesmen who think that the state can have an excellence of its own, and not merely as a means to the welfare of the citizens. I cannot see any reason to agree with this view. "The state" is an abstraction; it does not feel pleasure or pain, it has no hopes or fears, and what we think of as its purposes are really the purposes of individuals who direct it. When we think concretely, not abstractly, we find, in place of "the state," certain people who have more power than falls to the share of most men. And so glorification of "the state" turns out to be, in fact, glorification of a government minority. No democrat can tolerate such a fundamentally unjust theory.

Today the status of the individual is endangered by this concept of the omnipotent state. There were other ages in which the status of the individual was endangered by other social or even theological considerations. There were theologians who endeavored to exalt the omnipotence of God to such heights that they reduced man to a state of abject lowliness and worthlessness. We find that point of view challenged in the Book of Job. Job refuses to justify the ways of God by charging himself with sins which he knows he did not commit and which his friends are endeavoring to persuade him that he must have, knowingly or unknowingly, committed. Job would not do violence to the integrity of his own personality in order to vindicate the justice of omnipotence.

In the sight of God, I am important, you are important, to a degree undreamt of in modern society, where the individual is being reduced to an automaton, to a robot, to a frightened and abashed subject in a ruthlessly domineering society. The importance which my religion ascribes to me and to you does not derive from place or position, from wealth or ancestry. These are badges which men display from time to time to impress their fellow men. Intrinsically they are not indices of importance. Importance stems from within, from character, from our intellectual and spiritual aspirations. Importance wells up from the internal seas of our personality. A radiant soul is man's true dignity and is the real testament of his importance to himself and to society. "It is not the place which honors a man, it is the man who honors the place." My importance is to be found in what I earnestly and sincerely and worthily try to do.

Being important and feeling myself important does not mean feeling self-important or self-satisfied, self-sufficient or proud. God hates pride and arrogance. And so do men. Man's pride will bring him low. A man who is aware of his importance to himself and to others will have the imagination to be humble. "The greater thou art," we read in the Apocrypha, "the more humble thyself. Thou shalt find favor before the Lord." Torah, learning, and wisdom are acquired through humility. Humility is neither weakness nor self-effacement. Humility does not derive from timidity or servility, but from strength and wisdom. Humility, in the last analysis, is a kind of reverence before the majesty and the mystery of all that is baffling and unpredictable and impenetrable and glorious in life and nature and man. Humility is a kind of reverence in the presence of one's own place and role in this tangled skein of things, reverence in the presence of our own baffling destiny.

So a wise man is a humble man, a modest man. Now, a modest man is not a leaning willow. A modest man can be tempered steel. He knows his worth and will not permit anyone to trespass upon the sacred precepts of his being. But a modest man will never give offense by thrusting his self-estimate upon others, nor will he stultify himself or impede himself or embarrass himself socially by egotism, because egotism is really only the ugly rash of personality smallpox.

Because I am important, much is expected of me and much must I expect of myself. I must live up to the promise and the challenge of my life. I must educate myself to the utmost. I must explore every cranny of my heart and of my mind, for no one knows his true resources until he has explored them.

Because I regard myself as important, I respect myself. Reverence of self is the beginning of all virtue. Because I revere myself, I have reverence for my being. I will try not to stoop, not to truckle under, not to be cheap, not to sell myself cheap, not to do the things which degrade—not out of fear of being found out or fear of punishment, but out of reverence for myself and of the God that is in me. Because I think myself important, I will try to rely upon myself to the utmost, drawing upon my own confident strength as far as possible, remembering always, of course, that often we need the help or the strength of others. I must therefore be prepared to share my strength with others when they need it. No man is self-sufficient. But one must not build his life upon the backs of others, nor must one in every crisis of his life rely upon others and, failing to rely upon himself, resign himself to defeat.

Because I think of my life as important, I will on occasions make sacrifices for other lives which I regard as important as, and perhaps more important than, mine. Nevertheless, I will refuse to make needless sacrifices for the sake of others who may be less important and for causes which I disesteem. I will refuse to be exploited by others who would live off me. My life is as important as the life of my neighbor.

I will live for myself, but in so doing, I must live for others. "If I am not for myself, who will be for me? But if I am only for myself, what am I?" Because I regard myself as important, I must learn to stand alone sometimes and to differ with the people about me. When my convictions run counter to theirs, I must learn to defend my ideas, once I have assured myself of their validity. I must learn to speak the truth, in kindness, to be sure, but always to speak the truth. It is sometimes imperative for the salvation of my soul and for the vindication of myself to defy the whole world. I must learn the importance of being important. "In the place where there are no men," said Hillel, "strive thou to be a man," to be the man. And when we are constrained to do just that and the world's displeasures are visited upon us, we must learn to suffer and endure indignity as befits a son of God.

Now, in this vast, impressive world in which we find ourselves, we are prone to think of ourselves as more or less helpless beings. What can we do about all that is wrong in the world today? What can I personally do? I can do nothing. Many people feel that way about it. They are overwhelmed by the machinery, by the apparatus, by the organization, by the scale and mass of everything around them. They believe themselves inadequate to affect the course of things.

This kind of resignation is the end of democracy and of freedom, and it is the end of the development of human personality. We ought to remember at all times that whatever is done in this world is done by men like ourselves, for good or evil, for weal or woe, whatever happens in this world is the work of human beings, of men.

The Stalins and the Hitlers and the Mussolinis are just ordinary human beings, ordinary in terms of the common destiny which they share as human beings with all other human beings. So are the great and the good men of the world who have helped to advance our civilization. They, too, are human beings like ourselves.

We must not deprecate ourselves nor our importance. We *can* affect the course of things, if only within the little world in which we move and have our being, within the circumference of our life's influence.

If tens and thousands and millions of other human beings become aware of the strength which is in them and pour out their strength, that force becomes colossal and irresistible. We owe it to ourselves to regard ourselves as important, and then to proceed to acquaint ourselves with all that is happening about us, to ascertain the facts; not to be victimized by propaganda, not to howl with the mob, not to be stampeded by slogans and catchwords—that is, not to sacrifice our individuality, but to sift, screen, test, and analyze to the best of our ability everything that we see or hear or read. Not everything we read in the columns of our newspapers or hear over the radio is so. Much of it is not so at all. Much of it is only partially so. Use your knowledge, your insight, your wisdom, your moral sense to weigh and measure and balance and arrive at your own conclusions, and when you have arrived at conclusions, then learn to speak up—speak up unafraid. You will inspire others to do likewise. When the voices of men of good will are heard in the world, the action of the dark forces may be checked.

Organize with other men and women and express your power through your ballot, through other vehicles and agencies available to you. Activate your personality! Give it social significance by active participation in the life of your community, of your city, of your state, of your government. Because we are accepting what the dictators of the world want us to accept, namely, that individually we are of no account, can do nothing, we have been prone to shake off our personal responsibilities by loading government with all that is wrong in the world today. Whenever we find anything wrong, we blame authorities—the state government or national government. Well, it is not that they are free of all blame—far from it! But in the last analysis, if there is anything wrong in the world, if there is anything wrong in government which is permitted to endure for long, the wrong is with ourselves—us, you and me. We must begin the improvement of society with ourselves. The moral injunctions were given to us as individuals. "Thou shalt!" "Thou shalt not!"

What Are You Afraid Of?

SERMON, THE TEMPLE
JANUARY 21, 1940

There are men and women who are the victims of all kinds of phobias, people who are, so to speak, psychically allergic to certain things. Some have a phobia of open spaces; some of closed spaces. Some are afraid of crowds; some of being alone. Some are afraid of heights; some are afraid of crossing the street. Some are afraid of spiders, caterpillars, cats, snakes, or a little mouse. Some of these fears are not very serious, but there are people who become the victims of a continuous condition of mental strain and anxiety, of unreasoning and unaccountable fear bordering on hysteria. They require the attention of a physician.

That kind of fear I do not wish to discuss, because I am not able to discuss it with authority. Nor do I wish to discuss real fear, which is man's normal reaction to real danger. I do not wish to discuss it, because there is nothing to discuss. There is nothing wrong with real fear. Every normal human being experiences it at one time or another. Such fear is nature's danger signal. It is nature's warning to the individual to take steps either to get away from the danger or to defend himself from that danger. Such fear, when it is not extreme, is often the mother of wise caution.

Sometimes a good scare is worth more to a man than good advice. There is nothing wrong about that. The human race has inherited certain primitive fears. Infants are known to be afraid of certain things—loud noises, for instance, and falling; some say even of strange people and of darkness. These fears date back to the early life of the race. They date back to the infrahuman experiences in those long eons in the jungle, the experiences of man during his savage period, when he was hunted by men and by beasts. These experiences have left in the subconscious life of the

140

individual a dark deposit of what you might call instinctive reactions to certain stimuli, an instinctive sense of the fateful meaning of certain sounds, movements, and appearances and of how man must be prepared to meet them. It has been demonstrated that fear causes certain definite physical and chemical changes in the organism, changes which are necessary in order to equip man to defend himself against sudden assaults of danger. Fear, for example, causes an excessive glandular discharge of adrenalin which stimulates the nervous system, and more sugar is poured into the blood, creating additional energy. Blood is drained from the skin and the digestive organs and is channeled into the brain and muscles, where it is needed for defense. In other words, real fear prepares a man for necessary flight from danger or for necessary combat.

Such fear is not a cause for concern. It disappears with the danger which stimulates it, and it is commensurate with the danger.

But a man can have an excessive fear, out of all proportion to the danger which threatens him. Instead of equipping him for action, it paralyzes him. His defenses collapse. He becomes demoralized. His will is prostrate. Reason vanishes. He is a bundle of chaotic reflexes, a licked and shattered man. A human being caught up in such a panicky fear is frequently called harsh names, but the fault is not always a fault of character. Heredity and environment and training may have much to do with it.

Much can be done to keep these besetting fears of man within reasonable bounds. Much can be done to keep the phenomenon of fear from becoming destructive. Courage is a habit which can be developed. It is not true that courage is simply inherited. Courage can be developed like truthfulness and cleanliness. A person can be trained to have courage. Every soldier, for example, is afraid. Every man who finds himself in the firing line, danger lurking all around, ahead of him, beneath him, and over him, is afraid. But the discipline of training carries him along. At first it is hard; panic threatens to demoralize him, but it becomes easier as he time and again succeeds through force of habit, effort, and the exercise of will in mastering himself. A seasoned soldier, while he is not unafraid, is able to meet danger and curb panic and carry on.

From childhood on, men should be trained to face up to the dark and frightening possibilities in life. The trick is not to run away from fright-producing situations, but to confront them. This can be terrifyingly difficult, but life becomes increasingly less difficult as we face up to dangers which have a tendency to shatter and demoralize us. It must be done, this training in courage, because unquenchable fear, persistent, all-pervading fear is an ugly thing. Even when it does not betray itself in action, it is still ugly and dangerous, because it undermines character.

Fear makes us cruel, for fear makes men desperate, and desperate people are cruel in their panic. When you see a man who is cruel, you can write it down that man is weak, afraid of things perhaps unknown to himself. He may be physically powerful, but somewhere inside he has a gnawing fear which is undermining his spiritual strength, and that weakness is manifesting itself in desperation. A really strong man is never cruel.

Fear makes us hate, for we hate the people we fear. When you find someone who hates other individuals, or groups of individuals, or mankind, you can write it down that that man is afraid of that individual, or of that group of individuals, or of mankind, because if you hate life, you are afraid of life.

Fear makes us suspicious. It poisons all our normal human relationships, and fear betrays and defeats us in every decisive hour of our lives. You can move steadily on in life through months and years until there comes a great decision upon which all depends—and in that critical moment your fears will find you out and betray you.

Every great religion arose to deliver men from fear. Sometimes people who do not know, but think they know, make the observation that religion is born out of fear; that because men feared gods, they worshiped them and brought them sacrifices. Of course, these enlightened people have no fears, and they therefore do not need religion. The truth is that men turned to religion to be delivered from fear, to overcome fear. Men turned to religion to give them confidence and assurance and hope in the dark, danger-beset, fear-infested world in which they found themselves. They were beset by fear of the beasts, fear of the past, fear of the future, fear of life, and fear of death. Because of that web of entangled fears, the human being needed some focus of confidence and hope to enable him to live: hence God; hence religion. Men turn to their God not because they are afraid of Him, but because they need Him to help them surmount the fears which beset them.

From the Book of Proverbs we read: "The fear of man is like a snare unto him. But whoso putteth his trust in God, shall be set on a high and secure eminence." To save himself from the snare of fears about him, man turns in confidence to God. Our religion counseled men to exchange all their fears, their fear of life and of death, of pain, of poverty, of evils known and unknown—exchange them all for the one fear which is no fear at all, their trust in God. "Do not be afraid of the sudden fears that trap you, and from the destructiveness of the evildoers when they come to you. Have confidence in God. He will keep your foot from being caught."

There are a hundred admonitions in the Bible not to be afraid, and only one harsh admonition to be afraid. The single exception is: "Be afraid of your God." Such fear, of course, is no fear at all. Observe the moral law, lead the righteous life, and you need have no fear. When Adam disobeyed a commandment of God, the voice came to him in the Garden of Eden: "Where art thou?" Adam said, "I heard Thy voice and I was afraid." God said to Adam, according to the sayings of the rabbis, "When you heard My voice before, you were not afraid; now that you have sinned, you have learned fear." The prophet Isaiah turned to his people and said: "Fear ye not their fear, nor account it dreadful. The Lord of Hosts . . . let Him be your fear, let Him be your dread." In other words, faith is a dike against all fear, against all the dark waters of dread and terror and anxiety and worries which beset a human being.

"Though I walk through the valley of the shadow of death, I will fear no evil." Why? "Thou art with me." "The Lord is my light and salvation. Of whom need I fear?" That is the function of religion in the world —to substitute one fear, one trust, one reverence for the myriads of fears which undermine the happiness of the human being.

God does not want men to fear. When you come to think of it, to every great figure of the Bible, in the one crisis of their lives, there came the challenge: "Do not be afraid." When Abraham set out on his journey to the unknown future, he was told: "Do not be afraid. I will be your shield." To Isaac, God said: "Do not fear, I will be with you and I will bless you." When Jacob was about to leave the Land of Canaan to go down into Egypt, he hesitated, and was told: "Do not be afraid!" When the Children of Israel found themselves by the Red Sea with the waters in front of them and the pursuing Egyptians behind them, with death before them and death behind, there came the voice of God: "Do not be afraid! Stand firm!" When Moses was faced with the prospect of fighting every foot of the way for his Promised Land, the word of the Lord came to him: "Go up!" Conquer! Do not be afraid!" When Moses died and Joshua took command, the same words were spoken to him. It is amazing—the recurrence of the phrase. It is not an accident. "Be strong and be courageous! Do not be afraid! Do not be frightened!"

How often too the prophets, especially those of the exile, when the Children of Israel were scattered and dispersed and found themselves impoverished, hopeless, away from their native lands—how often these prophets repeated: "Do not be afraid. Do not be afraid, my servant Jacob!" Do not be afraid of the mighty forces about you.

That is the purpose of our religion, to emancipate human beings from paralyzing fears, known and unknown, and to set them free on the great heroic roads of adventure. Faith gives us confidence to move forward.

Many of our fears are imaginary. Human beings suffer far more from things which never happen than from physical pain. The imagination conjures up devils, ghosts, terrors not found in nature.

There is a famous story by Hans Christian Andersen called "The Emperor's New Clothes," which you will recall from childhood reading. Two weavers came to a country and announced that they could weave the most beautiful cloth imaginable. These weavers were rogues; they were out to get money. They announced that the cloth had the peculiarity of being invisible to anyone who was unfit for the office he occupied or who was hopelessly stupid. The emperor of the country was greatly intrigued by what the weavers told him, and he gave them a large sum of money to weave him some of this marvelous cloth. The two rogues proceeded to set up a loom and went through the motions of weaving the cloth, demanding the most delicate silk and the finest gold thread, which they promptly put away for themselves. After a few weeks had gone by, the emperor sent one of his ministers to find out how they were doing. The minister went to the weavers, and looked at the loom and saw nothing, for nothing was there. But he was afraid to say that he saw nothing. He did not want to be known as unfit, or a fool. So he stood there and admired the beautiful cloth on the loom. "How superb! What an admirable design!"

A week or two later the emperor asked another officer to see how the cloth was getting along. He too saw nothing, but knowing that the minister had been there before him and had praised the cloth, and not wanting to be known as unfit for the position he occupied, he too praised the cloth. Finally the invisible clothes were completed, and the two weavers took them to the palace. The emperor, of course, saw nothing, but then he remembered that the cloth was invisible to those who were unfit to occupy their positions. He remembered that his own minister and officer had praised it. He took off his garments, put on the invisible clothes, and stood before the mirror admiring himself. Attired in his new clothes, he marched through the streets of the city under a canopy, and all the people on the curb, not wanting to be known as fools and simpletons, looked at the emperor and said: "What marvelous new clothes!" But there was one little child who knew no adult pretensions who was startled by the emperor's appearance and said: "But he hasn't got anything on!" And that cry was whispered from one to the other: "The emperor has nothing on. The emperor is naked." Soon great laughter broke from the crowd. The emperor knew the people were right, but he could do nothing but go through with the procession.

How often do we deck ourselves out in invisible, unreal, fears—worries, anxieties, concerns for which there is no place in reality at all; fear of the future, fear of failure, fear of losing money, fear of taking a chance, fear of trying a new job, fear of starting out, fear of competitors, fear of being unpopular, fear of a crowd, fear of speaking our mind, all of these fears choking the energies, the daring, the adventure of which we are capable. These fears bog us down. They make us small men. If only we had the courage to speak up. These fears—they are frauds! Men today are afraid of the new world which has come to be. They anticipate collapse, some terrible catastrophe. They fear that mankind is going through some vast tribulation. Mankind has come through similar tribulations. Mankind will emerge from this one.

In 1803, when Napoleon was at his height, William Wordsworth wrote the following:

> When looking on the present face of things,
> I see one man, of men the meanest too!
> Raised up to sway the world, to do, undo,
> With mighty Nations for his underlings,
> The great events with which old story rings
> Seem vain and hollow; I find nothing great:
> Nothing is left which I can venerate;
> So that a doubt almost within me springs
> Of Providence, such emptiness at length
> Seems at the heart of all things.

One hundred and thirty-seven years ago, the poet saw the end of the world. Because of Napoleon he lost faith in the times and in God.

Jews today are beset with real fears, but many of us also have become afraid of what the Bible calls the "sound of a withering leaf upon the ground." That sort of fear may take us to our ruin. We have gone through the fiery furnaces before and we have come through cleansed, and strengthened. What we Jews need today is courage, the cool courage to fight that is characteristic of seasoned soldiers such as we are.

I hear of men and women saying, Oh, this is the end for us. The world is set to destroy us. We are not going to have children. There is nothing to look forward to. Our long past, the longest continuous experience of any people that has come down from antiquity—our past recalls many similar tribulations and ultimate victory for Israel. "Though I walk through the valley of the shadow of death"—and this day is the valley of death—"I will fear no evil, for Thou art with me." What are you afraid of?

If you are afraid, then you simply have not exchanged your fears—all of them—for the one reverential fear which should be yours, the fear of God, the God who sleepeth not, who has not forsaken His people.

Man and His Loves and Hates

SERMON, THE TEMPLE
DECEMBER 22, 1940

There is a curious phrase in the Book of Koheleth: "There is a time to love and a time to hate." It is rather strange to find in a book of the Bible something which looks like a mandate to hate. The answer may be found in the story told by one of the sages about the illustrious wife of Meir, a great teacher of the second century before the Common Era. Meir was frequently attacked by his enemies, so much so that once, driven to desperation, Meir begged of God that He might destroy his enemies. Beruria, his wife, said to him: "It does not say in the Bible, 'Let the wicked perish.' The Bible says, 'Let wickedness perish.' " In that sense there is a time to hate, to hate not the evildoer as much as the evil. There is a definite mandate to hate wrong, injustice, or cruelty—in fact everything that mars; not to tolerate evil, not to be complacent about it, not to come to terms with it, not to appease the wrongdoers.

From the point of view of Judaism it is not a quality of saintliness to ignore the oppression of mankind, to avoid doing anything about it, to concern yourself only with the perfection of your own soul and your own spiritual tranquillity. One must be intolerant of social evils. One must seek their eradication. At the same time one should try to be tolerant of men. One should try to make allowances for human frailties.

"Thou lovest righteousness—thou hatest wickedness." That is a supreme tribute written by the Psalmist to the ideal ruler. "I hate every way of falsehood." This hatred, unlike all other forms of hatred, derives from a higher love. You hate wrong because you love righteousness, truth, and goodness. This hatred has its roots not in the hatred of humankind, but in the love of humankind.

147

Our world suffers today not because it is full of hatred of evil, but because it is full of hate—simple hate. Hate, like fear, is being fostered deliberately, inspired and implanted in the hearts of men as part of the technique of total revolution and total war. The Germans are teaching men to hate Jews. When the Nazis decided to wage war on Poland, they incited their people to hate the Poles. Now they are teaching hatred of the English. Peoples you wish to conquer, peoples you wish to subjugate, you first try to make hateful so as to justify their subjugation.

War and revolution always introduce hate. Propaganda is largely a hate device. Anti-Semitism is the hate technique of the twentieth century which is being employed and most exploited by the Nazis today. Hitler is the great hater of our day. Those who know bear testimony to the fact that the man is consumed by overwhelming, sometimes uncontrollable hatreds. Hermann Rauschnig, who knew Hitler well, stated in his book *The Voice of Destruction:* "Every conversation, however unimportant, seemed to show that this man was filled with an immeasurable hatred. He seemed always to feel the need of something to hate. . . . Hatred, personal hatred, rang out in his words, revenge for early years of poverty, for disappointed hopes, for a life of deprivation and humiliation." Otto Strasser, a collaborator of Hitler's in his early days, says in his book *Hitler and I:* "He only knows what he wants to destroy; he pulls down the walls without any idea of what he will build in their place. . . . He hates without knowing love. . . ."

Because these hatreds are not hatreds of evil but devices for perpetrating greater evil, they have proved ruinous to our civilization. In the wake of these hates comes not a new or juster civilization, or reconciliation, but deeper hatreds, smoldering resentments, underground enmities. New dragon's teeth are being sown all over the face of the earth. Everywhere one is confronted with the ugly leer of shameless, naked hatred. New wars, strife, revolution are in the making. This hatred has filled our world with concentration camps, mass murders, mass expulsions, mass robbery.

And all this in a world which will in a few days celebrate the birth of the founder of Christianity, the founder who declared: "Love thine enemies, bless them that curse you, do good to them that hate you, and pray for them who despitefully use you, and persecute you." The Western world subscribes to this religion of love. It has built beautiful shrines and sanctuaries dedicated to this religious love. But the Western world is filled with hate, and the tragic contrast between what men and nations pay lip service to and what they actually practice has at no time been more dishearteningly displayed than at this Christmas, 1940.

The fault, of course, is not with the Christian teachings of human brotherhood and peace. The fault is with this age of apostasy which has turned its back upon religion, which has gone backward, back to the pagan world, to the pagan doctrines of force and tyranny: the rule of the strong and the rationalization that the end justifies all means.

Love is at the heart of every spiritual religion. The principle of love in Judaism may be somewhat more tempered, somewhat more settled, somewhat more practical than is the principle of love in Christianity. But it is there. Judaism taught men to love God: "You shall love God with all your heart, with all your soul and with all your might." Judaism taught men to love their fellow men: "Thou shalt love thy neighbor as thyself, for I am the Lord." Judaism taught men to love man. One of the famous mystics said that all the commandments have their roots in love. Their reality is the principle of love; without that principle, the commandments have no reality whatsoever.

Why did great religions emphasize the principle of love? Because it is the way to freedom, justice, and peace. Our tragedy is that man has been trying to find his way to these things—freedom, justice, peace—not through love, but through hate, through class struggle, through race hatred, through purges, through liquidations, through annihilation. And instead of justice and peace, we find only slavery, injustice, war, and death.

God has placed both love and hate in the heart of man. Both of these are to be refined by man. That is man's task upon earth—to refine both the love and the hate which God has placed in his heart. Hate is to be refined until it becomes hatred not of the wrongdoer but of the wrong, until it becomes the abomination of all that is morally abominable; until it revolts against every principle that shackles and oppresses mankind. Hate is to be refined through a process of moral self-discipline, until it is cleansed of envy, malice, and vengeance, until the chaff is separated from the wheat. And love is to be refined until it becomes not selfishness, or possessiveness, or jealousy, or lust, but a quality of living which uplifts, ennobles, makes strong, and liberates.

There is a common saying that love is blind. In a sense that is true: love *is* blind. But so is hatred blind. There is a fundamental difference between love which is blind and hatred which is blind; Moses ibn Ezra draws this distinction: "Love makes blind the eyes so that it cannot see the faults in the object of love. Hatred makes blind the eyes so as not to see the virtues in the object of hate." Surely it is far better for man to fail to see the faults in another man than to fail to see his virtues.

Love is blind in the sense that it overlooks faults, shortcomings, frailties. Thank God for that; otherwise no friendship or intimacy would survive. But in a deeper sense, love, like wisdom, opens our eyes to see more clearly, to see deeper. Love gives us a clearer and wider vision. Love is clairvoyant. Shakespeare says that love "adds a precious seeing to the eye." Love enables men and women to see beyond the normal range. It gives them a certain breadth of illumination. When we love someone, we are able to see in him or in her qualities unseen and unsuspected by others. We see beyond the surface into the depths; acts become more meaningful, words have larger significance for us. What may be unattractive to others comes to glow in the light of transforming love with a beauty of its own. For love sees much else. And unless love can see much else, it is not love.

In the same sense it is frequently said that man is a slave to love. Love enslaves a man and a woman, but it also sets us free. Love binds us irrevocably to the object of our love whether it is a human being or an ideal, because great love is never free. People who talk of free love have in mind barnyard mating. Great love is never free. Every great human devotion demands of us a full measure of exclusive and concentrated loyalty. Great love also frees our talents and our energies and capacities, because we wish to serve the object of our love to the utmost, and to the utmost be worthy of that love. We pour out our souls in generous abandon. We do not weigh, measure, or calculate. We become free in the boundless self-sacrifice, and because our love is prepared to sacrifice all, it conquers all.

Love knows its bounds, but it also knows its wings. The real difference between love and no love is the difference between speech and song. As long as it is song, it is love. When there are no more birds singing in Arcady, it is no longer Arcady.

The man who is deeply in love with his work, with his art, with his cause, not to speak of his beloved, his wife, his child, that man experiences a calm exaltation, a real intensification of life.

This week, the Jewish world is celebrating the eightieth birthday of a remarkable woman, Henrietta Szold. Here is a woman who loves her people, her people's literature. Here is a woman who loves her people's land so much that she has dedicated her entire life to her people. I have known Henrietta Szold for a quarter of a century. She was born in Baltimore, the daughter of an eminent rabbi. I knew her when she was engaged, in this country, in the work of helping to edit and publish the works of Jewish scholars. I saw her and observed her in Palestine, and I was always impressed with the amazing spiritual exaltation of this little woman, seemingly frail, but somehow possessed of an inner glow. Year by year she has carried on her arduous work with a spiritual serenity. With that great love for her people, she organized a remarkable woman's organization, the Hadassah, to bring healing to Palestine. She was responsible for the upbuilding of an amazing health program in that country. In her seventies, when the wrath of Hitler swept over Germany, this little woman went to Germany and there arranged for the transportation of hundreds of Jewish boys and girls to the shelter of Palestine. And now, at eighty, Henrietta Szold is still to be found at the docks in Haifa and Tel Aviv, welcoming every ship that comes into port bringing refugees. She welcomes them as a universal mother.

That is what I mean by a love which gives to a human being an intensification of life, a higher degree of living.

Finally, there is one other fundamental difference between love and hate. Love is always a refuge. Hate is never a refuge. Only a mentally sick person can find sanctuary in his hates. But love is the enduring sanctuary of life. Life may rob you of many things. It often does. Life may even bereave us of the object of our love. It often does. But it can never bereave us of love itself. That remains. The artist who loves his art may be tried by life and afflicted by life and may be denied reward or acclaim in life. The artist may know poverty, yet if he is a real artist, he will find within his art solace, comfort, refuge, sanctuary. That is his reward. That is his supreme reward. A man who champions a noble cause will in all probability be misunderstood. He will be mocked, hated. He will be persecuted. Yet if he deeply loves his cause, deeply believes in it, he will find real solace and tranquillity of spirit in it regardless of what the world thinks.

There is your real test of love. Is your love a refuge? Is your love a sanctuary? When your days bring you anguish and the nights bring you tears, can you retreat to the holy quiet of your deep and sacred love and find surcease from sorrow and balm for your spirit? If you can, you are in love. If you can, you have been granted the supreme gift of life. That is what the Psalmist who loved God meant when he said: "God is my strength and my fortress and my refuge."

Suffering and Death

SERMON, THE TEMPLE
FEBRUARY 14, 1932

There are many kinds of suffering to which mortal man is heir. The greatest of these is not physical suffering. Sickness and pain afflict all men at some time or other, and some men are called upon to suffer torments. Modern medical science can often relieve man of his pain by curing the malady which has caused the pain or, if cure is impossible, by deadening the pain. Courage, fortitude and patience, while they are not antidotes to pain, are nevertheless allies in helping man to master his pain.

I have known men and women with life-long afflictions, with total blindness or total paralysis, who were yet able to derive a great measure of contentment from life. Others whose afflictions were far less severe became so embittered as to derive nothing from life but resentment and unhappiness.

Physical suffering is of course the sharpest, most vivid kind of suffering. But I question whether it is as widespread as the other kind of suffering, the mental and the spiritual kind which corrodes the very substance of the inner life of a man—worry, defeat, disillusionment, bereavement, unrequited love, and a whole sad catalogue of human pain whose source is not physical.

These are terribly real forms of suffering, because a man lives not in his body principally, but in his emotions, his desires, his hopes, and his longings. In that psycho-physical world which is man, of which the body is only a part and not the most important part, what ailment, for example, is comparable to that ailment which we call a heartache, which eats and consumes all the vigor and joy of life and ultimately undermines the very foundation of living?

I am not now referring to the abnormal maladies of the human spirit. I am not referring to that which is morbid or pathological, the neuroses and the psychoses of sick people, to those ailments which require clinical attention. I am referring to the suffering of normal people who are called upon to bear heavy loads. I have known many people who have gone under, through mental and physical anguish. Here is a parent who has been dishonored by his child; here is a man who has been betrayed by his friend; here is a mother who has lost her child; here is a man whom life has defeated; here is another who is being ground down by poverty; here is another who feels himself persecuted by implacable enemies—a whole army of normal human beings who suffer to the very roots of their being.

Now, every great religion and every great system of philosophy has a message for such troubled hearts, and particularly Judaism, ancient and wise with the wisdom of years. Judaism is a realistic religion. It faces facts. It does not create fictions to soften the harsh reality of things. Judaism is not a demulcent theosophy which blithely and cheerily proclaims that all human suffering is but imagination, the product of the mortal mind of man. Judaism is not very much impressed with that theology which maintains that evil is negative, that evil does not exist with God, that evil is only relative to man. This is of course true, but it is cold comfort to those who suffer and are passing through heavy tribulations.

Judaism accepts and acknowledges the sad frustrations and limitations of human life. One of its greatest texts, the Book of Ecclesiastes, portrays man in his hour of agony both mental and physical. Judaism knows that "man that is born of woman is of few days, and full of trouble. He cometh forth like a flower and withereth. He fleeth as a shadow and continueth not."

Judaism knows of the passions, of the weariness, of the vanity, of the horrors and the tribulations of human life, and it therefore offers no philosophy of shallow optimism. Life is not a paradise. Happiness is not always within the reach of man, nor is it ever continuous. And the most contented and most righteous frequently are called upon to suffer grief, sorrow, and bitterness throughout their lives.

On the other hand, Judaism refuses to surrender itself to a philosophy of hopeless pessimism. Unlike Hinduism, Judaism does not believe that life is, by its very nature, hopeless. Judaism does not say that human suffering is meaningless, nor does it disparage civilization, progress, or the dignity or worth of man, the value of his striving and struggles. For the world, to Judaism, is not the result of a fatal accident, as it is to the Hindu. Nor is it the result of some irrational and inscrutable necessity, as it was to the Greeks. To Judaism, the world and all that is in it is the creation of the will of a wise and intelligent God, who meant human life to be just what it is—light and shadow, joy and sorrow and pain. Human life, in the mind of the wise and beneficent Creator, was meant, according to Judaism, to be a struggle against evil and ignorance: a struggle against the lower and an upreaching toward the higher. The whole significance of human life lies in the struggle, and all the satisfactions of human life derive from the struggle. Therefore Judaism sought to train men to prepare themselves for the struggle. Courage, fortitude, resoluteness, patience, these are the weapons with which the soldier of the spirit equips himself for the inevitable struggle of existence. The resolute heart, the stiff upper lip, yes, even the clenched fist—but always carry on. That is the teaching of our faith.

Judaism taught man, in his hours of struggle and suffering, to face reality, to see suffering as it is, for what it is, not to deny it, not to overestimate it, not to yield to it. And that is the important thing—courage and hope. "Why art thou cast down, O my soul?" "Hope in the Lord." "My flesh and my heart faileth, but God is the rock of my heart and my portion forever." In the midst of suffering, to be able to hope that light will follow the darkness, that is an act of will. Man must learn how to exercise his will so that in the hour of peril, when he is attacked by misfortune, by physical and spiritual suffering, he will be able to withstand the onslaught and come out the victor.

From this point of view, which to my mind is a sane and practical point of view, Judaism was able to reveal to man that suffering is not without its moral compensations. Those men who are not rebellious and those who are not crushed by suffering may derive a measure of strength and a full measure of wisdom from their trials.

Gold is tried by fire. The eyes of men see more clearly after they have been washed by tears. The hearts of men beat more truly after they have been pinched by anguish and tried by sorrow. The lips of men speak more kindly after they have tasted the cup of life's bitterness. Insight comes from plumbing depths. I know of men and women who have been drawn together by common sorrow and common bereavement as they had not been drawn together in life before. The wise may learn from their suffering.

Recently I read in a book of verse written by Lizette Woodworth
Reese, a poet of talent and profound insight, a group of poems dedicated
to a little girl, Henrietta, who had died. She was the delight of the home,
and all things lived in her presence. When she died, the light of life went
out for all who loved her, and darkness settled upon their habitations.
Miss Reese writes:

> Was life henceforth to be but days, days, days,
> That a few hundreds make into a year?
> Like coins to measure out with bargaining hand,
> Enough for roof, cloak, so much weight of bread?
> Had we been stripped for this and nothing more?
> For nothing more at all?
> Yet what was lodging without loveliness?
> Cloak without laughter, loaf without a song?
> Could one brief grave out in the autumnal wet,
> Serve us such scarceness, strip us down to this?
>
> We could not bear to see in the old grass,
> In the old walled yard, her new little grave.
> We could not bear it. Had we left her there,
> To kin with cold oblivion and the dark,
> Kept from her lovers and the good stout sun,
> And all the spinning year?
> Trapped underground to dole her April out
> For some end of the hard and aged dust?
> We could not bear it. One cry broke from all:
> "My God, my God, You have forgotten us!"

And thus they walked down their road of sorrow, groping in the
dark, seeking some comfort and solace in their hour of bereavement. And
it comes to them. The poet closes on this high note:

> Old days are over, and old sorrows gone;
> The unchimneyed fields, and the low mellowed house
> Set for a century in the four great winds
> Are perished with the nine trees in the lane.
> Yet still those quiet levels hold her grave,
> Old, now, in the old grass,
> A little sad. What have we kept of all?—
> That love, being lit of God, fails not or ends:
> That years are but His way to make us climb;
> And tears His way to make us understand.

"That years are but His way to make us climb; and tears His way to
make us understand."

What is true of suffering is true also of death. Some men fear death. More men fear dying. We have surrounded death with that which is dark and gruesome. Still more men fear, not their death or their dying, but the death and dying of their dear ones. That, of course, is the most tragic point of all fear. That belongs to the realm of suffering of which I have spoken, for which only courage and faith are man's allies.

Normal people seldom brood over their own death. The life impulse is too strong and drives the thought of death out of our consciousness. Even dangerously sick people think less of death than we imagine, and the old are generally quite reconciled to it and frequently welcome the swift consummation of their days. I have seldom stood at the bedside of the dying and beheld a dying man fear death.

How does every great religion, every great system of philosophy, how does our own religion teach men to meet death? With resignation, with nobility, with pride, and with hope.

An eminent rabbi was once asked what should one say to mourners when calling upon them for condolence. He said this: "Brothers bowed down in grief and suffering, put your ears to this consideration, this fact endures forever; it is a road which began with creation and will end with it. Many have drunk of this cup and many will drink of it, as with the first so with the last. May the Father of Consolation console you."

There is in this statement of the rabbi a calm and almost proud resignation to that which is inevitable. Our sacred literature teaches us and our faith has taught us from our youth to look upon death as we look upon life, as part of the cycle of existence. "We bring our days to an end as a tale that is told." "Dust thou art and to dust thou shalt return."

To face death with resignation and to face it with nobility, as one who apprehends some stupendous natural phenomenon, as one who sees something solemn and magnificent; to face death with pride, with the pride of one who has finished the task which was assigned to him, who has performed his duty to the best of his ability, who has persisted though the road was hard; with the pride of one who knows that he leaves after him a memory and a name; to face death with hope, as one who knew hope in life and will not lose it in death, as one who knows that God is the God of the living but also the God of the dead; as one who can say unto himself, "Yea, though I walk through the valley of the shadow of death, I will fear no evil for Thou art with me." That is how our religion teaches us to face death. Our religion has not laid heavy emphasis on the doctrine of immortality. There was much less of the doctrine of immortality in ancient Israel than there is in modern Israel. The ancient books have no definite teachings on the subject. The immortality of ancient Israel was built upon the here and not the hereafter. All the values of life had to be weighed in the balance of this mundane existence and had to be vindicated upon this earth.

In ancient times the group life of a people was tremendously strong, and the individual was absorbed by the group. He did not think particularly of his own survival. It was enough for him to know that his group, his people, would endure. There was in ancient Israel, as among all peoples in ancient times, some belief in the nonperishability of man. Man has always refused to accept his total annihilation. He could not conceive of it; he still is unable to conceive of it. But the existence of man after death, in the conception of our forefathers in ancient times, was a sort of sad existence in the nether world, a world of eternal silence, a world from which there is no returning. It was not a world of bliss or happiness or judgment or horror. It was just existence and nothing more.

The doctrine of immortality gained among our people with the centuries. It grew in the minds of our people; as the individual man discovered more and more his own personality and began to yearn more and more for his personal survival, as the race began to realize that righteousness is not always vindicated on this earth and evil not always punished, as the Messianic hope of the people for the Kingdom of Righteousness on this earth failed of realization, people began to think of the nether world as a place where these wrongs would be righted, where a balance would be established, where that which is crooked will be made straight. The doctrine of immortality, only the traces of which we find in the Bible, grew among our people under Persian and Greek influence. With the teachers of the Middle Ages we already find a well-defined doctrine of immortality which has become and now is an important teaching of Judaism—namely, that the soul of man is an entity of its own, deriving its eternal being from God, and therefore survives the dissolution of this physical body and continues its life uninterrupted.

But this should be said of the doctrine of immortality: among the best minds of our people it is a hope and a mystery. They claim to know little about the nature of that survival. The hereafter, to the great minds of Israel, is not a place of sensual, physical enjoyment, as it is in the Koran. It is a place of spiritual unfoldment, a place where the mind and soul of man continues its endless, unquenchable quest of perfection. "The righteous have no peace and have no rest either in this world or in the next world." "They go from strength to strength"—from one level of being to another, from one reach of perfection to another. That is the concept of immortality among the best minds of our people.

We are taught to face death with resignation, with nobility, with pride, with hope. Death is sad only when we have missed all the meaning and all the beauty of existence. Death is sad only when we go to our graves without having climbed the heights which we might have climbed, without having become what we might have been, without having raised the banners which we might have unfurled. Death is sad when we go down to our graves with regrets, regrets for joys which we might have shared, for love which we might have given, for beacons which we might have kindled. Death is sad, very sad, when the portals of the grave close over us and we leave no memory behind us, no one to ask and no one to answer who and what we were, no trace to mark our passage through time, no echo to hold, if only for a moment, the ardent song of our heart. Then death is sad. Otherwise death is not sad. It is the consummation of our days, the harvest which follows the seed-time, the fall and winter which follows the spring and summer. One of the most beautiful phrases of our sages which I am fond of repeating when I stand beside those who have loved and lost is this: "The righteous, the good, are alive even in death, for no one is dead until he has been forgotten."

I BELIEVE IN FREEDOM. I believe in the free exchange of ideas. I believe in man's inalienable right to dissent. I believe that it is only out of conflicting opinions, out of debate, out of exchange of ideas that all new truth is born. I want to be free, of course, within a full measure of social responsibility. Abuse of living is not freedom. Abuse of living does not make man free. It makes him a libertine.

As far as my private life is concerned, I prefer the old sanctities and the old loyalties. I am not impressed with the moral vagaries of our day. I have seen one or two revolts of youth come and go. I have seen the wild groping of our age outside the boundaries of self-discipline and responsibility where no freedom and no happiness can be found. The simple truth remains that given health and physical well-being, the enduring satisfactions of life come first from congenial work—any kind of work, just so it is congenial to your soul and to your mind.

The abiding satisfactions of life come from such work and also from warm friendships and from contact with the best that has been achieved by the hand and mind of man; and above all, from the love of a woman and the pride of children. It is from these worlds of beauty and of worth that the real satisfactions of life come. All else is vanity and a striving after the wind. Wealth is vanity. Fame is ephemeral. These are the real things: to live among your fellow men and to try to bring a little more of truth, justice, and peace into the world; to work at something that is significant, congenial; to have friends, not many friends, but some real friends; to keep in contact with art, music, books; and to love someone.

FROM A SERMON
"MY DESIGN FOR LIVING,"
THE TEMPLE, JANUARY 14, 1934

"If I Am Only for Myself, What Am I?"

Dr. Silver liked the story of the rabbi who was determined in his youth to remake the whole world. As the years passed, the rabbi decided to settle for the reform of his own community. Some years later, he gave that up in order to concentrate on his own family. Then, near the end of his life, he realized that even this was too ambitious and decided to spend the time he had left working on himself.

Abba Hillel Silver advocated a life which encompassed many worlds. But first one had to build his private, his family, world.

Rabbi Silver did not talk much in public about himself or his family. He believed that there were aspects of life which even a public figure had the right to keep private. But there was never any doubt in his mind that a man's life was fundamentally affected by the home in which he was raised, and the wife with whom he built his home.

"The knees of the father are the son," was a Talmudic phrase that he often quoted, and with it the interpretation he had received from his father. That means, his father had told him, that the knee is the one part of the body which can make a man tall or short. A parent must set his child a proper example. But the child must also feel the responsibility of making his parent "tall." This kind of co-responsibility was in Abba Hillel Silver's thought an axiomatic necessity in every relationship.

As to the values and virtues which Rabbi Silver stressed, they were indeed "old-fashioned." Balance, moderation, and foresight; hard work and belief in oneself; courage and will power; these were the guideposts for the individual and the happy family and for society at large. There were the moments when one had to stand "like an iron wall" against corrupting compromise and blatant evil. But reasonableness, patience, and the shunning of easy formulae had to accompany the effort to build the many worlds in which a person ought to be engaged.

The Seven Pillars of the Home

Part I

SERMON, THE TEMPLE
JANUARY 5, 1936

It is not necessary for me to extol the home. That is a favorite theme of poets. We are born into the home. We spend our infancy, our childhood, and our youth in the home. When we reach maturity, we set about building homes of our own. In other words, a complete home cycle engulfs the whole personality of man. Man is a home creature in the fullest and profoundest sense of the word. Whether one thinks in terms of heredity or environment, both of these influences derive from home and family. They may be good; they may be bad. But they are inescapable.

One word, however, may be said in our day to reveal the supreme importance of the home in the life of the individual. Our age is a mass age. We live in masses. We move in masses. We think and act in masses. In the mass, the significance of the individual dwindles. Each of us becomes an anonymous statistical unit in society. The thought of our age is cast in huge and round figures. When we talk about an unemployed person, we are not thinking of him as a unique unit. We are thinking of one among ten million unemployed. In business, in trade, in industry and labor, the personality and significance of the individual is subordinated to his economic function. He is a salesman. He is a machinist. He is a clerk. His value as a human being is calculated in terms of his economic worth. We are easily replaced and discarded and sometimes our value is nil. We are simply not wanted and we might as well not exist.

In our mass age, the significance of the individual dwindles whether we like it or not. But in the home, in that little world as father, as mother, as son, as daughter, we are ends in ourselves. We are supremely important and significant. That little world exists for us. It is our domain. We rule it. It is in the home that every one of us has an enduring and irreplaceable value and significance. In the home, in the family, we represent life's supreme meaning. I venture to say that in the modern world the home is the last refuge for the dignity, the nobility, the significance of the individual. It is in the home that a man can really live, figuratively speaking, under his own vine and his own fig tree with none to make him afraid.

What, then, are the pillars upon which the modern home must rest, if it is to rest securely? The old factors of authority, fear, law, and economic dependence, which used to be strong pillars in building a home, are no longer quite as cogent and valid as they were. There are few formal, traditional, authoritative pillars left in the modern world. Therefore, whatever pillars we can build to support a home must be of our own building and of our own volition. This extra burden which life places on our present-day generation is part of the price we must pay for our freedom. Because we do not accept the mandate of traditions and conventions, because old institutions are not binding upon us simply because of their antiquity, we must, out of our vision, hopes, and virtues, evolve other strengths and powers and supports, or our homes will topple over our heads in ruins and disaster.

The home is not a romantic institution, and home-building is not a romantic adventure. It is a day-by-day, everyday problem and task of free cooperative living. Home-building is as matter of fact as the bread we eat and the air we breathe, and, like the bread and air, among God's greatest gifts to us. The home rests not upon ecstasy but upon common sense, which, as you know, is the least common in the world. What do we mean by common sense? Common sense is that sense which is common to all men and all ages, that quintessential wisdom which mankind through long, long years of trial and error, of learning through suffering and failure, has gathered, particle by particle, and treasured. That is common sense: the accumulated, hard-won wisdom of humanity. There are intellectuals from time to time whose learning is bookish, fragmentary, recent, who think that they have discovered a profounder wisdom. When they finally come up against the grind and test of life, they find out that their little learning decked out in clever phrases is altogether futile and inadequate for life's practical problems.

Home-building is a difficult job but not an impossible one. It requires that common sense which includes knowledge and the basic truth of economics, of government, of education, of wealth, of the essential human relationships. It is a difficult job, and that is why you see so many people who know how to set the world right but do not know how to make their own home life right.

I should put as one of the important pillars in the security of a home the democratic spirit. What do I mean by that? I mean voluntary cooperative living on the basis of maximum freedom compatible with maximum responsibility. Every member in the home should be free— free to do not what he or she pleases, but free to develop his life and interests within the framework of the creative family responsibility. That is the only meaning which freedom has in families and society at large. No member of a family should consume the life of another member of the family. Each one has rules to live up to, privileges and duties and responsibilities. Each should be free to make his maximum contribution to the life and well-being of the family.

There are fathers who attempt to impose an unreasonable control over the life and destiny of members of their household. They like to exact obedience instead of winning willing cooperation. They are dictatorial. They are autocratic. They do what the rabbis caution a man not to do: "A man should not cast too much of fear into his home." There are mothers who overwhelm the lives of their children by excessive solicitousness, by an exploiting and consuming love which undermines the individuality of the child and saps his initiative. There are parents who like to prescribe and dictate the future careers of their children without regard to the children's own intrinsic talents and inclinations. There are children who look upon parents as perpetual pay-tellers. They exploit them. They assume that their parents are there to provide them with whatever they desire. They take! In fact their whole lives are series of taking— food, shelter, recreation, education. They seldom stop to ask the price which is being paid for this taking, the sacrifices which the parents have to make to provide them with what they want. These children have no sense of obligation, in terms of giving something to the home, even when they are able to give. They not only have no gratitude but they do not have the first idea of what is needed in team play. They are lone wolves, predatory omnivorous beings.

All this I put under the term "the undemocratic spirit of the home," the evil of domination, exploitation, and lack of responsibility. The reverse of this one finds in the happy homes where parents are content to guide their children instead of dictating to them. In such homes the father is head of the home—as every democratic institution requires one head—where he rules, so to speak, not by fear or by punitive authority, but by the spontaneous love and respect which his wife and children have for him. In such homes the mother is intelligent in her love, training the children in moral self-reliance and spiritual independence, not shielding them against the increasing trials and experiences of life. In such homes the children from earliest infancy learn teamwork by cooperating with the goals of the family and giving service. Homes like these rest on a great pillar—the democratic spirit of maximum freedom plus maximum responsibility for husband, wife, and children within the home.

As the second pillar of the home, I should like to nominate honor. One of the Ten Commandments, the foundation of our modern law, is devoted to this concept of honor: "Honor thy father and thy mother." Mind you, it does not say "obey." Honor is something far more important than obedience.

The glory of parents comes when children by their lives and conduct honor them. The unspeakable tragedy comes when children by their lives and conduct dishonor their parents. Parents hardly ever expect material return from their children. What they do want, their satisfaction in life, is for their children, when they grow up, to bring credit to their parents by the fine esteem which they win among men. That makes fathers and mothers brim full with joy.

Mutual honor and respect are essential ingredients of a happy home—respect of children for parents, of parents for children, of wife for husband, and of husband for wife. "He who loves his wife as himself, and honors her more than himself, and leads his sons and daughters in the straight path, to his house the words of Job apply: 'Thou shalt know that thy tent is in peace.' "

Every member of a household is entitled to a degree of respect and honor, first as a human personality, and second for what he or she signifies in the life of the others. Every soul is holy ground. One should not trespass on that holy ground, even if the soul is only a child's.

Ofttimes it is difficult to honor. Sometimes children find it very hard to honor a father when they know him to be guilty of dishonorable conduct in his private life or in his business or profession. Sometimes it is hard for children to honor a father when they see him, year by year, more and more consumed by ambition—even when that ambition is to bring more luxury and comforts into the home. Ofttimes it is hard for children to honor parents whose ambitions narrow their worlds, constrict their minds, deaden their generous impulses, tenderness, and good humor. If children are sensitive at all, their esteem and reverence for their parents will sink into the dust when they see that. Children love to be proud of their parents even as parents love to be proud of their children. I have never met a decent young man who boasted of the fact that his father had a million dollars. I have met many young men and women who are proud to say among their friends that their fathers are leading citizens of their communities, heads of institutions, workers in communal enterprises, respected citizens, men known for their goodness, generosity, helpfulness, social-mindedness. These good works children boast of and are proud of.

It is hard for children to honor a mother whom they know to be full of sham and whose standards and values are false, who spends her days in the pursuit of pleasure, who tries to rival her neighbor in style and cosmetics, a mother who at fifty tries to act the part of a girl of sixteen. A wise philosopher once said: "It is a great trial of wisdom to make our retreat from youth with propriety." Some people forget that what is pardonable and even clever in a young person of sixteen or seventeen is ridiculous in a person of fifty or sixty.

Every age has its own manners, its own demeanor, its own code, just as it has its own set of duties and responsibilities. To live outside of this age is to play a false role. People do not like that. Young people do not like that. To be true to your age, your station, your responsibilities, to be properly and sincerely adjusted to them—that is what we mean by dignity. Dignity is not formality. Dignity is not pomposity. Dignity is the charm and harmony which result when a person's conduct and deportment are in rhythm with his position, his duties, and his years.

Children like to find this dignity in their fathers and mothers. Of course, they want the direct, wholehearted, spontaneous friendliness of their parents. They do not want to see their parents across a gulf. They want to be able to look up to their parents as older, wiser, dearer friends whose lives and ways are steadier, more certain, more dignified than their own ardent, impetuous, uncertain ways.

When a father's standards are no higher than his son's, only more intense, when a father's pleasures are no different from his son's, only perhaps a little more circumspect, then the son has no one to look up to, and any reverence and respect he has for his father will be based simply upon the fact of parenthood.

Honor cannot be commanded any more than love can be commanded, but it can be evoked by our way of living, by our sincerity, candor, high standards religiously followed and unswervingly observed, by our fairness in every relationship, by our cultivation of the real things of life instead of the sham. If we are strong and dependable, then our children will form an image of us in reverence plus love. This image of us will remain their dearest legacy throughout their lives.

That thought brings me to a further aspect of honor—family tradition. In a new pioneering country like ours, where the majority of the population is composed of immigrants and children of immigrants, in a society where we move from town to town, it is difficult for us to grasp what is meant by family tradition. We have even confused it with wealth and aristocractic background. But it is not that at all. By family tradition we mean a set of standards which are developed during one generation and handed down to another generation. That is a spiritual inheritance, a legacy of a proud family loyalty which sustains young people when they set about building their own lives and families.

If Jewish home life in the past was exemplary, it was in no small degree due to the fact that the Jew placed no small emphasis on family tradition. "Do not pay heed to wealth or to beauty. Consider well family." "A man who marries a woman for money will have children that will lack honor." The whole tone of such a home is bound to be a false one. When these wise ancients spoke of "family," they had in mind character, respect, a family without blemish, where culture and the real values of life were cultivated. One of the rabbis said: "A man should always be ready to sell everything he has in order to marry the daughter of a cultured man, a scholar. If he cannot find a scholar, let him marry the daughter of one who has won recognition and honor in the community. If he cannot find such a man, let him marry the daughter of one who has been actively identified with religious institutions. If he cannot find such a man, let him marry the daughter of a man who is identified with philanthropic and charitable institutions. But never let him marry the daughter of a coarse, boorish, illiterate person." Now you have an idea of what people meant when they spoke of *yichus*: "Pay heed to families." Young people used to marry into families. People used to marry into families where there were long traditions, where there were proud memories. They were proud to prove themselves worthy. Young people used to revere the past, and they planned reverently for the future. These days young people come to the study of a rabbi to be married and you don't even see the families.

The home is built by many hands, not by any one man's hands. The invisible hands of the past had a great part and have a great part in the building of a home. Blessed is the man for whom parents and grandparents—they of the past—have laid up a marvelous tradition. Blessed is the man who has such a pillar that strengthens and sustains an individual. The home is a link between the past and the future. The home is the meeting place of the memories of the ages and the hopes of the future. Family tradition and honor, as well as the spirit of democracy, are the first two pillars upon which the modern home shall rest in security.

The Seven Pillars of the Home

Part II

SERMON, THE TEMPLE
JANUARY 12, 1936

In addition to the democratic spirit, to honor, and to the force of family tradition, there are other supports of stability in the home—for example, economic security.

Poverty is a dangerous foe in the home. There are families that rise above the handicap of continued want. They succeed in preserving family solidarity in spite of the wear and tear of continued deprivation. On the other hand, there are many families that buckle from continued and successive poverty. For poverty can make the home a focus of fretfulness, querulousness, and unhappiness. The frustrations which are caused by poverty, sooner or later may come to poison the wellsprings of natural affection between husband and wife, parents and children. The children, when they get older, may want to run away from such a home. It takes men and women of unusual qualities of character—fine qualities—to be able to live in contentment in the face of constant want and poverty. There still are some people in the world who sentimentalize about the upbuilding virtue of poverty, about its disciplining power. It is true, of course, that some people have been helped by poverty. It is equally true that many are hurt by it. Poverty is no blessing. In most instances it is a curse. Certainly, the institution of home has little reason to be grateful for the fact of poverty. And society, if it is earnest in its desire to make the home a wholesome place for the training of the rising generation, ought not to put severe handicaps on the home.

Every home is entitled to a measure of economic security: at least

168

the minimum in food, clothing, medical care, old-age insurance, unemployment insurance, and opportunities for education. Every home, if it is to be a wholesome one, if it is not to be a social liability where characters are destroyed—every home ought to have an income adequate for education and a wholesome amount of recreation.

The modern home needs a great deal of state support and protection, for the individual today is not always or often master of his economic fortunes. Frequently the individual breadwinner is thrown out of a job not because of delinquency of character but because vast economic forces beyond his control force unemployment upon him.

By economic security I do not, of course, mean wealth. Wealth is not a pillar of a home. There can reside, and often does reside, quite as much strife, bitterness, and hate in the mansions of the rich as in the hovels of the poor. In fact, wealth without the restraint of culture and tradition and a sense of honor has been a cesspool of social iniquity in all generations and in all civilizations.

A home requires a certain degree of comfort to make it pleasant and livable, but wealth has never been and is not today a requisite for the stability and harmony of the home. I know quite a number of young men who are unwilling to be married because they are afraid that too much will be expected of them in the way of maintaining expensive households. They do not feel equal to this. They do not wish to be reproached in later years by their wives' families, that they have not been able to become what is known as good providers.

Young people ought to have the courage—the splendid courage—to get married and begin life modestly; to begin not where their parents left off but where their parents began. They can enjoy life magnificently if, and this is a big *if*, they can throw overboard the whole set of false standards of their social set, cheap standards built upon false conceptions of the values of life, of material pleasure-seeking and false display. If they have the courage to throw overboard the whole set of false standards and values which belong to this age, if they have the courage to live true to themselves, they can be gorgeously happy. Fortunately, many young people are beginning to do just that, especially since the Depression. Young people are happy, joyous in the grand adventure of building a home together, frequently both working to contribute to the family budget. In such homes is the glory of a nation.

I should like to point to another pillar of the home. I call it reasonableness. Every sage of mankind has admonished people not to expect too much out of life. Life is not a fool's paradise. It is also not a wise man's paradise. It is not a paradise at all. Those who expect too much of life, whose expectations are fantastic and florid and excessive, are doomed to ruin, to cruel disillusionment. The sages of all times have admonished people to moderate their expectations in all things. It also applies to married life. "They were married and lived happily ever after" is a fairy tale. Marriage is no unfailing prescription for unending happiness. Nothing is. Life is checkered with beauty and sorrow, with pleasure and pain, with achievement and failure, and blessed is the man, or indeed, the woman, for whom life strikes a favorable balance.

There are not always present the favorable winds that drive the sails of our life to distant and sunny shores of happiness. Frequently there are storms and disastrous winds of adversity which drive the sails of our life to distant, darkened, and forbidding shores. It is all part of the bargain of life.

No home has a right to expect that it will enjoy continued health, wealth, and tranquillity. There are inevitable domestic cares and worries. Children are not always well and well behaved. They are frequently sickly and irritable. Husbands are not always considerate and even-tempered. Frequently they are harassed, worried, and befuddled, and they evidence that bewilderment and unhappiness in the home. Wives are often moody and are not always loving and sweet-tempered. They have their moods, days of extreme nervousness and irritability. These are normal phenomena in every home. No one has the right to expect perfection of wife, husband, or children, or of the home, for they are never perfect. When you marry a woman you love madly, you assume that she is the most wonderful woman in the world. That is as it should be. When you marry a man, you are quite madly in love with him. That is natural. After marriage, the wise man and the wise woman think less of the adjective *wonderful* and more of the substance—man and woman. For we are men and women and not angelic creatures. We have our tempers, our moods, our periods of forgetfulness. Our reasonableness within the home helps to bridge over these gaps without great difficulty.

A lack of reasonableness tends to widen the gap into a chasm, an abyss which may end in a broken home, in the divorce court. Hasty people sometimes call lack of reasonableness incompatibility. Such incompatibility is a frequent cause for divorce. There are men and women

who never should have married each other. They are completely malad-
justed. They have nothing essential and basic in common to hold them
together. Such people are better off apart. They injure the souls and minds
of their children by their open and equally by their covert hostility.
Those whom God never really joined together ought not to be forced to
stay together. On the other hand, in many cases, incompatibility is simply
an unwillingness on the part of men and women to learn the lesson of give-
and-take in life—an unwillingness to make the sacrifices necessary for
adjustment, a failure to realize that by marriage two people do not enter
a state of perfection and complete adjustment but a state which is a long
training in mutual understanding, not a career of mutual perfection and
not a career of reconditioning each other. What most people call incompatibility is generally a case of stiff-neckedness which borders on both
stupidity and arrogance.

Reasonable people try to reduce these misunderstandings and
occasions for irritation to a minimum within the home. They will try to
minimize their importance. A husband and father will try not to bring
into the home all the frets and worries of the business world. He will remember that home ought not to be a clearing house for all the trouble
with his partners or with his customers. A wife, too, must remember that
she can discipline herself, control her words, and that the home can be
and should be a place of refuge for her husband, who may have suffered
frustration in the world outside and comes to his home as a place
of solace, comfort, and understanding.

It is in the home that most men are either made or broken. That is
even more true of women. It is in the home that their morale can be
strengthened or destroyed. What helps the spirit of man to endure is the
home. A broken spirit—who can endure?

Children, too, ought to remember this lesson of reasonableness. I
know a lot of young people who put their best foot forward away from
home. Among older people, away from home, among business executives,
employers, even among the parents of their friends, they are modest and
attentive. They listen and very often take counsel from elders—that is,
away from home. At home they are the last word in impatient omniscience. They think their parents know nothing. Their parents are old-
fashioned. They have antiquated ideas. All that these children want from
their parents is an endorsement of their ideas and actions—and mainte-
nance. Frequently they do not even want endorsement but only mainte-

nance. Frequently they regard the counsel of their mothers and fathers as interference. Children want to be independent, forgetting that nobody is independent, nobody—certainly not young people whom life has not yet put through the hard-testing school of serious living. Reasonableness within the home—that is an important pillar upon which the stability of the home rests.

There is yet another, which I call good management. The home, of course, is a spiritual institution. But its successful administration is quite definitely a problem in home management, domestic economy. A poorly managed home is discouraging. A mismanaged home is a liability. In home-building and home management the woman is supreme. "The wise woman builds a home and the foolish woman destroys it with her own hands." That was said twenty-five hundred years ago. With skillful management a home can be made attractive and can be filled with beauty and charm by the wife and mother. It does not require wealth. It requires taste, skill, efficiency, competence, orderliness, neatness, hominess, coziness, and charm. These are the things which make a home livable. Vulgarity and extravagance destroy the inner dwelling place of which the home is the framework.

"She looks well to the ways of her household and does not eat the bread of idleness." The ideal mother in Israel was competent, a capable matron—not like the dreamlike, fragile dolls of medieval times nor the sheltered, prudish innocents of the Victorian Age, nor even the inconsequential, fussy, and irrelevant society ladies of our own day. You do not find them in the literature of Jewish life. The "mother of Israel" was the home-builder, the skilled craftsman in that art. She was not shut off from the world. Decidedly, she was a part of it, dynamically influencing it. But she realized that the supreme significance of her life was in the profession of home-building, of wifehood, of motherhood. She was the radiant center of the family. "She looked well to the ways of her household."

Show me a home in which there is joy, laughter, peace, happiness; show me a home where people like to be and to which they like to invite friends; show me a home which has been able to withstand misfortune, even impoverishment, and I will show you there a woman who has been a skilled, efficient manager, who has been a thoughtful guide of her children, who has looked after and reared her children, who has shown an intelligent interest in the affairs of her household. That is good management. It does not come of itself. It can be studied. It can be acquired. That is one of the great pillars of the home.

Finally, I should like to call attention to another pillar. That is religion, piety, God. "If God does not build a home, they who labor in it, labor in vain." The house without God is an endangered house; a secularized home is a weakened home. The home is more than a roofed edifice. It is a spiritual atmosphere, and that which contributes to its spirituality helps to strengthen it. Religion sanctifies all the qualities which contribute to the home. Religion places the seal of its authority, its sanction upon these factors which mankind has learned are indispensable to the home.

Worship in the home, observance of customs and ceremonials, helps to create a spirit of reverence in the minds of children. Sooner or later it becomes intertwined with the very idea of home. Worship, religious observance, ritual give tone to everyday life. They help to preserve the home. Children whose eyes have been filled and whose imaginations have been enkindled by the colorful ceremonies in the home, by the beauty and grace of festival observances, by the Sabbath-eve service, the Seder on Passover, the kindling of the lights on holidays; children who have had their lives filled with this beauty and loveliness of ancient customs and ceremonies come later in life to associate all this with the home. Their home will forever have for them a certain holiness and sanctity, and when they get older and set about building homes for themselves, they will reproduce them in terms of sanctity, in terms expressed in their early life.

The homes of our ancestors were much more modest than ours are today. Your forefathers and mine had fewer of the comforts of life, not to speak of the luxuries of life, than we have. Many lived in dark, dreary, harassed ghettos, and their homes were impoverished; but not really, for within their homes there dwelt the spirit of Godliness. When on the Sabbath eve, the father returned from the house of worship to his home and saw the festive Sabbath cloth spread on the table, the candles lit, his wife and children around him, he felt as if he were entering a sanctuary. He invited God and the angels of God to enter his home. "Welcome into my home. May your coming be in peace. May your going forth from my house be in peace." In this modest home God dwelt. His home was a little sanctuary.

This is a conception of the family which is the heart of the Jewish tradition—not beyond our means, not unreachable, not beyond the living of the average human being. Quite the contrary; it is a real, practical home, but one which was evolved through a religious interpretation, the way of profound faith.

"If God does not build a home, they who labor in it, labor in vain."

That is the sum and substance of it. These seven pillars of home are just seven expressions of the one basic truth. And our age, no less than the ages of long ago, needs this truth. There are classic ideals which endure. Regardless of the political and economic position of the Jew, there remains this one factor of home-building which is man's significant adventure and man's significant achievement. And it requires the supreme exercise of wisdom, intelligence, and spiritual devotion.

"Little Man, How Big Are You?"

SERMON, THE TEMPLE
MARCH 22, 1936

I had occasion, a few years ago, to pay tribute to a man who gave of his work in our community for a number of years. At that time I had occasion to say that in estimating the worth of a man, people are prone to think primarily in terms of a man's work, and that often it is not so much what the man gives that is important as what the man is. Sometimes it is the building of character, the fashioning of personality that is a greater and more difficult achievement than doing things in the outside world, doing things that people can see.

There are many men and women who win real greatness in this field of self-building who are nevertheless unknown and unnoticed in the world, because they have achieved no one outstanding thing that the world can see, no extraordinary exploit for which they would be known. These people who win greatness in their inner life and who are not known outside we are prone to call common folks. They do not make good newspaper copy. They belong to the large class of the anonymous, and because they are anonymous, people think they are unimportant.

Our histories, as a rule, tell of the dramatic things in life, the extraordinary, the catastrophic. The people who monopolize publicity today are the dictators, statesmen, real or imaginary, famous actors, actresses, prize fighters, kidnapers, quintuplets—unusual people, people who have plans for sharing your money. These extraordinary folks—these are the people that get into the papers! The average man seldom is given a chance at publicity. By the average man I mean the man who has man-

175

aged in his lifetime to keep out of jail, the man who has not donated a museum, the man who has built no depot or wrecked no bank—I mean the plain, ordinary folks who do their work in the world, build homes, raise families, keep their faith, and then quietly go out of the world, making room for other folks with but one bit of publicity—in the obituary column.

Because of this fact, because the extraordinary people are the ones who get the attention, there is a grave danger of our getting a distorted view of what are the real elements that make up society, of what constitutes real civilization.

Life in society is not made out of crises which call for extraordinary people, for heroes, leaders. Life is made up of common, everyday tasks which are nevertheless exalted in the beauty of faithful performance. A social life made up entirely of crises, emergencies, dramatic situations would break down quickly. A world of geniuses and heroes would be a madhouse!

The busy world is all too busy to notice common folks; it has time only for the unusual. If a man marries once, that is not news. He belongs to the great silent group—I use the word *silent* because he does not receive any particular notice. If a man marries four or seven times, that is news which is emblazoned in the newspapers. His picture appears surrounded by his entire matrimonial constellation.

The real work of the world is not done by celebrities. The man of genius may be the salt of the earth, but you cannot make a meal out of salt. The bread and the meat of life is the common people, the men who plow the fields, who forge the steel, the men who build homes and schools, the men who perform the everyday ordinary tasks in the ten thousand "Main Streets" of our lives. Anyone who thinks that "Main Streets" are nothing more than sprawling, ugly, raw streets with squat, unattractive buildings filled with people who are characterized by nothing but their intolerance, drabness, and gossip—anyone who thinks that has simply not looked into the "Main Streets" closely enough.

Among those who dwell in these towns and villages—the masses—you will find so much of courage, perseverance, loyalty, and sacrifice. You will find men and women who by their labor and devotion and sacrifice conserve the great tradition of a great people and transmit it to their children. You will find many souls who have passed through the deep waters of life, endured tribulations, men and women who have been subjected to the cruel buffeting of fortune but determinedly carry on and do their work.

Greatness is not show and sham and greed and pomp, but substance, inner spiritual strength, the power to endure, the power to carry burdens, the power to perform tasks however hard or cruel those tasks may be. Some people think of heroism as something flamboyant, impulsive. Real heroism is a thing of long endurance. You will find lawful martyrs, uncommonly heroic, among the common folks who make up the "Main Streets" of the world.

During the war, somewhere in Alsace-Lorraine where American soldiers were stationed, a general was decorating some of the soldiers for bravery. I commented on their heroism. His answer was, "Heroism in war—that is the most commonplace thing we know about here." When heroism is not a thing of impulse or of the moment, it is a thing of long endurance and infinite patience. It has to do with the faithful performance of duties even when duties are dull and monotonous and grind upon the heart through the years.

This nation was built by the anonymous. The noble folks remained behind in the Old World. The people who left the Old World, who plunged into the New World, were humble, unknown folks, many coming from the lowest station in life. Yet these folks—with a gun, an axe, and a sack of seed—entered the wilderness, endured loneliness and sickness without the aid of doctors, went through the miseries of cold winters, and with forked sticks broke up the ground and planted a nation. Common folks! No heroics! No one to applaud or acclaim them! But it is of such heroism that our nation was built.

This nation was settled by immigrants from all over the world, nearly all of them poor. The rich remained behind; the rich do not emigrate. These immigrants came into a strange new world. Many of them did not know the language. They were humble folks, nameless folks. It is these immigrants who built the cities, who girded the plains with paths of steel, who dotted the prairie lands with towns and cities and built schools and hospitals and made America—humble folks, unknown folks.

How they labored, these poor humble folks, to build a home for their families! You may recall a father or a grandfather who labored and sacrificed not for himself but for his children, to give his children what he had been denied. There is no record kept of such individual acts of greatness, of heroism. No history books will ever record them. Yet everyone, if you will stop to recall, knows of such stories, marvelous cases of greatness.

I recall, as a boy, one man who lived on one of the most thickly settled streets on the East Side of New York City. We children coming and going from school would ofttimes see him. He was a little old man with a gray, straggly beard, who dealt in coal and ice. He had his place of business in a dark basement underneath a huge tenement. In winter he sold coal and in summer he sold ice. He would sell coal by the bucket-load and would carry these buckets up three and four flights of stairs. In the summer, he would buy large cakes of ice, cut them into smaller cakes, and carry them up five, six flights of stairs to his customers. He was always bent under a load. We called him "Humpback," though he was really not humpbacked. This little man with the gray, straggly beard, "Jacob the Humpback," died quietly like all humble folks, as he had lived. A few years ago I learned that one of his sons, because of the labors of "Jacob the Humpback," had become a professor of mathematics in a large university, and another had become a surgeon. I suddenly asked myself, "Little man, how big were you?"

Think of the mothers of men—not the glamorous women but the plain, humble folks, the millions whose hands are more tender than soft, because they have no wealth, servants, leisure. They are the working mothers of the world, mothers whose faces are perhaps a little rough yet who have a skin people love to touch, mothers who are always there when there is washing or scrubbing to do. When there are lessons to study, stories to tell, they are there—mothers who are always there, who work for their brood, who sacrifice for them. Talk about heroism in common folks! There are plenty of fathers, many of them not educated properly, who had to leave school at twelve or thirteen, who are not always up on the latest novels or the latest fashions—but fathers who give up their lifeblood for their children. Who has counted the myriad acts of greatness of common folks?

There are startling evidences of bigness in the little people who make up the humble folks. I recall, a few years ago, coming home one afternoon, rather tired and fretful. The doorbell rang, and a middle-aged couple came in. The man said to me, "Rabbi, we would like to get married." I was a little impatient and I said, "Why all this suddeness? Why didn't you telephone first?" He took me aside and said, "This lady I am about to marry is on her way to New York to have an operation on her eyes. The likelihood is that she will go blind. I want to marry her so that I will be able to take care of her if she goes blind."

They were plain folks. I saw the hands of this man—hard with manual labor. There was nothing of grace and charm about either of them, but being with them was like standing in the presence of reverence.

I married them. A year or two later, a blind woman came to see me—the same woman—and told me that her husband had died. I asked her how she was getting along. "Why, all right," she said. There was no complaint, no bitterness. "I am working, I am doing odd jobs, getting subscriptions. I am getting along." Courage! Greatness!

The trouble is that we look for greatness where it really does not exist—often among people who destroy and whose feats of destruction we surround with nobility, while humble, honest labor is surrounded with anonymity and sometimes with indignity.

I have never forgotten a story told to me when I was a little boy about the old lamplighter who would go down every afternoon through the streets of the city and light the lamps. No one knew him. People did not even know his name. Hardly anyone stopped him or paid any attention to him. When in the fog or murk of the evening he went down the street, he left behind him a kindled light. How many myriads of such people are there in the world whom we take for granted, to whom we do not give a second thought, yet whose quiet labors light our own ways?

In the sight of God there is no bigness and no littleness. Of what significance is all this dressing up, all this puffing, all this strutting? None at all. "All alike, the prince and the pauper, the king and the slave, the rich and the poor lie together in the grave." There is no distinction.

If, however, you have ever felt the thrill of some deep devotion, the consciousness of some deep love, the exaltation of some noble sacrifice, if ever you have felt the pride of honest craftsmanship, if you have ever experienced the joy of doing well something you wanted to do, then you have come as close to real greatness as is within the reach of mortal man and in truth, you are blessed. Such blessed people are all around you. Just open your eyes. It may be your father, your mother, your sister, your brother—great souls!

I know a little woman who permitted life to pass her by because she wanted to insure the success of her brother, who is a fine artist. She labored day after day, week after week, month after month, and year after year in poverty, denying herself everything, stinting herself so that her brother, blessed with a talent, might have his chance in life.

How many such people do you know in the world? There are more than you imagine—your husband, your wife, your father, your mother, your brother; look around you! This world could not exist if it were not for the greatness of the common folk.

Friends—Enemies

SERMON, THE TEMPLE
DECEMBER 17, 1939

Friendship is not based on ties of blood, or conventional obligations, or vested interests. It is not established in law, or ordained or enforced by society. It is a purely voluntary and spontaneous relationship, and at its highest and best, uttery uncalculating and impersonal.

It is so fine and spiritual a relationship, so subtle, that many people never truly experience it. All men, of course, have acquaintances, but not all men have friends. All men have relatives. They are wished on us. Some of them are distantly related, but not far enough removed. And by convention, we are expected to lavish an uncritical, indiscriminate affection on each, an obligation, of course, which few really discharge.

Friends are not wished on us. We do not deliberately choose friends. We win them. And not every man or woman has that disposition, not every man and woman is possessed of that inner grace wherewith to win friends. Just as some ears are deaf to music and some eyes blind to painting—hearing but not comprehending, and seeing but not discerning—so there are hearts that are closed to friendship.

People who are busily absorbed in other relationships, who are too completely dominated by other interests, or too self-centered, too egotistical, too self-sufficient; or the contrary, people who are too timid, too locked up, escapists who run away from what they fear, from commitments and entanglements—all such people often miss the completing and exalting experience of friendship.

Friendship, like all other human forms of culture, takes time and thought. It must be carefully cultivated, and it requires time for seasoning and ripening. It is the old friends who are the true friends, just as it is the old wine that is the good wine. So we read in one of our sacred books: "Forsake not an old friend, for the new is not comparable to him. A new friend is as new wine. When it is old, thou shalt drink it leisurely." Those who are too busy with other concerns have not the time, therefore, for the proper husbandry of friendship.

These busy folks have many business associates and many social acquaintances with whom they exchange courtesies and social amenities. They invite, and they are invited. They exchange pleasantries around the dining board. It is all a pleasant and modish and worldly and conventional and certainly not harmful game. But it has little to do with friendship. All this is part of the etiquette of social life, and as such it is largely formal, somewhat artificial; a façade, and ofttimes a mask. For friendship, if it is anything at all, is revelatory, personal, intimate. It is a soul-to-soul contact. It is not a pleasant game but a wholehearted devotional experience. God spoke to Moses as a man speaks to his friend. There is something sacred in this relationship of friend to friend, whether it is expressed in speech, or acts, or just in unspoken comradeship.

In fact, when you come to think of it, there is something quite inexplicable, something almost mystical in this relationship we call friendship, something almost predestined. We do not know why we go out of the inner circles of our families to make friends, or why we choose, if choosing it is, those people who become our friends. Why these, and not others? There are other people in the world whom we know, whom we meet often, who may be brighter or as bright, wealthier or as wealthy, handsomer or as handsome, and yet it is just this particular one, or these particular few people with whom we somehow feel free to share our hopes, our anxieties, our joys and sorrows. There is something strange about this blending of human hearts and minds and souls. We do not know the catalyst that brings about this peculiar and amazing reaction.

All great religions and all great literatures stood in the presence of the phenomenon of friendship as if in the presence of something mystic, something magnificently great. Our literature abounds with passages on the subject of friendship, in praise of friendship, in characterization of friendship, and in caution and admonition concerning friends.

One sentence has always struck me as profound, among the many on this subject in our literature. It is in the Book of Ecclesiasticus, in the Apocrypha, those books not included in the Bible. Ecclesiasticus was composed by an eminent physician, Ben Sirach, in the second century before the Common Era. He was a wise man who traveled far, learned much, and gathered much wisdom, and he devoted quite a number of chapters to the subject of friendship. In one of them we find this sentence: "A faithful friend is the medicine of life." That I regard as a very beautiful and apt characterization. There is something healing and strengthening in friendship. There is something of renewal in friendship.

Francis Bacon, an Englishman who lived at the time of Queen Elizabeth, wrote on the subject of friendship and said: "A principal fruit of friendship is the ease and discharge of the fullness and swellings of the heart, which passions of all kinds so cause and induce. . . . No receipt openeth the heart but a true friend, to whom you may impart griefs, joys, fears, hopes, suspicions, counsels, and whatsoever lieth upon the heart to oppress it, in a kind of civil shrift or confession." In other words, both the wise Jew of centuries ago and the wise Englishman of a much later century felt that friendship is something which enables a man to unburden himself, to ease an overcharged mind or heart, and, by so doing, to "cut our sorrows in half and double our joys."

There is healing in friends. It is agreeable to have another human being to share with us those things which burden us, filling our hearts beyond their own capacity to bear them. In this way, a faithful friend is the medicine of life—and in another way, too. Not only by sharing our burdens with others, but by taking into our lives the griefs and the hopes and the problems of our friends, we cleanse our own souls of all the self-coddling, we save ourselves from becoming too wrapped up in ourselves. In other words, friendship acts as a sort of spiritual purgation, a catharsis for selfishness and egoism. In that sense, too, it is the medicine of life. We heal ourselves and make ourselves whole by giving and by receiving.

There is another profound comment on friendship found in the Bible: "Just as iron sharpeneth iron, so a man sharpeneth the countenance of his friend." One does not always think of friendship in that light. But it is of the essence of friendship that it is a challenge. Friendship not only helps a man to clarify his own ideas by talking them over with his friend, it not only gives a man the benefit of another man's counsel, of his judgment, of his point of view, but friendship, if it is the real thing, has a way of bringing out the best that is in us. For a real friend is always eager to remain worthy of friendship, to be held in unfailing high esteem. We are not on parade, of course, with our friends. We must be completely straightforward, open. We never want to be regarded by our friends as

commonplace. Friendship requires an overtone of splendor, style, ritual.
It must never become trivial. It must never fail in the element of pride.
We must be proud of our friends. They must be worthy of that pride.
The wise American writer Emerson, who wrote on friendship among
many other things—and it is of interest to note that there were very few
first-rate minds who failed to express themselves on this subject—wrote
this:

> We are to dignify to each other the daily needs and offices of
> man's life, and embellish it by courage, wisdom and unity;
> it should never fall into something usual and settled, but
> should be alert and inventive and add rhyme and reason
> to what was drudgery.

That is the transfiguring power of a friendship.

Friendship makes demands. A true friend will keep you up to the
mark. Friendship is not a matter of pleasant convenience. A friend is not
there just to be a receptacle for our confidences, to soothe us, to agree
with us always, to justify us always and to approve of us always. That is the
function of a sycophant, of a flatterer. It is true that "a friend loveth always," but true love is not always indulgent or complacent. There is such a
thing as the chastisement of love. Love must sometimes be a sharp censure,
a strong disapprobation, firm but of course without malice and without
bitterness. They who cannot endure what our Bible calls the "faithful
wounds of a friend," and who prefer the kisses of an enemy are unfit
for the higher regimen and discipline of friendship.

A friend is not called upon to underwrite all our pretensions, or
to subscribe to all our whims, or to sacrifice his convictions to ours—the
convictions of independence of judgment, of individuality.

I can recall some people whom I came to regard as friends, and who
heaped kindnesses upon me, courtesies which I sought to deserve; and
yet, when out of my convictions I felt called upon to challenge their attitude, to oppose them in certain measures which they regarded as vital
to themselves, they became offended, felt as if I had betrayed them. They
must have regarded me as ungrateful indeed. This proprietary type of
friendship must be shunned as a blight, for it is a subtle and most dangerous attack upon character. It is a perversion of loyalty. It corrodes everything that is intrinsically worthy. It is an exploiting kind of thing.

In our sacred literature, we are cautioned to prove and to test men
before we admit them into the sacred sanctuary of friendship. "If thou

wouldst get a friend, prove him first and be not hasty to credit him!" For there are those who are friends only in name. "There are those who are friends for their own occasion, who will not abide in the day of thy trouble. If thou be brought low he will be against thee; he will hide himself from thee." These are the fair-weather friends, our prosperity friends, our companions at the table. They are our "belly friends." They are the scavengers of friendship. They are the camp followers. Some people are taken in by them to their own hurt. But the wise are not beguiled by them.

Real friendship is possible only when there exists between two people a concurrence of interests and a genuine capacity for loyalty, for trust, for generosity, and an utter absence of any desire to dominate, monopolize, or exploit. When you have those conditions, you have a soil rich for enduring friendship.

As I said a moment ago, we must win friends. We must hold them and cultivate them. Enemies come of themselves. It is easy to acquire an enemy, but it is hard to acquire a real friend. Sometimes we ourselves are responsible for the enemies we make. Our injustice, our cruelty, our arrogance, our attitudes of contempt toward other people, our sharp dealings are sometimes responsible for that. But sometimes it is other people's vices that make enemies for us. Their envy, their malice, their evil eye make enemies of us.

Few men ever escape the gunshot of some enemy at some time in their lives. Some are decent foes. Others are dirty foes. Some are by nature traducers, maligners and mischief-makers. It is their nature. They cannot help themselves. Some are avowed enemies. Some are concealed enemies. It is only when a man has his back up against the wall that he discovers who are his friends and who are his enemies, how many friends he has and how many enemies he has.

Some enemies can be turned into friends. It takes a good deal of skill and strength of character and forbearance to accomplish this feat. It is a great achievement and a great tribute to a man if he can succeed in converting an enemy into a friend. Other enemies cannot be converted. There is no use eating out your heart trying to do it. Ignore them if you can. Fight them if you must. "Love thine enemies!" That is a doctrine which is not found in our religion. It is a psychological impossibility. But we are admonished that if we must make enemies, we should see to it that it is not our vices which call them into existence, but our virtues. "A man's greatness can be measured by his enemies," someone once said. If in the performance of your duty, if in the championing of righteous causes, if in battling against vice and corruption, you succeed in making enemies for yourself, bitter enemies, vindictive enemies, then they are as much of a tribute to you as the friends you have suceeded in winning. People who are afraid to make enemies, those who always want to be popular with everybody, those who always want to be liked by everybody, those who never want to take advice, those who are always neutral in their convictions involving inescapable moral issues are consigned just within the gates of Hell. These people cannot enter either Heaven or Hell.

Finally, we are admonished to remember that one's real enemies are within one's own self. I think it was Publilius Syrus who said: "Formidable is that enemy that lies hidden in a man's own breast." Fear is such an enemy. Cowardice is such an enemy, and avarice and selfishness. In fact, the whole complex of emotions which goes by the name of "the evil inclination"—those are our most dangerous enemies. The wise man seeks to vanquish them, and when he has vanquished them, he is fit to join in combat with his enemies without. He is equipped. He is armored. He is strong. The man who has subdued these enemies within—selfishness and unbridled ambition, the desire to master and dominate and exploit, always to amass and always to accumulate; when a man can subdue these rapacious, voracious passions—why, then he becomes fit for friend and foe. He becomes a dangerous adversary for enemies and a most welcome friend.

Friendship is the medicine of the soul!

What Is Justice? What Is Love?

SERMON, THE TEMPLE
OCTOBER 20, 1963

It is well to distinguish at the outset between legal justice and ideal justice. The two are, of course, not synonymous. There is a difference which we can observe almost daily between law and ideal morality. Law represents the minimum of moral requirements which a community at any given stage in its development regards as absolutely indispensable. Law reflects the average morality of a society. There are laws on the statute books which are clearly inferior to the moral sentiment of the best elements among our people.

Law lags behind ideal justice, though it often tries to catch up with it. The moral idealism of a people tries to bring its laws into conformity with the ideal moral standard. It is quite difficult, therefore, and unprofitable to seek to determine what is justice by reference to a people's legal code. A code of laws may be said to represent what has been achieved, but ideal justice represents society's outreaching for perfection. "The path of the just shines more and more perfect unto the day."

Even in legal justice, there has been marked progress in recent times. In the past, society assumed that a man's wrongdoing was exclusively the result of a deliberate evil intention. The wrongdoer was entirely to blame, and society was justified in inflicting maximum punishment upon him. Recent studies in sociology, and more particularly in psychology, have convinced men that there is such a thing as a social partnership in crime, that the community is, in a sense, partly responsible for the actions of the individual. Often a man's wrongdoing is the result not of his evil intention, but of an evil environment and upbringing. A man is frequently driven to do wrong by forces over which he has no control.

186

Our entire philosophy of crime and punishment has undergone a radical change in the last few decades. We conceive of justice today less in terms of the punitive, and more in terms of the corrective; and we look beyond the corrective to the preventive. Today justice seeks a change in social conditions to a point where society will help the individual to observe the laws and keep him from perpetrating antisocial acts.

This sound and commendable view has its dangers. Some have come to believe that the individual is without blame or responsibility; that when he commits a crime, the blame is entirely society's. This extreme point of view leads to moral anarchy. Justice should take into account all extenuating circumstances, but at the same time hold fast to the dogma upon which all morality is ultimately based, namely, that a normal individual is responsible for his actions.

We can go to the lawbooks and find out what legal justice is, in any given situation, but where shall we find a definition of ideal justice? Frankly, it is difficult to find such a definition. From the days of Plato to our own day, philosophers and students of ethics have sought a formula which would adequately define ideal justice, but no consensus has been reached. No writings anywhere in the world are so completely devoted to the concept of ideal justice as our Bible. Almost every page rings with it. Yet nowhere in the Bible will you find a concise definition of what really constitutes justice.

Throughout the immortal preachments of the prophets, the cry for justice reverberates. And an exalted conception of justice it is, alike for rich and poor, for subject and ruler, for native-born and stranger. When the great King David sinned, the prophet Nathan did not hesitate to go to him, point an accusing finger, and cry out: "Thou art the man!" When Ahab robbed Naboth of his vineyard and had him put to death, the prophet Elijah did not hesitate to go to him, denounce him to his face, and proclaim doom upon him.

It is told in the Talmud that the head of the Sanhedrin Simeon ben Shetah, a famous Pharisaic teacher who lived in the first century before the Common Era, was such a stern, rigorous, and implacable defender of the law that he made many enemies. One day two of his enemies conspired to bear false witness against his son for a crime punishable by death, and on the basis of their false testimony, the son of Simeon ben Shetah was condemned to death. As he was being led to the place or execution, he protested his innocence so loudly that the witnesses, who accompanied him, repented and confessed that they had borne false testimony against him. The judges who had sentenced him were ready to reverse their sentence, and even Simeon ben Shetah, the father, now convinced of his son's innocence, was ready to reverse the sentence. But there was an ancient law in Israel which refused to accept the recantation of witnesses after sentence had been decreed. Witnesses who had once given their testimony could not be trusted when later they reversed their testimony. The son of Simeon ben Shetah, who was being led to execution, turned to his father and said: "Father, if you wish to become the salvation of Israel, see to it that my sentence is carried out. Look upon me as a doorstep over which you must pass to your great destiny, without compunction."

We find in the Talmud the principle, "Let the law pierce through the mountain. The law of justice must endure." So great was Israel's passion for justice that in its name they dared even to challenge God Himself. God Himself must be bound by His own laws of justice.

Yet in spite of the truly exalted conception of justice which we find in the Bible and among our rabbis, nowhere do we find a definition which will help us in determining exactly what justice is. Perhaps such a definition is not to be had. But we may approximate an understanding of it if we ask ourselves, "What is the goal of justice? What does justice aim to accomplish for society?" I suppose that here we can all agree that the aim of justice is to make possible a good society in which all men may develop their talents and capacities freely and fully. A good society is one in which every man does what he wishes to do, but wishes to do only what will contribute to the happiness of others as well as to his own. Ideal justice aims to ensure responsible freedom for all men which will help them build the good society. Ideal justice is that which grants a man freedom to develop his capacities to the utmost. If a man is equipped to become a first-rate mechanic—and in the economy of God's world a first-rate mechanic is as important as a first-rate musician—society ought to make it possible for him to develop himself in that capacity to the utmost. The way to make this possible is to afford him the opportunities of education and training. If a man is endowed to become a great musician, society ought to make it possible for him to develop his gifts. Whether he belongs to this or that class, to this or that race or religion, does not matter; society must see to it that such considerations in no way interfere with the free unfoldment of that man's talent or career. In other words, ideal justice demands that every man should be given not an equal share but an equal chance, a chance to realize all the potentialities of his being.

Many revolutionary implications flow from this definition. If justice means freedom to develop, then everything which keeps a man from enjoying that freedom is injustice. What are some of the impediments which keep a man from enjoying that freedom? One is poverty! You have often heard it said that poverty is a spur to ambition, that need incites to greater effort. That is true up to a certain point. A pinch of poverty may prove a stimulus, but continuous, crushing want will starve and stultify personality and ultimately destroy it. There is little to be said for poverty. Poverty is a form of slavery; poverty is a prison house; want is so many shackles upon the human spirit.

A society which is pursuing the ideal of justice will set about to destroy poverty, by increasing the social goods and by distributing these social goods equitably. The task of a society which aims to establish ideal justice is to eradicate poverty—not by charity, not by philanthropy, not by doling out gifts to the poor, but by establishing an economic order where every man who labors will receive a fair recompense for his labor and will have enough to protect himself and his family against want, sickness, and the material disabilities of old age.

The destruction of poverty is the first requisite for the establishment of ideal justice among men. Another factor which makes for injustice is unearned wealth. The only justification for our present economic order is the merit system. Unearned wealth destroys the merit system, and by so doing destroys justice in society. No man who does not contribute to the assets of society should be privileged to draw upon its treasures. There ought to be, if not a rigid, at least a fair correlation between service and reward, or the whole system becomes infamously unjust.

How can you determine whether a given act is ideally just? How can you tell whether an act which you have performed, or are about to perform, is just? Ask yourself: Does this act represent me in my capacity as a free agent, working for the common good, or does it not? If it does, then it is a just act. If it does not, if it represents me at the lower levels of my enslavement to passions, to lust, to desires, to cupidities, to envies, then it is an unjust act. The way to determine whether I am doing the right thing is to ask myself: Suppose every other living human being did the same thing; what would happen?

That is the test which, you may recall, Immanuel Kant set. Universalize the act! Say to yourself: Suppose every living human being would do the same thing; would it contribute to social well-being or would it not? Long before Kant, Hillel set the same test: "That which is hateful to yourself do not do to your neighbor." Ask yourself whether the act which you are about to do would be congenial if someone else did it to you. Would it contribute to your well-being?

Both of these tests are valid tests. Perhaps Hillel's is the more practical one. You may not know how a given act will affect humanity, but you pretty well know how a given act will affect you. If you are about to rob a workingman of his just hire, put yourself in his place and ask yourself: If I were the workingman and this act were perpetrated on me, would I like it?

If this is ideal justice, what is ideal love?

Love is the supreme motive of human life, and ideal justice is its supreme instrument.

It is quite difficult to define or analyze a sentiment as complex as love. It baffles thorough description and all analysis, and yet there is no doubt about its reality or its potency. Of all motives in human life, love is the most powerful. The author of that marvelous love lyric The Song of Songs says, "Love is as strong as death. Its flashes are flashes of fire. It is the very flame of God."

There are many other motives in human life besides love. There is ambition; there is hate; there is fear; there is compassion. But the motive which produces the noblest results, whether in art or literature, in religion or character, in families or in society, is unselfish love, which is the supreme achievement of the human race.

Whether or not unselfish love is an original endowment of the human race is really of little moment. We might be able to trace back this love of which I speak to its humble beginnings in physical and material considerations. That would make no difference at all, for the beginning of a thing is not the thing itself. The oak tree begins in the acorn, but the oak tree is infinitely more than the acorn. Cynics are frequently tempted to deprecate the value of a human institution by pointing out its humble origin, but that is fallacious reasoning. An institution should be judged on the basis of its value at the time it is being judged, and not on what its beginnings were. It is folly, for example, to run down a great man, or deprecate his importance, by pointing out that once upon a time that man was a helpless, drooling infant. We know that there is such a thing as disinterested love in the world, and when we see it in action we stand before it as before a holy thing, rapt in adoration.

There is this to be said about true love: that it is never without its compensations, though compensation is never the motive of real love. The mother who loves her child, the man who loves his friend, the idealist who lives for his ideal are not thinking in terms of possible rewards. In fact, they would not know what you were talking about if you spoke to them about a reward for their love. They love because it is the most necessary, the most desirable, and altogether the most spontaneous thing in the world for them.

But while compensation is not the motive of real love, it inevitably follows real love. The compensation of love is inner joy! He who loves finds joy in the object of his love. Love is encompassing joyousness. Her love for her child makes the heart of a mother sing for joy. This does not mean that there are no deep sorrows or anguish in the lives of those who love. There are. There are the inescapable sorrows which are part of our common destiny.

True love rejoices in the object of its love. The love of knowledge, the love of beauty, the love of God is an inexhaustible source of joy. "I rejoiced when they said unto me, come let us go into the house of the Lord." The greater the love, the higher the ecstasy of joy. And here, perhaps, is the first real test of love. Do you find joy in the object of your love? Without an element of happiness there is no love. You may respect, you may admire, you may tolerate, but if you do not find joy, you do not love. Marriage, or friendship, or the pursuit of knowledge, or philanthropy, or the love of God; in fact, every emotion which we assume to be based on the sentiment of love which does not bring with it an overwhelming sense of joy is not the real thing. It is a plaster imitation of it.

I repeat, this fact does not preclude the possibility, or even the probability, of great grief and misery and tragedy. There are many eddies and crosscurrents in the tides of life, but love is the deep channel which carries the river of life, steady and strong, to its appointed destiny. Because true love brings great joy, it is powerful. Sorrow and grief constrict, enfeeble, inhibit. Sorrow paralyzes our power of volition and of action, but joy releases energy. Happiness is really the dynamics of inspiration. The rabbis were profoundly wise when they said "Inspiration does not rest upon a man who is depressed."

Love is the supreme motive of human life, and ideal justice is the supreme instrument of love. Great love works great justice. Very often a distinction is made between love and justice. Theologians are fond of making such a distinction. Apologists for one religion or another are given to drawing this rather artificial distinction. It is said, for example, that the religion of Israel is a religion based on rigid justice, and that Christianity came into the world to teach men a new principle—that of love. This is an unreal distinction, because there can be no real love without justice, and there can be no real justice without love. We cannot be just if we are not kindhearted; we cannot be kindhearted if we are not just. Love which does not work through the channels of justice—and here again let me remind you that I am not speaking of legal justice, but of ideal justice—love which does not seek to express itself through justice frequently becomes a serious roadblock in human life. Love may become clannish.

Love is also in danger of being unreflective and impulsive. You see a poor man, you pity him and you give him alms. That impulsive giving may do more harm than good. It may be socially harmful. Love will frequently condone and be lenient where it should be corrective. I am ready to subscribe to Paul's dictum that love is the greatest thing in the world, but only when it is qualified by the idea that justice is its supreme instrument. I cannot subscribe to that other dictum which it attributed to the master of Christianity, "Love thine enemy." That is psychologically impossible. We cannot love our enemies. We ought to be just to our enemies; we ought not to hate our enemies, but we should try to check their power to do evil, and to persuade them, if at all possible, that they should cease to be our enemies. "Thou shalt rebuke a man and not bear grudge against him." Great love, I repeat, works through great justice.

The man who loves mankind will not remain content with mere charity. He will set out to help bring about a full measure of justice in society which will make his charity unnecessary. It is not enough to feed the hungry, clothe the naked, pity the unfortunate. Love demands that we should devote our energies to the reconstruction of society so as to prevent hunger and want and misery among men, to restore every child of God to his divine patrimony; to enable every man to live under his vine and under his fig tree with none to make him afraid; to make it unnecessary for a human being to come knocking at our door for alms. The greatest love works through the greatest justice. I do not crave the privilege of doling out alms to the poor in order to express my love for mankind.

Love also develops responsible freedom in the object of one's love. A man and a woman who are deeply in love will not seek to subjugate one to the other, or to drain the personality of one in order to feed the other. They will make possible the fullest development of each in the comradeship of freedom. A man who is a real friend will not try to make of his friend a reflection of himself, an echo of himself, but he will try to develop both himself and his friend to the fullest freedom, each one living his own life, developing his own capacities, and yet helping the other to grow.

This brings me to the second test of real love. The first test is joy; the second test is growth. A love which does not stimulate growth and unfoldment in the person one loves is not love at all. Young people who are in love find in their love a stimulation to the best that is in them. It will evoke the strongest and the finest in both of them. When husband and wife deeply love, they will go through life growing and developing, refining and upreaching. One of the great tragedies of married life is just this: that married folks settle down to a pedestrian existence. They stop growing, and very often the one who stops growing first drags the other one down. True human fellowship is an inspiration to growth. "Iron sharpeneth iron." And so does man's friend; and that is true of every human relationship.

The husband who looks upon his wife as an annex to his own personality, as a convenient foil to his own life, is not truly in love. True love asks for an even greater measure of responsible freedom in the object of love than in itself. Many parents are ultimately without the love of their children because they failed to develop in them the responsible obligations of freedom, because of too much unreflective love for them. Many parents are cruel to their children when they are overly protective. They keep their children from developing into responsible freedom, either by overly shielding them, by overly indulging them, or by attempting to dictate too long and too often to them—out of love, of course.

The rabbis say, "God loved Israel greatly. Therefore He gave Israel the Torah and many mitzvot—many laws and commandments." God manifested His love for His people not by indulging them but by permitting them to develop freely through many obligations and responsibilities. This is the essence of love. Love is the driving impulse of all the noble adventures in human life; it lends color and charm to human existence; it robs sorrow of its sting; it heals wounds; it softens the harshness of all experiences; it makes life a joyous and eager pilgrimage, but only when it expresses itself through supreme justice, justice to ourselves and to those whom we love.

True love does not indulge, does not cater, does not exploit, does not make unreasonable demands. True love is strong and oftentimes exacting, but it always seeks the happiness of the object loved. "And thou shalt love the Lord thy God with all thy heart, with all thy soul, and with all thy might." This is true of all love, sacred or profane, for there really is no profane love. All true love is sacred, because all true love is of God.

III. THE PEOPLE

I STOOD with Abraham in his lonely vigil and read the destiny of my people in the stars. With Isaac I built the altar of a patriarch's stern faith and ultimate sacrifice. At Jabbok's ford I learned to wrestle through the night with the dark angel of despair and to wrest a blessing at the break of dawn. With Joseph I dreamt of sheaves and of stars and climbed the steps from the dungeon's pit to a prince's throne.

I wandered with Moses, an alien prince among an alien people. Unshod, I knelt with him before the vision in the wilderness, and from within the inextinguishable fires of God I heard the Voice summoning to duty and freedom. I saw the lightning and the clouds and heard the thunder roll around Mount Sinai, and witnessed the everlasting covenant between my people and its God. I learned how to suffer and hunger in long and weary marches to reach the Promised Land.

I was with Joshua fighting at Gibeon, and with Deborah by the waters of Megiddo, when the stars in their courses fought against Sisera. I stood with the blind Samson in his agony, and heard the wild cry of his desperate courage as he pulled down the temple over the Philistines. I heard Samuel admonish his people to remain free, and not to reject God by enslaving themselves to a king. I listened to the harp of the shepherd king, David, and saw the great king bow before the righteous wrath of the prophet, and before the majesty of the overarching Law of God. I prayed with Solomon in the Temple which he dedicated as a House of Prayer for all peoples, and I learned of a God whom Heaven, and the Heaven of Heavens, cannot contain, and whose compassion extendeth to all, even to the stranger who cometh out of a far country.

I marched with the resolute band of the prophets who came to destroy old worlds and to build new ones. I shuddered at the wrath of their spirit as they lashed out against oppression and injustice, against false gods and gilded idols, against blind leaders and lying prophets. I warmed at their infinite compassion for the weak, the denied, and the wronged. From them I learned the nature of mission and what a raging fire within one's bosom an unfulfilled mandate of God may become.

I wandered with my people by the slow-moving rivers of Babylon, and I heard their oath of deathless loyalty: "If I forget thee, O Jerusalem, may my right hand forget her cunning." I entered their humble and improvised synagogues, and discovered that prayer and devout study are beautiful, and as acceptable to God as the sacrifices of the priests in the Temple, and the songs of the Levites.

I returned from captivity, and standing with those who rebuilt the

197

walls of Jerusalem, I learned how a people can build upon ruins. I sat with the sages and scribes who piously taught and interpreted the word of God, and molded a people's reverence for its spirit enshrined in a timeless Book. I moved among the mountains of Judea, pulling down the heathen altars, with the lionhearted sons of Maccabees. I saw the miracle of a single cruse of spiritual oil inexhaustibly illumine the rededicated Temple of their faith. I was a companion of the gentle Hillel, who revealed to me the whole of the Law in the single kernel of neighborly love; and of Akiba, who knew how to inspire a revolution, defy an empire, and die a martyr.

And then into the long dark exile I wandered with my people, into many lands over which cross and crescent reigned, and I walked with them the weary highways of the world. I was with them when they drank deep out of the bitter chalice of pain, humiliation, cruelty, and hate. But never did I fail to sense the stress of their imperious vision, their pride of a great past, their hope of a greater future, their superb courage, their unflinching faith. Philosophers, poets, and saints never failed them in the lands of their dispersion, and the light of their Torah was never extinguished.

And then I saw the night lift and the dawn break; and into a reborn world, drenched with a new light of freedom and justice, I marched with them exaltingly. I heard the shackles fall from off their limbs. I saw the radiance of their emancipated minds and hearts. I beheld them, mounting as on eagles' wings, rising to bless the world with matchless gifts of heart and mind in every field of human creation.

And now I see the night descend again, and into the dark and the storm my people are wandering forth again. Shall I leave them now? Can I leave them now? Shall I part company with this immortal band? They have become too dear and precious to me. The urgency of their pilgrimage is now coursing through my own blood also. Their beckoning is now the shrine of my quest also. Like unto the first pilgrim, out of Ur of the Chaldees, I, too, seized by the hand of God, am listening to the divine summons: "Get thee out of thy country and from thy father's house unto a land which I will show thee . . . and I will bless thee, and thou shalt be a blessing. . . ."

FROM AN ADDRESS
"RELIGION IN PRESENT-DAY JEWISH LIFE,"
BIENNIAL CONVENTION
UNION OF AMERICAN HEBREW CONGREGATIONS
JANUARY 17, 1939

"Look to the Rock Whence You Were Hewn . . ."

Abba Hillel Silver, as a religious thinker and sage, is persuasive and effective. But Abba Hillel Silver, when he speaks of his own people—their history, their literature, their great souls—rises to a different level of feeling and discourse. The words come from the depths. Dispassion, objectivity, reasonableness give way to burning pride, to love. The discipline of logic and reason is still there, but it is used to structure the form of a full-blooded, passionate commitment.

His discourses on the genius of his "race" (the term had not yet acquired the opprobrium of later days), his insistence that Jewish nationalism, Zionism, and the Hebrew language were integral aspects of Judaism—and religion its central component—must be appreciated in the context of the environment and time in which he spoke. It takes no courage today to hold that a Jewish homeland is important to Jewish survival, or to say that Jews are a distinct people with a special destiny. This has been demonstrated by history as well as theory. But it was by no means obvious to the American Jewish community when Rabbi Silver began preaching. Indeed, the claim that "nation, race, land, and language were always vital and indispensable concepts in Jewish life" was not acceptable to many in the ranks of his liberal religious movement. The Central Conference of American Rabbis still clung to the Pittsburgh Platform of 1885, which disclaimed any necessary connection of Judaism with Palestine or Zion. But it was not only Zionism that was unpopular. Anything that seemed to make Judaism sound parochial and alien, anything that tended to expand it beyond a set of monotheistic beliefs and worship patterns congenial to the American scene was intensely resisted, and often by the very circles within which Abba Hillel Silver lived and spoke. Rabbi Silver—and a very few colleagues—were lonely voices in this environment. But his was just as lonely a voice in many of the Zionist, nationalistic circles of his day, which were committed to a secularist ideology. He felt no rapport with those Jewish "intellectuals" who advocated a "cultural" Judaism "emancipated" from both religion and "narrow" nationalism.

It is against this background that Rabbi Silver's essays and sermons should be read. His was often a minority voice. But he was convinced that what he was saying was Judaism—historic, authentic Judaism. A half-century has passed, and it is no longer difficult either in the Reform rabbinate or in the American Jewish community to speak as Silver did. Hitler had something to do with this. So did the establishment of the Jewish National Homeland. But so also did Abba Hillel Silver. The role which he played in the Zionist movement and in the establishment of the State of Israel is a subject for a later volume. What we will quickly sense in the following selections is the pride and love for his people and the deep commitment to Israel's tragic and glorious destiny which were the wellsprings of Abba Hillel Silver's efforts as a rabbi, leader, and statesman.

"Eli! Eli!"—the Soul of a People in Song

SERMON, THE TEMPLE
NOVEMBER 21, 1920

The legend of "Eli! Eli!" is wrapped in darkness. Yet it is a comparatively new song. It was, in all probability, a song taken from a Yiddish opera, based upon a story of the Inquisition. "Eli! Eli!" is a song which the heroine sings just before she is led to be burned at the stake. The first line, of course, is taken from the twenty-second Psalm—"My God! My God! Why hast Thou forsaken me!" The rest is in Yiddish, the language of the greater part of our people for centuries; and the dramatic finale, the climax of it, is the creed, the confession of faith, the battle cry of our race.

I have always loved this song "Eli! Eli!" I heard it years ago in the murky theaters and music halls of the ghetto in New York. I have heard it sung at many gatherings. Yet somehow, I never plumbed the real depths of the song; I never realized the almost palpable tragedy, the magnificence, the grandeur of it; the passion and the pathos and the pain of it, until but a few days ago, when I heard it entoned by that golden-voiced daughter of Israel, Rosa Raisa. I seemed to catch a breath of another world, and the whole, vast, somber panorama of my people's experiences down through the ages was revealed to me on the rising waves of impassioned song.

I had thought up to then that "Eli! Eli!" was a song of lament only —a great dirge, a suppressed sob, the eternal suffering of an eternal people; but as I listened to the message which she found in that song, I was able to catch new meanings. I saw in it then not only the cry of a people in distress, but a superb challenge; I caught the undying faith, the unquenchable hope, the eternal faithfulness and superb endurance of a people. And all of that rising in a spiral wave of impassioned emotion up to the magnificent climax, that superb phrase which is at once the hope, the faith, the creed, the destiny of our people—"Eli! Eli!"

I reread this song; it is a very simple thing. It is almost primitive in its directness. Yet it is not naive. It knows the depths of human experience. But it has all the unpremeditated directness of the love declarations of little children—spontaneous and almost impulsive. It has nearly all the essential qualities of our people, dramatically scored; it has been successful in seizing swiftly upon the fundamental and the elemental things of Jewish life, giving them overpowering and forceful expression.

First comes the refrain of the song, "My God! My God! Why hast Thou forsaken me!" This is not a solitary phrase in the Psalms. It echoes and re-echoes like a litany, not alone through the Psalms and the prayers of our people, but throughout its vast experience. I open the Book of Psalms and I come across similar expressions: "Why dost Thou forsake my soul and hide Thyself in time of trouble?" "Why wouldst Thou forget me forever?" "Why dost Thou stand far away in time of great distress?" Throughout the Psalms one catches this refrain, "My God! My God! Why hast Thou forsaken me!" One is able to see the captives by the rivers of Babylon, hanging their harps upon the willow trees, unable to sing the song of Zion in a foreign land; one seems to catch the sad, melancholy refrain sung then by these broken and beaten captives—"Eli! Eli!"

One is able to stand with them before the smoldering ruins of the Temple, beside their fallen dead, vanquished and captive, with the night settling over their lives; one is able to hear that chant in that night—"Eli! Eli!" One is able to stand with our forefathers in that night of terror and dread in the graveyard of Frankfurt; one is able to stand with them, wrapped in shrouds, awaiting death, while the infuriated mob is breaking through the gates of the cemetery determined upon their destruction. One can hear their trembling lips mutter in prayer, in despair, in confession—"Eli! Eli!"

One can go with them, the old men, young men, and maidens, up to an auto-da-fé in Cordova or Toledo, and one can see the vast crowd of merrymakers howling their delight as each unfortunate is marched to the fire. One can hear the hiss and crackle of the flames, and in the terror-stricken, questioning eyes of these men and women one can read that phrase—"Eli! Eli!"

Today one can go to little scattered villages on the steppes of Russia, and in the silence of the night one can hear suddenly the howling and the shrieking of men bent upon the destruction of their fellow men; and one can hear the breaking in of doors and the smashing of windows; and one can see the trembling men and women ferreted out of their hiding places and killed by sword, or axe, or kris. And one can hear the cry—"Eli! Eli!"

There is no other such superb phrase in the whole of the literature of the world, and that is why the artists of the New Testament, who constructed the figure of Jesus, placed upon his dying lips these words "Eli! Eli!" I suppose that every servant of God, every idealist, every dreamer among men who has walked the path of sorrow that leads to the grave has found himself in the last moments of his life bereft, forsaken, alone, crying in the midst of his despair, "Eli! Eli!"

But it would be a mistake to think that this song is only a song of despair. It would then not be true to the soul of our people, because the soul of our people is not completely filled with the spirit of dejection and hopelessness.

Let me read you a translation of the Yiddish poem:

> My God! My God! Why hast Thou forsaken us! With fire and
> flame they tortured us; everywhere they made us to shame and
> mockery; yet none of us did turn away from Thee, O God, from
> Thy holy Torah and from Thy commands.

Notice how quickly the poem seizes upon the two kinds of persecution to which our people were subjected—the fire and flame of physical persecution and the mockery and insult of spiritual persecution. One thinks of the physical persecution in terms of the scenes which attended the ravages of the Black Plague in Europe and the extermination of Jewish communities as a result of it. One thinks of the physical persecutions in connection with the Crusades, which left behind them countless exterminated, charred, and burnt communities; one thinks of the physical persecutions in terms of the Cossack rebellions, which destroyed three hundred thousand of the best of Jewish manhood and womanhood in Poland; one thinks of physical persecutions in terms of expulsion and the Inquisition; one thinks of it in terms of modern pogrom and persecution; of your brothers and mine, who stood some years ago waiting for the dawn, asking themselves, "O Watchman, what of the night?" And the answer must be given to them, "The morning has come, but it is night again."

But of the spiritual persecution one is forced to think in terms of ghettos; one thinks of Cologne, Speyer, Worms, Frankfort, Prague, Rouen; one thinks of the sunless, cheerless ghettos, enwalled, enslaved, encased, isolated, like festering sores; ghettos on the banks of some dirty river, ghettos where grottos were placed to add insult to injury. One thinks in terms of the badge, the brand, the peaked hat; one thinks of every device to crush and break and humiliate; one thinks of legislation, of one council after another prohibiting the Jew from holding office, from eating with his Christian fellow men, from conversing with them, or appearing on the street during Passion week, or walking through the parks of the city, or having Christian servants and nurses in the home. One thinks of those ingenious devices that only man in his moments of absolute depravity can think of. One thinks of the name that was given to them: *servii camera,* "the servants of the chamber of the king." Men who prided themselves on being "the servants of God" had become the chattels of the king, to be traded off and bartered as slaves, to be handed over from one prince to another, or from one bishop to another, in order that taxes might be extorted.

"And yet no one was able to turn us from Thee, O God, and from Thy holy Torah and Thy commands." I think now of what happened in the Jewish quarter of Worms in 1096, when the First Crusade swept over Jewish communities on the banks of the Rhine. The Jews sought refuge in the castle of the Prince of Worms, and he had protected them. But the mob grew in number and fury and threatened to destroy the castle. The prince came to the eight hundred souls that were in hiding and said to them: "There is but one choice open to you: you must either convert or be slain." The Jews asked for twenty-four hours in which to deliberate. The prince left them, and after twenty-four hours he returned, and as he entered the vast banquet hall of the palace he found the eight hundred men, women, and children lying dead. They had killed themselves.

These memories recall that beautiful phrase of the Siddur:

> Look down from heaven and behold, for we have become the mockery and the scorn of the nation. We are accounted as the sheep that are led to the slaughter; and in spite of it all, Thy name we have not forgotten. Please do not forget us.

Now, the miracle of Jewish life is not that we endure; the miracle of Jewish life is that we are able to sing in spite of all. It would be a mistake to think that Jewish life was at all times somber and sad and full of weeping and lamentations. We had those moments, and all too many of them. But it would be a mistake to think that we did not have moments of light and cheer and happiness. Jewish life had its humor, its leisure, its freedom, its love and joy. The miracle of Jewish life is that in spite of the terrible onslaughts of a harsh fate, Jews were able, in the midst of their suffering, to sing out of contentment and joy: "How fortunate are we! How beautiful is our heritage!"

Their bodies may have been torn, but their souls have not been lacerated. When there was darkness without, there was light within. When the storms raged about them, there was peace and contentment at home, in their family circles, among their loved ones. One thinks of the Sabbath among our people; one hears the song of joy sung on the Sabbath eve. One thinks of the Jew hounded and hunted, an outcast of the world—a king in his own home. One hears him sing, "Peace and joy and light for the Children of Israel." One thinks of Jewish festivals, filled with sweetness and real happiness and joy. One wonders what it was that made a people sing in spite of its suffering.

The Jew, thank God, never made a cult, a virtue of pain, as other religions have done. We never enthroned suffering as itself glorious and holy, or as, of itself, a road to salvation. We met suffering and we endured it; we were tested and tempered and improved and forged by it, but we conquered it and sang in our triumphs.

Do you recall that phrase of the Psalms: "When I said my foot hast stumbled, Thy kindness, O Lord, supported me." Out of the depths, even when he cried, "My God, My God, why hast Thou forsaken me!" the Jew, in the innermost parts of his soul, knew that God had not forsaken him. "Thou alone, O Lord, canst help." The burning experiences of our people brought to us the undying conviction that only One can bring help and redemption and happiness in life, and that is God alone.

> My God, My God, why hast Thou forsaken me! By day and by night I yearn and pray for Thee. Anxiously I keep Thy holy law, but I pray save me, save me once again, even as Thou hast saved our fathers of yore. Listen to my prayer and my lament, for Thou alone, O God, canst help; Thou alone, O Lord, canst help.

I think for a moment of Heine, one of the resplendent singers of Israel—Heine, the scoffer; Heine, the pagan; Heine, the cynic; Heine, who toyed with all the sanctities of life and religion; I think of Heine in the last years of his life, on his mattress grave in the attic of some old house in Paris—tortured by the ailments of his body, scorned by his friends, broken in spirit. And I read the words of his confessions:

> I ask that my funeral should be as simple as possible, and that the expenses of my interment should not exceed the amount of the smallest citizen. Although I belong to the Lutheran confes-

sion by the act of baptism, I do not desire that the ministers of that church should be invited to my burial, and I object to any other sort of priest officiating at my funeral. This objection does not spring from any spirit of freethinking or prejudice. For the last four years I have renounced all pride of philosophy and returned to religious ideas and feelings. I die in the faith of one God, the eternal creator of the world, whose pity I beseech for my immortal soul. I regret having spoken, sometimes, of sacred things without any due reverence in my writings, but I was led astray more by the spirit of the time than by my own inclinations. If I have unwittingly offended against good morals and morality, which is the true essence of all monotheistic doctrines of faith, I do ask pardon of God and man.

Can you not hear in those last words the old refrain of his people—"Eli! Eli! . . . Thou alone, O God, canst save."

I think of the men and women who leave the faith of their fathers, who set out into the world in a spirit of adventure, who are hurled into the maelstrom of existence, who are engaged in furious enterprise—doing, planning, climbing, struggling, striving; and then suddenly, in the midst of their lives, they realize that they are beaten and their vision is darkened, that their hopes have not been realized, that men have turned against them. Then they come back, like lost sheep, to the fold, and then they recall that phrase of the Psalms: "Even when father and mother forsake me, God will take me in." Then they realize that there is but one faithful friend in all the world, one last refuge, one eternal hope—God.

"Thou alone canst save . . ." That is the climax; that is the consummation; that is the explanation of it all. God is one. All is of God. Pain, suffering, persecution, misery—all are of God. The tear and the smile; the day and the night; the darkness and the sunshine—all are of God, and all serve some unknown purpose in God's grand scheme of life. The Lord is one. All is of God, and God is for all—for all men. Oh, His children may yet be blind, and they may yet hurt and bruise one another in blindness, in ignorance; His children may not know His truth and His life as yet, but they are all His children, and in His own time they will come to recognize that God is for all. "God is one."

"Hear, O Israel, thou more than any other people, for unto thee was this glorious fact first revealed." "Hear, O Israel, the Lord is one. And it is thy holy duty to glorify, to preach, to proclaim unto the world that God is one."

That is your burden; that is your sorrow; that is your sacrifice; that is your cross. But that is your glory and that is your triumph.

My People

I am not a chauvinist. I do not condone the deficiencies and the short-comings of my race, and I do not exalt it beyond its just deserts. I believe chauvinism is contrary to the spirit and the tradition of our race. Indeed, I do not know of any people that is so self-analytical, so critical, so intro-spective—to the point, oftentimes, of morbidity.

Certainly no prophet ever indulged the people. The seers and the sages and the rabbis and the prophets of our people loved Israel; they were true and loyal sons of Israel, but they loved it with a love that cleanses and purges, that often hurts, because of the rigors of the discipline which it exacts.

I know the deficiencies of my race, and I oftentimes attack them. But I do so, I hope, in a spirit of comprehension and sympathy, for actions must be measured in relation to the circumstances from which they spring. You must understand the seed of an act to judge it rightly, and because I know and understand I can be sympathetic. The marvel to me is not that our people has this flaw or that flaw; the almost miraculous thing to me is that our people has so few radical, vital deficiencies. I believe this was born from contact with the soil for two thousand years; from contact with the stabilizing, balancing, normalizing influences of the agricultural life. A people that was driven into the lowest, most noisome, and most pestilen-tial sections of cities, and then caged in as beasts in ghettos; a people that was driven out from the multitudinous occupations in which people may engage and forced into a few, and those few not of the kind that develop character; a people that was subjected for fifteen centuries to all the cruel devices that the cunning of vindictive men could think of—devices calculated to break their spirit, to destroy their manhood, to make of them outcasts, pariahs, gypsies; the marvel of it is not that we have one weakness or another, but that we have succeeded in spite of this organized, studied hostility in preserving so much of the inner glory and grandeur of our character.

I am not a chauvinist. Other races that may have achieved great things in the world have attributed those achievements to their natural gifts and capacities. The Greeks did that. The Romans did that. The Prussians do it now. The present-day Anglo-Saxon is launched upon such a delusion. But the prophets never permitted our race to indulge in any such fatuous illusions. If Israel produced great things, it was not to be attributed to Israel's natural excellences, but simply to the fact that a great God had selected this people to be the vehicle for His revelation. "Are ye not as the children of the Ethiopians unto me, O children of Israel?" I brought you out of Egypt, it is true, but "have I not brought the Philistines from Caphtor and the Syrians from Kir?" You are all my creatures, alike, and every race serves a specific purpose of mine.

Israel can no more pride itself upon its achievements than an artist who becomes the channel through which the divine inspiration addresses man can pride himself upon his achievements. We are all tools in the hands of an omnipotent power, and some are chosen to carry a larger measure of beneficence and glory than others.

But whether my people is perfect or imperfect, whether it is flawless or full of flaws, it is my people; and I would no more think of denying it or deserting it or despising it than I, or you, would think of despising our kith and kin if they do not happen to have that refinement or that culture that we would like them to have. To despise one's own is to despise oneself; to be ashamed of one's own is to confess the lowest moral degradation and spiritual debasement.

I mean to chastise my people when they follow strange gods, but I love them. I am proud of their steadiness during the weary centuries and the dark nights. I am proud to repeat my faith with those who worshiped in caves and in secret hiding places, with those who carried upon their shoulders the badge of infamy and sublimity, with those who ascended the scaffold and faced the Crusader; I am proud to be able to repeat with them: "In spite of all these things Thy name we have not forgotten."

I would not have you think that my love of my people is based on pity. My pride does not grow only from my people's heroic suffering. I think it is a sign of a neurosis when a people seeks refuge in suffering. The sick and the martyrs have no claim upon us simply because of their sickness or martyrdom. It is the cause that suffering serves that ennobles it.

My people does not exert its tyranny upon me simply because it has suffered. Other peoples have suffered; suffering is a commonplace event in our world for individuals and for peoples. Rather it is because of the unique character of its suffering that I love it. Its suffering was self-imposed, voluntary, and vicarious. Its suffering was sacrificial, an atonement for the sins of others. It suffered so that other peoples might say: "Verily he bears our illness and he suffers for our wickedness." The Jew chose to die that others might live. He chose to perpetuate with his tears and his endurance the glory of the kingdom of God, and such suffering becomes an object of pride. When suffering becomes a sacrament, it becomes majestic.

And quite apart from the tragic grandeur and the majestic scope of my people's suffering, the achievements of my people make me proud. I hold a few convictions that have for me the potency of a creed, and one of the convictions which gives purpose and meaning to my life and labor, and to that of every Jew, is this: that the Jew as a Jew has benefited mankind, and that the world needs the Jew as a Jew.

When that wanderer from the little city of Ur left his home, his kith and kin, his friends, his comforts, he asked of the God who troubled him, who urged him out to seek a new land: Wherefore and why? Why need I now become an exile and a wanderer upon the face of the earth? And God answered: "That all the nations of the earth may become blessed through thee and through thy seeking."

And I believe that our people has remained true to God's charge. I do not have in mind now the individual achievements of individual Jews in the arts, the sciences, or literature. Gifted sons and daughters of Israel have given abundantly to the cause of the advancement of mankind in every age and land. I have in mind the achievements of our people as a people. As a people we have abundantly blessed mankind; as a people we shattered the idols of the world in order to enthrone the one God; as a people we looked above and saw God, and we looked below and saw suffering mankind. We taught mankind how to look above: "Lift up thine eyes and see," even while we prayed to God to look down: "Look down from heaven and see." We drew religion and morality into the inseparable union; we brought God and suffering mankind together in the unity of father and son.

As a people we saw hate rampant, peoples suspicious of one another, seeking one another's undoing, and we said unto them: "Have we not all one father? Hath not one God created all? Why then should we deal treacherously with one another?" As a people we saw war and bloodshed and the blind struggle of nations, and we projected a vision to the world of the day when "they shall beat their swords into plowshares." "Peace be unto those who are weary and unto those who are afar off."

As a people Israel saw oppression and injustice. We saw the millions who were submerged and denied, in shackles and in slavery, and we cried aloud for freedom, for the opening of the gates of the dungeons, for the bringing forth of all who were imprisoned and incarcerated, for justice and truth and equality and freedom. "Justice, justice shalt thou pursue!"

As a people we became the ever-present heretics of the world, because as a people we denied the divinity of any one man in order to assert the divinity of all men.

And because of these achievements we won many friends and we won many enemies. Would you know who are the friends of my people? The friends of my people are all those, who, in every corner of the world today, are fighting for justice, truth, and humanity. Wherever there is a freedom-loving son or daughter of the human race, wherever there are men who believe in progress and advancement, there are the friends of my people. Wherever there are peoples who wish to break chains, there are the friends of my people.

A people whose God could say unto them, "Ye are my servants but not servants unto servants, for unto me belongs the world," such a people is the friend and the plighted kinsman of every man who loves freedom. Wherever there is a liberal in the world who needs comfort and inspiration in his lonely struggle, why, all he needs to do is to look upon this little people—"For ye are but few"—this challenging and protestant minority that has defied for centuries an overwhelming majority, and that, in spite of untoward circumstances, has endured. He finds in Israel the symbol of truth triumphant, of truth crushed to the ground rising again, and out of Israel he draws inspiration for his own work and his own trials.

Do you know who are the enemies of my people? Wherever there are ghouls in the night; wherever there are those who prefer the Stygian gloom of medievalism; wherever there are the entrenched and privileged who live on the exploitation of their fellow men, there you have the sworn enemies of my people. When such a one comes to the United States to begin a campaign of propaganda to restore the bloodstained Romanoff dynasty, who does he first attack? The Jew. When those hooded ghouls of the night spread over this land the bedraggled hates of medievalism, that vileness which the war has spread forth, they too are the enemies of my people. Wherever there are people who hate the prophet and who hate prophecy, who cry that "the spiritual man is mad and a menace"—there you will find the enemies of our race.

These enemies we know how to meet. We have developed through the years a strategy, a defense which they have never succeeded in downing. Persecution, opposition, and ostracism steel us and strengthen us and make us the more determined. It is the enemy within, "the destroyers who come from within you" that are the most menacing of our enemies.

Who are they? There are just two classes of them; one is the Jew who has lost his vision, the Jew who has sold his birthright for a mess of pottage, the Jew who has lost his soul in the passion for acquisitiveness, the Jew who has become a traitor to the vision which sustained and preserved our people, the Jew who has dethroned God and enthroned wealth, money, and pleasures—the predatory Jew, the materialistic Jew. He is not alone a menace to Israel, but he is a veritable menace to the whole human race. The enemy within is the man who has forgotten that the keynote of our race is to give and to sacrifice, not to amass and to hold. "The world does not exist but for the sake of the sacrifices," said one of our rabbis. When your forefathers and mine lived in want and uncertainty, in penury, in the hated and dirty ghettos, they were able still to dream of "the city of universal peace," to dream of a "kingdom of God." They could still look up and look beyond; they had dreams, they had visions, and they lived by the light of their visions. In this age of freedom and prosperity so many of us have become choked in the obesity of plenty that we have lost the gift, the one holy gift of our race—that of being able to dream and to project visions that would astonish mankind. The tragedy of our day is that our children are growing up obsessed by an un-Jewish, anti-Jewish, antisocial passion for things, for money, for dress, for wealth, for position! The glory, the enthusiasm, the sacred duty to go out into the highways and byways of life to serve and give and help—that is fast passing from the lives of the children of my people.

The other class of such enemies of my people are the terrified Jews, the weasel Jews, those who are Jews by sufferance, those who feel the burden and not the glory, who scurry down back alleys and who have not the courage openly to acknowledge defeat and suffer it. Somewhere from among that group of terrified Jews comes the clamor: "The world does not like the Jew, the world does not like the name 'Jew.' It is rather unpleasant to carry around with one the title of 'Jew'; let us change it; let us call ourselves by a different name; perhaps we can fool people." Weasel Jews!

Why should I change my name—a name drenched in the tears and the blood of a race, a badge of sacrificial idealism? Change it because, forsooth, some blind or stupid or malicious creature does not like the sound of it? I suppose that the Quakers, that band of sacrificing, serving, holy servants of God, when they began their ministry of compassion and mercy in the world, and people derided them and mocked them and jeered at them and called them in contempt "Quaker," might have said to themselves: "Let's change our name; perhaps people will forget about us." But no, they hung on to their service and to their name, and today the name "Quaker" is a name not of reproach or of contempt but of dignity, of beauty.

Surrender my name? Ah, no. When mine enemy says "Jew," I say "Aye, Jew!" and I shall continue to say "Jew" and the children of my people shall continue to say "Jew" until that day "when God is one and His name is one." My people, slaves of a deathless vision, masters of an ancient wisdom! My people, dreamers from Chaldea and Galilee, dreamers lost in the sorry traffic of Rome and London, hostages alike of God and men! My people, the risen people of an immemorial crucifixion, in their hearts the promptings of an ancient splendor, in their blood the rhythm of a mighty song, and in their hand a torch! My people! God, what a heritage, what a burden and what a glory!

Nationalism —
the Struggle for Survival

SERMON, THE TEMPLE
FEBRUARY 14, 1926

This subject of the status of the Jew, be he race, nation, or religion, is at best academic, and I am concerned with the realities of Jewish life. The reality of the situation is that the Jew has, since the beginning of his career, looked upon himself as a distinct people, and that he still regards himself as a distinct people. There have been a few who have wished that the Jew would lose his physical identity. There are still a few here and there who wish that the Jew would assimilate and lose his identity, or who wish to consider themselves no longer of a nation but only of a religious community.

But this is at best only a wish—a wish of what might be rather than a statement of what is. A wish cannot undo history and a wish cannot obliterate facts of history. The fact of history is that for the first thousand years of his existence the Jew possessed all the essential characteristics which we are wont to attribute to a nation. He had a common land, a common language, a common religion, a common racial ancestry. In the last two thousand years of his existence he has lacked a common center and a common land; to a degree he has lacked a common speech. I say to a degree and only to a degree, because Hebrew has continued to be the universal language of Jewish prayer and Jewish literature. He does possess a common religion, and to a remarkable degree he has maintained common racial antecedents.

Destiny surrounded the Jew with so many restrictions and so many oppressions that his life of necessity and by force of circumstance became isolated, and to that extent was conserved. In place of a common land or a

212

common center the Jew substituted an embracing Messianic ideal—a hope of restoration and rehabilitation, a common vision in which the people rejoiced during the years of exile, waiting for the restoration to its own home.

So that the Jew comes down to the twentieth century very much an integrated people held together by ties racial, religious, historical; enjoying common memories, common traditions, common loyalties, common aspirations; and these, we maintain—in deference to the realities of the situation—are the essentials of nationality.

Another reality which we must accept is that the non-Jewish world regards the Jew as a distinct people. The non-Jew sees in the Jews a people possessing those distinctive qualities which he is wont to attribute to a people, and he accepts them as such. So that really a metaphysical or intellectual discussion of the problem of the status of the Jew is altogether beyond the point.

So potent was this idea of nationalism in Jewish life that when the Jew lost his political independence and became scattered to the four corners of the earth, he refused to disappear. He posited two tremendous dogmas in his life as an expression of his will to persist. The first is the dogma of the eternal people, and the second is the dogma of the Messiah.

The dogma of the eternal people was first enunciated during the first exile—the Babylonian. When the First Temple was destroyed in 586 B.C.E. and the Jews were exiled to Babylon, they sensed then and there the menace of disintegration. There were many forces about them tending to break them up and to destroy their national self-identity. So they established in their exile the dogma of the eternal people, and through the voice of their great prophet, whom we call for lack of a better term the second Isaiah, this national will to live expressed itself most perfectly. "As the new heaven and the new earth which I make endure before me, saith the Lord, so shall your race and your name endure." "For the mountain shall depart and the hills be overthrown, but my kindness shall not depart from thee, nor shall my covenant of peace be overthrown, saith the Lord that hath mercy on thee." "When thou shall pass through the waters," cries this prophet in anger in a magnificent and heroic passage, "I shall be with thee; and through the rivers, they shall not overflow thee; when thou shall go through fire, thou shalt not be burned, and the flames shall not be kindled against thee. For thou art an eternal people."

This dogma of the eternal people was never logically proved. Yet if logic has not established its truth, experience, to a degree, has. The Jew is warranted in believing that somehow in him there is resident the quality of eternity; for what has not the world done to him in order to break and to destroy him? When he stands today and scans the purview of all his yesterdays; when he considers what the armies of Babylon and Assyria sought to do to him, and the chariot armies of Memphis and Thebes, and the hoplites of the Greeks and the iron legions of the Romans and all the followers of the cross and the crescent, who mistook and misinterpreted the ideals of their own faith; what the rack and the stake and the Inquisition and exile and ghetto and yellow badge and pogrom and massacre have sought to do to the Jew; I say, when the Jew scans his past and sees what instruments of destruction were brought to play upon him, and that in spite of them all he is, he persists, he lives, perhaps he is justified in believing in the dogma of the eternal people.

The second dogma which the Jew established as an expression of his will to live was the dogma of the Messiah. In a way it derives from the dogma of the eternal people. The belief in the Messiah began with the Roman conquest and oppression of Palestine. It gained tremendous impetus at the time of the destruction of the Temple and the loss of national independence, and from that day to the day, almost nineteen hundred years later, when the Hebrew University was dedicated on Mount Scopus, in sight of the Temple mount, this faith in the coming of an era of redemption, of emancipation, of reconstruction, physical and spiritual, was never wanting in the life of the people. At every crisis in its life it flared up; during every revolutionary moment or event it came to the surface, whether it was the collapse of the Roman Empire or the rise of Islam or the Crusades or the Black Death, or the Protestant Reformation or the Cossack uprisings, or the French Revolution or the World War. Whenever there took place an event which stirred the world, the Messianic hopes in Israel surged to the surface and the embers glowed with rare expectancy. The finest minds in Israel dreamt of the return, prayed for the coming of the Messiah, and even calculated the time when he would come. Whether they were rabbis like Jochanan ben Zakkai and Akiba, or philosophers like Saadia and Maimonides, or poets like Gabirol or Jehuda Halevi, or statesmen like Hasdai ibn Shaprut or Isaac Abrabanel, or mystics like Abraham Abulafia and Isaac Luria—whatever type, whatever profession, the finest minds in Israel hoped for the return, prayed for it.

And why? Because in them the national, the racial will to live a fuller and richer and quieter life was never dead; and modern Zionism, I make bold to say, is an expression of this selfsame Messianic hope. It may be less mystic. It may be more realistic. Its technique and apparatus may be more scientific. It may be paying much more attention to the realities of the international situation, but the rise of the movement is the same, the faith which inspires it is the same, the driving impulse one and the same.

Nationalism is a basic instinct, but the Jew gave the idea of nationalism a unique turn, a distinctive definition, and that perhaps is one of the great contributions which Israel has made to civilization. To the Jew it is not enough for a nation merely to survive, to exist, or to grow through conquest. That is not enough: to the Jew a nation must vindicate its existence through some social, creative purpose. Just as no individual fulfills his destiny merely by living or by growing great through acquisition, so a nation does not justify its existence merely by surviving or by growing imperial through conquest and aggrandizement. A nation must—so says the philosophy of Jewish nationalism—find its highest motif and its highest goal in some form of human service.

Early in Jewish history the Jew found his motif and his goal, and early in his history the Jew came and spoke of himself as the "servant of God." The Jew was of "a kingdom of priests and a holy people." Not a people which arrogates unto itself a priesthood and a holiness, but a people which strives to be priestly and holy. That same great prophet who announced the dogma of the eternity of Israel also announced the dogma of the mission of Israel. "Behold my servant, whom I uphold; my chosen one in whom my soul delighteth; I have put my spirit upon him; he shall make the right to go forth to the nations. He shall not fail nor become weary until he shall have established justice in the earth." Again: "I, the Lord, have called thee for salvation; I will hold thee by the hand; I will defend thee and make thee a covenant of the peoples, a light unto the nations."

Why? To open the eyes of the blind, to bring the prisoners out of the prison house, and they that dwell in darkness out of the dungeons. Think of it! Twenty-six hundred years ago, in exile, a broken people was in a position to define a conception of nationalism which so far transcends modern conceptions of nationalism.

Israel's task in the world was not to grow great and conquer, not to establish a vast empire, not to exploit the resources of the earth, but to be a light unto the nations. That is the mission of Israel. Some have spoken flippantly of it; some have spoken cynically of it; yet it is one of the real facts of Jewish life. The mission idea does not at all, as has been frequently maintained and is still being frequently maintained, preclude the idea of nationalism. The great prophet, the second Isaiah, who gave the classic expression to the ideal of the mission of Israel, was himself the supreme nationalist and the supreme Zionist of his day.

The Jew need not be scattered to the four corners of the earth in order to carry out his mission, any more than the Greeks had to be scattered to the four corners of the earth to carry out their national mission, which was to teach mankind how to think logically and critically, and how to feel the beauty of the world. But it would be a mistake on the part of the champions of Jewish nationalism to push to the background this inspiring motif of Jewish life. I would not wish my people to become another little statelet, another little Montenegro somewhere, merely for the sake of existing as a separate entity there. I wish my people to continue its historic mission as a light-bringer unto mankind, and as a reclaimed and integrated people on its own soil carry on this great work which destiny seems to have outlined for it from the beginning of time.

It is of interest to note that the four great tendencies of Jewish life—prophecy, legalism, mysticism, nationalism—received their consummate expression in Palestine. I do not mean to say that in exile during the last two thousand years the Jew did not create any values and did not contribute to society. He did. He gave much to the world even as he received much from the world. He participated in every major cultural movement. But somehow the real stamp of creative genius, of originality, of world-conquering truth are possessed by those things which were born on the soil of Palestine.

It is not that the soil of Palestine is any more inspiring or holier than the soil of any other nation or any other land, but in exile the Jew lacked freedom, and freedom is at the very root of creative genius. Freedom alone enables a man to express, without let or hindrance, the gifts which are latent in his soul, which he can express. Throughout the last two thousand years the Jew has lacked that complete freedom, that spaciousness, that stability, that sense of belonging which enables a people to create for it grand and lasting things.

In exile the Jew has lacked the stimulating environment which makes for greatness. In the Diaspora his greatness is either crushed and stultified as he is forced in upon himself, or is weakened and distorted as he seeks to exceed himself. Either is dangerous to creative greatness.

The fact of the Zionist ideal is, I take it, just this wish to regain the authentic mood in Jewish life and the authentic voice, to recapture greatness by finding freedom and the stimulating environment which it had in its ancient days.

The Jew in Palestine may create in the years to come values comparable to those which he created there in the past. It is not at all certain that he will. Perhaps people will say the Zionist is hoping for miracles; the past cannot be recaptured. Perhaps so. But Israel's life has been so full of miracles, its existence and survival has been such a marvelous miracle that I am ready to take a chance upon this miracle. As for those Jews who will remain in the Diaspora—and the majority of our people will always remain outside of Palestine—they can do three things and remain contributing forces to civilization. First, they can remain loyal to their faith. Second, they can preserve their racial and historical identity. In other words, in this beloved land of ours the Jew can completely Americanize himself, share in the common life of America, obey its laws, participate in its government, contribute to its national life, love it, serve it, and at the same time keep from destroying himself, from assimilating himself beyond recognition.

Third, the Jew in the Diaspora, here and elsewhere, may continue as a contributing force to civilization by living up to the ideals of his race, the moral teaching, the mission of his people; then he is, in a sense, a missionary to mankind, an apostle of truth, a messenger of good tidings, a champion of justice and truth.

I hear a great deal today about anti-Semitism, and I hear these complaints most in those circles which somehow seem to have drifted away from Judaism. When I come into a circle of people who are not affiliated with a temple or a synagogue, who do not participate in Jewish educational movements or in any movement of Jewish interests, the first subject of conversation is anti-Semitism. That is the one thing that hurts them, the one thing that disturbs their bovine peace. If that were removed, why, they would be in paradise.

My great concern is not anti-Semitism. I am used to it; my people is used to it; we have experienced it for twenty centuries; it is not a novel experience in our life; we are reconciled to it; we have developed a strategy for meeting it; we have seen it in uglier forms than now; we shall see it in the future; we shall abide as we did in the past. It does not bother me. What bothers me, what hurts me to the quick is to see the moral debacle of our people, the breakup of moral idealism, the encroaching of materialism and the saturation of the whole body of Israel in this land with all the vileness and the corruption which comes from prosperity too quickly gotten and not readily assimilated. That is the tragedy of Jewish life in America, and it is a growing tragedy for which the non-Jew is not responsible, for which we ourselves are responsible. When I see the rising Jewish generation, steeped in sensuality, in materialism, thinking only of the day and of success and of prosperity and of pleasure and the hectic chase after material things; when I look about me and see the standards which have been set up in Jewish life, I say to myself how tragically we have failed in our mission as the priest people of mankind.

Oh, I know you will tell me everybody else is doing it; the non-Jew is no better. Of course he is no better; we have no monopoly on vice; we have no monopoly on materialism. I know that. But we burdened ourselves twenty-six hundred years ago with a world-revolutionizing career of service; we were to make the right prevail on the earth; we were to establish justice; we were to be a light and a leader to the nations. We are not doing it. When I see the number of Jews in the professions who fall below the line of the ethics of the profession; when I see the number of Jews, adult and juvenile, who are crowding into our courts; when I look about me and see the number of Jewish homes that are breaking up; when I look about me and see the hundreds and the thousands of young Jewish boys and girls growing up without God, without Torah, without ideals, I see before me the greatest tragedy in Jewish life, and all your wealth and all your prosperity and all your beautiful homes and all your sense of ease and peace do not for a moment compensate for this tragic loss.

I believe that American Israel needs a stirring revival, an awakening, a return to fundamentals, a taking of stock of its spiritual life. If we are to continue as a people, as a distinct group, then we ought to continue as a worth-while, helpful, creative group in American life. In other words, we shall have to go back and pay an attentive ear to the mighty phrases of our sages and prophets of old; we shall have to think a little more of spirit, of ideal, of God, of worship, of prayer, of service, of education, and a little less of pleasure and money and wealth and display.

That is our task and our challenge for tomorrow.

The Mystery of Our Survival

SERMON, THE TEMPLE
PASSOVER, APRIL 11, 1936

I wonder what passed through the minds of Pharaoh and his hosts as they pursued the Children of Israel who were fleeing from Egypt; I wonder what thoughts passed through their minds as their chariots rolled on and their swords and spurs flashed.

The beautiful song of Miriam in the Book of Exodus tries to portray the ideas which flashed through the minds of the enemy. The enemy said: "I will pursue, I will overtake them. I will divide the booty. My desire shall be satisfied upon them. I will lay bare my sword and my sword will destroy them." This was Pharaoh four thousand years ago and this is Hitler today.

Where are they now, these men for whom our ancestors built the citadels of Pithom and Raamses, these mighty swordsmen and charioteers who pursued the people of Israel? The sands of time have completely covered them up. Nothing remains of them. What remains of other enemies of Israel, those who laid waste to the kingdoms of Israel and Judea—proud Assyria and mighty Babylon? They are of interest only to students of archaeology.

The miracle of this little people that never conquered the world and never erected pyramids or empires is that it continued an unbroken chain of historical continuity, outlived all great empires and is now, twenty centuries later, even more numerous and energetic, more hungry for life than in the past.

How often as you read Jewish history do you come across the phrase, "We have swallowed her up this day"? How often do you come across the cry echoed in Germany, "The Jew shall perish like a beast"? What weapons were not forged and used against this people, from the laws of Pharaoh in Egypt which destroyed every male Jewish child to the Nuremberg laws which threaten every Jewish life? And yet here we are, living, achieving, creating, fighting our foes as valiantly as in the past—sixteen million strong.

If you ask for any miracle in history, here is the supreme miracle. The Christian world is celebrating this day the miracle of the resurrection of its master, who was crucified and descended into the tomb but rose again. I submit in all humility this greater miracle—an arisen people, an often crucified people, which more than once was nailed to a cross; a people which descended into the valley of the shadow of death time and time again, and arose, again resurrected.

We are a people sharply critical of ourselves. Think how often the prophets of Israel despaired of Israel and called it a sinful and backsliding people! Yet the miracle has happened—the miracle of self-redemption, a miracle of repentance and refashioned ideals. The Jews who left Egypt and wandered through the wilderness for forty years—what a miserable lot they were! How frequently they complained to Moses and plagued him. They did not have enough food to eat. They did not have water to drink. They wanted the fleshpots of Egypt. They were a people that regretted that it had left Egypt, because the freedom of the desert brought hardship. They were a discouraged people. Yet a generation later, the descendants of these same people fought and died like heroes, conquering and building up the land. That miracle of self-redemption has happened over and over again.

Jeremiah at the time of the exile of the Jews in Babylon complained bitterly of the sinfulness of the people, and of backsliding and idolatrous practices and false prophets. Yet two generations later, the sons of these same people returned to Judea, rebuilt their nation, purified their religion, and gave to the world the most exalted monotheistic faith that it has ever had.

The Jews of Spain had lived there for centuries and had become rich and prosperous. They were rich and proud. Yet when expulsion came and these same people were given three months to decide between being baptized or exiled, between leaving all their possessions in Spain, their homes and comforts, or going out into the world as paupers facing danger, torture, exile, most chose exile. A miracle of self-redemption—and I say that this generation of Jews, after its testing time, will rediscover within itself that same primal race loyalty and strength.

What is the key to this strange survival of our people? I would like to point to a few facts. In the first place, just as there are individuals who possess love for life, vitality, energy in greater measure than other people, so there are groups of people who possess this life hunger, this will to live, and this capacity for living in larger measure than other peoples. The people of Israel have always had an amazing capacity for life and an indefeasible will to live. "Choose thou life." That has been the mighty principle of Jewish survival. When the rabbis called us the toughest and the hardiest people of the earth, they knew what they were talking about. This will to live has always been strong enough to evolve strategy to protect Jews against the forces which threatened to destroy them. Those who love life never relax their vigilance against forces which might cause their disintegration.

In the second place, there is the life-giving faith of our people, a faith which does not stultify and strangle religion but which has enabled it to make new adjustments, to advance. The Egyptians worshiped the god of the nether world. Their scripture was the Book of the Dead. The God of Israel is a "king who desires life." Our faith was the sort of faith that made Jews seekers, men who go out in quest of the new, the undiscovered. Get thee out from the rut, from the conventional. Go to the new land which I will show you, and there you will become a blessing and all nations of the earth will become blessed through you.

Third, there is the Jew's capacity to adapt himself to his environment, to adopt the best in other cultures without destroying his own, without becoming submerged, without being completely assimilated. The Jew never ghettoized himself intellectually or spiritually. If he had, he would have vanished a long time ago. He took the best from other cultures and incorporated it into his own. He never permitted himself to be completely immersed and erased.

I should like to point to another factor which has enabled the Jews to survive—loyalty to our own group. Jews have a strong sense of responsibility. Every Jew is responsible for every other Jew. This strong tie of brotherliness has never been broken.

Another factor is the survival of the Jewish home. A few days ago a newspaperman called me up and said: "Rabbi, I know all about the history of the Passover holiday. I know about the redemption. I would like to have you tell me something about that rare and admirable thing that we know exists today—the beauty and nobility of Jewish home life.

That is something from which non-Jews can receive inspiration." This is a rare thing in the world, and I hope it is not becoming rare among our people.

The interesting thing is that all these factors are still with us in 1936. We can still use them. They are still functioning as the bulwarks of survival, and that is why I am not a pessimist though so much is happening to make men depressed and dejected. We shall outlive Hitler as we outlived Pharaoh. The story of Pharaoh is exactly the same as the story of Hitler.

They know—the Hitlerites do—that they are doomed. Hence their cruelty and desperation. They know that the spirit of Israel which they fear will ultimately triumph. That love of justice which speaks from every page of the Bible they must read today in every church in Germany. They cannot help themselves. What they would like to do is to revise that Bible. They would like to forget that every page is written by Jews. They would like to obliterate every reference to freedom, tolerance, and fair play and substitute for it war, hatred, intolerance, and racial bigotry.

You cannot forge a religion. You can be pickpockets, as the Nazis have been, and take the wealth which the Jews achieved through their labor in Germany and rob them of it. You can cheat. You can lie. You can break treaties. But you cannot undo history. Every time the Bible is read on Easter morning in a church in Germany, the thought will sink into the minds of the listeners that the Bible is the book of the Jews, whose descendants are today being degraded and humiliated and persecuted in their very midst, that the founder of the religion they follow that morning was a Jew, was of the race of Israel, of a race which Hitler tells them to regard as an inferior race—a race which teaches not of hatred nor war but of freedom and peace and justice and love of thy neighbor.

Ultimately these things will undermine this regime of wickedness. Unto Abraham it was told and repeated unto Isaac, who repeated it unto Jacob. "And I will bless those who bless you and those who curse you, I will curse." That is the law of Jewish history and one of the laws of Jewish survival.

To us and to our ancestors, all history is revelation and testimony. We hold history in great reverence. We were the first people to write history, and to interpret it. "The Book of Chronicles was given for the sole purpose of interpretation." Our people were encouraged to rehearse and to cogitate upon the great moments of their national history. "The more one expatiates upon the story of the Exodus the more praise is due him"; for in it is guidance and prophecy for the future. "The last Redeemer will be like unto the first." Our spiritual leaders based their faith in God not upon any cosmological proofs, but upon history—upon those significant events in their own and in the world's history and those processes of the unfolding spiritual life of man which revealed the presence of God. History to them was evidence for faith far more valid than philosophical proofs!

The Jewish people today is therefore warranted in drawing deep draughts of confidence from its past history. What we were able to do over and over again in the past, under all conceivable circumstances and in all parts of the world, we may yet do again, and again in the future. Nothing has fundamentally changed for us, neither the world's mania for persecution nor our own unbroken will to live. Our forces are not less today, but more. Our powers of adaptability, which the strong life-sense of our people developed, have not been dulled. We were able in the past to adapt ourselves to all forms of economic life and activity—the pastoral, agricultural, commercial and industrial—and to all forms of political systems and arrangements. We adjusted ourselves to conditions of utter rightlessness, to restricted rights, and to equality of rights. If in the future Jews will be faced with the necessity of adjusting themselves to new economic and political arrangements, to new forms of capitalism or socialism, or to new conditions of restrictions and disabilities, or if they will be again confronted, as many of them already are, with the necessity of emigrating to new countries and of establishing a new Diaspora, they will be able to make their adjustments in the same way as their people have done throughout the ages.

FROM AN ADDRESS
"THE WORLD CRISIS AND JEWISH SURVIVAL"
JUNE 1951

"Let Us Now Praise Famous Men"

A people reveals its soul in many ways, said Abba Hillel Silver—through its music, its dance, its literature. But the clearest revelation of that soul is through the lives of certain individuals, its leaders and poets, its saints and heroes, and also through *amchah*—its masses. In describing these individuals, Rabbi Silver's extensive scholarship and talents as a teacher combined with a flair for sketching of character and mood to produce dozens of historic silhouettes. Through them he described the variegated facets of the Jewish soul. He had favorites, like Moses, whose character is drawn and redrawn from the pulpit almost every year. But a mystic like Baal-Shem and a "heretic" like Nordau receive equally fascinating treatment. These lecture-sermons on historic Jewish figures represent some of Rabbi Silver's most interesting and effective creations.

Israel Baal-Shem Tov:
On the Place
of Mysticism in Religion

SERMON, THE TEMPLE
MARCH 5, 1922

It is as difficult to define the term *mysticism* as it is to define almost any other psychic phenomenon. The difficulty entailed is not a reflection upon the reality of the thing that you want to define, but rather is it an indictment of the shortcomings of our intellectual equipment; we are not sufficiently equipped, intellectually, to define all reality and all spiritual values.

It is a fact that every great religion contains a mystic element. Professor D. B. Macdonald, an authority on Islam, has said that every sincere Moslem was a mystic. Buddhism is, of course, one vast system of mystic experience. Christianity began as a mystic religion, and found its noblest expression among the mystics of the Middle Ages and the Reformation; and our own religion, in spite of the fact that so many have attempted—to my mind needlessly—to prove that Judaism is a rational religion, our own religion has a deep and rich vein of mysticism running right through it from its beginnings to the present day.

We find it in the Bible, in legend and myth and song and in the visions of Ezekiel and Daniel; we have a more luxuriant crop of mysticism in post-Biblical literature, in the Apocrypha, the hidden writings; in the Apocalypse; and in the Talmud. In the Talmud we have, alongside of the law, the Halakhah, a vast amount of lore, and the Aggadah, full of mystic teaching concerning the soul, concerning the Messiah, concerning the mystic value of numbers and the alphabet.

The authoritative religion, the formal religion, tried to keep these things out, to keep them beyond the pale. The Mishnah, for example, which is the code of Jewish law of the first two centuries of the Common Era, deliberately omits any reference to an angel or to the Messiah. But in the Aggadah, in the lore which is scattered through all the Midrashim or commentaries on the Bible of a later period, we have an abundant and profuse mystic speculation.

The popular religion demanded mysticism. It is the food which the human heart and soul craved for, and the rabbis had no hesitancy in providing that meal. In the period of the Gaonim, in the eighth, ninth, and tenth centuries, we have mystic lore developing. Even a profound scholar like Saadia, who wrote one of the classic philosophic treatises on Judaism, had no hesitancy in writing a commentary on the Sefer Yezirah, the Book of Creation, which became a textbook of later cabala and later Jewish mysticism.

From the tenth century on, philosophy rather than mysticism holds the stage of Jewish thought, and the philosophic movement, the attempt to define Judaism as a system of philosophic thought, of metaphysics, gained strength, and culminated in that titan, that master mind of Jewish thought—Moses Maimonides. Maimonides attempted to show that Judaism is a rational religion, completely in harmony with the teachings of Aristotle. Unfortunately he reduced the full content of Jewish thought and Jewish faith to a system of dry, spiritless, fervorless syllogisms: logic.

Then the reaction began to set in. People realized that such a religion is not the religion that is food for human souls and hearts. Such speculation may drive men away from God, even as it tries to bring them nearer to God. So in the fourteenth century the cabalistic movement began. In 1305 the Zohar appeared, the textbook of all later-day cabala. For centuries thereafter, with the decline of philosophy, cabala and mysticism grew and developed in Jewish life. The mystic movement reached its culmination in the sixteenth century in the school of Safed in northern Palestine, with teachers like Moses Cordovero, Isaac Luria, and Chayim Vital.

From the sixteenth century the movement began to degenerate into mystery, into miracle-mongering, into Messiah-hunting. That degeneracy reached its most tragic expression in the movement of Jacob Frank, the false messiah. Then for a hundred years cabala was relegated to the background; people were beginning to be afraid of it, and the philosophic and the legal phase of Judaism again came to the forefront until the middle of the eighteenth century, when the mystic spirit, always present in Jewish religion but submerged and at times eclipsed, again pushed forward in a movement which engulfed half of Jewry. This movement, which came to be known as Hasidism, was founded by Israel Baal-Shem, the subject of this sermon. The historian Simon M. Dubnow estimates the number of Hasidim living today as five million, so the movement is something to be reckoned with in Jewish life.

As you scan Jewish history, you cannot help but come to the conclusion that the definition of Judaism as a rationalistic religion, is, to say the least, imperfect. Judaism has more than one system of ethics, and Judaism is much more than a system of abstract principles concerning God; Judaism is also a religion of divine intimacies, a religion of human pilgrimage to the dwelling place of divinity; a religion of glow and fervor and enthusiasm; a religion of prayer.

Philosophy and theosophy—philosophy and mysticism—may be said to have run side by side in Jewish thought; they supplemented one another, or corrected one another. In philosophy the Jewish intellect never permitted mysticism to run riot, as mysticism has done in some religions. In mysticism the heart of the Jew never permitted philosophy to starve the content of Jewish life, to reduce it to a formula, to a syllogism. So the two have proved that marvelous synthesis, that marvelous union in Jewish life, which, to my mind, has preserved Judaism.

You find that synthesis in the best Jewish thinkers of all times. I mentioned Saadia, the philosopher, who wrote a commentary on a mystic book. I could just as well have mentioned the famous legalist of the thirteenth century, Nachmanides, who was also a mystic; I could have mentioned the classic example of Joseph Karo, the famous author of the Shulchan Aruch, the code of law in force today in Orthodox Jewry. Joseph Karo was the most noted jurist and the most scholarly Talmudist of his day, yet he too wrote mystic treatises. He claimed to have been informed nightly by a spirit which was the angel of the Mishnah, concerning vast and profound and mystic truths which he incorporated in his writing.

So in Jewish life you do not find that conflict between reason and mystic speculation that you find in other religions. Judaism, somehow, found that spiritual alchemy that blended the two to make them one.

Now, then, what is mysticism? It is not mystery. To be a mystic is not necessarily to be mysterious. Mysticism is much more than vagueness. Jewish philosophy or Jewish mysticism comes from two kinds of mysticism: one is called the speculative mysticism, the Cabala Iyunith, and the other is called the practical mysticism, the Cabala Ma-asith.

Now, the practical kind of mysticism has to do with things like charms and formulae and spells and the medicinal value of herbs and healings; with speculations concerning the coming of the Messiah, and the interpretation of dreams—which, by the way, was the beginning of the science of psychoanalysis, just as alchemy was the beginning of the science of chemistry. This practical mysticism very often degenerates to the level of the mysterious, because it is veiled in secrecy; these are the hidden things, and every charlatan, every quack, finds in this practical cabala an opportunity to exploit the credulity of men and women. Cabala produced its charlatans. Every garden of flowers produces its weeds. That sort of mystery you find in all religions from primitive days to the present day. You find it among the savages, with the medicine man who puts a vile-looking mask over his face and paints himself and shakes the totem and beats the drum.

Well, that is the lowest form of cabala. That is really not mysticism at all; real mysticism has nothing to do with the mysterious; it has nothing to do with secrecy; it always speaks of light. The one word most often in use among all mystics of all religion is *light*—illumination, brilliancy. The task of the mystics was to seek the real light, the illuminating truth.

Mysticism is nothing else than the intense personal contemplation of reality. Mysticism is the pilgrimage of the human soul to the shrine of unity with God; mysticism is the quest for the inner reality of things and for their inner harmony; and mysticism is the discipline which leads a man to find this hidden meaning, this hidden light, this inner truth, and this inner harmony. Mysticism is the successive stages of the development of the soul and the successive states of exaltation and ecstasy which a human being climbs to reach the throne of God.

I said it is a quest for the inner reality. Let me try to make myself a little clearer. Here all around me is a world—the universe of God. I can see but little of the world; I can apprehend less because my five senses, the avenues of cognition, the channels through which I apprehend truth, are imperfect and faulty, untrue; they can give me but a limited view of reality, and they can show me, perhaps, but one or two phases of it, while there may be an infinite number of phases of reality to the universe which is about me.

But the world is there and God is there, and somehow I ought to be able to get beyond myself, beyond these five senses, to force my way through the walls that confine me, that incarcerate me, that keep me from seeing the light beyond. If I only had the key, the mystic key with which to unlock the doors leading to the great truth beyond, if I only had the divine intuition, I would see the real essence of things, I would see truth and reality—and God!

Now, there is a way of finding this mystic key, and that comes through discipline of self, through conquest of self, through subjection of all that is material and animal within me, through the subjection of all the passions and the desires and the craving and the ambitions that enslave me, holding me bound to the earth. If I can free myself from this bondage of the flesh, which is a sort of *klipah,* as the cabalist calls it— a shell, a husk which keeps my soul from merging with the great Soul beyond and my life from losing itself and, in a sense, from finding itself in the great life of the eternal; if I can destroy by an effort of will this earthly self of mine; if I can lose all pride and all vainglory and all opinions I may hold that are really not opinions concerning truth, then there may a way of finding this mystic key.

Then some day the light will break through upon me, even as light comes to a blind man who has never seen it before; it will come like an inundation, like an influx, like a revelation. I will then know reality, I will then know the essence of things. I will then know God; and, knowing Him, I will have found the greatest good in the world.

That is the underlying faith of the mystic. It is difficult, very difficult, to understand it; even as difficult as it is for one who has no ear for music to understand a symphony. But to the mystic it is the essence of life. You see that mysticism is not a system of doctrines; it is a temperament. You must have the temperament to be a mystic; you must have the temperament to be an artist. If you do not have it, you simply cannot be a mystic. If your mind is absolutely logical, you will have real difficulty in fathoming the profoundness of the mystic soul.

The mystic cares little for authority, for books, for creeds, for dogmas, for churches, for ecclesiastical forms: he has one authority in his life, and that is the God that dwells within him; He is his one source of authority, his one inspiration. Books and Bibles and creeds and dogmas may have value; they may be necessary for the uninitiated; they have a pedagogic value, they help to train the masses, but they are only symbols after all—symbols of an inner truth. That inner truth comes to the real mystic directly, immediately, intuitively, by the contact of his soul with the all-Soul of the universe.

The one basic principle of mysticism is love. A Moslem, Sufi, uttered this thought: "Oh, my God, when I speak of thee in public, I invoke thee as one invokes a Lord; but when I speak of thee in private, I speak of thee as one invokes a beloved one. In public I say unto thee: 'Oh, my God'; in private I say unto thee: 'Oh, my beloved.' " That sums it all up.

The Jewish mystic phrased it somewhat differently when he used that beautiful sentence of the Song of Solomon to express his relationship with God: "I belong to my beloved, and my beloved belongs to me." One of the three cardinal principles of Hasidism was to cling unto God, identifying one's whole life and the experiences of one's whole life and all the needs and all the longings of one's life, merging them all in the unity of the One—clinging unto Him as one clings to a dear friend, to a kinsman. That is mysticism.

Lastly, the mystic saw God everywhere and in everything. The philosopher may say God created the world and then somehow removed Himself from the world; the philosopher can speak of God as transcendent —removed, little concerned with the affairs of men, with their struggles and their strivings. The mystic, on the other hand, says: "No. God created the world, but God is indwelling in the world, in every blade of grass, in every wave of the sea, in every longing of the human soul, in every tear that falls from the sinner's eye, in the place of sin and in the place of evil—everywhere! everywhere! there is God!"

"Matter is not only the garment in which God clothes himself, but it is of the very essence of divinity. God had to restrict Himself; God had to confine Himself; God had to express His greatness so that human beings could see Him and understand Him partly; and so the world was created. But God is there indwelling, within reach of every human soul, and everything sings of God, and everything bespeaks God."

There is a beautiful folk song that came down from these pious men known as the Hasidim, which reads something like this:

Master of the world, where shall I find thee,
   And where shall I not find thee?
East and west and north and south, thou art there;
   Above thou are there, below thou art there.
Everywhere thou, only thou, thou alone.

Now, that is pantheism, but pantheism with a living, providential God permeating, controlling, and guiding the world. That is the faith of the mystic, and that is real religion.

This mystic faith that is found in the religion of the Hasidim was propounded by the founder, Israel Baal-Shem. The word *hasid*, by the way, simply means "a pious man." The Hasidim were men of exceptional piety. *Baal-shem* is an interesting word. The word is found in Jewish history as early as the eleventh century. *Baal-shem* means "the master of the name." It does not mean a man of good name; it means the master of the name, the miracle-worker, the man who could perform wonderful things through the medium of God's name; who knew the secret of the manipulation of the letters of God's name, and so could perform marvelous deeds.

And so from the eleventh century down to the eighteenth, of which we speak, there was a series of these pious wonder-workers, of Jewish men of piety and great devotion who won for themselves a reputation among peoples. People came to them for counsel, for advice, for healing; and they were known as the *Anshe-shem,* "the men of the name."

Israel Baal-Shem was one of them, but he was the greatest of them all. Israel was born of poor parents in the year, we will say, 1700; we do not know exactly. He was born in a little village on the border between Poland and Walachia. Little is known about his life; legend has veiled it in mystery. The few things that stand out are these: at an early age he was orphaned; he received a poor schooling; he was never a student; he was never a scholar. He married rather early in life; his wife died young; he removed to a village in the Carpathian mountains, settled there, and remarried there. For seven years he lived among these beautiful mountains, imbibing the love of nature and the love of the world and the joy of life. Through all these years of humble and pious activity he dug lime for a living, and his wife wheeled the lime on a wagon to the village to sell it. He was a workingman, and in those days a workingman was rather looked down upon by the aristocrats of learning.

At the age of thirty-six, the legend says, he revealed himself; that is to say, becoming conscious of a great psychic gift that was in him, he went from village to village, and from town to town, healing, counseling, helping, and spreading the gospel of a new type of Judaism. He was not a reformer; he did not introduce any new dogmas or any new sects; he did not challenge any old dogmas or any old creeds. It was altogether a matter of emphasis; it was altogether a matter of soul.

He left no books. All that we know of him has come down to us from the writings of his disciples, principally Dov Baer and Jacob Joseph Ha-Kohen.

You ought to know Israel Baal-Shem. He is a great figure in Jewish thought; he has a message for us today. Just as in the thirteenth century cabala arose as a reaction to the rationalism of Maimonides and of all who preceded him, so five centuries later Hasidism arose in the personality of this man, Israel Baal-Shem, as a reaction to the dry rot which had set in in rabbinical legalism and speculation.

Judaism had for generations become starved, dry, hackneyed, scholastic, a matter of casuistry, a matter of dialectics; Judaism had become almost exclusively a matter of study—the study of the Talmud. Learning was the test of character and the test of piety. The condition of the Jew of the time was terrible. Suppression, exploitation, uncertainty were the order of the day. The Cossack uprisings fifty years before in Poland, in 1648, had destroyed the economic life of the Polish Jew; his life was harsh, crude, unattractive, and his soul was starved and empty. He asked for soul food, something to inspire him, something to sustain him, something to give him a little hope in life; and the rabbis gave him laws and disciplines and duties and nothing else.

Israel Baal-Shem preached a new gospel to these hungry souls. It was a simple faith, a faith of divine intimacy, a faith of warmth, of *hithlhavut*, of enthusiasm, a faith of hope. Israel Baal-Shem brought a message of life. They welcomed him, and his teachings spread throughout Israel.

First of all, he said, it is a good thing to be learned, but it is not the whole of life. To know the Torah is a meritorious thing, but to pray with intent so as to establish communion with the spirit above is even more important. God desires not so much the brilliant mind as the devout soul. "God desireth the heart of man." If circumstances have kept you from becoming a scholar, you are none the less the child of God, in His presence daily; and God is as near to you as He is to the student.

Now, think what a message of hope that brought to the tens of thousands of the ignorant and the illiterate among Israel, who looked upon themselves as outcasts and were so regarded. Here was a man who brought God nearer unto them, and who brought new life, new hope, and a new faith.

And then he said: "Religion is not a matter of duty and fear; religion is a matter of love"—the mystic speaking again. There are three great loves that everyone ought to have in life, he said. There is the love of God, there is the love of the Torah, and there is the love of Israel. That is all there is in life for the Jew: just three devotions, just three supreme loves—God, the Torah, Israel.

And that is the way to serve God—through love. Let others speak of duty, let others speak of fear; we will speak of God as our friend, a friend to whom we can bring the broken bits of our hearts to be made whole again. A friend who suffers with us and who rejoices with us and who is our kinsman—that is our God.

Think what that meant to those people, hounded and hunted, the prey of every whim of a tyrant. A great and good friend came into their lives—God, who was with them all the time and near unto them when they called unto Him. That was his second teaching.

And his third was this: What is all this sorrow that has come into Jewish life? Why this poignancy and penitence and self-castigation? Why has religion become a matter of such solemnity? Why all this fasting? If you have such a friend with you as God, rejoice and be glad! To do good is not a painful task; it is the supreme joy of life. Baal-Shem began to preach "the joy of doing good," the joy of being a Jew; to preach that in spite of persecution, in spite of suffering, and in spite of exile and poverty, the Jew still had the one absolute perfect good in life—God! They still had the Torah; and nothing else counted. And so he built for them a paradise amidst their poverty and squalor; he built for them a fairyland where they could find solace and comfort and cheer when all about them was gloom and darkness.

Lastly, he brought to them again the message of the mystic.

Think not of God, my children, as a great tyrant sitting away up there in Heaven removed from you. Why, look down! There is a flower, and a blade of grass, and a stream, and a grain of sand—and that is God, too! He is there! He is everywhere!

There is no place where He is not. In every movement of your soul there is God; in every reach of your thought there is God.

Why, even in your misdeeds, in your sins, God is there. Wherever there is life there is the breath of God!

The artist can take silver and fashion a beautiful goblet and put his soul in it. And when he is through, when the goblet is finished, the artist can step aside and remove himself to a distant land. The goblet is there. But not so with God. God fashioned the world out of His soul, but He does not remove Himself and leave His handiwork. The artist, the human artist, creates something out of something else; he creates a reality, a substance out of another substance. But God created the world out of Himself, and so He is always present in the world.

That is the parable which Baal-Shem brings. God is everywhere, God can be seen everywhere, if men knew but how to look for Him. The trouble is, he said, that the eyes of human beings are trained to look for other things, and so they cannot see God.

A king built for himself a beautiful palace of many rooms, and filled them all with gold and beautiful stones. He placed himself in the last of the chambers of his palace, and people came from all parts of the earth to see the king. Some went into the first room and found gold and silver, and they were satisfied and left; some went into the second room and found precious stones, and they gathered in all they wished and left. Nobody saw the king, until the king's own son came. He really wanted to see the king, and his eyes were not dazzled by the gold and the silver and the jewels. He walked right by, right into the chamber where the king was. It was a simple thing to see the king if you really wanted to see him.

That is Baal-Shem's parable of how God can be found. That was his teaching; that was the wisdom that he brought to a suffering race. He brought to them joy, life, hope, inspiration. He was a glorious influence for many decades. In time, of course, Hasidism, like all good things, declined. It outlived its usefulness; a new day was dawning. But for generations it served a wonderfully effective and beneficent purpose in Jewish life; it was a stream of new faith poured into the soul of Israel. Baal-Shem will remain a saint in our history.

One word in conclusion. I said that Baal-Shem has a message for us. I believe he has, because we Reform Jews are becoming guilty of the same mistake that Maimonides and his predecessors in the thirteenth century were guilty of, and that the rabbis in the eighteenth century were guilty of: we are trying to make of our religion an ethical code, a system of theological abstractions, metaphysics, speculation. A religion of that kind is doomed.

No religion can live on a syllogism. To make of our faith a dynamic faith, to make it purposeful and real in our lives and in the lives of the generations to come, we must introduce into it those same three loves, those same three devotions of which Israel Baal-Shem spoke—the love of God, and the love of the Torah, and the love of Israel.

We must become saturated with an unconquerable love for these three eternal verities—God, truth, and Israel! The servant of God and the message of truth! We must bring back warmth, devotion, consecration, enthusiasm into our fold. Our religion, too, must cease to be only a matter of mind: it must reach down and touch our souls!

Max Nordau

SERMON, THE TEMPLE
FEBRUARY 18, 1923

On the twenty-second day of January, 1923, there died in the city of Paris, in comparative poverty though not in obscurity, a man who is destined to live long in the grateful memory of his own people and that of the entire world—Dr. Max Nordau.

In the death of Dr. Nordau there passed away a prophet who summoned men and nations to repentance, and warned them of impending doom; and in his death there passed away a champion of Israel, a staunch defender of his people—a modern Maccabee, who heralded, and labored for, the rebirth of his people.

Dr. Max Nordau belonged to the giant spirits of the human race. In him a brilliant mentality, an encyclopedic mind, a linguistic gift, a literary endowment, a brilliant wit, and a courtly manner were wedded to a high moral passion, a fine idealism, and vast courage.

I call him an iconoclast. Perhaps I should call him a prophetic iconoclast. He shattered idols—which seems to be the task providentially assigned to all the outstanding prophets of the human race, and more especially to the prophets of Israel from the days of Abraham to this day. He shattered these idols furiously and in high passion, and yet not willfully nor petulantly.

Dr. Nordau's intellect was not a destructive intellect; he was not merely a rebel, a disgruntled, discontented, fretful personality raging and storming against all the social values and all the social conventions and all the institutions of mankind. He was not a "bull in a china shop"; he was a prophet; he knew that the mission of the prophet was as Jeremiah con-

236

Abba Hillel Silver
1962

Abba Hillel Silver, the son of Rabbi Moses and Dinah Seaman Silver (above), attended Hebrew Union College in Cincinnati and was ordained in 1915. He was awarded the *Academic Palms* in 1918 for his work on behalf of the American Red Cross (below, with French officers on a battlefield near Verdun).

Holmes

The young rabbi (above, left) served from 1915 to 1917 at the Eoff Street Temple in Wheeling, West Virginia, before beginning his lifetime rabbinate at The Temple in Cleveland. By 1923 his leadership had brought him wide public recognition (above, right: a Cleveland *Plain Dealer* cartoon) and resulted in completion of a new Temple edifice (below).

Perry Cragg

Rabbi Silver was a lifelong champion of the cause of a Jewish homeland in Palestine. His writings, his skillful leadership, and his powerful addresses at Zionist rallies were a major influence in guiding the movement.

Victory for an independent Israel: As chairman of the Jewish Agency for Palestine, Rabbi Silver testifies before the United Nations in November 1947. At his right (above) is Andrei Gromyko of the Soviet Union; seated behind him are Emanuel Neumann, Mrs. Golda Meir, and Moshe Sharett. Enthusiastic followers embrace Rabbi Silver (below) in the moments following the U. N. vote.

Rabbi Silver conferring with World Zionist leaders: at a London meeting in 1940 with Chaim Weizmann, first president of the State of Israel (above); at a state dinner in Israel in 1962 with David Ben-Gurion, first Israeli prime minister (below).

Presidential candidate Dwight D. Eisenhower met with Rabbi Silver during the 1952 campaign (above). Candidate John F. Kennedy shared the rostrum with him at a Zionist Organization of America rally in 1960 (below).

Brownspigel

Rabbi and Mrs. Abba Hillel Silver in the library of their home in Cleveland.

ceived of it—"first, to break and to shatter and to destroy the old, and then to rebuild and to replant."

He shattered idols because he wished to enthrone true values. He hated above all sham and fraud and hypocrisy, whether the sham and the fraud of ancient institutions and ancient movements, or the sham and the fraud of new institutions and new movements. He hated the hypocrisy of monarchy even as he hated the hypocrisy of democracy. All that glittered, all that was not real, all that was pretense, all that was fraud, all that was not relevant to a fundamental, underlying truth, all that did not emanate from something that was essentially real and sound and sane and moral— that Nordau hated and viciously, bitterly attacked.

But just as he was an iconoclast he also was a builder. The dynamics of his soul were not exhausted in destructiveness; he had much left for constructive work. He was the physician—as in very truth by profession he was a physician; he diagnosed the malady without any reference to the likes and the dislikes and the prejudices of the patient; and once having diagnosed the malady he proceeded to suggest the cure, if a cure was possible.

He was a builder, and a very orthodox one. People are prone to think of Nordau as a radical. Yet in the modern connotation of the term, Nordau was orthodox; he based his views on those ancient foundations of the ancient wisdom upon which the prophets of antiquity had based their convictions. And Dr. Nordau shared the prophet's fate, and more especially the fate of a Jewish prophet; he was persecuted during his lifetime. All these groups and classes and individuals whom he so vehemently attacked and ruthlessly exposed turned against him and embittered his life. His life was passed in storm and in struggle, and it ended in near tragedy.

Dr. Nordau, though an Austrian subject, lived in France for over thirty years. He loved France; he loved the sweet temperament and the mellow culture of France. After the War of 1870, he denounced the venality of Germany in taking Alsace-Lorraine from France. But during the World War these reactionary elements that Nordau had attacked turned against him, and influential as they were in the circles of the government, they succeeded in having Dr. Nordau humiliated. First he was imprisoned, then exiled, and then his property, the accumulations of a lifetime, the little bit that he had gathered together, hoping to leave it to his wife and his daughter, was confiscated by the French government, and, up to this day, has not been returned. Dr. Nordau experienced the tragedy of the Wandering Jew in the twilight hours of his life. He died in Paris in a little room on the fifth floor of a humble dwelling—a poor man but not an obscure nor a forgotten man.

Dr. Max Nordau was a Jew in yet another sense: he was the child of two cultures and two civilizations, which, in a sense, is the tragedy of Jewish life. He was born of Orthodox Jewish parents. His father was a rabbi, and in the early days of his life he was imbued and saturated with the spirit of Orthodox Jewry, with all its romance and all its poetry, and the learning of his people. In youth and in manhood he went out into the world, entered the universities of Europe and came in contact with a new civilization and a new culture and a new environment, totally different from, and in many ways hostile to, that civilization in which he was reared as a child. He struggled throughout his days to effect (as so many of us try to do) a synthesis of these two cultures and these two civilizations. So there is much that is almost anomalous, much that is difficult to understand, much that is contradictory, apparently, in the life of Nordau.

For example: Nordau was an irreligious man; Nordau was an anti-religious man; Nordau denied God, Nordau denied the soul, Nordau denied immortality, Nordau scoffed at religious customs and religious practices; but when he died a *talis* was wrapped about his body, and the Kaddish was pronounced by the Chief Rabbi of France at his grave, at his request.

Nordau was an internationalist, as so many of our brilliant minds were during the past generation in Europe. He was a cosmopolitan. His ideal was, as he called it, the solidarity of the human race. He hated national chauvinism, and he hated the spirit of nationalism, which led to national prejudices and hate and rivalries and war. He was a broad, free, untrammeled spirit, a citizen of the world; and yet Nordau was the founder of the Zionist movement, together with Dr. Theodore Herzl. Nordau became the eloquent spokesman of Jewish nationalism; and Nordau was a passionate Jewish nationalist.

Very strange—nearly anomalous; very contradictory; and yet very human, isn't it? For, after all, free as the spirit of man might wish to roam and, in the early days of our youth, does roam, after a while, our wings become tired and we would like to have a place to rest. We can speak of the human race and the solidarity of the human race and the love of our fellow men, but, after all, there is the pull and the tug of our own, our own people, flesh of our flesh and bone of our bone; who know us, who understand us, who can sympathize; and that tug and that pull brought Nordau back to his people.

And, after all, a man may have an intellect that is absolutely emancipated from all religious convention and from all religious conviction,
and yet the longing soul remains unsatisfied and hungry and thirsty. A
starved soul cannot be fed by a brilliant intellect, and Nordau craved for
the poetry and the beauty and the romanticism and the soul food of his
youth, and in his later life he came back to them.

I want to speak this morning first of Dr. Nordau the thinker, the
philosopher; the man whose voice shook Europe and startled the peoples
of the earth; and then of Nordau the Jew.

Dr. Nordau's philosophy is embodied in a trilogy of books—the first,
The Conventional Lies of Civilization, published in 1883; the second,
Paradoxes, published two years later; and the third, *Degeneration,* pub-
lished in 1893.

There are two main theses in the thought of Dr. Nordau, and only
two; and to express these two fundamental convictions and to call dramatically the attention of the world to all their implications, Nordau wrote
this trilogy. His first thesis was this: that our present-day civilization is
crumbling, crumbling like the civilization of the ancient Romans before
the invasion of the barbarians, and crumbling because of an all-pervading,
destructive pessimism, which is evidenced in all departments of life—in art,
in literature, in philosophy, in religion. This pessimism is caused by one
fact: that there is today a rift, a discrepancy, an incongruity between the
things we do and the things we believe in; between the institutions in
which we live and our opinions concerning these institutions. There is this
tragic disharmony between theory and practice in every department, in
every sphere of civilization today. In other words, says Dr. Nordau, we
consistently live a lie.

We no longer believe in the things which we do out of habit, out of
convenience, and because of compulsion; we no longer believe in the basis
of our religious life; we no longer believe in the basis of our economic life;
we no longer believe in the basis of our social life. And yet we keep on
living these things as though their bases were still true and as though we
still believed in them. Dr. Nordau says:

> This is the tragic side of our contemporaneous civilization, that
> the ancient institutions have no longer the courage and self-
> confidence to maintain their positions before mankind, in the
> stiff and unyielding forms in which alone they are true to logic
> and history, repeating the Jesuits' motto: "As we are or not at
> all." They attempt an impossible compromise between their

premises and the convictions of modern times; they make con-
cessions to the latter, and allow themselves to be penetrated by
intellectual elements, foreign to their constitution, and sure to
disintegrate it. The new ideas to which they are trying to conform
themselves are in direct opposition to every one of their fundamental principles, so that they resemble a book containing on
the same page some ancient fable with footnotes criticising, rid-
iculing, and abusing it in every possible way. In this shape these
institutions, denying and parodying their true character, seem
objects of ridicule and scorn to cultivated minds, and even to
the uncultivated, sources of annoyance and painful perplexity.

The present era of science, claims Nordau, has destroyed man's
faith in these institutions; and yet these institutions continue. With what
result? With the result that character is destroyed. What is character? Character is an integration, a unity of self; character is brought about when an
individual possesses certain simple, dominant convictions which are true to
him, which are sufficient to guide and influence and determine him. A man
has character when he has what we call principle, when he has in his life a
unified, harmonizing, ingrowing conviction.

Today in European civilization convictions have been destroyed;
faith has been undermined; character has been destroyed. And where there
is no character, says Dr. Nordau, degeneration must set in, as it is setting in
(so he claims) to destroy civilization.

He goes into detail to prove his thesis. On these conventional lies of
our civilization he has five chapters: one called "The Lie of Religion,"
another "The Lie of a Monarchy and Aristocracy," the third "The Political
Lie," the fourth "The Economic Lie," and the fifth "The Matrimonial
Lie." Of these five, his first chapter, "The Lie of Religion," is perhaps the
least constructive and the least helpful to us today. Perhaps in 1883, when
the book was written, there was enough dynamite in this chapter to set
men to thinking, to awaken them. But as we read it today, the chapter
seems rather naive—perhaps we might say antiquated. Nordau lived during
the period when the theory of evolution had first burst upon mankind and
had not yet been understood in its deeper significance. The theory of evolution was accepted as dogma. Its implications were clear: nature was ruled
by blind, unchanging forces, controlled by constant and unyielding laws;
nature was not possessed of a will power or an inner intelligence; natural
law dethroned God, dethroned the soul, dethroned religion.

Nordau accepted all these naive early conceptions concerning the theory of evolution. He calls religion "a physical relic of the childhood of the human race." At best it is a functional weakness of mankind. Religion is based on fear; God is the creation of that tendency in man to anthropomorphize, to place a conscious will power, a somebody, back of every natural phenomenon. The soul is an illusion; immortality is merely an expression of man's disinclination to die, of man's inability to conceive of his annihilation; religion is a figment of man's imagination.

Nordau presents a religion of his own. In place of God the ideal of the solidarity of the human race; in place of the church the lecture hall and assembly room; and in place of the ritual, the ballot. Nordau was even more vehement in his denunciation of religious forms than of the content of religion:

> I can understand why some people are religious; there is a sentimental yearning for it. Well and good. But for people today to believe in religious forms and in religious ceremonies, in churches, in rituals, in a Bible, in priests and dogmas, that is a lie—a living lie.

He had a very misguided estimate of the Bible, did Dr. Nordau, and he recanted in later life. He said: "The morality of the Bible is revolting; the concept of the universe in the Bible is childish; its literature, its second-rate ceremonies, are coarse; their origin is in barbarism; they are Asiatic or African. They have no meaning for people today."

Of course it is too late in the day to begin a refutation of these contentions. Suffice it to say that we know now that the theory of evolution, at least, does not dethrone God; that science does not prove the non-existence of God or of the human soul; that it does not deny immortality. Suffice it to say that we know now that the lecture hall can never take the place of the church, nor can the ballot box replace the ritual of the church. Suffice it now to say that the origin of things does not determine the value of things. Because a ceremony was begun ten thousand years ago in the jungle life and in the jungle instincts and in the jungle needs of the human race, it does not necessarily follow that that ceremony or that practice or that rite or that custom no longer has value and relevancy for us today.

It is not what the beginnings of a thing are; it is what the thing itself means for us—how it reaches our soul, how it touches the mainsprings of our emotions, what function it has in our life. You might as well look with disfavor and contempt upon a symphony of Beethoven because, forsooth, music began with the beating of a tom-tom in some hut or cave of a primitive. You might as well hold Shakespeare in contempt because, forsooth, literature began in some rhythmic singsong of a battle hymn of savages; you might as well look with contempt upon a magnificent cathedral because the first architecture of the human race was a miserable hut of reeds and rushes and twigs.

It is not what the beginnings of a thing are that counts: it is what it has come to be. And civilization is just this: the real interpretation which every age puts upon things which somehow seem to be, in their essence at least, eternal.

There is not very much, I think, that is constructive in Dr. Nordau's attitude and opinion concerning religion, and I fear me that he felt that most deeply in his declining years. But there is much more of meat in his second chapter on "The Lie of Monarchy and Aristocracy." There all the brilliant wit of Nordau (which I had the good fortune to see in action in London in 1920), all his gift of satire, his destructive satire, comes into play. And that chapter won for him the undying hostility of all these classes.

Of course he hates monarchy, but, he says, absolute monarchy is a logical thing; constitutional monarchy is a lie. Absolute monarchy is based on the theory of the divine right of kings, and one who accepts the premise that kings have a God-given right to rule ought to believe in absolute monarchy. Where people insist upon loyalty to a constitution and at the same time upon loyalty to a monarchy, there is that conflict, there is that incongruity, and there is that rift, says Nordau, which makes for a living lie in our civilization.

He was not a ranting democrat. If there is anything true about Nordau it is that he was an aristocrat in the finest sense of the word, not only in his bearing and in his courtly manner and in his speech, but in his thinking. Nordau did not believe in human equality. He said that that, too, is one of the conventional lies of democratic civilization. Liberty? Yes. Fraternity? Yes. Equality? Oh, no. Nature is against it. It is an intellectual fiction. The struggle for existence denies equality; our whole progress in civilization depends upon leaders—the leadership of the few exceptional, gifted ones.

Republicanism, he said, is a good thing, "but do not be captivated by words and slogans and catch phrases. A republic, if it is to progress, must be founded upon a number of social, political and other institutions, entirely different from those existing at present." At present a republic is a lie because the ground has not yet been cleared for a real republic. "As long as Europe continues to live in its present form of civilization, a republic is a contradiction and an unworthy play upon words. A simple political revolution, which would turn any one of the existing monarchies of Europe into a republic, would be merely imitating the acts of the apostles to the heathen during the early part of the Middle Ages, who converted the pagans from their false forms of worship, by simply giving their gods, festivals and ceremonies Christian names." It is only a question of the juggling of names between present-day monarchies and present-day republics.

> The entire effect of such a revolution would be limited to pasting upon the shop-worn, unsalable goods, a lot of new labels, which would deceive the people into thinking a new stock of goods had been procured. A republic is the last link of a long chain of development. It is the form of government in which the ideal of self-government finds realization—the supreme power residing ultimately in the whole people and directly exercised by them. This form of government, if it is organically genuine, and not merely an external, pasted-on or painted resemblance to a republic, is inherently incompatible with hereditary privileges and distinctions, with the enormous influence wielded by accumulations of capital and monopolies, with the power of an army of office holders and with any restrictions to the free liberty of thought, speech and action of the grand masses of the people. But to leave the organization of the State as it is, and merely to change the name of the government from a monarchy to a republic, is like the well-known trick of the publishers who manage to smuggle forbidden works into another country, by substituting for the title-page another, taken from some innocent fairy-tale or prayer-book. What was the Italian republic of 1848, or the Spanish republic of 1868, and what is the French republic of 1870, but monarchies with their thrones standing vacant for a while, monarchies parading under the mask of republicanism.

I said that Nordau was an aristocrat. Nordau even believed in hereditary aristocracy; he believed in families of aristocratic bearing and culture and prestige, in which the trust of aristocracy, the pledge of aristocracy, the promise of aristocracy was handed down from generation to generation. He believed in that kind of aristocracy—that it makes for finer bodies and finer souls, that it makes for character. The aristocracy of today, our nobility, he says, is sham, an anthropological fake, as he calls it. They are not the fittest. They are not the *aristos*. They are not the best.

They are not the most capable. They are not the most heroic. They are not the standard-bearers. They do not excel in body. They do not excel in character. The aristocracy of today is aristocracy made by patent, by the will of a monarch or a king; it is aristocracy made by wealth, and that is a lie.

There should be an aristocracy, but it should exist on one condition: namely, that it remain true to the tradition of the *aristos,* and welcome into its ranks everyone who has evidenced exceptional ability of character and mind and soul—an aristocracy that assumes the burden and the responsibility of leadership. That is the kind of aristocracy he believed in.

Nordau speaks of the political lie. He hated government interference; he hated the inequalities which resulted from taxation, where the poor man is taxed heavily while the rich man is taxed nominally. He hated the idea of representative government which is not representative. He was not an anarchist; he believed in government: "You cannot get three people together but what, before long, there will be a certain set of regulations or agreements of mutual subordination for a common purpose, which is government." But he believed in a simplified government; he did not believe in all the cluttering, confining, annoying restrictions which bureaucracy (which Spencer called the coming slavery) imposed upon men.

Government, said Nordau, should function like a traffic officer—to keep the traffic moving, not to interfere with traffic; to keep the traffic of the human soul moving and not to interfere and inject itself into the lives of individual men. That is a condition to which we are coming in the United States today. There is a passion for government interference; there is a passion for law-making; there is a passion for petty regulations that slowly but surely, even if unconsciously, are circumscribing and may ultimately destroy the elemental human rights which men ought to enjoy in a democratic government. And Nordau foresaw this tendency in 1883.

Nordau speaks of the economic lie. He speaks of the inequalities which bring so much misery and unhappiness into the world; he speaks of what city life has done to men. Our civilization is an urban civilization; and the city life has created a wage-earning class. Our factory system has created a class dependent not upon the soil, not upon something which they command, not upon something real and constant, but upon a shifting, uncertain job; and that has brought uncertainty and instability into the lives of workingmen.

Nordau is not a Communist; Nordau exposes the folly of Communism. He says that the love of property and the influence of property is fundamental, even as the influence of sex in the human race, and it is one of the essential things in civilization. A man is entitled to his property, to the things he owns and the things he has acquired; he is entitled to the use of that property; he is entitled to protect his offspring so that in their early years they will be amply provided for. But no man has a social right to bequeath to his offspring a fortune which society has helped him to make, to hand a fortune down through generations, thereby creating an idle, parasitic, lazy class, thereby creating men who live for luxury and not for productiveness.

Nordau believes that the cure of all our economic ailments can be effected only through the abolition of inheritance. He says that this is not a radical idea. England has had a law for hundreds of years that only the first-born inherits his father's wealth; all others are disinherited. "I want to apply that same law even to the first-born." And he has a warning at the close of his chapter on the economic lie, and as I read it anew, I knew that the man spoke in 1883 as a prophet speaks.

> Great catastrophes are looming up on the field of political economy and it will not be possible to ignore them much longer. As long as the masses were religious, they could be consoled for their wretchedness on earth by promises of unlimited bliss in the future. But today they are becoming more enlightened and the number of those patient sufferers is daily growing less who find in the Host a satisfactory substitute for their dinner and accept the priests' order on the place waiting for them in paradise with as much pleasure as if it were some good terrestrial farm of which they could take immediate possession. The poor count their numbers and those of the rich and realize that they are constantly growing more numerous and stronger than the latter. They examine the sources of wealth and they find that speculating, plundering and inheriting have no more rational justification for existing than robbery and theft, and yet the latter are prosecuted by the laws. The increasing disinheritance of the masses by their deprivation of land and by the increasing accumulations of property in the hands of a few, will make the economic wrongs more and more intolerable. The moment that the millions acquire in addition to their hunger, a knowledge of the remote causes to which it is due, they will remove and overthrow all obstacles that stand between them and the right of satisfying their appetite. Hunger is one of the few elementary forces which neither threats nor persuasion can permanently control. Hence it is the power which will probably raze the

present structure of society level with the ground, in spite of its
foundations of superstition and selfishness—a task beyond the
power of philosophy alone.

Do you see Russia in all this? That was Nordau's first thesis—we are
living a lie. And his second thesis was that our present-day art and literature give evidence of the fact that we are degenerating. Nordau applies the
science of psychiatry and psychology to art and literature and finds that
they are rotten to the core, that they are suffering from a malady, and that
malady is simply this: that our civilization is so involved, that our civilization today is so cluttered up, that it has exerted too much of a strain upon
the nervous system of the human race. We cannot bear the burden of civilization because we have not cleared the ground for a healthy, normal civilization. We have speeded up life; we have put tremendous mechanical
forces to work producing things and things and things! But our emotions
have not kept pace with our intellect. Emotionally we are still five hundred
or a thousand or five thousand years in antiquity; intellectually, mechanically, scientifically, we are living at breakneck speed, and this incongruity,
this rift, is telling upon the nervous system of the human race. It is breaking it, it is demoralizing it, it is making for degeneracy!

He talks of Tolstoi and Ibsen and Brandes and Swinburne and
Nietzsche, and shows, rightly or wrongly—I am not defending his thesis
now—that the writing of these men, their style, their teaching, their points
of view are those of degenerate criminals, of men who have lost their hold
upon reality, of men who have lost the restraint and the discipline of real
culture and real civilization, of men who are drifting aimlessly because
they cannot control their emotions, even as a nervous person cannot control his muscles.

He speaks of the so-called modernists, the so-called realists, and of
all the filth that has come into modern-day literature, which is exalted as
being evidence of the emancipation of the human soul from the shackles of
convention. He says that that is a lie, that these are not evidence of emancipation; they are evidence of enslavement to all that is corrupt in the body
politic. And like a prophet of old, with the passion of an Isaiah, he calls on
sane, healthy, normal human beings to organize and stamp to death that
snake which is poisoning the whole system. For six hundred pages he diag-
noses, with the close reasoning of a mathematician and the close analysis of
a physician, the maladies of the present day; and he concludes his great
work with this tremendously powerful paragraph:

We in particular, who have made it our life's task to combat antiquated superstition, to spread enlightenment, to demolish historical ruins and remove their rubbish, to defend the freedom of the individual against State oppression and the mechanical routine of the Philistine; we must resolutely set ourselves in opposition to the miserable mongers who seize upon our dearest watchwords, with which to entrap the innocent. The "freedom" and "modernity," the "progress" and "truth," of these fellows are not ours. We have nothing in common with them. They wish for self-indulgence; we wish for work. They wish to drown consciousness in the unconscious; we wish to strengthen and enrich consciousness. They wish for evasive ideation and babble; we wish for attention, observation, and knowledge. The criterion by which true moderns may be recognised and distinguished from impostors calling themselves moderns may be this: Whoever preaches absence of discipline is an enemy of progress; and whoever worships his "I" is an enemy to society. Society has for its first premise, neighborly love and capacity for self-sacrifice; and progress is the effect of an ever more rigorous subjugation of the beast in man, of an ever tenser self-restraint, an ever keener sense of duty and responsibility. The emancipation for which we are striving is of the judgment, not of the appetites. In the profoundly penetrating words of Scripture, "Think not that I am come to destroy the law, or the prophets; I am not come to destroy, but to fulfill."

And that is why I speak of Dr. Max Nordau as truly orthodox. He is not a preacher who has come to denude and destroy the moral foundations of our system; he is the man who has come to preserve; to preserve not the sham, not the externalities, but to preserve the foundation, the heart, the soundness of our moral law; and in that he is one with all the seers and the prophets of the human race.

And he is an optimist, an extreme optimist. He believed in the regeneration of society even as he saw its degeneration. He believed that there is in this vast cosmic scheme an urge, a vital urge, which is constantly evolving new and higher forms and which is driving man, if man would not stop it, to higher levels. Nordau asks for a clearing of the jungle so as to permit this clean, fine, wholesome spirit to be given free expression.

That is Nordau the thinker—a modern prophet in every sense of the word. A word about Nordau the Jew, and I shall be through. Nordau was a Zionist, a nationalist. He believed in the regeneration of Israel as a people upon Israel's ancient soil in Palestine. There was no compromise in his position; it was to him a dogma, a creed—even as he did not believe in dogmas and creeds in anything else. Nordau became the champion and the spokesman of this renaissance of Israel.

Nordau hated the sham and the hypocrisy of Jews. He hated the Jew who denies himself, because that, to him, showed lack of character, which makes for degeneration. Nordau hated what he calls the *Luftmensch*, the materialistic Jew, who was losing his soul in the obesity of wealth, who was corrupting himself through the gifts bestowed upon him by his emancipation.

Nordau called with a clarion voice for an enlightened, proud, purposeful Jewry the world over. He knew the tragedy of Jewish life. He witnessed the pogroms of 1882; he witnessed the Dreyfus affair; he knew the condition of eight millions of Jews in Eastern Europe. He called them *Luftmensch*—the "men of the air"—men who had no solid foundation upon which to stand. He knew their tragedy and he knew their needs; he loved his people and he returned to them from the glittering civilization of western Europe, and from the academies and the universities, from the life and light and sweetness of French civilization. He went back to the bleakness and the gloom and the poverty and the misery of his own people. He returned to help them, and it is no wonder that when he died after years of service, universal Israel stood by his open grave and mourned the passing of a prophet and the passing of a Maccabee.

Sholem Aleichem

SERMON, THE TEMPLE
MARCH 22, 1959

When Sholem Aleichem died in May, 1916, in the city of New York, hundreds of thousands of Jews turned out for his funeral. Seldom has any writer, Jew or non-Jew, been so honored. Simple folk followed the funeral procession and wept as though they had lost a very dear and intimate friend.

This month, which marks the hundredth anniversary of the birth of Sholem Aleichem, is being commemorated by the entire Jewish world; even in the Soviet Union, where Jewish writings and writers have not been held in high repute, this centenary is being observed with the friendly approval of the government, and a new edition of his work—short stories, novels, plays—has been published.

During the lifetime of Sholem Aleichem and since his death, his writings have been translated into numerous languages, including Japanese and Esperanto. He has been likened to Cervantes, to Charles Dickens, to Mark Twain.

Now, who is this writer who has been known far and wide by his pen name, Sholem Aleichem? His name means "peace to you." Whence is his great and lasting appeal even to those who do not understand the Yiddish language in which he wrote? The world about which he wrote has since vanished almost completely. The language in which he wrote, which in his day was spoken by some ten or twelve million Jews, is known today, I am afraid, to less than one-fifth that number. Evidently there is something perennial and universal in the stories and the types and characters of Sholem Aleichem's writings, something that lives above and beyond time and place which insures him immortality in mankind's literary pantheon.

Solomon Rabinowitz, for that was his real name, was born in a rather small town in southern Russia one hundred years ago. In many ways the life of eastern European Jewry in Sholem Aleichem's day was still medieval, but new winds had begun to blow through the Pale. Czarist tyranny was still pressing down very heavily upon the people. Their lives were hemmed in and insecure. Many occupations were closed to them; they lived in constant dread of hostile decrees and ruthless government officials. It was not long before violent pogroms broke out and drove the masses to despair and sent them into headlong flight to other countries, especially to America.

Jewish life was still within the framework of orthodox, traditional Judaism. It was still largely controlled by the detailed provision of the Shulchan Aruch, the rabbinic code of Jewish practice for all occasions. The cheder, the elementary school, and the yeshiva, the higher rabbinic seminary, had changed very little through the centuries in content or in method, and their curricula included very little of the learning and the science of the new age. Nevertheless, this was no longer a static world. Here and there, especially in the larger cities, Jews were reaching out for the enlightenment and the education and the opportunities and the teachings of the modern world which they knew to exist beyond the borders of the Russian Pale. They were reaching out for the revolutionary ideas of human freedom and basic human rights. Some, like Sholem Aleichem himself, began to study the Russian language, and that helped them to look towards new horizons. Some were secretly joining revolutionary political movements, and were working for the overthrow of the Czarist tyranny. Others were escaping the Pale of Settlement and were making their way westward to the schools and the universities of the Western world and to the new world which had begun to beckon to them, the golden land of America.

Sholem Aleichem was a child of this world of the Pale of Russian Jewish Settlement. His early life was spent in a small old-fashioned town called Voronkov, in Poltava in southern Russia, near Kiev, which he later immortalized in his writings as Kasrilevke, and which he himself described as a "small town of the little people." Sholem Aleichem was a product of the cheder but he also, as I said, learned Russian. His father was a Maskil, one of the intellectual Jews, who believed in giving his children a modern education. In fact, by the age of seventeen, Sholem Aleichem was supporting himself by giving private lessons in Russian, and he fell in love with one of his pupils, a daughter of a rich Russian landowner. Later on, against the violent opposition of her father, they were married.

Sholem Aleichem as a young man was bright and gay and light-hearted, bent on all kinds of innocent mischief. He loved to poke fun at people and make them the source of merriment, but never with any malice —never with any bitterness. When his father-in-law died, Sholem Aleichem became the administrator of the estate of this Jew—an estate which amounted to a quarter of a million rubles, a substantial fortune in those days. But Sholem Aleichem began to trade on the grain and stock exchange and soon lost his fortune. He never came within sight of so much money again the rest of his life. Most of his life he lived very modestly or in actually straitened circumstances, and toward the end of his life in the Bronx in New York City, he was an unsuccessful insurance agent and could not make a living.

Among the famous portraits of Kasrilevke which Sholem Aleichem so skillfully and artistically depicted, there is one character, Menachem Mendel, a *Luftmensch,* a man who is up in the air all the time, his feet never on the ground; a speculator, a man who has amazing plans afoot, a man who tries a thousand and one occupations and never makes a cent; a speculator, always in a hurry. Menachem Mendel was a broker, a real-estate agent, a dealer in timber and mines, in oil, and whatnot; and in that character one can find a very sly criticism of the author.

As Sholem Aleichem's fame grew as a writer, he traveled through-out the Pale of Jewish Settlement of Russia, Poland, and Lithuania, and read his stories. He was a skillful reader and became extremely popular. He traveled to Galicia, to western Europe, and everywhere he was warmly received by the masses of the people, who loved his stories. When the pogroms of 1905 broke in Russia, Sholem Aleichem left Europe and came to the United States, and here too he was received with open arms. But he stayed in this country only a short time; he could not acclimatize himself to the New World, and returned to Europe. There he traveled about, writing, reading his stories, trying to earn a living. He spent some time in Italy. His health was not the best. When the First World War broke out, he again returned to the United States. And here for a while he did well as a writer for one of the Jewish newspapers, but after a time he lost his contract with that newspaper and, as I indicated a moment ago, spent the rest of his life in relative poverty, in spite of the great adulation which was given to him by the masses of the people. He died, as I said, in 1916.

Sholem Aleichem was seventeen when he began to write, and his first writing was in Hebrew, not in Yiddish. Hebrew was the language of the intellectuals. Yiddish was the common speech of the masses, the *mama loshen,* the vernacular; it was not as high-toned as Hebrew. Jews had been speaking Yiddish for hundreds of years, ever since the Jews of Germany first adopted it in the Middle Ages, but it had never displaced Hebrew as the language of study, of worship, or of literary composition. And that is true, if you will recall, also of the German language and of nearly all the Romance languages of Europe: they could not displace Latin as the language of scholarship and learning and writing until comparatively recent times. But around the middle of the nineteenth century, Yiddish began to come into its own and three great writers were largely responsible. The first was the famous writer Sholem Abramowitz—Mendele Mocher Seforim, which means "Mendele the Bookseller." The second was Isaac Loeb Peretz and the third Sholem Aleichem. It was they who made Yiddish a respectable and effective language of literature. These writers—Abramowitz, Peretz, and Sholem Aleichem—soon found that if they wished to reach the masses of the Jewish people and not merely the intellectuals with their messages and social criticism, they had to employ Yiddish, which was understood by everybody. Sholem Aleichem's style soon captivated large sections of eastern European Jewry; it was folksy, lively, richly idiomatic, and easy-flowing, yet artful and cunningly wrought, and the style revealed how colorful and how flexible and how perfectly adequate this so-called jargon, this ugly duckling of a dialect, Yiddish, could be.

People loved his style and people loved the people about whom Sholem Aleichem wrote—themselves. He wrote about their life as they knew it: their environment, an environment which was made doubly revealing to them because of his skillful artistry. He wrote about their hopes and their foibles and their sufferings. He wrote about Kasrilevke, their *shtetl,* their little town, the people they knew—familiar faces, all of them, and they loved Sholem Aleichem for the way he wrote about them. He did not laugh at them—he laughed with them. He did not mock or deride them as others have done or could easily do. He did not make sport of them. He knew the unseemly side of their lives; he knew all that was grotesque and all that was absurd and he did not withold his pen from writing about it. But he also understood the why and the wherefore of things as they were, what had gone before, what went on, poverty, misery, and oppression, and he did not hold them up to ridicule. They felt that he was one of them; he included himself in all the sly, compassionate humor which he directed at his fellow citizens of Kasrilevke, and he could weep with them. He was their brother, their big brother, perhaps a more understanding brother, but a brother all the same.

Sholem Aleichem describes the city of Kasrilevke in *The Old Country,* and I want to read you a paragraph or two which may give you a taste of his style and his approach to the subject and to the people about whom he wrote. He was always interested in little people. Big people did not interest him; they had other writers, they could look after themselves.

The town of the little people into which I shall now take you, dear reader, is exactly in the middle of the blessed Pale, the Pale of Settlement in which Jews have been packed as closely as herring in a barrel and told to increase and multiply. The name of the town is Kasrilevke. How did this name originate? I'll tell you. Among us Jews, poverty has many faces and many aspects. A poor man is an unlucky man, he is a pauper, a beggar, a schnorrer, a starveling, a tramp or a plain failure: all kinds of names for a poor man. A different tone is used in speaking of each one but all these names express human wretchedness. However, there is still another name, kasril, or kasrile. That name is spoken in a different tone altogether—almost a bragging tone— for instance: "Oh, am I ever a Kasrilic." A Kasrilic is not just an ordinary pauper, a failure in life. On the contrary, he is a man who has not allowed poverty to degrade him. He laughs at it; he is poor but cheerful. Stuck away in his corner of the world, isolated from the surrounding country, the town stands, often dreaming, bewitched, immersed in itself and remote from the noise and bustle, the confusion and tumult and greed which men have created about them and have dignified with highsounding names like culture and progress and civilization. A proper person may take off his hat with respect to these things, but not these little people. Not only do they know nothing of automobiles and modern travel and airplanes, but for a long time they refused to believe in the existence of the old railroad train altogether, refused to believe in its existence. "Such a thing could not be," they said. "Why," they said, "it is a dream, a fairy tale; you might as well talk of a merry-go-round in heaven." But it happened once that a householder of Kasrilevke had to go to Moscow. When he came back he swore, with many oaths, that it was true—there was a railroad; he himself had ridden in a train to Moscow, and it had taken him, he shrugged his shoulders, less than one hour. This, the little people interpreted to mean that he had ridden less than an hour and then walked the rest of the way. But still the fact of the train remained. If a Jew and a householder from Kasrilevke swore to it, they could not deny that there was such a thing as a train. It had to be true. He could not have invented it out of thin air. He even explained to them the whole miracle of the train—he drew a diagram on paper. He showed them how the wheels turned, the smokestack whistled, the carriage flew. People rode to Moscow. The little people of Kasrilevke listened, nodded their heads solemnly, and deep in their hearts they laughed at him. What a story, the wheels turn, the smokestack whistles, carriages fly, people ride to Moscow and then come back again.

That's how they are, these little people, none of them are gloomy, none of them are worried little men of affairs; but on the contrary, they are known everywhere as jesters, storytellers, a cheerful, lighthearted breed of men—poor but cheerful. It's hard to say what makes them so happy—nothing—just the sheer joy of living. Living? If you ask them "How do you live?" they will answer with a shrug and a laugh, "How do we live? Who knows, we live." A remarkable thing: whenever you meet them they are scurrying like rabbits—this one here, that one there— they never have time to stop. "What are you hurrying for?" "What am I hurrying for? Well, it's like this, if we hurry we think that we might run into something, earn a few pennies, provide for the Sabbath." Provide for the Sabbath. To provide for the Sabbath—that is their goal in life. All week long they labor and sweat, wear themselves out, live without food or drink just so there is something for the Sabbath. And when that holy Sabbath arrives, let Yehupetz perish (Yehupetz is the name for Kiev), let Odessa be razed, let Paris itself sink into the earth—Kasrilevke lives.

And this is a fact: since Kasrilevke was founded no Jew has gone hungry there on the Sabbath. Is it possible that there is a Jew who does not have fish for the Sabbath? If he has no fish then he has meat; if he has no meat then he has herring. If he has no herring, then he has white bread. If he has no white bread, then he has black bread and onions. If he has no black bread and onions, then he borrows some from his neighbor. Next week the neighbor will borrow from him. The world is a wheel and it keeps turning. And the Kasrilevke repeats this maxim and shows you with his hand how it turns.

To him a maxim, a witty saying is everything. For an apt remark he will forsake his mother and father, as the saying goes. The tales you hear about these little people sound fabulous, but you may be sure they are all true. For instance, there is the story of the Kasrilevke who got tired of starving in Kasrilevke and went out into the wide world to seek his fortune. He left the country, wandered far and wide, and finally reached Paris. There, naturally, he wanted to see the Rothschilds. How can a Jew come to Paris and not visit the Rothschilds? But they didn't let him in. "What's the trouble?" he wants to know. "Your coat is torn," they tell him. "You fools," says the Jew, "if I had a good coat would I have gone to Paris?" It looked hopeless, but a Kasrilevke never gives up. He thought a while and then he said to the doorman, "Tell your master that it is not an ordinary beggar who has come to his door, but a Jewish merchant, who has brought him a piece of goods such as you can't find in Paris for any amount of money." Hearing this, Rothschild became curious and asked that the merchant be brought in. "Sholem Aleichem," said Rothschild. "Aleichem Sholem," said the merchant. "Take a seat; where do you come from?" "I come from Kasrilevke." "What good news do you bring?" "Well, Mr. Rothschild, they say in our town, that you are not badly off; they say that if I had a half of what you own or only a third, you would still have enough left. And honors, I imagine, you do not lack either, for people always look up to a man of riches. What do you lack? One thing only: to live forever, eternal life, and that is what I've come to sell you." When Rothschild heard this he said, "Well, let's get down to business. What will it cost me?" "It will cost you 300 rubles." "Is that your best price?" "My very best. I could have said much more but I've said it so it's final." Rothschild said no more—counted out 300 rubles, one by one, and now the Kasrilevke slipped the money into his pocket and said to Rothschild, "If you want to live forever, my advice to you is to leave this noisy, busy Paris and move to our town of Kasrilevke. There you can never die, because since Kasrilevke has been a town, no rich man has ever died there."

Sholem Aleichem brought cheer to an oppressed and distraught generation of Jews. His purpose was never to hurt but always to heal. He was not a reformer. He was not a moralist. He was not interested in reproving or chastising or exposing the evils which an ordinary loveless satirist might have done. Whatever criticism he had to offer he always offered in the form of a capsule of good humor.

Someone summed up the message of Sholem Aleichem to his generation in these words: "You take the world too seriously; you think more of it than it is worth, you demand of it more than it can give. The things you complain of are merely trifles. If you looked at them from a proper distance, you would see that there is more to laugh than to cry over. You are justly displeased with the world, but there is something which transcends justice: it is mercy. You are a pessimist because of your overabundant optimism. You think that the world deserves to be rebuked; all it really deserves is to be forgiven."

I wish I had time to tell you more about Sholem Aleichem, and some of his amazing characters, but you must read him yourself. Sholem Aleichem should be read rather than talked about, and many of his works are available in English translation.

Sholem Aleichem loved his people and they loved him, not only for his humor but for his humanity. He loved children greatly. He wrote some of the loveliest children's stories in Yiddish literature—and, for that matter, in all literature. He loved the common people, and in his last will and testament he wrote: "No matter where I die, I am to be buried not among aristocrats, men of high lineage, or men of great wealth, but among common Jewish workmen, with just ordinary folk; so that the tombstone to be put up on my grave will honor the ordinary graves around mine, and the ordinary graves will honor my tombstone, in the way in which the plain, honest people honored their folk writer in his lifetime."

And so it came to be—Sholem Aleichem found his last resting place in the Arbeiter-Ring Cemetery in Brooklyn, but he also found his last resting place in the hearts of his people everywhere throughout the world.

Four Great Choices
Which Moses Made

SERMON, THE TEMPLE
PASSOVER, APRIL 22, 1962

A man is known by the choices which he makes at the critical junctures of his life. It is then that a man's true character reveals itself, for it is then that the total man makes a decision—the man as he finally emerges from a long, inner struggle. The debate is now over, the pros and cons have all been weighed, and the irrevocable choice is made. It is a once-for-all choice, for it is not quickly or lightly made. And as the decision is, so will be the man's destiny.

There are people who are incapable of making decisions. There are people who are unable to meet the challenge of choice. They go limping through life with two or more opinions about the same subject. They cannot trust themselves to make up their minds. They persist in weighing and considering so long that performance comes to nothing. Action falls between the two stools of unresolved choices. Of such men the Bible says: "He who observes the wind all the time will not sow, and he who regards the clouds constantly will not reap."

Now, the failure to make a decision is in itself a decision—though an involuntary one. And that failure to make a decision also reveals character, the vacillating character of irresolution and timidity. Man must pay the price for both decision and indecision, but the one is noble and the other quite ignoble.

Every great human soul experiences what you might call the agony of prolonged inner struggle preliminary to making a final choice and a final commitment, but, once the choice is made, once the commitment is

257

made, after a prolonged heart-searching struggle, it remains for all time and under all circumstances, firm, constant, and undeviating.

Now, a great human soul informs our festival of Passover—Moses, the man of God. There is so much that is appealing in the life of this hero not in armor, this conqueror who never built a city which time would ultimately destroy, nor an empire which would someday be traced in ruins; this great man whose tomb would never know a monument, but whose name would forever remain sweet upon the lips of all men in all ages who love freedom, who love justice, who love goodness!

Kings and rulers, the mighty of the earth, have often built for themselves magnificent tombs, tombs which Job quite properly called "ruins"; for they all end up in ruins, no matter how magnificent they may be. One thinks of the ancient pyramids, the vast desert tombs of the Pharaohs which tens of thousands of slaves helped to build; one thinks of the tomb of King Mausolus of Caria, the king whose name is embedded in our word *mausoleum,* the tomb which was erected by his widow, Artimisia, and which was considered by the ancients one of the seven wonders of the world. One thinks of the resplendent tomb of Cyrus at Pasargadae in ancient Persia, which was carved out of a steep mountain slope painstakingly and at enormous cost, but which was finally plundered and abandoned; one thinks of the majestic tombs of the Medici in Florence, which Michelangelo sculptured and adorned; and of the Escorial, one of the most remarkable buildings in the world, which contains the richly decorated pantheon where the kings and queens of Spain lie buried; and of the tomb of Napoleon in Les Invalides, on the banks of the Seine.

Tombs in all parts of the earth, monuments to man's vanity, even in death, and to his vain conceit that massive blocks of stone and marble heaped high will ensure his immortality or the affectionate and reverent regard of posterity! Of Moses, whose name outshines all others in the annals of mankind, and who will outlive them all—of Moses the Bible says: "No man knows the place of his burial to this day." No tomb. No monument.

One of the most appealing qualities of this man Moses, whom the Bible calls the greatest of the prophets and the humblest of men, was the manner in which he arrived at the important and critical decisions of his life, the manner in which he made four decisive choices of his life. The Bible describes them in detail, and because of them we celebrate today the festival of Passover.

The first choice which Moses made rather early in life was between palace and hovel. Moses, as you will recall, was born in a hovel among slaves. His kith and kin were the slaves of the Egyptian Pharaoh; they and their ancestors had been slaves for nigh unto four hundred years. Their burdens were heavy. They groaned under their bondage. Their lives were made bitter by hard labor with mortar and brick. Moses, who was born among these slaves and who was doomed to die, as were all male children born to the Hebrew slaves—Moses was by his mother secreted in a basket of bulrushes and hidden among the tall reeds of the Nile, from where he was rescued by the princess of the Pharaoh. Moses was raised as a prince in the palace of the king. His youth and early manhood were spent amidst the splendor and luxury of the royal palace. He was given a princely Egyptian education. His future was full of the promise of all good things— power, glory, wealth, and all the delights of man.

But Moses knew that he was a Hebrew! Not far from the palace where he was reared were the miserable slave-pens where his family and his brethren lived and groaned under the lash of the taskmasters. Moses grew up. His mind and soul developed as he matured, and now he was confronted more and more with a problem, a problem which would not let him go: What should he do? Should he go back and cast in his lot with his suffering brothers, become a slave like them, live with them amidst the filth and the poverty of their slave-quarters, or should he continue to dwell as a happy, pampered prince amidst the pleasures and delights of the Egyptian court? His mind and his soul were in constant turmoil. He could not evade the problem. He must make a choice. Palace or hovel! Prince or slave! The young Moses finally made his fateful choice: he went back to his brethren. So, as between status and loyalty, Moses chose loyalty. As between pride and obligation, Moses chose obligation.

That choice determined his entire career and all the momentous events which were to follow. This was the first heroic choice of Moses. It involved a sharp break with his past, and a desperate plunge into an unknown future. Ask yourselves: How many men would make such a choice?

Years later, Moses was to make another decisive choice. You will recall that he fled from Egypt. In his anger at seeing an Egyptian taskmaster mercilessly beating a helpless Hebrew slave, he struck the taskmaster and killed him. When his act became known, he had to escape, and he fled to the land of Midian. There he remained for many years. He dwelt with Jethro, a priest of Midian, tending his flocks, and in the course of time he married Jethro's daughter, and children were born to them. Moses dwelt peacefully in a peaceful land. In the quiet and the freedom of the oases, far away from the noise, the corruption, and the horrors of Egypt, Moses was at peace and he was happy. But something in his soul continued to trouble him and would not give him rest. Memories of his kinsmen, enslaved in faraway Egypt, kept recurring. How was it with them? Once before some obscure and unaccountable force had pulled him back to his suffering people. Should he return to his brethren again, share their fate, perhaps help them, but in so doing face the danger of a fugitive whose life the Egyptians were seeking? The prolonged turmoil within his soul finally culminated in a revelation—in a flame of fire out of the midst of a bush which burned without being consumed. With it came the call to return to Egypt and bring forth his enslaved brothers. And here Moses found him-self again in the dread valley of decision. He must make a choice. There was no escape. Should he return? Should he remain? Moses did not arrive at his decision quickly, without great soul-searching, without great hesitation. "Who am I that I should go to Pharaoh and bring the sons of Israel out of Egypt?" Again we read: "Oh, my Lord, I am not eloquent, I am slow of speech and of tongue, send someone else . . ." and again, "Oh, my Lord, send, I pray Thee, some other person." But the call finally overpowers him. He makes his irrevocable decision. He returns to Egypt. What follows is world history. Moses was to set in motion the first great revolution in behalf of human freedom.

And so between ease and mission, Moses chose mission! Between personal comfort and the service of his fellow men, Moses chose the service of his fellow men. Would we make such a choice? How many people would make such a choice?

There is yet a third choice which Moses was to make which revealed his true character. He had at last brought the people out of Egypt across the Red Sea, and across the wilderness to the foot of Mount Sinai. Painfully he had led them. Patiently he had instructed them. For their sake he had suffered much. But, as soon as he was gone from them, gone to the top of the mountain to receive the Torah, the same people for whom he had labored so much and suffered so much flouted all his instructions. They quickly made for themselves a golden image, a golden calf, and they danced around it in licentious abandon and cried out: "This is your god, O Israel." Moses, on descending from the mountain, was crushed by this evidence of the futility of all his work, the terrible failure of all that he had tried to do. At that moment he hears the voice of God: I will destroy this people. They are worthless. They are irredeemable serfs. Their souls are still in Egypt even though their bodies are not. They are a stiff-necked people. I will destroy them, but of you, Moses, I will make a great nation.

Here again Moses is faced with a fateful choice. Should he consent to the destruction of his people, this ungrateful, sinful, and inconstant people which had betrayed him and his life's work, and allow himself to be spared, to become the progenitor of a new nation? Moses made his choice. Moses said to the Lord: "Alas, the people have sinned a great sin, but now, O Lord, if Thou wilt forgive their sin it is good—but if not, blot me, I pray Thee, out of Thy book which Thou has written."

Between hurt pride on the one hand and love on the other, Moses chose love and pity. Between love of self and love of his people, the immortal leader chose the love of his people. How many men, when they feel themselves abused and wronged, would choose pity and compassion and understanding as Moses did? How many would rather sulk in their tents and say: "Well, I have done my best by these people and now I am through"?

There was a fourth and final choice which Moses made. Moses is on the top of Mount Nebo just outside the Promised Land. He is now an old man, a very old man. He is within sight of the Promised Land. For forty years he had trekked through an awesome and terrible wilderness with his people. For forty years he had endured the heat and thirst of the desert, the rebellions, grumblings, and complaints of his people; for forty years he had had to fight enemies without and rebellion within. But now here is the Promised Land into which he will enter. This will repay him for all the hardships and heartaches of the weary years; this will crown his life's work.

At that very moment the voice of God comes to him: "Moses, look well over this Promised Land from a distance. Look it over to the north and the south and the east and the west; look long, for only with thine eyes thou shalt see it, but into it thou shalt not come." Why, this cannot be! To be robbed of victory on the threshold of attainment? To be frustrated at the point of victory? To die of thirst in the sight of springs of fresh water? Is this just? What will Moses now do or say? Will he turn bitter? Will rebellion and bitterness well up in his soul, all the accumulated complaints of his life—will they rush to his lips? After hearing his doom announced, the first words that come to the lips of Moses are not words of rebellion, of complaint, or of challenge. Slowly he begins to intone a blessing, his last sweet blessing of his people: "Let Reuben live and not die." Let Israel live and not die. What am I? I am mortal; I must die. What matters it if I cannot enter the Promised Land? I do not count. "Let Reuben live and not die." Let Israel live and not die.

And so between rebellion and faith, between defiance and submission to God's inscrutable will, Moses chose faith. This is the last of the four great choices which Moses made. As between position and loyalty, he chose loyalty. As between ease and duty, he chose duty. As between selfish interests and the love of his people, he chose the love of his people. As between rebellion and faith, he chose faith. Would you? How many people would make those choices?

"Once to every man and nation comes the moment to decide," wrote the American poet Lowell shortly before the Civil War in his poem "The Present Crisis." "Once to every man and nation comes the moment to decide, in the strife of truth with falsehood, for the good or evil side." Perhaps more than once! Great is the man who has the courage to make his decisions, and having made them, to abide by them and act upon them. "The king of Babylon stood at the parting of the ways," declared the prophet Ezekiel. How often do we find ourselves standing at the parting of the ways . . . What shall I choose? Shall I choose ease? Shall I seek my own good? Should I shut out the clamor of the unhappy world around me, and turn a deaf ear to the call of duty, or shall I choose duty, loyalty, and commitment? Shall I listen to the sad music of humanity, and seek ways to give other men an ampler life with my labors and sacrifices? Shall I choose me, or shall I choose the God in me? Shall I constrict my soul within the narrow confines of my bodily cravings and appetites and ambitions, or shall I take the wings of the morning and soar to the uttermost regions where truth and goodness and beauty eternally abide? "The king of Babylon stood at the parting of the ways." In a sense, every normal human soul is king, is sovereign, possessed of the right of sovereign choices. "Behold, I have set before you life and the good, death and the evil . . . choose life!" Moses chose exile, suffering, ingratitude, misunderstanding, vilification, betrayal—the hard choices, but he also chose life! For himself, and for his people. And out of this beautiful holiday of Passover, Moses speaks to us and summons us through all the symbols and ceremonies to make the right choices in the significant moments of our lives.

I would like to call your attention to some choices which the people of Moses made, inspired by his example. The Jewish people in the course of their long history were confronted time and time again with critical decisions upon which their survival and the survival of Judaism depended. The first one was at the foot of Mount Sinai. They were asked to choose, asked to accept or reject a covenant with God which would make of them a different kind of people. And they were told what this covenant would entail: relentless warfare with all the surrounding peoples whose way of life was different from theirs and who persisted in holding on to their own cherished way of life, their creeds, their cults, their practices. If they accepted this covenant they would become a hated and resented minority in the world. Would it not be better, on the other hand, to be like all other peoples, to adopt their beliefs, conform to their customs, to float along, as it were, with the currents, instead of buffeting the waves of controversy? What would be their choice at Mount Sinai? Moses put the entire matter before them. The people decided. They answered as with one voice: "All that the Lord spoke we will do." And so an everlasting covenant was entered into, between Yahveh and the people of Israel, which made of them a different kind of people to this day.

Let me give you the example of another choice which our people, the people of Moses, made. Centuries later, the Jewish people found themselves in exile in Babylon, and there they were confronted with another choice. Their state in Judea had been destroyed, their Temple was in ruins; they found themselves amidst a proud and conquering people. What should they do? Should they break their ties with the past, forget Judea and Jerusalem and Yahveh, who seemed to have forsaken them, and assimilate and cease to be Jews? It would be much easier for them and their children. There were among them many whose morale broke, and a wave of apostasy swept over them. They returned to all the forms of heathen worship in Babylon. But the majority clung loyally to their covenant. They would not assimilate. They would not become submerged. So, amid the ruins of their national disaster, they proclaimed with increasing fervor their faith in Yahveh, who forgives the iniquities of His people, who does not visit the sins of the fathers upon the children, who does not require a Temple for His dwelling place nor altars and sacrifices for His worship. By the rivers of Babylon they lifted up their voices and said: "If I forget thee, O Jerusalem, may my right hand wither." Because they made their choice we are here today; because they made their choice, Western civilization inherited from them the spiritual and ethical values which are molding the lives of people.

Finally I should like to call your attention to another great moment in Jewish history when our people found themselves at a crossroads and had to make a decision—a fateful, dreadful decision. In Spain our fore-fathers had lived for centuries. They increased in numbers and in prosperity. They came to occupy high positions in government; many became advisers and treasurers to kings. Many of them dwelt in mansions and palaces such as Moses had dwelt in as a young man in Egypt. There was little to distinguish these Jews of Spain from the proud grandees of the country, but the Church was unwilling to have infidels, those who refused to accept Christ, share in the prosperity of the country. They would dese-crate the sacred soil by their presence. And the Church had no difficulty in persuading Ferdinand and Isabella. So on March 31, 1492, a royal edict was issued which gave the Jews of Spain—the hundreds of thousands of them—the dread choice either of abandoning their religion, their ancient faith, or of abandoning their country, their homes, their property, their positions, their security, everything, and go out into exile and face the unknown dangers of homelessness and wandering. Three months were given them to make that choice—apostasy or exile. History records that very few Jews accepted Christianity. The overwhelming majority of them went into exile and faced the tragic experiences which overtook them. And because these men, these Jews, made their fierce and desperate decision, our people have survived.

Even now, in our own day, in spite of savage persecutions, terror, and death visited upon millions of our people by the Nazi beasts, in spite of the destruction of tens of thousands of Jewish centers and communities, the Jewish people chose not to succumb, not to give way to despair—"I will not die, I will continue to live." They surmounted their appalling trag-edies by a powerful act of will, and they proceeded to build a new hope and a new life and a new homeland in Israel. Because they made this deci-sion, Jews of this generation will grow in strength and our people will awake better and freer in happier days. We co-opted for life. We could have co-opted for disappearance. We co-opted for life, and therefore more abundant life will be given unto us. Moses, our great teacher, taught us to make the right kind of decisions, to choose wisely. We may be called God's chosen people, but equally, as someone said, we are a right-choosing, truth-choosing, life-choosing, God-choosing people, and this is the secret of our survival.

WHAT should, therefore, concern us today is not whether the Jewish people will survive, but how. Shall it be affirmatively and challengingly, as in the great periods of our past, holding our banners high in a day of battle and storm; or negatively, creeping into the nooks and crannies of the earth, waiting for the wrath to pass and grateful for the mere gift of existence and survival? We can do either. Apart from all else, apart from the mighty energies which the past has stored up in us, mere inertia and social lag can keep us going for an indefinite period. Many Jews, especially the more prosperous ones, out of fear and personal interest, are choosing the latter course. But the Jewish people as a whole, I believe, will not, because it cannot, consent to such a role of passivity, abdication, and escapism.

There is too much leaven in its spirit, too powerful a dynamic in its faith, and too much of the unquenchably prophetic in its traditions. When dangers threaten, when the enemy appears on the horizon, then the Ark of the Covenant begins to move—the Ark which "carries those who carry it," the Ark which rests with the people, and marches with the people, and the cry goes up: "Arise, O Lord, and let Thine enemies be scattered!" and a militancy, a bitter stubbornness, a sharp defiance comes into the hearts of our people, and they are ready for battle. . . .

FROM *THE WORLD CRISIS AND JEWISH SURVIVAL*
AN ADDRESS BEFORE
THE CENTRAL CONFERENCE OF AMERICAN RABBIS,
JUNE, 1939

"Number the Days of Old, Consider the Years of Many Generations . . ."

Every January, Dr. Silver offered a review of the year from the pulpit. It was an event eagerly awaited by the community. Often, he would prepare a sermon series outlining ten or a hundred or a thousand years of cultural, economic, or political highlights.

Personally, he found history, ancient and modern, a perpetually fascinating subject and enjoyed the role of a commentator, selecting, analyzing, and then presenting in dramatic form the events of a particular epoch. His public addresses were rich with apt historic allusion and parallels.

He also turned to history for validation of his basic faith. In doing so, he was following Jewish religious tradition. For, quite obviously, an individual life, or the fate of an individual generation, cannot always offer proof that good prevails over evil. But the larger perspective, the experience of many generations—this, the Jew has always claimed, can yield evidence of a moral universe. It is, then, to history that Abba Hillel Silver appeals again and again when he tries to comfort Israel in its doubt and agony. We must "endeavor to appraise our present hour in terms of what has gone before. In so doing we shall gain perspective, confidence, and courage."

The Democratic Impulse in Jewish History

SERMON, THE TEMPLE
NOVEMBER 4, 1928

I have selected to write and to speak on the theme "The Democratic Impulse in Jewish History" because the conviction has been growing upon me in recent years that not enough stress has been laid by students upon the role which democracy, or, as I choose to call it, the impulse of democracy, has played throughout Jewish history, and that not enough stress has been laid upon what I regard as perhaps the outstanding contribution of Israel to the thought of mankind. This contribution is democracy—democracy not only in political life but in social, economic, and religious life as well.

When our forefathers appeared on the frontiers of Canaan ready to begin their amazing career in the world as an historic people, they had already been fashioned and molded by countless centuries of desert life. You know, of course, that our forefathers before they came to Palestine were nomadic peoples wandering through the great Arabian desert for endless centuries. The home of our forefathers was that vast mysterious land known as the Arabian desert, the Arabian wilderness.

Now, in the desert there are no kings. In the desert to this day there is no aristocracy of birth or of wealth; no military hierarchy, no priestly hierarchy. The leader of the tribe was the *shofet*, the *primus inter pares*— the first among equals. Among wandering tribes there is a rude elementary democracy, and our people was fashioned and molded by that democratic spirit for endless cycles of time before they came into the settled agricultural life of Palestine. They never lost their desert tradition of equality and mutuality.

All through their history to this very day, our people, which had been imbued through countless generations with a democratic passion, never quite lost it throughout a checkered and turbulent career. When our forefathers entered Palestine, during the centuries of turbulent conquest and settlement, they lived without rulers and without kings. Whenever an emergency presented itself and they were compelled to ward off an invading enemy, they would choose one of their numbers to be their *shofet*, their judge, their general, who led them into battle. When the emergency was over, that *shofet* returned to common civil life. There was no king in Israel.

It was only with the menace of a new and desperate enemy—the Philistines—that the scattered tribes of Israel in Palestine were compelled to consolidate. It was then that the demand arose on the part of the people for a king. "Let us be like all other people. Let us have a king who will be the symbol of our unity." At that time the prophet Samuel was the judge, the *shofet*, and when they came to him and asked for a king, Samuel was outraged. It was unheard of that the Children of Israel, these freeborn men of the desert, should permit themselves voluntarily to be enslaved by a king and a dynasty. He told them that their demand for a king was an apostasy from God. It was a culpable mimicry of the heathen. He told them that a king would enslave them. He pointed out to them what the exploitations and the spoliations of royalty are. He warned them not to ask for a king, and through Samuel that genius of the race, that democratic genius of the race, spoke. But necessity compelled Samuel to yield to the clamor of the people, and they chose a king.

But the king in Israel, from the time of Saul to the time of the last king, Zedekiah, never, never occupied that role of Oriental potentate and despot which was held by the kings of Egypt, of Assyria, of Babylon, of Syria or by the other kings of antiquity. Frequently you read in the Bible of revolutions and rebellion; frequently you read in the Bible that the prophet, who was the monitor of that desert tradition of freedom, denounced the king to his face; and it was in the name of a law greater than that of royalty that Samuel faced Saul, that Nathan denounced David, that Shemaiah imprecated Rehoboam, that Elijah cursed Ahab, and that Jeremiah pronounced doom upon Zedekiah, because "he hearkened not to the voice of the prophet speaking in the name of God."

The king in Israel was always subject to the same moral law binding upon common man. There was no king worship in Israel. That is significant, because among all the peoples of antiquity the king was worshiped as divine. The Pharaoh of the Egyptian was always addressed in the following terms: "Lord of heaven, lord of earth, sun, life of the whole world, lord of time, creator of the harvest, maker and fashioner of mortals, giver of life to all the host of gods."

The king of Israel was denounced by a prophet. The highest compliment which the Bible can pay to a king is this: that he did that which is pleasing in the sight of God. When the Syrian general Naaman came to the Hebrew king to be cured of leprosy, thinking that the Hebrew king possessed the same divine attributes that the kings of other peoples were said to possess, the Hebrew king replied: "Am I God to kill or to make alive?" You will understand exactly what I am trying to emphasize when you contrast this point of view of Israel as regards royalty with that of the enlightened and the advanced Greeks—Plato and Aristotle, the finest flower of Hellenic thought. Plato in his *Republic* declared that the ideal polity was a monarchy and that the ideal ruler was a king, who was at the same time a soldier and a philosopher. Aristotle maintained that kingship is the most divine and primary form of political organization. When you contrast Plato and Aristotle with Samuel, who looks upon kingship as apostasy from God, you will realize the essential difference in outlook between Israel and other peoples.

After the destruction of the First Temple and the Babylonian exile, when our forefathers returned from Babylon to Palestine and rebuilt their country, they had no kings at all. For hundreds of years, for nearly a half of a millennium, they governed themselves by the political autonomy they possessed. Then there was the interlude of the Hasmonean dynasty, which lasted for a comparatively short time. After the destruction of the Second Temple took place and Israel was exiled from Palestine, for nearly nineteen hundred years Israel has lived, scattered to the four corners of the earth, a fairly united, a fairly integrated people, but possessing no king and no potentate and no pope, no central authority in the hands of a privileged group or a privileged individual. That is an amazing thing. For Israel has not lived during these last nineteen hundred years as a host of gypsies without any internal organization or control or discipline. There has been a very strong inner control and inner discipline, but not a control superimposed by a reigning family or a feudal lord or by a religious autocrat. It is the authority voluntarily assumed by people in a democratic organization. For Israel believed—and this is essential to an understanding of our religion—that every human being had a worth and a dignity comparable to the worth and the dignity of the highest human being, and therefore Israel declared: "All the children of Israel are sons of kings!" To look upon every human being, the humblest of the humble and the lowliest of the low, as the son of a king, a prince, is to get a totally different conception of life from that of peoples who enslaved millions, and who had castes and gradations and social stratification. Israel established a perfect equality, a basis, a level of supremacy for all human beings.

When you leave the realm of the political and enter the realm of the economic, you find that same democratic impulse at work. When you read your Bible, you come across social legislation enacted to protect the individual against exploitation, against monopoly, against the loss of patrimony. The Bible is full of this progressive legislation; I say "progressive" because these laws were far in advance of their day, and they are far in advance of our day. When you read them you will understand them only as you know that they are based on the conviction that all human beings are entitled to the same rights and privileges and opportunities. "For unto Me are the children of Israel slaves; they are not slaves unto slaves."

Unless you bear this fact in mind, that in the soul of Israel there was always a vibrant, democratic passion, you will not understand the prophets of Israel at all. Because it was in the name of that imperishable and invincible desert tradition of democracy that the prophets of Israel denounced the oppressors of mankind, those who ground the faces of the poor into the dust and turned aside the way of the humble. It was in the name of that democratic principle that they wielded the scorpion whip of their fury upon all those who exploited their fellow men, and it was in the name of that tradition of equality and human responsibility that they championed the cause of the denied and the dispossessed and the broken and beaten of life.

The whole struggle between the priest and the prophet which rings through the pages of the Bible is comprehensible only as you remember that the priest represented a privileged class, and that the prophet was the spokesman of the Jewish laity who challenged the prerogatives and the privileges of the priesthood. Prophecy in Israel was not merely a protest against idolatry. It was that. It was not merely a protest against the supremacy or primacy of ritual and cult in religion. It was that. Prophecy was not only the upreaching of the sensitive soul of the race "for the Kingdom of God." It was that. But it was something more, too. Prophecy in Israel was the passionate crying of the Jewish layman for full lay participation and leadership in the life of the people.

The priest maintained that he is to be the teacher of the Law. Well and good. Let him teach the Law. But so may a layman not of the Aaronic family become a teacher of the Law and of the religious life of the people, provided he is prepared for it; provided he has prepared himself for that function. You will probably recall from your reading of the Bible the story of the rebellion of Korah. It is a story that has been frequently misunderstood.

Who were the rebels under the leadership of Korah? They were not a nondescript people. The Bible speaks of them as the elect men of the group, men of renown. What was their complaint? These princes of the congregation, these men of renown, these leaders of the laity assembled themselves and said unto Moses and unto Aaron, who are here assumed to be the representatives of the priestly class: "Ye take too much upon yourselves seeing that all the congregation are holy, every one of them, and the Lord is among them; wherefore, then, lift ye up yourselves before the assembly of the Lord."

The whole congregation is holy, not merely the priest. There you have one reflex of that bitter struggle that was waged through the ages between the class and the masses of the people. When, later on, two laymen, Eldad and Medad, began to prophesy in the camp, Joshua cried unto Moses, "Moses, shut them in!" Here are laymen trespassing. They dare to prophesy. They have no right. Moses replied: "Art thou jealous for me? Would that the whole people of the Lord were prophets, and that God, the spirit of God were upon them."

That same struggle between democracy and autocracy is reflected again in the centuries-old struggle between the Pharisees and the Sadducees. What was the struggle between these two sects? Why, it was simply this: the Sadducees, who, as the name indicates, were the party of the priesthood, maintained that the priests were the sole monitors of religion and the sole legislators in matters of religion; that laymen had no right to trespass. The Pharisees, who represented the masses, whose rallying place was the synagogue, just as the Sadducees' rallying place was the Temple—the Pharisees maintained that God gave to all the Law and the sanctuary. "The Torah which God gave unto us is the heritage of the whole house of Israel." And every layman, every human being has a right to read the Law, to teach the Law, to interpret the Law, and to evolve new laws to meet the advanced needs of life.

The attitude on the part of the masses of Israel that the Torah was given to all, not merely to a small group of functionaries, led to a remarkable fact in Jewish life. The Jewish people was the first to establish a universal system of education, for young and old, for rich and poor. Josephus two thousand years ago makes the statement: "Our chief concern is to educate our children well." There was hardly a town in ancient Palestine that could not boast of a school or of an academy. In fact, the town which did not have a teacher and a school was looked upon as accursed.

Learning was democratized. There was no small group at the top that monopolized learning and study and religious authority, and handed down its decisions to the masses. The faith and the lore and the learning of Israel became the possession of the whole house of Israel; and that has continued to this day. When people tell you that Jews are individualists; when people tell you that Jews are more or less rebellious; when people tell you that Jews question always, that is part and parcel of a racial temperament which has been developed through endless centuries of education. Every individual Jew was encouraged to be an individualist, to be an authority by himself.

Had I the time I would indicate to you how such an important movement in the Middle Ages as Karaism, the movement of the Scripturalists, those who challenged the authority of the rabbis, denied the authority of the Talmud, and claimed that our only authority is the Bible—how that movement and the later mystic movement during the Middle Ages both had their source in this democratic passion of the people.

Had I the time I should indicate to you how a movement like Hasidism also had deep roots in the democratic life of the people. For at that time, 150 years ago in eastern Europe, the rabbis had become an aristocratic class possessing tremendous power and influence in Jewish life, and they looked upon those who were not rabbinic scholars with a certain contempt. The masses of the people, who could not, because they did not have the time, devote themselves to rabbinic dialectics and to the finesse of rabbinic speculation, felt themselves spiritually excluded. There arose a movement among the masses, led by Israel Baal-Shem, who said that real Judaism is not this dry, sunless, cold legalism of the rabbis. Real Judaism is the warmth and the passion of faith, and that belongs to everybody. The essence of Judaism is to worship God with sincerity and without any sublety. And Hasidism swept like wildfire, through the communities, a movement which was nothing more than an upthrust of the same ever-present democratic passion of the race claiming that the glories of faith belong to all, to the rich and the poor, to the learned and the unlearned—to all.

There is this one final thought I should like to leave with you. You have heard it said that liberal Judaism emphasized the ideal of the mission of Israel, and some of our luminant fellows of the intelligentsia have, in recent years, elected to make sport of this ideal of the mission of Israel, thinking thereby to attack liberal Judaism at its most vulnerable point. Now the fact of the matter is that in making the ideal of the mission focal in its ideology liberal Judaism placed itself in direct line of descent from the prophets and the Pharisees. For what is the ideal of the mission of Israel? It is nothing but democracy applied to religion. That is all it is in its profoundest implications. Among all peoples of antiquity there was a small priestly class who were looked upon as possessing a certain exclusive sanctity. The priest was singled out as a man possessing a higher degree of sanctity and holiness than the rest of the people. But the genius of Israel would not tolerate that distinction; the genius of Israel maintained that if there was anything at all to this concept of holiness in life, if human beings can truly raise themselves to a level of holiness, then that holiness is the prerogative not of the few but of all. And so the democratic genius of Israel placed as its goal to make of the whole people of Israel "a kingdom of priests and a holy people."

Here was an amazing and revolutionary concept. Among no people in antiquity or in this day do you find this thought dominant: that a whole people, mind you, not merely a few within the people, but a whole people, young and old, men, women, and children, are to become priests of the living God, holy men devoted to an ideal. That is the ideal of the covenant of Israel. God made a covenant with the whole people of Israel to be his emissaries, his missionaries, his spokesmen, his prophets in the world.

It may be that we are no longer fit to be God's spokesmen in the world. I do not know. It may be that the time has come for us to abandon our historic role of a covenanted, consecrated people. It may be that we no longer have the desire or the will or the capacity to function as the shock troops of the Almighty. That may be so. But we must always remember that we cannot rewrite history or revamp that which has already taken place. What has been is. The Jew throughout the ages did conceive of himself as a covenanted people, as being subjected to a mission in life. That mission was the work not of the rabbis but of the whole people. Why our synagogue? What was it but a layman's institution? At the altar any layman could come up and worship and lead the congregation in prayer. At the reading of the Torah any layman of clean hands and pure heart could come up and read and preach to the congregation.

That democratic religious conception you find among no other people in the world, and that is the most exalted expression of the genius of our race. Whenever ten people met they could build a synagogue; they could take a room and convert it into a synagogue—anywhere. We have no sacramentalism in Jewish life. The whole people became a people of priests. Liberal Judaism's great mistake was not in retaining the ideal of the mission of Israel, not in challenging every Jew to a type of life consistent with the role of a religious teacher and leader but in underestimating the importance of the people of Israel, the group discipline. It spoke of the mission of Israel, but it forgot to preserve or to develop a mode of living which would constantly remind the Jews that they are a covenanted and a consecrated people.

Liberal Judaism began under the influence of the ideas of the French Revolution—liberty, equality, fraternity. When modern Reform Judaism began, many people actually believed that the great day of Jehovah was near at hand: a new dawn was breaking for mankind; the old order was giving way to a new one; all religious differences would be wiped out; all national antipathies would disappear. Consequently they felt that Israel, instead of retaining its distinctiveness and its uniqueness in custom, in observances, in practices, ought to give them all up and join in the one family of mankind.

Every revolution is a seedbed for apocalyptic dreams, for vast impractical vision. Well, those who followed that thought through were soon lost to Israel, because the day of liberty, equality, and fraternity did not materialize. It has not materialized yet. And the same apocalyptic dreams are in the air today as a result of the World War. The World War, too, spoke in terms of universal peace and universal brotherhood and universal righteousness—one mankind, one great family, one great religion. Some of our Jews have been stampeded into a pathetic self-abdication. Why remain Jews? Why insist upon our own identity when the world is fast marching to a day of universal peace? Other people do not believe as the Jews do. Why not join in one great family?

But the patient, sober Pharisee, the patient, sober Jew who knows his history, who knows what has happened and can draw conclusions about what will happen, that patient, sober Jew will not permit himself to be stampeded. He will know that many and many a sharp and desperate battle will yet have to be waged before the ideals of our people, for which we shed our blood, before the sacred dreams of our race will ever be approximated. That patient and sober Jew will bethink himself not only of the abstract ideals of his people but of his people itself. He will think not only of the faith of Israel but of Israel. He will think not only of prophecy in Israel but of Israel which gave birth to prophecy and to prophets. In other words, he will die to maintain a strong group loyalty, a strong group discipline which will conserve him for his tasks of tomorrow.

In a legend of the rabbis, the prophet Elijah was approached by a Jew who said, "Prophet, I have two great loves in my heart, and I do not know to which one to devote myself most. One is the Torah and the other is the people of Israel. Which of the two is greater?" The prophet answered: "Most people would say to you the Torah is more important. I say unto you the holy people of Israel is more important." For it is of that people that prophets came to mankind, and it is that people that may yet give another Bible to mankind. It is out of the soul and genius of that race that many a new and startling revelation will come to mankind.

In a renewal of Pharisaic Judaism lies the hope of our faith. In the renewal of a democratic, disciplined, religious community lies the hope and the promise of Judaism. There is, to my mind, enough of power and enough of beauty and enough of glory in the three major concepts of Israel —the faith of Israel, the people of Israel, the land of Israel—there is enough of beauty and power and magnificence in these three concepts to enkindle the enthusiasm of our people and of our youth. We must conserve them all. Everything which contributes to the enrichment, to the intensification of Jewish life—our customs, our tradition, our hope of national rehabilitation, our language, our law, our literature; everything which can serve as a bulwark, a prop, and a mainstay in Jewish life, liberal Judaism ought to preserve, and we ought to challenge our youth with a faith exalted, imperial, majestic, "a flaming faith," if you will, a faith in a mission.

We ought to train our young people in the unflinching and invincible conviction that they have been born into a community of priests, into a household of a holy people dedicated to the holy ideals of mankind; that it is their crown and their immortality to be identified with a group of men who long ago, at the foot of Mount Sinai, pledged themselves to be "the servants of God." Their lives must be different, finer, nobler, harder. The weak among them will reject it; the strong and the high-spirited will accept the challenge and the opportunity.

This is what I mean when I speak of the democratic impulse in Jewish history. A real Jew is a passionate democrat, not only in regard to political life but in regard to economic and social and religious life. In all the departments of the world he seeks the fulfillment of the individual's life; he seeks expansion, growth, freedom, opportunity for all the children of God. It is the peculiar mission of our people to be the spokesmen of that democratic ideal to mankind.

"But Mordecai Bowed Not Down!"

SERMON, THE TEMPLE
MARCH 8, 1936

"The Jews rejoiced—in joy, happiness, and honor." That is the keynote of Purim. Purim is a festival of relaxation for the Jewish people. The Jew, in spite of the strain and tension of his life in the Galuth, in the exile, knew how to relax. He knew how to distill some joy and gladness out of his life's experience, however somber and tragic it ofttimes was. For the Jewish people was always a healthy people, not given to moodiness, moroseness, pathological depressions. The Jewish people always believed in a God of whom it could exclaim time and time again: "Thou hast turned my mourning into rejoicing." A bow which remains constantly strung taut sooner or later breaks. Our people knew how to unbrace, how to relax.

Israel had its Sabbaths, its festivals, its seasons of gladness. And the happiest day of all its seasons of gladness was Purim. Purim was a carnival, a festival of hilarious joy, masquerade, dancing, singing, feasting. On Purim the spirit of revelry was introduced into the most sacred of places, and during the reading of the Megillah, the Scroll of Esther, pandemonium broke loose in the synagogue when the name of Haman was mentioned.

"These days shall be remembered and observed in every generation," you read in the Megillah. And the days of Purim were observed and remembered in every generation. Why? Because the festival of Purim is so characteristic of Jewish experience in the exile; Purim is our one festival whose locale is in the exile, outside of Palestine, and everything connected

277

with the story of Purim is typical of Jewish experience in exile from those days to these.

First of all the story of Esther is a story of the uncertainty and impermanence characteristic of Jewish life in the Diaspora. For years people had lived at peace in the vast empire of Persia. Suddenly out of the clear sky came this desperate fact into their lives—that a man close to the king had been angered by a Jew and, because of his anger, he had persuaded the king to destroy not merely this man and his family, but the entire Jewish people. The tragic insecurity of the Jews in the Diaspora is brought out most dramatically in the Megillah: "And thy life shall hang in doubt before thee." You will have no assurance in your life. That has been the mark of the exile.

In those days as in these days, there came a recrudescence of anti-Semitism. Haman was not the first nor the last of the anti-Semites. A thousand years before Haman, Pharaoh sought to destroy the Jews of Israel, and twenty-five hundred years later, another anti-Semite in Germany is seeking to annihilate the Jews. In a few weeks we will celebrate Passover and will read in the Haggada this rule of exile life: "Not one man alone arose to destroy us, but in every generation people will arise to seek and destroy."

From a reading of the Book of Esther, we learn how little originality there is to these foes of Israel—how identical are all their motives and their methods in those days as in these days. For example, Haman was not at all of Persia any more than Hitler is of Germany. Haman was an Amalekite, an immigrant. The naturalized must prove their loyalty. Because Haman was an Amalekite, and a stranger, he was a super-patriot. Haman started out on his anti-Semitic career with a personal grudge against Mordecai. Mordecai, who sat in the gate of the palace of the king, would not kneel to Haman as did all the other people. The rabbis explained Mordecai's boldness by saying that Haman carried upon his garment the symbol of an idol, and as a Jew Mordecai was forbidden to kneel to any idol. Be that as it may, Haman became angry at Mordecai. Hurt pride led him to turn against Mordecai and his people. Haman was not satisfied to put his hand out toward Mordecai alone; he turned against Mordecai's people. How characteristic this is of Jewish experience in exile! The anti-Semite starts with a personal grudge against some individual Jew and ends up as an enemy of the entire people.

There is no originality among the anti-Semites. Haman, like all anti-Semites preceding and following him, found high-sounding titles and phraseology for his spite and enmity. He masked greed and malice under the cloak of patriotism. Because of his personal grudge against Mordecai, Haman proceeded to incite charges against the Jews on the ground that all Jews are disobedient, traitorous, dangerous to the empire. Today in Germany, economic rivalry, competition, hatred of the competitor, and envy of the Jew cloak themselves in the garb of patriotism, nationalism, and pride of race and blood. Haman resorted to bribery: he offered ten thousand talents of silver to the king in order to win his signature on an edict of annihilation. The anti-Semite either bribes outright or with promises of the great boon which will come to the nation if the Jews are expelled or annihilated. Hitler promises golden days of glory for a Germany *Judenrein*.

Haman appealed to the king on the basis of differences which exist between the Jew and the non-Jew—a favorite device of all enemies of Israel. "Theirs is a scattered people and their religious customs are different from ours." Suspicion and fear of the unknown can easily be stimulated in the masses. The masses love conformity, unity. When you arouse them to a sense of fear, a sense of difference, you are on the way to victory —in those days as in these days in Germany.

Haman did not persuade the king at once. The king was unwilling to destroy the Jews. Our Midrash tells us that Haman carried on a protracted campaign of propaganda before he finally persuaded the king, just as the Nazis have carried on fifteen, eighteen years of propaganda to poison the German mind against the Jews. If you repeat something often enough, the people come to accept it as an axiom, something which requires no proof, no investigation: that is the dangerous power of propaganda and its appeal to the anti-Semite.

There is no originality in the anti-Semite even in his ruthlessness. Pharaoh in Egypt was satisfied with the destruction of children. Every male child that was born was to be thrown into the Nile. Nebuchadnezzar destroyed the First Temple, and rooted out a nation. Haman, too, tried to uproot, to annihilate. He wanted to uproot the last germ of the house of Israel. Haman then and Hitler now. There is little imagination among our enemies.

And from the same Book of Esther, we read how deliverance comes to our people, how our people are saved from hate. Deliverance comes as a result of the loyalty of the Jews. Mordecai was strong, proud, persevering; Mordecai would not bow down, would not court toleration through kneeling. Esther, at the risk of her life, intercedes for her people. Courage, faith, loyalty—these are the factors which will save our people whenever persecution comes. The Jews in these trying times must remember the lesson and not kneel, must not bow down to untoward circumstances, must not become servile or stampeded.

Our strategy must always be to join forces with all the liberal elements in the world and fight this recrudescent barbarism with every power at our disposal, to harass, to undermine, and ultimately to destroy it. The German problem will be solved when the Nazis are destroyed, not before, and in no other way. Any Jew who, because of his timidity or complaisance, does not enter the struggle today to save the precious values of civilization, who does not fight for democratic human life, is underwriting his own suicide.

There can be no peace for sixteen million Jews in the world if the program and the policies of the Nazis spread throughout the world. It is not going to spread if the Nazis are destroyed. Even if we get two or three million Jews out of countries in Europe and settle them in Palestine, that does not solve the problem for the rest of the Jews who are going to remain in the Diaspora. So, our problem is to fight for an order of society which will allow us to live any place, anywhere on the face of the earth.

It is not enough to raise money for relief. It is important to raise money for relief, but it is more important to raise money for war against the enemies of civilization.

Haman prepared the gallows for Mordecai, and on those gallows not Mordecai but Haman was hanged. The Nazis prepare destruction for the Jewish people, but there is a law of history which operates not only in Shushan but in Berlin. And that law of history says that in the long last, bigotry, intolerance, and hate do not win the day. Haman, the symbol of hate, is led by Mordecai, the symbol of faith, in triumph through the capital. In the long last, it is the ideals of freedom, good will, and tolerance that will win in these days.

So Purim comes to us with a reassuring message. When Mordecai heard the decree that the king had issued on the thirteenth day of Adar, that all the Jews of Persia were to be destroyed, he was, of course, terribly depressed. He put on sackcloth and ashes and went through the streets wailing and bemoaning the fate which was to overtake his people. He met three little Jewish boys coming from school. He stopped one and asked him: "What did you study in school today?" And the lad recited to him a verse from the Book of Proverbs which he had learned that morning: "Do not be afraid of a sudden terror and the wickedness of thine enemies, for God will be kind and He will keep thy foot from being caught." Mordecai turned to the second lad. "What did you study in school this morning?" And the boy quoted a verse from the prophet Isaiah: "You enemies of Israel take counsel together but your counsel will be destroyed. Speak the word of destruction but it will not come to pass, for God is with us." And he turned to the third little lad and asked: "What did you study in school this morning?" And he also quoted a verse from Isaiah: "Listen to me, O House of Jacob: unto old age I shall be with you. Even to hoary hair I will carry you. I made you and I will carry you. I will bear you up and I will deliver you."

When Mordecai heard what these three little Jewish lads had learned on that day, on the day of the dire decree, he laughed long, loud, and joyously. Mordecai laughed on that day, and for the twenty-five hundred years since that day, Mordecai's fellow Jews throughout the world, however dark the world around them may be—on the festival of Purim, on this festival of reassurance, on this day which reminds them of recurrent threats and of the deliverance of the people, the brothers of Mordecai laugh joyously and confidently, and, laughing, they face the future.

Seeing Our Problem
Against the Larger Background

RADIO ADDRESS, UNITED JEWISH APPEAL
FOR REFUGEES AND OVERSEAS NEEDS
MARCH 18, 1939

Czechoslovakia has ceased to exist as an independent country and the situation has again changed for the worse. Hitler destroyed it. The Czech nation has been absorbed and politically obliterated within the Third Reich. Slovakia, too, is now a German protectorate. Thus the Nazi Government, which in six short years has made stateless and homeless two million people, Jews and non-Jews, is now shattering the lives and fortunes of hundreds of thousands of new victims in a conquered land which is non-German by race, and which until recently was a free and tolerant democracy. Another half-million potential refugees, Jewish and non-Jewish, have been created overnight. All who had loved their country too dearly, and had resisted too loyally Nazi propaganda and penetration, all who belonged to a differing political faith, all who had fled from Germany to Czechoslovakia for refuge, and all Jews, and those who are declared to be Jews by the infamous Nuremberg race laws, are tonight marked and doomed men—they and their wives and their children. Many are already in concentration camps. Many more are on their way there, to taste the savage brand of Nazi sadism and *Schrecklichkeit.*

A veritable manhunt is on. No one will escape. The borders are closed. The occupation of Czechoslovakia was as swift and unexpected as that of Austria. There was no chance of escape. Men are trapped. The March horrors of Vienna are tonight being re-enacted in Prague. Many are committing suicide. Frightened people are seeking temporary sanctuary in the consulates and legations of foreign nations. The notorious and well-oiled Nazi routine of expropriation and confiscation, of robbing men of their businesses and possessions, is in full swing. When that process is completed, another half-million or more of "plundered, profaned, and disinherited" human beings will be cast out as human debris upon the mercy of the world.

Close upon the heels of this disaster comes the news of further anti-Jewish legislation in Hungary. Hungary has now absorbed one of the dismembered parts of Czechoslovakia—Ruthenia—which has a substantial Jewish population. Many Jews of Hungary will be forced to emigrate as a result of the new legislation which sharply restricts and, in many instances, completely destroys their opportunities to earn a living.

Likewise during this week, Great Britain, following the breakdown of the London Round Table Conference, announced its own tentative plan for Palestine. By the terms of this plan, Jewish immigration into Palestine will be reduced to an average of some fifteen thousand a year for the next five years. Jews had hoped that Palestine would serve as a ready and welcoming haven for the vast number of homeless refugees from all parts of Europe. Palestine is capable of absorbing a hundred thousand new immigrants a year. Under the terms of the mandate, Great Britain had undertaken to facilitate Jewish immigration into that country and to assist in the upbuilding of the Jewish National Homeland. It is now contemplated to reduce Jewish immigration drastically in order to ensure that the Jews shall forever remain a minority in Palestine.

Thus, at a time when a tragic and overwhelming catastrophe has overtaken the Jewries of Europe, forcing myriads of them to wander forth in search of new homes, the doors to their own homeland are to be steadily closed to them. The same wrongheaded and bankrupt British foreign policy of unilateral appeasement, which has been responsible for the dismemberment and annihilation of the brave and gallant little democracy in central Europe, is now visiting a similar fate upon the Jewish National Homeland in Palestine. In both cases, terrorism and lawlessness have been rewarded, and loyalty, labor, and law have been flouted and betrayed.

The prospect for millions of our people in Europe today seems hopeless indeed. But our history knows no hopelessness. We have passed through the deep, dark waters many times before. We are an ancient people. Thirty-five centuries have hardened us. We have learned how to draw strength from danger and defeat. In every testing hour of our history, in every time of wrath, we found our sure and strong defense in a reinforced loyalty and solidarity, in great love and ready sacrifice. And above all, in confident faith in the Guardian of Israel who neither sleepeth nor slumbereth:

"My flock was scattered for want of a shepherd, and became food for all the beasts of the field; my flock wandered over all the mountains and over every high hill; my flock was scattered over all the face of the earth, with none to seek or search for them. . . .

"Thus saith the Lord: Behold, here am I, and I will seek and search for my flock. As a shepherd searches for his flock on a day of whirlwind, when his sheep are scattered, so will I search for my flock; and rescue them from all the places to which they have been scattered, on the day of clouds and thick darkness."

The tragic fate which has now overtaken Czechoslovakia should make it clear to all men that the organized attack upon the Jewish people in many parts of Europe is not an isolated phenomenon, to be explained in and by itself, but rather part of a larger sinister design. It is part of a major offensive, along the entire front, not alone against the rights of all minorities, but against the rights and independence of all smaller nations. Imperialism is on the march again in Europe—and in that part of Europe which has always been the bloody arena of rival imperial ambitions. Minorities and small states are pawns in this desperate and infamous game of empire. They are first enmeshed in a web of scandalous intrigue, conspiracy, and propaganda, and then ruthlessly and cynically sacrificed to power politics. The smaller states, which lie across the path of expanding empire, are systematically disrupted from within, disintegrated, and then absorbed.

In this skillfully elaborated technique of disruption, anti-Semitism has served as one of the handiest and most effective weapons. Anti-Semitism of the postwar era in Europe has been purely political and governmental. It is neither religious nor racial. It is not the attitude of peoples but the incitement of politicians and Fascist adventurers and agents of imperial intrigue. The racism of the Nazis was only a grotesque façade for a cunning and conscienceless political strategy by which to divide the German people, discredit liberalism and democracy, and disrupt the German Republic. Since their coming to power, the Nazis have consistently employed anti-Semitism to confound the political life of those countries which they have marked down as steppingstones in the imperial-expansion program of the Third Reich. By means of it, they succeed in destroying their democratic forms of government. They sow discord and disunion among their people and undermine their power of resistance to Nazi aggression.

Some of the smaller nations and minority groups of Europe be-guiled themselves into believing that it was only the Jewish minority which would be singled out for persecution and destruction. They were immune. Some of them even introduced within their own borders some of the anti-Semitic tactics and practices of Berlin, and consented to act as Nazi marionettes. They erred grievously. They should have taken warn-ing from the Nazi persecution of the Jews. When the elementary rights of one minority group are flouted with impunity, the rights of all minority groups are endangered. When law is denied to one, tyranny is likely to overtake all. When there is no respect for the inalienable rights of men or religions or races which are too weak to defend themselves, there will be no respect for the inalienable rights of nations which are too weak to defend themselves. Hitler, the arch anti-Semite, has now finally revealed himself in his true colors as the archenemy of all minority groups and small nations in Europe. The rape of Czechoslovakia is part of the same outrageous scheme of power politics and empire-building as the robbing and looting of the Jewish group in Germany, and the shameless exploita-tion of anti-Semitism.

The Jewish problem in Europe is thus bound up with the whole problem of the protection of the rights of minorities and of smaller na-tions. It is part of the problem of collective security in the world. It is also bound up with the classic ideals of liberty, peace, and brotherhood, whose progress has been so sharply interrupted in our day. When this progress will be resumed it is difficult to say. Hard and desperate days lie ahead for mankind—for Jews and non-Jews alike. The forces of reaction and blackest tyranny are triumphantly on the march. Democracy has suffered one severe defeat after another. The League of Nations lies shattered and discredited at our feet. The free spirit of man stands shaken and frightened today in a dazed and apocalyptic mood, as if awaiting some crash of doom.

But though our hearts are heavy and our minds perplexed, we should not despair. We should try to understand our age against the back-ground of the ages. We should endeavor to appraise our present hour in terms of what has gone before. In so doing, we shall gain perspective, confidence, and courage.

What seems like Armageddon at first is in reality but another bitter skirmish in the age-old and irrepressible conflict between the religious and moral traditions of mankind, as represented in Judaism and Christianity, symbolized in the concepts of law, freedom, peace, brotherhood, and the inviolable rights of man—and the indurate traditions of paganism symbolized in the concepts of power, state idolatry, autocracy, militarism, conquest, and war.

The outcome of this conflict cannot be in doubt. Man, though frequently yielding to fear, pressure, and panic, will not permanently submit himself to intellectual and spiritual serfdom, however great the deceptions and beguilements which a cynical government, bent upon power, will through a thousand and one forms of propaganda, practice upon him. In the long run, man will accept no substitutes for the autonomy of his spirit and the sovereign freedom of his questing and adventuring mind. Man does not wish to be a robot, or the blind instrument of some usurping state bureaucracy. Man wants freedom and dignity and a sense of personal and inherent worth. There is also something in man which at long last revolts against the mystic adoration of force, the everlasting brandishing of fists, and against national and racial chauvinism and exhibitionism. There are deeper sources of human inspirations whence well up irrepressibly the redemptive power of compassion, love, and goodwill, the ideals of human solidarity, justice, and peace.

Mankind will sooner or later return to these classic ideals of civilization. We are not at the end of a way, at the edge of a wilderness, but on a long broken detour. We shall return to the golden highway. But this return will not come about automatically and as a matter of course, but only as the result of the patient labor and the heroic faith of those people who, in spite of the world's vast turmoil, still think with a minimum of bias and feel with a maximum of self-restraint—who have lost neither their vision nor their perspective, who are conscious both of their strength and of their mission, and who are determined to carry on, even as a saving remnant, in these times of spiritual crisis and tribulation. Upon these people, working faithfully each in his sphere to preserve the precious values of a free society, rests today the ultimate salvation of our world.

There are periods in human history when conditions become so bad and problems so involved and seemingly impossible of solution that whole generations are seized with a desire to escape. Men begin to yearn for some distant hermitage of tranquillity from which the urgencies and anxieties of the world would be excluded and wherein all life would be beautifully simplified. Here and there an individual may free himself from the coils and involvements of his day and age and find sequestered peace on some isle of ease. But for the millions of men, this is quite impossible. There is no running away. There is no peaceful valley to which the masses of mankind can retire and, amidst peace and pleasant labor, live unhurried and unharassed lives, savoring all the loveliness of existence.

It is only out of the hard and bitter realities of life, through struggle and suffering, by means of hard planning and building, slowly and with many heartbreaking setbacks, that men can construct a cleaner and lovelier order of life for themselves and for their children. For all men of spirit, this age should be a challenge, not a disillusionment or a despair.

We Jews, especially, should learn to see our problem against the background of the entire world's problem and also against the background not of the last few years, but of generations, nay, centuries. We are bearing today a double load of the burdens which all free men are bearing. Frequently that has been our fate in the past. It is our cross and our crown and our immortality. Perhaps it is the key to our strange destiny so underlaid with grandeur and with pain. We never succumbed, and as long as we remain faithful to the God whose name and nature our seers revealed to mankind, as long as we serve Him in simple truth, in justice, in love, and in sacrifice, dealing our bread to the hungry, bringing the poor that are cast out to our homes, and satisfying the afflicted soul, so long will light ever rise in our darkness, and the gloom shall be as the noonday . . .

For us Jews, too, this age of surge and thunder, of suffering and menace, should be a compelling and undeniable challenge, not a disillusionment or a despair.

Religion in Present-Day Jewish Life

ADDRESS DELIVERED AT THE THIRTY-SIXTH
BIENNIAL CONVENTION, UNION OF
AMERICAN HEBREW CONGREGATIONS
CINCINNATI, JANUARY 17, 1939

Many factors have tended to make religion of secondary importance in the life of our people.

Religion, generally, has been pushed into a subordinate position in the Western world. Science has steadily divested it of many of its franchises. The satisfactions which men have derived from the increase of power, wealth, and material well-being brought about by science have placed science upon the pedestal which was formerly occupied by religion, whose gifts are now less prized and sought after. Science has successfully refuted many pronouncements which were made by religion in its sacred texts concerning the universe, nature, and man. This has cast suspicion upon much else in religion. The separation of church and state, the growth of civil authority and the contraction of ecclesiastical authority, the secularization of education, and, in the realm of speculative thought, the divorce of philosophy from theology—all these have been both cause and effect of the diminishing importance of religion in modern society.

Other forms of loyalty have clamored for supremacy—loyalty to nation, country, race, class. Each of these derived its sanctions and mandates from sources other than religion, and proceeded to construct systems of thought with little or no reference to it.

The Jewish people left the ghettos of the Western world at a time when these secular movements were unfolding. The world from which the Jews emerged was thoroughly pervaded by religion. It had been thus pervaded for centuries. Every phase and activity of life was bound by its discipline. Nevertheless, the Jews yielded to the new temper of the age as readily as any other people. In some countries they not only caught up with the new secular mood of the Western world but outdistanced it in dogmatic ardor and intensity.

There transpired among the Jewries of western and eastern Europe not only reform movements designed to revamp their religious ideas and practices, to "modernize" them and to bring them into consonance with the new outlook of Europe, but also strong centrifugal movements away from Judaism altogether, movements of flight, not toward other faiths so much—these latter flights were dictated, as a rule, by careerism and social escalade—but toward religious negativism and indifference, expressed in non-affiliation with the synagogue and in a renunciation of the entire religious regimen of Judaism.

This flight from Judaism was also motivated by strong political and economic considerations. Throughout the nineteenth century, Jews struggled for emancipation. They reached out after complete equality. They believed that their distinctive religious beliefs and traditional way of life segregated them and disadvantaged them among men. They further believed that by surrendering their beliefs and traditions they would succeed in acquiring those rights and privileges which other peoples possessed. This political and economic motif behind the flight complex was soon rationalized into a system of thought, conveniently neutral and agnostic, which discounted religion generally and proclaimed that the scientific progress of mankind had finally outstripped religion, and that while religion might still have a certain usefulness for the young, the poor, and the unenlightened, cultured and prosperous folk could get along very well without it. All religious and racial differences were certain to be merged very soon in a common brotherhood of men, dedicated to the life of pure reason. The mighty accents of the American and French Revolutions and the other upsurging political struggles of the century reverberated through all this hopeful and wishful thinking. Thus enlightenment and emancipation were the Pied Piper whose music beguiled many Jews away from their ancient loyalties and spiritual securities.

The wealthy and the well-placed Jews especially pampered themselves with these comforting notions. The richer they became and the more important positions they occupied, the less need they had for religion. The upper classes, which had succeeded in reaching, if not the center, then at least the periphery of the non-Jewish world, were the most supercilious in their attitude towards Judaism. When men are prosperous they find it easy to dispense with God—especially with a Jewish God.

Fortunately not all Jews were of the same mind. Many refused to exchange spiritual treasures for material advantage. They saw neither the need nor the wisdom of it. They were of the opinion that if freedom and equality are to come to all men, they should come also to the Jews as a matter of right, as a restoration of that which belongs to them and to all men as a natural endowment, and not in payment for unwarranted sacrifices of religious convictions, a distinctive culture, and a historic way of life. They suspected, furthermore, that the new millennium might turn out to be quite as much of a mirage as many others in the long past of Israel, and, on the basis of past experiences, they feared that should another such reaction in their political and economic fortunes set in, Jews would find themselves spiritually shattered, homeless, and utterly bereft, unless they had the secured sanctuaries of Jewish life and faith into which to retreat for refuge and solace. Many other Jews, out of force of habit or because of the strong appeal of ancient ties and memories, remained constant. So Judaism was not lost.

Throughout the nineteenth and the early twentieth centuries, wide and ominous cracks appeared in the beautiful façade of European enlightenment and emancipation. Startling eruptions of violent anti-Semitism occurred, at one time or another, in nearly every country of western Europe. Medievalism raised its ugly head over and over again, either as a Magyar blood libel or a Germanic literary pogrom or a Gallic *cause célèbre* or an outright Slavic slaughter of Jews. The rains sadly disfigured the wall "daubed with whited plaster," and the foundations thereof were uncovered.

Some Jews were quick to read these warning signs. They returned to their faith and to their people as to a shelter from a gathering storm. Others, however, persisted in their hypnosis, discounted any evidence of an underlying menace, and blithely proceeded on their way. In the generation before the World War, Judaism in western Europe touched bottom, and languished also among vast sections of Jewry in the United States.

Then came the World War, which unleashed all the furies. Who can number the high hopes of mankind which perished upon its battlefields? What was apparently won was actually sunk and lost in their bloody bogs—freedom, democracy, the self-determination of peoples, the rights of minorities, and the vision of an international order based upon law, justice, and peace. Out of the ten million graves of the needlessly slain, there arose the dread ghosts of hatred, of national and racial passions, of arrogance and vindictiveness, of widespread want and bitter class struggle, and of a dread stampede towards force, violence, and terror as life's sole technique. These ghosts are dancing today their *danse macabre* in the hearts of men and nations. Civilization is plunging into darkness and chaos. A paganism far more crass and cruel than that of antiquity is engulfing the whole Western world.

For the Jewish people, the World War and its aftermath spelled Golgotha! A quarter of a century of mounting disasters and calamities culminating in the unprecedented horrors of recent months. Great Jewish communities, rich in history, culture, and achievement, among whom the dream of a free, enlightened, and tolerant humanity was most ardently cherished, have been plunged into Hell. Gone for them are enlightenment and emancipation. Gone are the dreams of human brotherhood and equality. Gone are the beckoning horizons of great careers and great service. Gone are all shelter and all security. Gone, even, the scant and tenuous security of the ghetto! Into exile, broken, stripped, and impoverished, they must go, even as their forefathers before them, who knew neither enlightenment nor emancipation. From countries and homes where they had known dignity, honor, power, and wealth, Jews, in their mounting legions, must now wander forth, bewildered and disillusioned, into a bewildered and disillusioned world.

For the world, generally, stands today bewildered and disillusioned. The strong and sure foundations upon which it had builded its life have been rudely shaken. That high optimism which fed upon truly remarkable achievements in every scientific field has vanished. Marvelous were the vistas which opened up before the eyes of men in the nineteenth century. Men could dream then and men did dream, unabashed, of a glorious and uninterrupted progress for mankind, of an unending conquest of nature, and of building, in a world of abundance, a civilization free from all poverty, ignorance, and war. "In the nineteenth century," wrote Victor Hugo, "war will be dead, the scaffold will be dead, hatred will be dead, frontiers will be dead, royalty will be dead, dogmas will be dead, man will begin to *live!*" But here we are in the twentieth century, and war is not dead, the scaffold is not dead, hatred is not dead, frontiers are not dead, royalty is not dead, dogmas are not dead, and man is beginning to *die*. The vista which stretches before our generation today ends at the edge of a wilderness. For twenty-five years now, men have lived in a world of mounting hate, intolerance, and bigotry, of revolutions, invasions, wars, of the rise and fall of empires amidst the slaughter of millions of their kind. Great peoples have destroyed their liberties and enslaved themselves. Millions of men cower today in terrorized submissiveness. The wealth of nations is being drained in preparation for wars which will also drain the lives of their people. The mind of man, trained and sharpened by generations of scientific education, is now applied to the perfection of the war technique. So that the discoveries which science records in our day in such great numbers no longer fill the hearts of men with pride or enthusiasm. They suspect that these things will not contribute either to their happiness or to their security, or to greater decency in the world. The human spirit stands today frightened, weighted down with apocalyptic foreboding, as if awaiting the crash of doom.

The thoughtful among men have accordingly begun to search earnestly for some way of salvation—a road away from disaster. They are seeking desperately hard to rediscover that vision which was somehow lost amidst the brilliant pageantry of scientific achievement in the last century, to the hurt and sorrow of the world. They understand now what the wise men of the earth have always known: that increased knowledge does not necessarily mean increased goodness or happiness, that facts are not in themselves blessings, that "truth can make us mad as well as free," that the prolongation of human life is not the same as the improvement of human life, that the acceleration of a process does not always insure a finer product, and that change does not necessarily spell progress. They realize now that the fault is not with science or education or democracy, as such, but with the interpretation which men put on them, with the omnipotence and autonomy which they ascribed to them, and with their failure to understand that science, education, and democracy are means and not ends in themselves.

What has been tragically missing in our civilization has been the compelling and coordinating belief in the great human goals which religion, and religion alone, has set for mankind, and towards the attainment of which science, education, and democracy must contribute if they are to fulfill their sole function. Mankind lost sight of these goals. Therefore human progress today has no clear direction. Good material and good tools are not enough for the builder. He must have a plan. To build a noble and enduring society, it is not enough to have wealth and intellect. Mankind must be possessed of the architectural plan, which the spiritual vision of man designed, and it must have the will and loyalty to follow that plan. That will and loyalty only the moral sense of man can provide. Without faith in God, the reality of spiritual vision as well as the sanctions of morality are quickly denied and rejected in the world.

Mankind's way of salvation is the way which leads back or forward to God.

In the same way, and even more earnestly, are thoughtful Jews reaching out today for the religious vision of Jewish life. For ours is a double measure of disillusionment and a double measure of misfortune. More than any other people do we require today the everlasting arms of a great religious conviction to sustain us.

To thoughtful Jews it is becoming increasingly clear that there are no substitutes in Jewish life for religion. Neither philanthropy nor culture nor nationalism is adequate for the stress and challenge of our lives. All these interests can and must find their rightful place within the generous pattern of Judaism. But the pattern must be Judaism, the Judaism of the Torah, the synagogue, and the prayer book; the Judaism of the priest, the prophet, the saint, the mystic, and the rabbi; the Judaism which speaks of God, and the worship of God, and the commandments of God and the quest of God. Most eloquently did Moses Hayyim Luzzatto, in his *Mesillat Yesharim*—the Path of the Upright—define Judaism in terms to which every classic teacher of Israel, I am sure, would have subscribed:

> We thus see that the chief function of man in this world is to keep the commandments, to worship God, and to withstand trial. The pleasures of this world should be only the means of affording that contentment and serenity which enables man to apply his mind to the fulfillment of the task before him. All of man's strivings should be directed toward the Creator, blessed be He. A man should have no other purpose in whatever he does, be it great or small, than to draw nigh to God and to break down all separating walls, that is, all things of a material nature, between himself and his Master, so that he may be drawn to God as iron to a magnet. He should pursue everything that might prove helpful to such nearness, and avoid everything that is liable to prevent it, as he would avoid fire. In the words of the Psalmist, "My soul cleaveth to Thee; Thy right hand upholdeth

me fast" (Ps. 63:9). Since man came into the world only for the end of achieving nearness to God, he should prevent his soul from being held captive by the things which hinder the realization of that end.

Our leaders would do well to understand this. Now that Jewish life is entering again upon an age of persecution and martyrdom, our people, and more especially our youth, require more than the example of generosity towards our unfortunate brothers overseas, and more than the example of a valiant defense of Jewish rights at home. They require the example of the practice of Judaism, as Luzzatto defined it: "to keep the commandments, to worship God, and to withstand trial"—the example of religious discipline, piety, and sacrificial loyalty. These leaders must help us to rebuild our inner world, now that our outer worlds are beginning to crumble again.

There have been many false prophets of ersatz Judaism in our midst who have frequently misled our people. There were those professional social workers who announced that a full complement of scientifically administerd hospitals and orphanages and other social agencies was a sufficient vade mecum for the Jewish people, and that the synagogue and the religious school were quite unnecessary. At best they were to be tolerated only as a concession to those who still take such things seriously, and in order not to create unpleasant friction in the community. Such social workers had many ready adherents among our would-be assimilated and rich Jews.

There were certain Jewish educators who resented the intrusion of religion in their ultra-scientific curricula. Judaism, they said, was not a religion, but a way of life—that is to say, *their* way of life, which, of course, was non-religious or anti-religious. Jewish education should, therefore, not be religious at all, only nationalistic and linguistic. At best the religious note might be smuggled in, but only as a concession to old-timers and cranks who do not know any better.

There were those Jewish spokesmen who offered Jewish nationalism as a substitute for Judaism, forgetting that nationalism as such, unredeemed by moral vision and responsibility, has sadly fragmentized our world, provincialized its peoples, and is driving nations madly from one disaster to another; forgetting, further, that there is a widely felt and widely answered need for religion and religious institutions even among peoples whose national life is already fully established in their own lands and who are possessed of a rich national culture. Amos, Isaiah, and Jeremiah felt the need to preach religion—God and obedience to God's moral law—to their people even though they were established as a nation in their own land and spoke their own language. It is not possible to brush aside the spiritual needs of Jews in the Diaspora and their problems of survival as Jews in lands outside of Palestine, where most Jews will continue to live, merely by talking long, loud, and enticingly about Palestine. The upbuilding of a Jewish National Homeland in Palestine is one great, urgent, and historically inescapable task of Jewry. The upbuilding of Jewish religious life in America and elsewhere throughout the world, inclusive of Palestine, is another. One is no substitute for the other. One is not opposed to the other.

Again there were other Jews who advised their people that Judaism can well be laid aside, now that the proletarian Messiah has already appeared in the land of the Slav, riding in a droshky, and the Kingdom of Heaven is near at hand.

All these false prophets have had their clamorous hour among us. But their hour is over. Thoughtful Jews are turning to the sure and classic highways of Jewish life and thought. We are not likely to be beguiled again, at least the men of this generation, by these prophets and their alien teachings.

Humanity has sickened of its Godless civilization. Because the spiritual interpretation of human destiny was allowed to languish, other interpretations have come to life and are now driving mankind mad. For when God is dethroned, His throne does not remain vacant for long. Some false god, some Wotan, Moloch, Mammon, or Mars, soon occupies it. Because the ideal of the imitation of God was banished from the hearts of men, the imitation of some Satan is now the ideal. In place of piety, reverence, humility, compassion, and self-sacrifice, other qualities—insolence, cruelty, aggression, and combativeness—are now extolled. Because men have rejected the ideal of the sanctification of human life under God, they now have a world in which human life is cheap, in which the stature of the individual has been reduced, his rights usurped by the state, his labor a commodity, and his life just a statistical item. Because the world rejected God, it rejected also man, fashioned in the image of God, possessed of a sacred and inviolable personality, endowed by his Creator with certain inalienable rights. Because men have ignored the sovereignty of God's moral law, they have a world in which men, parties, and governments have set themselves up above all law. Where there is no longer the Law of God, there ensues the law of the *duce*, the *Fuehrer*, or the commissar, before which all men must tremble.

Now that lights are going out everywhere in the world, men are turning to the Light of God.

Jews can do no less. Jews will do no less. I sense an incoming tide of faith among our people, a faith charged in some instances with deep mysticism. It should not surprise us, and it would be in keeping with similar moments in our past history, if our age should witness a strong mystic movement among our people. Such mystic movements followed the expulsion of the Jews from Spain and Portugal at the close of the fifteenth century and the appalling disasters which overtook Polish Jewry in the seventeenth century. The present-day expulsions of the Jews from Germany and Austria, the dismal plight of Jews throughout eastern Europe, the stress under which Israel finds itself everywhere, coupled with the distressed mood of mankind generally, may give rise to a strong mystic movement which will express itself in religion, literature, and art and in personal habits of thought and conduct.

In a sense, the problem of the survival of Judaism is much simpler in our day than at any time in the past. Our leaders need no longer expend the energy which was expended during the last century to persuade Jews to remain Jews. The doors of escape from Jewish destiny have been shut. The choice confronting intelligent Jews today is a very simple one. They have realized that God has not placed the shears of destiny—to be, or not to be—in their hands. Forces which they have not summoned are driving all would-be escapists back upon their people. Somehow there has always been an element of unavoidable compulsion, of the inevitable, in Jewish experience. It is the *baal korcha* element, the quality of shunless destiny. It was under such compulsion, the rabbis declared, that our forefathers accepted the Torah at Mount Sinai. "And that which cometh into your mind shall not be at all; in that ye say: 'We will be as the nations, as the families of the countries, to serve wood and stone.' As I live, saith the Lord God, surely with a mighty hand, and with an outstretched arm, and with fury poured out, will I be king over you . . . And I will cause you to pass under the rod, and I will bring you into the bonds of the covenant."

The choice today is not between survival and extinction, but between doom and destiny, between burden and mission. Shall we live our Jewish lives greatly or meanly? Shall Jews walk "darkling to their doom" or advance confidently and exultingly to their destiny along the eternal road which stretches from Ur of the Chaldees to the distant Messianic lands of *acharit ha-yamim?* Shall we quarrel with our fate and beat helpless hands against the unyielding bars of circumstances or shall we, by a miracle of faith, remembering that "stone walls do not a prison make," cease to be the unwilling prisoners of circumstance, and in the service of God, and of God in man, become magnificently free?

"The slave of God—he alone is truly free." Our choice today is between the *ol malchut* and the *ol malchut shamayim*—between the yoke of earthly kingdoms, which is grievously hard to bear, and the yoke of the Kingdom of God, which makes all other yokes easy to bear.

What hands shall weave the loom of our future years? Our own hands, tender and skillful, drawing the golden strands from our own treasures of wisdom, piety, passion, and dreams, which all the goodly folk from Abraham to our own day have stored for us? Or shall alien hands, rude and unsympathetic, weave the web of the destiny of ourselves and our children?

Now that many doors are closing, should we not open wide to our children the doors leading to the treasure-troves of their own people's spiritual and intellectual wealth, for their future sustenance, inspiration, solace, and pride? The days ahead will be hard days for them. Until the world completes the latest stage in its economic transformation and steadies itself again, after a long, violent period of readjustment, Jews, because they are everywhere an exposed minority, easily blamed and easily victimized, will be hammered on the anvil of every world event. The days ahead will be hard days for our children, but they need not be ignoble or unrewarding days. Give them their total heritage, the copious bounty of Judaism—the Torah, the synagogue, the prayer book, the noble literature, and the beautiful language of their people. Give them the millennial companionship of their kinsmen and their kinsmen's heroic faith and dreams and their matchless saga, and they will be matched with their great hour. They will then come to understand what it is in our heritage that has kept us alive; what it is that laid waste the paganism of the ancient world and now finds itself again in mortal combat with another paganism which it is also destined to destroy; what it is that makes their people the brunt of attack whenever privilege, power, and reaction make a major onslaught on the precious hopes of mankind, and why the ancient ideals of their people are forever the battle cries of upstruggling humanity. They will then come to understand that it is not because we are weak or unworthy that barbarous governments have vowed to destroy us, but because we are strong, and they fear us. Not us, but the faith which is in us, the torch which is in our hearts and the passion which is in our blood for the prophetic mandates of our Jewish heritage, for justice, freedom, brotherhood, and peace, for the vision of *ir ha-tzedek, kiryah ne'emanah*, "the city of justice, the city of faith," in place of the *ir ha-damim*, "the city of blood," built upon the pride of blood and upon glory drenched in the blood of the conquered, the despoiled, and the slain. These reckless adventurers of power, who have put all ethics, all science, and all religion in the service of a design for power, who have made all ethics relative to tribal temperament and national interests, who have forced upon civilian life the discipline, the dumb obedience, the drill, the barrack room, the court-martial, the censor, the espionage system, the whole code, complex, and outlook of the military, and, by so doing, have destroyed civilian life completely; these present-day heirs of the tradition of Ishmael, the Wild Man, "whose hand is against every man and every man's hand is against him," these heirs of the traditions of Esau, the Hairy Man, the *ish tzayid*, who sees life only as the hunter sees the hunted, and who delights "to live by his sword,"—these men abhor and dread the tradition of Jacob, the *ish tam*, the man seeking perfection through rational and moral pursuits, *yoshev ohalim*, content to live in the peaceful tents of work and study, devoted to the greatness of morals instead of the morals of greatness . . .

And understanding this—and understanding further that they must now become the active trustees of this classic tradition of civilization—they will, along with all other men of good will, feel themselves challenged. They will not be ashamed or cast down. They will face their world without fear or apology. They will not seek the world's approval—only God's. They will not be afraid of hostile voices—only of their own voice when silenced in fear. The insolence and naked impudicity of the heathens who rage will never humiliate them, only their own apostasy, backsliding and fear. They will try to be worthy of their great hour of testing!

The Questions That Await Us

TERCENTENARY ADDRESS
DETROIT, MICHIGAN
OCTOBER 17, 1954

This is an occasion to look backward and to look forward. We look back with pride and gratitude. We look forward with confidence and high hope. Our beginnings here were humble, as were the beginnings of all peoples who came to these shores. Steadily through the years, and more rapidly in the last three-quarters of a century, our numbers have increased and we have shared eagerly and gratefully in the growing and evolving life of America. Our people have become in outlook true children of the New World and, in service and devotion, loyal and proud citizens of the United States. They have served it patriotically in peace and in war. They have made creditable contributions to its material prosperity, to its political and social progress, to its democratic institutions, to labor and industry, to its arts, science, literature, and music. They have supported generously all the philanthropic and social agencies and institutions of their communities—Jewish and non-Jewish alike. They have been not an unworthy or unimportant part of the colorful, unique, and noble mosaic pattern which is America.

Nor have they ignored or forgotten their own religious heritage. They have remained faithful to it. Upon the shores of the new land they built their synagogues, their schools, and their institutions of learning and philanthropy, which have always embodied the ethical ideals and the way of life of our people. They did not isolate themselves from the lot of their fellow Jews in other parts of the world. They remained bound to them in fraternal solicitude. They helped them in their needs. They came to their defense when attacked. They poured out their generosity when tragedy overtook them. They rallied to the task of building the State of Israel when the historic moment arrived, and they have undergirded it with their support and unflagging interest since then.

They remembered why those twenty-three Jewish pilgrims came to Nieuw Amsterdam. They came here for the same reason that a generation before them another group of men and women came from England to Plymouth Rock. They wanted to remain loyal to their faith. They continued the noble tradition which was set by the founder of their faith, Abraham, who was the first pilgrim of mankind, for conscience' sake. Among the first things which the twenty-three Jewish pilgrims requested of Peter Stuyvesant, the governor of Nieuw Amsterdam, was permission to build a synagogue and to purchase a burial plot. They wanted to found a Jewish community.

Very few indeed were the possessions which these refugee pilgrims brought with them to the New World. But they did bring their most precious possession of all, the Bible. This book contained a verse which a century and a quarter later the founding fathers of the American republic had inscribed upon the Liberty Bell, a verse from the Book of Leviticus—"And ye shall proclaim liberty throughout the land unto all the inhabitants thereof." Liberty is the key idea in Judaism, along with the ideas of unity and compassion. Kings in ancient Israel were never permitted to be autocratic and absolute. They were never deified or worshiped, as they were throughout the rest of the ancient world and in the Greco-Roman world. All men—king, nobleman, priest, and common man— were subject to the same overarching moral law of God. A prophet in Israel could bring a king who had grievously sinned down to his knees by confronting him with the words, "Thou art the man." The passion for freedom was strong among our people throughout the ages. An eminent rabbi declared: "Every human being has the right to say, 'For my sake was the whole world created.' "

It was this same Bible which inspired the Puritans, who justified their anti-monarchial position and their demand for civil and political liberty by the words of the Old Testament. It was this same Bible which inspired the Declaration of Independence, the anti-slavery movement in the United States, and every movement for the economic and social advancement of the working masses of the people in the United States.

Many have been the contributions of our people to the progress of America during these last 300 years, but none has been as momentous as our spiritual contribution in fashioning its basic institutions and its dominant traditions. I venture to say that we Jews of America can make no more significant contribution as Jews to the advancement of our beloved country in the future than to preserve and express these basic spiritual elements in our historic faith which have molded the great civilizations of mankind.

We have now closed three centuries of living in this country. In no other land have our people been privileged to enjoy so long a period of uninterrupted and peaceful dwelling and labor. Can we think hopefully of the future as Jews and as Americans? I believe that we can. I believe that we have every right to do so, though we cannot be dogmatic about it, for progress is neither guaranteed nor automatic, nor can we ignore the fact that time and again the unforeseen and unpredictable in history have upset all man's most careful calculations.

Ours is a great age, and I believe we are entering into an even greater age. The wave of the future, the true direction of man's pilgrimage and destiny may, from time to time, be thwarted and opposed, dammed up, as it were, and obstructed, drawn off and retarded, but it cannot be permanently estopped.

In our day this moral forward thrust of man has encountered the stubborn and insolent resistance of Nazism, of Fascism, and of Communist dictatorship. These have violently resisted the spiritual aspirations which constitute mankind's wave of the future. They put shackles on man, even when they promised him larger freedoms. They divided and stratified men, even when they prated about a classless society. They fomented war even when they preached peace. But the onmoving tides of man's irresistible spirit have now swept over the shattered ruins of some of these sinister aberrations and dark conspiracies of the rebels against light— though they have not as yet entirely obliterated them. And the tides are now whirling around the bastions of the remaining dictatorships of the earth. They will surely succumb. They cannot, in the long run, win in the contest for man's heart and man's loyalties. Man has struggled through the long, weary centuries to free himself from the bondage of nature. He will not voluntarily and for long submit to the bondage of man. Neither dictatorship nor racialism nor statism nor militarism can or will command the fortunes of the human race. They represent the sunk wreckage of the past which the storms of our day have dredged up again from the bottom of their buried depths and have set afloat again dangerously along the ship lanes of the world.

The coming age will be a great age for America. The next hundred years at least seem likely to be known, I believe, as "The American Century," in the same sense as the nineteenth century was "The Century of Great Britain." Destiny has singled out our beloved country, the foremost democracy on earth, to give leadership to the world and to lead mankind out of the grave social, political, and economic predicament in which it finds itself. I believe that American leadership will prove itself equal to the challenge, if it will take counsel of faith and not of fear, and if it will be guided by the prophetic insights and the wide perspectives of the founding fathers of this republic.

I believe that our age will find the formula of toleration which will enable the many evolving and fluid forms of capitalism and socialism to work out their destinies in the one world in which we live. They may be irreconcilable in theory; they need not be in practice.

America will lead in finding the way. The way is not that of a global armament race which will impoverish the peoples of the earth—ourselves included—and end as such races always end—in the catastrophe of war. The way is rather that of conference, of courageous diplomacy, of giving urgent leadership in the United Nations to a program of speedy and balanced reduction of armaments and of help to the backward peoples of the earth.

I believe that the American people will earnestly strive to be worthy of the challenge and opportunities of the American Century.

And I believe, too, that it will be a great age for American Jewry if the catastrophe of war does not shatter its security and life. As a minority, we are helpless against the ravages of hate and demagoguery which war and economic depressions unleash. But given peace and economic stability, the American Jewish community will move forward and develop. It will expand its cultural and religious life and institutions, and will make worthy contributions to the total life of America.

If the American Jews of the coming decades will carry on uninterruptedly and with wisdom and discrimination, putting first things first, and accentuating the positive and indispensable enterprises of Jewish life, they will make the numerically largest Jewish community in the world also one of the greatest in terms of faith, culture, and scholarship. What may endanger our Jewish future here is not conscious escapism or deliberate assimilationist tendencies such as characterized Jewish communities elsewhere and at other times. Rather, our future may be endangered by an unconscious drift and a carefree relaxation of all disciplines, not out of conviction but out of sheer indifference—such as belonging to synagogues but not attending them, or sending children to Sunday schools which are so limited in time that they cannot really give an adequate Jewish education, or, as often happens, not giving children any religious instruction at all, or emptying the home of all Jewish content.

Too many of our people want an easygoing religion, one which does not challenge or disturb them, a religion without any spiritual travail, without any stab of thought or conscience, without any sacrifices, the religion of a self-pampering people. No religion can ever survive in that kind of emotional and intellectual vacuum, Judaism least of all.

It is a great virtue in our people that they are generous in heart—charitable and responsive to all human need and suffering. It is a noble tradition of Israel, a by-product of a religion which, foremost among all the religions of mankind, made charity and loving-kindness central in its code of human conduct. But Judaism is much more than charity, and the charitable impulse alone will not preserve our faith and our people. "This Book of the Law shall not depart out of your mouth, but you shall meditate on it day and night, that you may be careful to do according to all that is written in it; for then you shall make your way prosperous, and then you shall have good success." No Jewish community ever survived for long which did not cultivate Jewish learning and study and which did not cultivate the prescribed way of Jewish life, at least in its essentials. The axe must never be permitted to exalt itself over the man who wields it. . . .

What we should fear most is the rise of a generation of prosperous Jews who have no spiritual anchorage, or a generation of clever, restless Jews of quick ferment and high voltage, rooted in no religious tradition, reverent of no moral code, ignorant of all Jewish learning, and held to social responsibility by no inner spiritual restraint, who will rage and bluster all over the American scene from literature and art to politics and government and will commit their fellow Jews in the eyes of the American people. Such floating mines are a danger to any people, but especially to a minority group. Some of these mines are already exploding.

If American Jewry of tomorrow will restore to the center again what has become peripheral in our life—the synagogue, the school, the academy, and the religious disciplines of Judaism; if it will recapture the wisdom of our ancient teachers, who admonished us that the study of the Torah outweighs all other commandments, for it leads directly to them all, then American Jewry is destined to enjoy a resplendent century of spiritual growth in this gracious land.

THE ONE UNIVERSAL GOD does not require one universal church in which to be worshiped, but one universal devotion. In the realms of ascertainable facts, uniformity can be looked for. In the realms of art and philosophy there can be only sincerity of quest and expression—only dedication. Religion is the supreme art of humanity.

Judaism developed through the ages its own characteristic style, as it were, its own view of life, its code and forms of worship. It possesses its own traditions based on Torah and covenant.

Its adherents today find inspiration and spiritual contentment in it, as did their fathers before them, and wish to continue its historic identity within the configuration of other religious cultures. Other religions, too, developed their characteristic ways based on their unique traditions and experiences. There is much that all religions have in common and much that differentiates them. Their common purpose in the world will not be advanced by merger or amalgamation. Were all arts, philosophies, and religions cast into one mold, mankind would be the poorer for it. Unwillingness to recognize differences in religions is no evidence of broad-mindedness. To ignore these differences is to overlook the deep cleavages which existed in the past and to assume a similarity of doctrine and outlook which does not exist in the present. The attempt to gloss over these differences as a gesture of good will is a superficial act which serves neither the purposes of scholarship nor the realities of the situation. It is far better and more practical to look for ways of working together on the basis of a forthright recognition of dissimilarities rather than on a fictitious assumption of identity. Indifference to one's own faith is no proof of tolerance. Loyalty to one's own faith is part of a larger loyalty to faith generally.

SERMON, THE TEMPLE
FEBRUARY 3, 1952

"Where Judaism Differs"

From the very beginning of his preaching career, Rabbi Silver made a point of offering his congregation glimpses into the beliefs and traditions of other faiths. He would describe and analyze the great religions of the world in order to reveal their truths and also to define Judaism by contrast.

In his presentation of Judaism, Abba Hillel Silver is a "mainstream" Jew. He was fully aware of the fact that strong religious currents are not always or easily contained by straight banks. They make sudden twists, shoot outward into diversionary streams. They carry travelers into unexpected places. Abba Hillel Silver knew that a thirty-five-hundred-year-old river of faith like Judaism had produced its share of powerful side streams. But he preferred the mainstream.

Early in his career he marked out what he thought were the directions of this mainstream and often compared them with other religious and philosophical currents. His conclusions are embodied in his book *Where Judaism Differs*, published in 1956 by Macmillan. These conclusions differ in depth and subtlety from his youthful convictions. But the basic ideas hold firm. The flow of Rabbi Silver's religious thought is just as steady and straight as his conception of "mainstream" Judaism.

On the other hand, it is clear that Rabbi Silver was fully appreciative of Judaism's "happy inconsistency," and felt that each Jewish generation had the obligation of selecting and emphasizing those elements of its history and faith which most sharply underscore its uniqueness and its consequent *raison d'être*.

Sinai, Olympus, and Calvary

SERMON, THE TEMPLE
MARCH 13, 1921

Sinai, Olympus, and Calvary are the three mountain heights of revelation. None of these three represents an unusually high altitude as far as physical height is concerned. Calvary is only a hillock; Sinai is not the towering mountain of our early imagination; nor is Olympus that mighty heaven-reaching peak that we thought it to be when we studied the mythology of the ancient Hellenes. But these three mountains—Sinai, Olympus, and Calvary—represent the three highest peaks in human thought. They represent three distinctive revelations, three distinctive attitudes to life and to the problems of life, three distinct messages unto the children of man.

These three peaks belong to the same mountain range; they reach up to the one aspiration—God; and they rise from the one common level—the soul of man. Yet between these peaks there are valleys which separate them, and each mountain peak is distinctive and separate, unique in itself. The revelation which came down from each may touch at one point or another the revelation of the other two; and yet each revelation has a personality, a distinctiveness all its own. And it is well that there be more than one truth in the world. It is well that there be more than one revelation in the world. The same precious stone may have many facets, and the light may reach it from many sides. Progressive truth is made possible through the meeting and the clashing of conflicting ideas, and the spark of human inspiration is born out of the friction of opposing truths.

Religion is very much a matter of temperament. A philosopher once said a man is what he eats. That is not entirely true, but there is much of truth in it. Physical conditions—geography, climate, and environment, have much to do with the qualities of one's mind, with one's temperament, with one's religious aspirations. So peoples that live in different parts of the world, under different physical circumstances, will evolve different God concepts and will receive different revelations.

I believe that there is not a religion upon God's earth that has not served the needs and has not satisfied the longings of His children. I am not one who believes that my religion is the only true religion and that all other religions have no truth in them whatever. I do believe that the faith of Sinai has perhaps more of livable truth, more of practical truth, more of applicable truth than the faith of Olympus or of Calvary. And yet I know that the faith of Olympus made beautiful the lives of hundreds of thousands of God's children in the days gone by; and I know that the faith of Calvary is making sweet the lives of millions of men today. One is justified in having his own attitude and preferring his own revelations, provided he credits the man who has a different revelation with sincerity and with honesty of motive, and is kindly and gentle and tolerant toward him.

It is difficult to summarize in a few words the revelation of Sinai, the revelation of Olympus, and the revelation of Calvary. To summarize a thing is to delimit it and circumscribe it, and, in a way, to do injustice to it. Besides, these truths and revelations overlap one another, and each grew and was modified over the centuries. These mountain revelations are often surrounded with clouds—the clouds of ages.

Yet it may be well to ask ourselves what meaning the instinctive sense of the people has given to the heart of these three revelations. When you speak of the revelation of Mount Sinai, what doctrine does that call up in your mind? One sees Mount Sinai wrapped in clouds, with thunders rumbling round it, with lightning brightening the darkness, one hears the shofar blasts sounding, and then one hears a mighty voice—the voice of the One Omnipotent, revealing His will and His Law unto the children of men; a stern God, a stern Law, a God whom one must approach in reverence and in awe, because there is might, and there is wisdom, and there is eternity.

The revelation of Mount Sinai speaks of God and of Law.

When you speak of the revelation of Olympus, what picture does that call up in your mind? Why, a mountain bathed in sunlight, with graceful and beautiful gods moving about it; gods who are glorified and superb; human beings who while away the idle hours in song and dance, quaffing nectar and ambrosia. The revelation of Olympus speaks of beauty and the joyousness of life.

When one thinks of Calvary and of the revelation there, one thinks of a suffering and a dying God; a crown of thorns, a bleeding heart. One thinks of a God drinking not nectar or ambrosia, but a cup of bitterness and gall; one thinks of a God nailed to a cross, crying in the bitterness and anguish of his soul: "My God, my God, why hast Thou forsaken me!" One thinks of tragedy, and human suffering, and sacrifice, and salvation.

These are three distinct God concepts, and three distinct attitudes toward life. The God of Sinai is the stern judge of the world; the God of Sinai rules the world in wisdom and in might. One cannot approach Him in levity of spirit; one cannot brook His wrath and His anger. He is the God of Nature in her sterner moods. He is the Ruler—the King.

The gods of Olympus—Zeus and Apollo—are kindlier, more human deities, subject to all the frailties of human beings, to all the moral lapses and weaknesses of human beings; an aristocracy of gods, who have their political arrangements and their intrigues, but beautiful gods and joyous gods, who are not concerned very much with the lives of mortals nor with ethics, and morality, and justice.

The God of Calvary is a God who inspires love and pity, a God who inspires compassion, a God of tragedy, whose life belies the futility and the sinfulness of this world, and holds the promise of the glories of the kingdom come. He is the sadness of the world, and the misery of the world, and the compassion of the world.

Recently I read a Hebrew poem in which the poet complains about the religions that mankind is suffering under today, and asks for the return of that religion of light, and beauty, and song, and freedom—the religion of Olympus. He pictures in his beautiful way the twilight of the gods on Mount Olympus; he pictures the time when song sounded in the little hamlet of Bethlehem, announcing the birth of the new messiah, a song which sounded a dirge in the palaces and dwelling places of the gods of Olympus, because in the birth of this God—that man of sorrow—they saw their own death.

Pan, the god of life and the god of love and the god of laughter, must die, because the new God has come into the world. "What," says this poet, "has this new God brought into the world but self-denial, self-abnegation, monasteries, hermitages, nunneries, sorrow, sin, and the sense of sin, while all the beauty, and all the love and light and laughter which were associated with the gods of Greece have passed out of the world."

This poet complains bitterly also about the God of the Hebrews—

"the hidden God." He says, "When I grew older I sought my God; I asked for him; I wanted to love him, but I could not love a God whom I could not see."

Hellas gave unto mankind beautiful, graceful, charming gods that men could see, and love, and worship. Israel gave unto the world an un-known God, a Spirit dwelling everywhere but nowhere. The God of Israel, says the poet, was born out in the wilderness, amidst the storms and the harsh winds of the wildernesss, and so there is a God of anger, and a God of wrath, and a God who appears in thunder and in lightning. But the gods of Olympus were gods who came with sunshine, with smiles—the gods who moved with men kindly.

Apparently, then, there is a radical difference between these three revelations. If I were to try to express in single phrases the dominant thought, the chief characteristics of these three religions, I would say that the spirit of the Greek religion is stoicism, the spirit of the Christian religion is asceticism and pacifism, and the spirit of the Hebrew religion is prophecy.

If I were to express the dominant thought of these three religions, these three revelations, I would say that the dominant thought of the Greek religion is fate, the dominant thought of Christianity is salvation, and the dominant thought of Judaism is moral conduct. The Greek religion had no dogma, no creed, no hereditary priesthood, no prophets, no preachers, no sacred writings; it was a free religion and a beautiful religion. It had its beautiful temples and its shrines, its solemn rituals, its wonderful processions on the occasion of festivals or national holidays. But the gods of the Greeks were not the gods that could satisfy the inner long-ings of the human soul. They were glorified human beings, and when a man came face to face with the hard facts of life, when he was bruised and beaten by the untoward and cruel vicissitudes of life, he could not go to his gods for comfort and solace, for cheer, for inspiration, because the gods themselves were powerless and impotent, because they also were the play-things of a controlling fate.

The gods were just as much subject to the fate and the necessity of life as man. And so the whole of life was overshadowed by this sense of a blind, unyielding fate against which the hands of mortals could but knock in vain. So the life of the ancient Greek did not have all the glitter and the joy and the laughter that we associate with it; it had its moments of deep solemnity and seriousness, and it had its moments of deep pathos.

Homer likened life to the seared and withered leaves in autumn. Life had no purpose; there could not be a purpose to life if all was controlled by fate. There was no far-off definite event toward which all men could strive. Therefore, there was no lift and inspiration in achievement, in aspiration, in struggle; life was inevitably bound to sink to the dead level of a cold stoicism, even of a cynicism. And so the dominant thought of the ancient Hellenes was stoical and cynical. There was nothing in life, and there was nothing in afterlife. After death, according to the religion of the ancient Greeks, men, both good and bad, lived a gloomy, shadowy, cheerless existence in some realm which they called Hades; an existence without consciousness, without purpose, without peace, without bliss. That was the attitude towards life resulting inevitably from the revelation of Olympus.

Christianity and the revelation on Calvary resulted in another attitude towards life: life is sinful and man is enmeshed in sin; man fell from grace back in the early dawn of human history with the fall of Adam. Ever since that first disobedience, men have labored under this original sin, and nothing that they themselves do can free them from this millstone, this yoke, this terrible, oppressive yoke of original sin. Life is sinful, the flesh is sinful, all matter is sinful; this world is just a vale of tears and suffering, only a preparatory stage to the world to come—the world of eternal bliss and perfection. It needed the sacrifice of a God to wash the sinful tribe of man clean of its sins.

Christianity constantly held before the eyes and the minds of men the thought of sin, the consciousness of sin, of wickedness. It led men to deny life and the needs and demands of this world, separating themselves from human relationships, from the concern of society, isolating themselves and trying to gain salvation through the purification of their souls by denying the demands of their bodies.

Christianity resulted in monasticism. Worldliness hampered the soul. Hermitages and nunneries and monasteries were established where men and women tried in purity of spirit, in fine idealism, superb idealism, to gain that salvation for which their spirits yearned. Christianity was a religion concerned primarily with individual salvation, with the soul of the individual.

The revelation of Sinai resulted in an attitude entirely distinct from that of Olympus. I believe that it is a much more practical and sane and satisfying attitude toward life. The revelation of Sinai stressed two ideas:

first, that God is not a vague abstraction, not a principle of the philosopher, not a metaphysical notion, but that God is a reality—living, omnipresent, personal, an all-powerful Creator, the great Architect of the Universe, whose spirit informs and controls and whose purpose is the destiny of the universe; and second, that God is not like unto the gods of Olympus—weak, mortal in a sense, subject to all the frailties and weaknesses of human beings, a god made in the image of man, but a good God that the mind of man, and the senses of man, and even the imagination of man cannot reach and comprehend in His fullness and in His perfection; a God who can become the object of reverence, of worship, of awe, and yes, of fear.

Men and women today speak with great trepidation and a certain hesitancy concerning the idea of fear as associated with Divinity. It is well to feel that we can love our God, that God is kind and forgiving, but it is also well to remember that we must fear our God; that he can punish; that he can visit the sins of the fathers upon the children; that there is a social responsibility that is handed down from one generation to another. It is well to feel that Nature and God have their sterner moods, even as they have their kindlier moods of mercy, and compassion, and forgiveness.

We have spoken too little in the last generation concerning the fear of God. The God of Sinai is a God to be revered. The gods of Olympus could be made fun of. Aristophanes spoke lightly and with great levity and fun and humor about the shortcomings of his gods; Euripides doubted the powers of the gods of Hellas. But no one can speak lightly and slightingly of the God of Sinai.

The revelation of Sinai speaks of Law and conduct; it is a religion for men who live, for men who wish to live in society, in the world of men. It is not the religion of the man who runs away from the responsibilities of the world. Judaism has never said unto men that they are burdened with an original sin; that whatever they do or may hope to do cannot save them from the consequences of the one act of disobedience performed by one man ages ago.

Judaism says unto mankind: Life is made up of sin and of good, of light and of darkness, of sweetness and of bitterness. It is for man to hew for himself a pathway through life and, by dint of his own efforts and his own labors and sacrifices, to fashion for himself a world of beauty in which to live.

Judaism says unto the children of men: God has put sin and suffering and disillusionment in the world not to break us, not to crush our spirits, not to remind us of our weakness, but to remind us of our strength, of our capacity for greatness, of our ability to take the cold, crude clay of life and with the fingers of our own inspiration mold it into a shape of true divinity.

Judaism reminds man that in spite of the mortality of his body there is dwelling within him the spark of God's own fire. "The spirit of man is the light of God." The soul of man is made in the image of God; man is of God—Godly. He himself may become a co-creator and co-worker in God's grand scheme of creation.

Judaism aims to tell every one of us that the hammer of our aspirations, striking forcefully upon the anvil of life, can fashion a new heaven and a new earth. Man need not go through life oppressed constantly with the consciousness of sin; and man need not look with revulsion upon the beautiful body that God gave him, as though this body were the deadliest enemy of his spirit.

Judaism says unto man: Purify your spirit through and by your body; live in the world, by the world, and for the world, and you will reach the heights of salvation. Judaism is concerned not so much with the salvation of your own soul so that you may be prepared for the world to come; Judaism is concerned with the problem of how you can live in a spirit of amity and good will and righteousness with your neighbor, so that both of you and myriads like unto you may constitute a kingdom of heaven upon earth.

Judaism is concerned with social problems, with problems of justice, with problems of politics, and with problems of economics. Judaism is concerned with problems of international relations, with group morality. A few days ago I heard a speaker say that the need of society today is to emphasize not the thought of sinning by the individual, but the sinning by groups; that the greatest sins perpetrated upon the human race have been perpetrated not by the individual man or woman but by groups, by racial passions and racial antipathies, by racial ambitions. In each group the individual feels himself righteous because his group is committing the act in the name of some great ideal or some noble civilization.

Well, Israel caught the significance of that centuries ago. The New Testament has nothing to say concerning the relations of one nation to another. The thought of international morality does not enter the purview of the writers of the New Testament; but the works of the prophets are saturated with the thought that nations are subject to the same immutable laws of righteousness as individuals are. The prophet calls unto Assyria, Babylon, Egypt, Greece, Persia, and all the peoples to submit to the will of God, to abide by His will, for God is the judge of nations, even as He is the judge of men.

Judaism is prophetic, and prophetism means but two things—God and morality; God and good. Judaism is faith in God, in a living God, in a good God, but in a righteous judge. And prophetism believes that God is the source of our moral life, that He revealed the moral law unto the children of men, and unto Him we hold a responsibility for our conduct upon earth.

Judaism is prophetic inasmuch as it has a mission unto the children of men. The Greeks never had missionaries; the Greeks never had apostles; the Greeks were never bothered with the problem of sending forth their light unto other peoples. Christianity had its missionaries; Christianity had its apostles. But the message they brought to the world was: "Repent ye, for the kingdom of God is at hand." Prepare yourself for the great cataclysm that is bound to come; a frightful revolution is at hand which will destroy this world, its wickedness, its order, its arrangement, and will bring suddenly the new kingdom.

Judaism made of the whole people of Israel an apostle people and an apostolic race—a prophetic people. "Get thee out from thy land and from the home of thy people unto the lands that I will show thee." And preach the gospel of what? Of another world? No! Of another kingdom to come suddenly? No! "Do justice!" "Righteousness shalt thou pursue!" That is the prophetic message of Sinai.

And so when one meditates upon these three great revelations that have come to the world, one is prone to say that while each has been a boon and a blessing to mankind, while Olympus has emphasized the beauty and symmetry and joy of life and Calvary has stressed magnificently the thought of vicarious atonement, of dying that one may be reborn anew into a higher life of love, of compassion, and of pity; one is prone to say, however, that as far as the organization of human society is concerned, as far as the foundations of our social life are concerned, as far as the problems of human relationships are concerned, the revelation of Sinai, speaking of God, of justice, of law, of righteousness, is perhaps the most essential, the most basic, the most applicable, the most needed revelation in the world.

Olympus belongs to mythology, and the gods of Olympus have long since left the mansions and the palaces. Night has fallen over the pantheon.

The God of Calvary is worshiped by millions the world over, but the spirit of these millions is fast turning in hope to the spirit of the God of Sinai, to the spirit of the Old Testament, to the spirit of prophecy, because they have realized that the perplexing needs of life today can be satisfied not by a religion of asceticism, not by a religion of pacifism, not by a religion of mysticism, not by a religion which denies life and escapes from life, but by a religion which faces squarely all the problems of life and wrestles with them in the faith that God lives and that truth will ultimately triumph.

The spirit of the Hebrew, the spirit of Sinai, is today marching triumphantly through the world.

The Jew to Jesus

An Imaginary Colloquy at the Christmas Season

SERMON, THE TEMPLE
DECEMBER 20, 1936

O Man of mine own people, I alone
Among these alien ones can know thy face,
I who have felt the kinship of thy race
Burn in me, as I sit where they intone
Thy praises—those who, striving to make known
A God for sacrifice, have missed the grace
Of thy sweet human meaning in its place,
Thou who art of our blood-bond and our own.

Are we not sharers of thy Passion? Yea,
In spirit-anguish closely by thy side
We have drained the bitter cup, and, tortured, felt
With thee the bruising of each heavy welt.
In every land is our Gethsemane.
A thousand times have we been crucified.

This moving sonnet by Florence Frank called "The Jew to Jesus" is not inappropriate for the season of the year when the Christian world begins the celebration of the nativity of its founder. A Jew comes into this season with mingled emotions, for Jewish experience in the last 2,000 years has been inseparably intertwined with the story of Christianity. The Jew has lived much of the time in Christian lands, and his history is the story of the attitude of the Christian world toward his existence in its midst.

To this poet, the thought which seems to be uppermost is the similarity in the fate which overtook the founder of Christianity, Jesus, and the fate which overtook his race—the Jewish race.

Are we not sharers of thy passion? Yea,
In spirit-anguish closely by thy side

315

We have drained the bitter cup, and, tortured, felt
With thee the bruising of each heavy welt.
Every land is our Gethsemane.
A thousand times have we been crucified.

And that, of course, is too too tragically true. Our people have been forced to take the "via dolorosa," the sorrowful road of persecution, of misunderstanding, of hatred, of suffering, and our "via dolorosa" has not yet ended. The whole race of Israel, because of its vision, became in the language of the prophet Isaiah the "man of sorrow," and whole generations of our people agonized upon the cross of persecution. Upon the head of the man who became the master of the Christian world they placed a crown of thorns, and upon his race the clown cap of humiliation and the yellow badge of shame. True it is that Israel has been the risen people of an immemorial crucifixion.

To us this season suggests another similarity—the similarity of defeat. How tragically both Christianity and Judaism have failed to redeem the world, to regenerate mankind, to build the kind of a world we hoped to build.

If a Jew were to meet Jesus on this Christmas Eve of 1936, he would greet him, of course, with the old Jewish greeting *"Shalom aleichem"*— "Peace be unto you!," the only greeting that Jesus knew, the ancient greeting of ancient Israel. And soon both would be startled to realize how strange that greeting sounds in the world of 1936.

The Jew would remind Jesus that according to the legend sacred among his disciples and followers, the heavenly host on the night of his nativity sang "Glory to God in the highest, peace on earth, good will toward men." And the Jew would ask, "Now that nineteen centuries have rolled by and your followers have grown from a humble little company into tens and hundreds of millions, and have mastered the Western world, where is this peace on earth? Where is the good will among men?"

The Jew would perhaps say then to his brother Jesus, "You will have great difficulty in walking across the face of Europe because of the number of graves and the rows of crosses of Christians, millions of them who killed each other in hate and fury in the last World War." And then he would ask:

"Brother Jesus, are you on your way, perhaps, this Christmas Eve, to Madrid, Spain? There you will find no heavenly hosts chanting the hymns of peace. From the skies flaming death rains down, bombs to kill men, women, and children. You will see an old Christian city with magnificent churches turned to shambles, where brother Christian is slaying brother Christian, and here they will invoke your name even as they drive bayonets into each other's bodies. Some say they kill to save your religion. Is that your religion, Brother?

"Or perhaps you are on your way to Rome this Christmas Eve, where there is the most magnificent church in Christendom, and the seat of one of the greatest Christian communions. You will find a people celebrating not Christmas but the conscious, ruthless conquest and destruction of another Christian race, and they will celebrate this bloody conquest of Ethiopia and the fact that they defied the whole world and won.

"Or perhaps you are on your way to Berlin, this Christmas Eve? There you will hear the bells tolling and in numerous churches you will hear your story told—the story of how you were born in Bethlehem in Judea of a Jewish father and a Jewish mother. They will hail your birth and hail you as the leader of mankind who saved the world. They will chant praise and hallelujahs. But Brother Jesus, if you were born today in Berlin, you would be a marked and branded child, forever an alien among these people. You would be regarded as a member of a worthless race. You would be born under a flag which carries not your cross, but a crooked cross, the swastika, which is the symbol of Aryan racial purity and superiority, the symbol of the impurity and degradation of the Semitic race of which you and I are children. Brother Jesus, you loved children. You said many beautiful things about children: 'Suffer little children, and forbid them not to come unto me, for of such is the Kingdom of Heaven.' But in Berlin, Brother Jesus, they do not suffer little children to come in joy to their rightful patrimony. Our Jewish children are shunned as lepers, segregated, isolated, humiliated.

"You used to love to preach, Brother Jesus, in the synagogues. You were welcomed. Christian Germany will not let you preach in church or synagogue, for you are a Jew. They do not like Jews, even when they turn Christian.

"Do you recall how your followers were persecuted, how your disciples and faithful ones met with the hatred and contempt of the people, how they were charged, the early Christians, with being enemies of the great Roman Empire, how they were charged with practicing every conceivable abomination and violation, every vice, in the name of God? Remember the awful charges that they killed children and drank their blood in rites of initiation, that they performed shameful orgies in performance of their religion? Do you remember Julian, who charged your followers with being a sect of fanatics, and do you remember how all Christians of the Empire were deprived of their professions? They were forbidden to hold office, to teach; they were forbidden employment in state, army, or province. Brother Jesus, your followers, centuries later, say the selfsame things and lay the selfsame restrictions against your people. Today your race is being accused, as your followers were, as conspirators against the state. You destroyed Rome, they said. We ruined Germany, they say, and the same measures are being enacted against our people as were enacted against your followers centuries ago. How little the world has changed, Brother Jesus, in all these centuries!

"In 1936, Brother Jesus, they really do not know what to do with the Jews. They cannot forget your greatness. The world has acclaimed you. You have been so much a part of the history of the Western world, and yet they would rather that you had been born at Potsdam. They would rather have had it that you were born the offspring of some Prussian corporal than of a Jew in Galilee.

"They do not know what to do with your teaching, Brother Jesus. The world has hailed you as a gentle teacher who loved peace and forgiveness. Yet in Berlin today and in many other countries of the world these are not the virtues extolled. They adore the iron fist. It is force they love. They despise the pacifist. They love to hate. They want a God who can thunder and make their enemies quake. Somehow, Brother Jesus, you do not fit into their Valhalla. No, in Berlin, on Christmas 1936, you will hear no heavenly hosts preaching 'Peace on earth!' You were a pacifist. In Palestine, in the ancient days, they did not persecute you because you were a pacifist. But in Germany you would be sent to the concentration camp, and the iron heel would be dug into your face. There was a humble and gentle disciple who lived in Germany, Carl van Ossietzky, one of the true faithful ones. They took him and placed him in a camp and kept him there until he was worn to the brink of death, a broken frame, and then they left him to spend the rest of his life on a bed of suffering. That is how they treat pacifists. They want war. They starve their people so as to have provender for their guns. They have rejected the Jews—men of peace.

"Do you remember how you warned people against the abuses and dangers of wealth, against laying up treasures upon earth; how you warned people that you cannot serve God and Mammon at the same time and how you told them that a rich man shall hardly enter in the Kingdom of God?

"You had a dream, we had a dream, of a perfect society that would be ushered in by God, men preparing themselves by meekness and right-eousness and purity, and you said, 'These people were the blessed ones.' And you said, 'Blessed are the poor'—not the strong, not the mighty, not the rulers of the earth, but these. What has become of this dream nineteen centuries later? Everywhere they are worshipping Mammon, everywhere they are worshipping Mars. Everywhere they despise the weak. Everywhere they wage war to conquer and to possess. Whenever the poor rise to de-mand justice, the rich and the mighty set about destroying them.

"They have rejected you, Brother Jesus, in the Christian world. You are an alien, a prophet not without honor but what is worse, a prophet honored but not listened to."

Now, in this colloquy, on the road this Christmas Eve, 1936, what would Jesus answer? What would he say? He would say, "You are right, Brother. I know that thy road through these long, weary centuries has been long and hard, harder by far than the road I once traveled to Golgotha. Often have I had to drink the vinegar mingled with gall as you have. Oh, my brother, I know that not all who prophesied in my name obeyed my word. I know that 'not every one that saith unto me, Lord, Lord, shall enter into the Kingdom.'

"I had a dream of a world swiftly regenerated, of a blessed new world. I proclaimed that faith. I summoned men to regenerate in order to re-enter my wonderful new Kingdom of God. I failed. But have you, my brother, succeeded? You too had a dream, the dream we shared, the dream of Isaiah, Jeremiah, and Micah, of great teachers, of those words I read in the synagogue; the dream of the 'coming day when the earth shall be full of the knowledge of God,' when 'men shall beat their swords into plow-shares, and their spears into pruning-hooks.' What of your dream, O brother of my people? Are the Jews today all God-fearing, all peace-loving? Are they free from intolerance and hate and pride? Are they free from ex-ploitation and the worship of Mammon? Are they unhappy because of the wrongs of mankind or because of their wrongs? Are they seeking the King-dom?"

And what would the Jew answer? "You are right, Brother Jesus. We too have not lived up to our vision. Perhaps the world's redemption has been retarded so far because neither your followers nor my people have had the courage to confess their failures, the courage to be honest with themselves. Neither Christianity nor Judaism has been easy. Hard has been the road for both of us. But both our roads are only at the beginning. Our work in the world is still to be done and what we both need, Brother Joshua, are new and faithful disciples, men who will be afraid neither of hate, nor misunderstanding, nor persecution, nor death, nor torture, men to whom faith will be an exaltation, a consecration, a rising consuming passion. With such disciples our dream would conquer the world.

"You uttered some great truths to your few followers in Judea. Those few you chose to follow you 'feared not them which killed the body, but are not able to kill the soul' and you warned them, 'Ye shall be hated of all men for my name's sake.' Our prophets and your prophetic forebears likewise admonished the faithful, 'Those that put all trust in God will renew their strength. They shall mount up with wings like eagles. They shall run and not be weary. They shall walk and not faint.' That breed of followers we need, Brother Jesus, to make our dream come true.

"Where are you going, then, on this Christmas Eve, Brother Joshua?"

And Jesus' answer would be: "I am not going to the magnificent cathedrals to listen to the pealing of the organ, to see the splendid robes of priestly functionaries. I am not going to smell incense. I am going through the byways of the world, even as once I walked along the shores of the Sea of Galilee seeking a few simple folk, fine honest men to help me build a Kingdom."

"So am I," the Jew would say. "I, too, am seeking such brothers. *Shalom aleichem*—Peace be unto you!"

"And unto you, Brother."

The Parting of the Ways

A SYMPOSIUM ON THE OCCASION OF THE
FIFTIETH-ANNIVERSARY CELEBRATION OF THE
DROPSIE COLLEGE, APRIL 29, 1957

When we speak of the "parting of the ways," in referring to the separation of Christianity from Judaism, it is clear that we do not have in mind comparative assessments. We are interested in an objective analysis of the differences which have led these two great religions to follow independent courses through history. Each system of thought has its own texture and pattern, and each faith its own perspectives. Differences should not obscure the underlying unity of the human race or the common needs of human life which all classic institutions and beliefs of mankind aim to serve or the urgency of their close cooperation to achieve their common purposes.

When Jesus came to Galilee, "spreading the gospel of the Kingdom of God and saying the time is fulfilled and the Kingdom of God is at hand," he was voicing the opinion widely held that the year 5000 in the creation calendar, which was to usher in the sixth millennium, the age of the Kingdom of God, was at hand. It was this chronological fact which inflamed the Messianic hope of the people.

Jesus appeared in the procuratorship of Pontius Pilate (26–36 C.E.). The first mention of the appearance of a Messiah in Josephus is in connection with the disturbances during the term of office of the procurator Cuspius Fadus (c. 44 C.E.). It seems likely, therefore, that in the minds of the people, the millennium was to begin around the year 30 C.E.

Be it remembered that it is not the Messiah who brings about the millennium; it is the inevitable advent of the millennium which carries along with it the Messiah and his appointed activities. The Messiah was expected around the second quarter of the first century C.E., because the millennium was at hand. The time spoken of in Daniel "for a time, times and a half," was now fulfilled. Prior to that time he was not expected, because according to the chronology of the day the millennium was still considerably removed.

The central theme of the preachment of Jesus and of John the Baptist, whom Jesus hailed as the Elijah who was to announce the advent of the millennium, was repentance. The day of repentance will precede the actual millennium. Only those who would repent would be spared the purging and cleansing process antecedent to the millennium—"the wrath that is to come."

Jesus' essential mission was apocalyptic, not prophetic. His concern was not to reconstruct society but to save it from the winnowing and retributive judgment which was imminent in the van of the approaching millennium. The ethical counsel which he gave to his followers was for a world *in extremis*, and it was to help them survive the terrors to come and to be admitted into the Kingdom, the new order of existence which the millennium would usher in.

Jesus was impatient because the people did not seem to realize its imminence: "Ye hypocrites, ye know how to interpret the face of the earth and the heaven; but how is it that ye know not how to interpret this time?" "Verily I say unto you, there are some of them that stand here, who shall in no wise taste of death till they see the Son of Man coming in his Kingdom."

Jesus' attitude toward the Law was determined by his views concerning the approaching End. He did not oppose the Law in part or in whole. He did not seek to abrogate it. It was not necessary. The incoming millennium would of itself do away with the Law entirely. However, "until all things be accomplished," the Law must be obeyed. Not, however, as most men obey it, formally and mechanically, but with a soul-searching intent and intensity, so that it may prove a real help to that spiritual lustration required for initiation into the Kingdom. Jesus' real attitude to the Law is admirably summed up in Matt. 5:17–20:

> Think not that I am come to destroy the Law or the prophets; I come not to destroy but to fulfill. For verily I say unto you, till heaven and earth pass away, one jot or one tittle shall in no wise pass away from the law, till all things be accomplished. Whosoever shall break one of these least commandments and shall teach men so, shall be called least in the kingdom

of heaven; but whosoever shall do and teach them, he shall be called great in the kingdom of heaven. But I say unto you, that except your righteousness shall exceed the righteousness of the scribes and Pharisees, ye shall in no wise enter into the kingdom of heaven.

Jesus proceeds to indicate what he means by a righteousness which exceeds the righteousness of the scribes and Pharisees. In no instance does he call for a new Law or the abrogation of the old Law, but for the correct "intensive" attitude toward the existing Law.

Why should men fulfill the Law with such inner intentness? Not that they will thereby bring the Kingdom about. The Kingdom comes through the grace of God, not through the works of men: "For it is your Father's good pleasure to give you the Kingdom." Its advent is preordained in the cosmic scheme. It is inevitable. It cannot be hastened or retarded. But those who will fulfill the Law in truth and in sincerity will be spared the "pangs of Messianic times" and will be privileged to enter the Kingdom.

There is nothing in all this that would bring about a parting of the ways with Judaism. While these beliefs did not constitute essential Jewish doctrine, they were part of fairly familiar Aggada, legendary lore, whose time, according to the belief of Jesus and his followers, had finally come.

But a parting of the ways did take place, and that fairly early, perhaps within half a century of the crucifixion. Why?

Paul, alone, is not responsible for the break. It would have taken place without Paul. Paul found Christians and apparently even organized Christian societies already in existence in some of the cities which he visited in his missionary activities. These may still have regarded themselves as Jewish, but already as hyphenated Jews—as Jewish-Christians—and were swiftly moving toward the inevitable separation.

Paul insured the spread and, to a large extent, the survival of Christianity, by adding to the simple, unblended Messianic message of Jesus and of his followers in Jerusalem or by intensively stressing a redemptive, salvationist message, which was more familiar and appealing to the gentile world. He directed his message principally to the pagan world or to Jewish proselytes from the pagan world, who were fully acquainted, through the numerous mystery cults about them, with similar salvationist hopes. By combining Judaism's monotheism, its relentless attack upon polytheism and idolatry, its lofty and cleansing moral idealism, with a

Messianic faith, strongly salvationist in character, whose major accent was upon redemption and the promise of immortality, Pauline Christianity was able to make a strong impact upon the Greco-Roman world, long in the throes of a spiritual crisis resulting from the breakdown of its ancient beliefs. Where Judaism, in its proselytizing efforts—and they were not inconsiderable—could attain only a limited success, because it would not yield in its requirements for the total acceptance of the Law on the part of those who sought full proselytism, Christianity of the Pauline school, making no such requirements, scored heavily.

But even without Paul, a parting of the ways would have taken place, earlier, of course, in the Diaspora, but not much later in Palestine.

A Messianic movement must either succeed, which in the very nature of things is not possible, or, failing to convert the parent body to its Messianic views, must separate from it or be rejected by it.

Messianic beliefs, in a variety of fluid forms, were current among Jews—not necessarily all Jews—around the beginning of the Common Era. Such beliefs are reflected in pre-Christian apocalyptic literature and are also to be found in the Dead Sea Scrolls. They made an especial appeal to the mystically minded among the people. They were not frowned upon by the authoritative Judaism of the day, nor were they regarded as unorthodox. On the other hand they were not held to be dogmatic teachings of the faith, denial of which was heretical. Some Jews rejected the whole Messianic complex; others were simply indifferent to it. As long as no Messiah appeared, and no practical consequences were drawn, the believer would go unchallenged. It was a phase of folk-faith, of popular tradition, of Aggada.

But the actual appearance of a Messiah meant, apart from its political and social implications, a concretizing of this revolutionary Aggada into a definitive creed, sect, and discipline within the nation. This, official Judaism could neither ignore nor accept. For very serious consequences for faith and practice flowed from such a Messianism, now translated from an expectation into a reality.

The coming of the Messiah meant the ushering in of the millennium. With the millennium all the laws of the Torah, as we stated above, are automatically abrogated. There is no longer any need for them when the Kingdom of God has been established. The sole purpose of the ceremonial law, of rites and rituals, was to purify the hearts of men. It is a matter of history that antinomianism in one form or another, timid or audacious, attended every important Messianic movement in Israel. In the early propaganda of such movements the abrogation of laws served the purpose of a symbolic demonstration that the millennium was definitely on the way, if it had not actually arrived.

This was the case with the first Christian fellowship in Jerusalem. There were conservative elements in it who hesitated to take the bold step of abrogating some or all of the basic ceremonial laws of the Torah. There were others who remained ambivalent in their attitude, denying freedom from the Law to themselves, but permitting it to gentile converts. The strong trend, however, by the very logic and dynamics of the movement, went rapidly and inevitably toward abrogation. Paul himself wrestled tortuously in his soul, long and unsuccessfully, with the problem of remaining loyal to the Torah and at the same time carrying on an energetic universal evangelism for his Christ faith. He finally concluded that the gospel and the Law were irreconcilable, and that the coming of Jesus spelled "the end of the Law" (Rom. 10:4). He accordingly "died to the Law" (Gal. 2:19).

"Dying to the Law" meant a rejection of the Torah. A rejection of the Torah meant a decisive break with Judaism, for no sect could remain within Judaism, or ever did remain within Judaism, which rejected the Torah completely. Paul's break came within two or three decades of the death of Jesus. Other Jewish-Christians in and outside of Palestine did not make the break—and it was a voluntary break—that early. They "died to the Law" more slowly—the Ebionites, for example, as late as the second century—but they died nevertheless. In the tense interim period between the appearance of the Messiah and his expected early return, a Messianic movement which was bent upon the rapid conversion of the gentile world would not long impede itself with the Mosaic ceremonial law, so alien and so burdensome to the gentiles—a Law which the approaching millennium would soon do away with anyhow.

The parent body of Judaism did not accept the Messianic views of Jesus' followers. The latter remained a relatively small group within Palestinian Jewry; but it was from the very start a separate group. It was made so in the first place not by any external pressure, but by its own distinctive fellowship as a mystic union with their risen Lord; by its special rites of initiation which probably developed very early—baptism and the Communion meal; by its own manual of instruction and recruiting; and by its separate prayer meetings as well as by the form of its social and economic life, wherein all things were shared in common. The Jerusalem fellowship came to be linked with similarly minded communities outside of Palestine and was dependent upon them for support. These communities, because of their large infiltration of gentile converts, became increasingly less "Jewish" and less Torah-minded.

There were also, of course, external pressures which progressively isolated this Jewish-Christian brotherhood. It was suspect and held in disfavor by many from the very first. Its Messianic faith was a discredited one in the eyes of the people, for it had failed of its objective. Jesus, whom his followers proclaimed as the Messiah, had been crucified, and the millennium had not materialized. That this Messiah had risen from the grave and was now seated at the right hand of God and would soon return to judge the earth—a conviction now held by these Messianists, no longer as part of an indefinite and visionary saga but as a present fact focused in the specific personality of a man by the name of Jesus—must have outraged many Jews, both Pharisees and Sadducees. Any Aggada, however inspiring and beautiful, when suddenly presented as an actual and concrete reality, may grievously shock and offend even those who had previously cherished it. To the Sadducees especially, this claim of the Jewish-Christians was particularly obnoxious, for the Sadducees denied the resurrection of the dead altogether.

Furthermore, there were some among the Jewish-Christians in Jerusalem who shared views about the Law similar to those which Paul came to express so vigorously and to more receptive ears in the racial melting-pot cities of the Diaspora. Any such denigration of the Torah, or any attempt to abrogate any of its laws, either by the authority of a new revelation or by the technique of allegory employed to suspend the literal meaning of a law, would naturally arouse sharp hostility, especially in Jerusalem, though violent opposition and riots developed also elsewhere.

The Apostles and the early disciples in Jerusalem had come to claim, by virtue of the power given to them by Jesus, or through a direct revelation, or by the very fact of baptism, the gift of prophecy. This too was held to be an inevitable by-product of the Messianic age. The prophet Joel had proclaimed that in the latter end God would pour out his "spirit on all flesh; your sons and your daughters shall prophesy; your old men shall dream dreams and your young men shall see visions; even upon the men-servants and the maid-servants in those days, I will pour out my spirit" (Joel 3:1–2). The miracle of Pentecost—on the very day commemorating the giving of the Law at Sinai—which was attended by extraordinary natural phenomena reminiscent of Sinai, as recorded in Acts, Chapter 2, when the Holy Spirit suddenly descended upon the Apostles and some hundred and twenty disciples—was intended to substantiate the belief that the Messianic age had actually arrived, and that the Apostles and disciples were now possessed of prophetic power and authority.

At the time of Jesus, the authoritative teachers of Judaism, while they did not deny the possibility of the reappearance of prophecy, the Bible clearly certifying such a contingency, were no longer willing to stake the future of their faith on the chance appearance of men who might pretend to superior divine authority and who might utter prophetic oracles which would not be in keeping with the long-established principles of Judaism and perhaps might even be in defiance of them. They were unwilling to base a law or doctrine or its abrogation upon reputed miracles which might be exploited to confirm heresies. They therefore maintained that prophecy had actually ceased in Israel with the last three Biblical prophets, Haggai, Zachariah, and Malachi. They held that at the time of the destruction of the First Temple, prophecy was taken away from the prophets and given to the sages (B.B.12b). An extreme view was expressed by one rabbi: "At the time of the destruction of the First Temple, prophecy was taken away from the prophets and given to fools and children." This was as if in pointed rejoinder to Paul and other Christian preachers, who exhorted their followers to prophesy: "Now I want you all to speak in tongues, but even more, to prophesy" (I Cor. 14:5). It might be noted in passing that the Christian church itself, which soon came to be plagued with false prophets, impostors, and pretenders who endangered its own orthodox doctrine, soon put prophecy under restraint.

The position came to be held in normative Judaism, that the sage, the skilled interpreter of the Torah, was superior to the prophet (B.B.12a). The purpose of the rabbis was not to deny the prophetic spirit but to insist that whatever further truths or new insights were required by subsequent ages could very well be drawn by trained and devout minds out of the deep well of the Torah itself, whose waters were inexhaustible.

The claim of the early Christians therefore to have come into possession of the gift of the Holy Spirit, to have prophetic authority and the authority of revelation, carrying with it the authority also to abrogate or suspend Biblical laws, was a direct challenge to the accepted views long held by the authoritative representatives of Judaism.

A prophet was assured privileges under the Law which were not possessed by any other religious teacher. A prophet whose credibility was well established could, for example, order the temporary suspension of any law of the Torah, short, of course, of the prohibition of idolatry, in order to meet an emergency, and the people were obligated to obey him (San. 90a). The claims of the early Christians were therefore a challenge not alone to Pharisaism, which was then energetically developing a system of Halakhah based on a carefully devised technique of interpretation, as opposed to new revelations, but also to Sadduceeism, which would naturally resent any modification of the written Law.

The early Christians were, of course, aware that Jesus had abrogated no law of the Torah. But, as the need for relenting upon the rigors of the Law, especially the laws of Sabbath observance, circumcision, and prohibited foods, became urgent in the rapid process of winning over gentile converts, the authority of new revelations was rapidly invoked. The gentile brethren in Antioch, Syria, and Cilicia are informed by the Church in Jerusalem that on the authority of the Holy Spirit they need no longer practice the rite of circumcision (Acts 15:28; see also Col. 2:11). Peter sees a heavenly vision which declares unto him that all foods are permissible (Acts 10:10 ff.). And on the authority of Jesus himself, it was soon maintained "that the Son of Man is Lord also of the Sabbath" (Mark 2:28) and that, therefore, it is a matter of personal preference for Christians whether they wish to observe the Sabbath or not (Rom. 14:5 ff.).

The admission of gentiles to full membership in the ecclesia of the faithful without the necessity of observing any laws of the Torah except the so-called Noachian laws (Acts 15) and the free sharing by them of the Holy Spirit (Acts 10) meant to all intents and purposes the early abandonment of the Law for nearly all its members. It would be found impossible to maintain a united fellowship—one church, the dream of all the faithful —with one part committed to Torah observances and the other uncommitted and, in fact, critical of them. The opening of the doors of proselytism to the gentile world on the sole basis of faith in the resurrected Christ (Rom. 10:4 ff.) whose revelation superseded the Torah, was a critical innovation which was bound to turn what was at first a Jewish sect into a new non-Jewish religion.

It is difficult to establish exactly when the concept of Incarnation became part of the Christian faith, probably very early. Paul thinks of Jesus as the pre-existent Christ, identified with the Holy Spirit, who had now assumed a human body: "God sending his own Son in the likeness of sinful flesh, and for sin, condemned sin in the flesh" (Rom. 8:3). John thinks of Jesus as the Logos—the Word which was made flesh, "and dwelt among us" (John 1:14). Matthew and Luke speak of Jesus "as begotten of the Holy Spirit" (Matt. 1:18; Luke 1:35).

Certainly, no one who is acquainted with the determined and persistent struggle for a pure monotheistic faith among the people of Israel since the days of Abraham, Moses, and the prophets could have assumed for a moment then or since that Judaism would find lodgement for the concept of a God who came down to earth, assumed human form, and suffered death for the salvation of men—a doctrine which Jesus himself never taught. These ideas were known to the Jews long before the time of Jesus, and had been rejected by them. They were popular and current in the ancient world. Judaism had resisted these notions for centuries. The Jewish people could not but reject such a doctrine unless it were prepared to abandon the most treasured and essential conviction for which it had struggled through the centuries and of which it believed itself to be the covenanted guardian and spokesman to the world. It could not accept a renewed mythologizing of God, which it had resisted for a thousand years, even though the concept of a born, dying, and resurrected God might now be presented as a metaphysical idea and not as a concrete event which took place on a specific date in history or as a trinitarian conception of monotheism.

A contributing factor, too, to a parting of the ways was the fact that the Jewish-Christians were pacifists, and would have no part in the people's resistance movement which culminated in the revolt against Rome. In the beginning of the Jewish revolt against Rome in 66 c.e., the Christian group in Jerusalem fled to Pella, a gentile center in Transjordan, as they did once again, later on, during the Bar Kochba revolt in 135 c.e.

The destruction of the Temple severed another important link between Jewish-Christian and official Judaism. The event was quickly seized upon by Christian propagandists as proof of God's displeasure with and rejection of Israel.

All these factors combined to surround the Jewish-Christians in Jerusalem in quick time with a host of enemies. Many clashes ensued. The first fateful outburst resulted in the slaying of Stephen.

Basically a parting of the ways was inevitable also because normative Judaism of the first century was not apocalyptic in character, or salvationist, or pacifist, or otherworldly. Its main concern was not with sin, grace, redemption, and justification, but with a way of life which would express in practice the prophetic ideals of doing justly, loving mercy, and walking humbly with God, and the building of the good society on earth.

In its historic evolution, Judaism moved not from prophecy to apocalypse but from prophecy directly to the men of the great synagogue, from the Torah to its interpretation at the hands of scribes and sages. The Five Books of Moses are not an apocalyptic text. There were of course mystic and apocalyptic elements among Jews of the Second Common-wealth, the Essenes and other groups—the Anavin ("the humble ones"), the Hashaim ("the silent ones"), the Zenuim ("the chaste ones")—and their numbers probably increased in the turbulent post-Maccabbean centuries, but their numbers were always very small and their ideas never constituted the mainstream of Judaism.

Prophetic and rabbinic Judaism was predominantly interested in the mundane progress of man and society, while the apocalyptists were interested in the timetable of the approaching End. The one sought a moral reformation of society; the others hoped for its miraculous transformation through divine intervention.

As we indicated earlier, there were expectations among Jews in the first century of the coming of the Messiah, because of a popularly entertained belief that the year 5000, the beginning of the millennium, was at an end. Many Jews entertained the hope of a national Messiah who would bring to Israel freedom and to mankind universal justice and peace. That this belief constituted the keystone in the arch of first-century Judaism is nowhere indicated. There were rabbis as late at the fourth century who denied the coming of a Messiah altogether. "The Jews have no longer any Messiah to expect, for they have already had him in the days of Hezekiah" (San. 99a). There were others, like Rabbi Samuel, who stripped the Messianic idea of all of its apocalyptic accretions: "There is nothing that will be different in the Messianic times from the present, except freedom from foreign domination" (Ber. 34b). The social order will not be subjected to any radical change.

It is very significant that while entertaining the hope of the coming of a Messiah, Judaism never accepted any specific Messiah. The Jewish people must have sensed that the idea, inspiring as a hope, was hopeless as a reality. An actual Messiah is always an unfulfillment, an anticlimax. His appearance in history has time and again had disastrous consequences for the people. Judaism does not stand or fall with the belief in the Messiah.

Thus any group which made a materialized Messianism central in its belief would find itself inevitably drifting outside the mainstream of Jewish life and thought. Judaism, in spite of Messianic and eschatological hopes which were maintained by some or by many Jews around the first century of the Common Era, continued as a religion dedicated principally to social progress and to the duty of men to reconstruct themselves and society to conform to the ethical precepts of the Torah.

Judaism is not constructed around any drama of redemption. There is no term in the Hebrew language for "salvation" in a sacramental, redemptive sense. The idea that man needs to be "saved" either from the toils of life or from some original sin or from the prison house of matter or from baleful astrological influences is not part of Judaism.

"Saviour" and "Redeemer" in the Christological sense are not to be found in the Hebrew Bible.

Judaism's primary concern was to teach man not how sin came into the world, but how to avoid sin and how to repent of sin once having succumbed to it. All men are capable of sinning because all men are endowed with free will.

Because there is no original sin, there is no need for a redeemer. The doctrine of atonement through the suffering of another is nowhere found in the Hebrew Bible.

Man does not need saviours. Nor does man need mediators between himself and God. "No one comes to the Father, but by me" (John 14:6) is a concept alien to Judaism. Man needs help in his moral struggles—encouragement, hope, confidence. Such help comes from turning to God, and it is at all times available. Through repentance and amendment man's moral effort becomes the channel for the inflow of the grace of God.

Nor is faith alone sufficient to make atonement for man's sins. It is "deeds which make atonement for men" (M. Ta'anit 16a).

In Judaism a man is made upright both by his faith in God and by his good works, the former being demonstrated by the latter. His spiritual life is not consummated by faith in God—it begins there, and it is ethical conduct which brings him near to God.

Asceticism, non-resistance to evil, and otherworldliness were never strong features in the pattern of historic Judaism, as they undoubtedly were in the pattern of first-century Christianity.

A faith predominantly eschatological gives rise to a way of life and a set of precepts different from one which has no such sovereign interests. The former will urge men to forsake this world, to be in it but not of it. It will urge them to abandon their possessions, to choose poverty, to seek escape from the trammels of society in the life of religious seclusion, to avoid, wherever possible, marriage and the begetting of children. It will instruct them not to resist evil nor to revolt against any form of tyranny or slavery, for all these evils will soon pass away in the new world order which is swiftly approaching. Judaism, in which the eschatological element played no decisive role whatsoever, would naturally reject such a code in its entirety—and did.

Christianity from the outset was overwhelmingly ascetic in outlook. Even marriage was disapproved of in the early Church. In fact, among the great religions of mankind, it is in Christianity and Buddhism that celibacy received its highest endorsement. At best marriage was tolerated as a concession to human frailty.

To marry and to beget children in order to preserve the race is a divine command in Judaism. "Be fruitful and multiply" (Gen. 1:28) is the first commandment of the Bible.

Judaism, rejecting all forms of dualism, did not encourage acts of mortification or self-removal from society as a way to holiness. One need not and should not renounce what is lawful.

In Jesus' mystical outlook, the world was fast coming to an end and there was no point in resisting evil. It would automatically cease with the millennium and the imminent establishment of God's Kingdom. Man's chief concern should therefore be not to fight evil, but to prepare himself for the new age.

Normative Judaism did not subscribe to doctrines of non-resistance and pacifism. It demanded action from its devotees. It taught that there is evil in society and that it is man's duty to overcome it, by force, if need be, though force is by no means the only way by which evil can be overcome. It is not enough to improve oneself; one must also seek to improve one's environment. The only refuge from the cruel wrongs of the world is in the effort to set them right. There is no ethic of resignation in Judaism.

When Jesus declared, "My Kingdom is not of this world" (John 18:36), he correctly defined the nature of his gospel. But Judaism's Kingdom of God referred to the reign of the one true God on earth, to the conversion of all peoples to faith in Him alone, and to the establishment of universal justice and peace.

Where Judaism Differs

Part I: "That Man Should Be Saved"

SERMON, THE TEMPLE
FEBRUARY 10, 1952

When we speak of Judaism, its doctrines and its principles, we should bear in mind that we are dealing with a religion nearly 4,000 years old, which has spanned nearly two-thirds of the recorded history of mankind. Clearly, therefore, Judaism experienced changes and modifications through its long history—changes which were induced from within and from without. Organic evolution accounts for some of these changes; contact with alien cultures and civilization accounts for others. Jews found themselves time and again in new environments, both in Palestine and outside of Palestine, and faced the necessity of making adjustments to new social, political, and economic conditions and to new ideas, moral and spiritual. For Judaism is no more the product of one country than it is the product of one age. Judaism is not a precise, formulated creed of some sect or some denomination. It is the emergent spiritual way of life of a people, of an historic people. Many streams poured into the main channel of the religious evolution of Israel, some more decisive than others; some of considerable and others of negligible influence.

It should be borne in mind that Jews never built an iron wall about themselves or isolated themselves intellectually or spiritually, except in periods of the direst persecution when they were driven behind walls, or when in a desperate effort to survive forces which threatened to annihilate them or to submerge them completely, Judaism barricaded itself for a time behind measures of exclusiveness. But at all other times Jews were receptive to the cultures of other peoples. They freely received and as freely shared spiritual ideas. They were always zealous, of course, to protect and to keep intact what they regarded as intrinsically, essentially, and specifically Jewish.

To expect unfailing consistency and unvarying uniformity in this 4,000-year-old compendium of Jewish doctrines and teachings, and to expect constant agreement among its teachers on all matters is, therefore, to expect the impossible. In the vast literature of Judaism, one can find opposing opinions on many subjects, contradictory accounts of certain things, considerable controversy and debate over the most basic theological and ethical concepts. And if one is eager to do so, one can find stray references and sayings and dicta of rabbis and sages to prove almost any thesis he wishes to prove.

There were many sects in ancient Israel which differed among themselves sharply and, at times, irreconcilably on what they regarded Judaism to be, both in doctrine and in practice. One of the rabbis of the Talmud declared: "Israel was not dispersed before it broke up into twenty-four sects of heretics." Numerous sects flourished during the Second Commonwealth—that is, between the destruction of the First and the Second Temples, nearly six hundred years. Some stressed one phase of Judaism and others stressed another phase. Some were strictly literal in their interpretation of the laws of the Bible; others were more liberal; still others were more mystic. Some were influenced by the philosophies prevalent in the non-Jewish Hellenic world of antiquity, and merged Greek or Buddhist or Zoroastrian ideas with their own. Others emphasized otherworldliness in their religious thought, and austerity and asceticism in their manner of life. Still others were confirmed pacifists. Some were taken with extreme ideas of ritual cleanliness and kept themselves away from all contacts which would contaminate them. We had a great variety, a great diversity among our people. But the remarkable thing to remember is that in spite of all this variety, Judaism retained an unmistakable character of its own. In spite of the many byways which frequently led off from it, the highway continued clear, steady, and undeflected. Judaism never deviated so far from its essential self as to become something else. Its reverence for the past ensured for it a historic continuity. Thus, the religious monotheism of the rabbis of the Talmud and their code of ethics differed in no essential regard from those of the prophets who lived nearly a thousand years before them, and they differ in no essential regard from those of their successors to this present day. Here and there one finds a difference of emphasis, a weightier or a lighter accent. Here and there there is a nuance, significant but not critical. But there is no transvaluation of values.

Judaism was fortunate in what Dr. Solomon Schechter called "a happy inconsistency." It never permitted itself to follow an idea, even a good idea, through to its logical conclusion, which often means a *reductio ad absurdum*—making a thing absurd or ridiculous. For example, Judaism loved peace. It was the first religion of mankind that proclaimed the ideal of "beating swords into plowshares and learning war no more." Yet normative Judaism never passed over into pacifism, as some small sects in ancient Israel did, and as Christianity did, because it was clear that the theory could not sustain the practice. Again, Judaism accepted the idea of a Messiah, but it never accepted any Messiah, for the idea was inspiring as a hope but hopeless as a reality. An actual Messiah is always an unfulfillment, always an anticlimax.

Or take the matter of the Bible. The Bible was looked upon by authoritative Judaism as the revealed word of God, and in the Bible it was clearly stated that there must be nothing added to it or detracted from it. Yet Judaism, true to the spirit of the Bible and desirous of keeping its laws vital, relevant, and not obsolete, found ways of interpreting Scripture so that much was added and much was detracted without doing violence to its spirit and to its integrity, although there were sects in Israel—some of them very influential sects like the Sadducees, like the Karaites—who clamorously insisted upon the literal interpretation of this law that nothing shall be added to the Bible and nothing taken from it.

There was the idea which was prevalent among our people that man was made in the image of God. Man was called in the Bible the "child of God." "Ye are children unto the Lord your God." No faith stressed so strongly man's kinship with God, *every* man's kinship with God—not just that of kings and rulers, which ancient people likewise stressed. But Judaism rejected every attempt to give a literal meaning to this idea of a "child of God," or a "son of God." It rejected every attempt to call any man divine, or the doctrine that the divine ever assumed the form of a man. Judaism kept religious imagery within bounds.

There is a remarkable balance and sanity and pragmatic quality to Judaism. While not discouraging deviations, either deviations into spiritual extremes or into the mystic or into excessive zeal, Judaism nevertheless kept these in their place, as it were, and reduced their importance. The periphery is never confused with the center, with the core; and the surface eddies were never mistaken for the deep carrying channels.

In this regard Judaism differed from many of the other great religions of mankind as sharply as it differed from the universal polytheism of the ancient world. Though polytheism was the religious form of many nations that in many ways were far superior intellectually, scientifically, and artistically to the Jewish people, Judaism never wavered in its faith in monotheism, and it also differed in many important regards from the other classical monotheistic religions of mankind. There is a quality to Jewish ethics and to Jewish religious doctrine which set it apart.

Take this concept of salvation, this idea that man needs to be saved. In nearly every religion there is the idea that man needs to be saved. But in nearly every religion the idea takes on a different coloration from what it has in Judaism. In Buddhism, for example, man needs to be saved from the toils of life itself—from existence; man needs to be saved from his own individuality. It is the will to live that is at the root of all man's suffering and unhappiness. Man needs to be saved from the world of the senses, because the world is wholly ill and evil, and anxiety is always at the core of all existence. Therefore, man should not strive for self-preservation, for self-development, for the integration of his personality; man should strive for self-extinction, self-denial. To be saved is to forego all desire, all ambitions, even good ambitions, to transcend one's individuality and lose one's self in Nirvana, in self-extinction, as a drop of water loses itself in the ocean.

That is one conception of how a man is to be saved; it is not Judaism's conception of salvation. Judaism is a strong affirmation of life. It is a prophetic faith which believes that while there is evil in the life of man and of society, it can by moral effort and exertion be overcome to a degree where man's life upon earth may yield him a large measure of happiness and satisfaction. Judaism does believe in the development of the individual through education and through moral exercise. Judaism does believe in social progress and in the value of social progress. Salvation, therefore, is to be found in action and in living, not in escape or denial. Salvation is to be found in spiritual self-confidence, and not in self-destruction.

In Christianity salvation took on another specific meaning. A man is saved only through faith in Jesus Christ, whose death upon the cross atoned for the original sin which the first man, Adam, by his disobedience committed. In Adam all mankind sinned and was condemned. That original sin had to be removed before God could forgive man and be reconciled to mankind, and this was achieved by the sacrifice of Jesus, by his suffering and his death. Man's reconciliation to God was achieved by a vicarious atonement for this original sin. In this sense Jesus is the Saviour; those who believe in him and accept his sacrifice are saved, and no one else. Salvation is thus achieved not by good works, not by merit, not by self-effort, but by an act of faith and an act of grace.

Man himself has not the strength or the will to save himself. God had to intervene by incarnating Himself in the personality of Jesus, and by making the blood sacrifice which reconciles man to Him. Salvation is thus a gift of God to sinful man, not the achievement of man himself. This thought is central dogma both to Catholicism and to Protestantism, though in some instances modern liberal Christianity has deviated from it to the point of maintaining that salvation is achieved through man's embodiment in his life of the character and the ideals of Jesus. But overwhelmingly it is the doctrine of salvation through faith in atonement as proclaimed by Paul, the true founder of the Christian church, that is authoritative for Christianity. "Therefore we conclude," said Paul, "that a man is justified by faith without the deeds of the law." Again he said, "As by the offense of one man, Adam, judgment came upon all men to condemn them, even so by the righteousness of one [Jesus], the free gift came upon all men unto justification of life."

Judaism rejected this conception of salvation. To be sure, we find occasional references in Jewish literature to the idea of original sin, but it never came to hold such a central or indispensable place in Jewish theology as it did in Christian theology. It was never made an article of faith in which a Jew must believe. It belonged to what we may call Aggada, the non-authoritative and fluctuating popular religious lore of Judaism, which never became part of the essential credo of the Jew. You could accept it or reject it. Your status as a believing Jew remained unimpaired, or for that matter, unimproved.

In the same category with the idea of original sin belonged the idea of original merit, or what is known in our literature as "the merits of the Fathers," of the patriarchs, of Abraham, Isaac, and Jacob, whose good deeds were so great that from their treasury of accumulated merit, a subsequent generation could borrow toward their own salvation.

In the Ten Commandments we read that God "visits the sins of the fathers upon the children until the third and fourth generation and showeth mercy unto the thousandth generation of them that love Me and keep My commandments." Here the idea of transmitted guilt and transmitted merit is accepted, but with a clear statement that the relationship between the influence of merit and the influence of guilt upon subsequent generations is in the ratio of one thousand to four. Nevertheless, even this Biblical judgment embodied in the Ten Commandments was challenged very early by the great prophets of Israel, by Jeremiah, for example, and Ezekiel. Ezekiel says, "Therefore, I will judge you, O house of Israel, everyone according to his ways, saith the Lord God." "The soul that sinneth, it shall die; the son shall not bear the iniquity of the father, neither shall the father bear the iniquity of the son." If fathers have eaten sour grapes, the teeth of the children will not, therefore, be set on edge.

The religious leaders of all subsequent times accepted this prophetic view of moral responsibility, of guilt or of merit. Thus, they brush aside the notion of "merits of the Fathers" by declaring that it was discontinued long ago in the days of King Hezekiah. The account was closed. "Let not a man say, my father was a pious man; I shall be saved for his sake. Abraham could not save Ishmael, nor Jacob save Esau."

In other words, Judaism did not hold that man was lost because of any inherited depravity from which he had to be saved, nor that his salvation depended upon the vicarious sacrifice of some saviour. Judaism did hold that man is born imperfect and that his destiny is to perfect himself. Man must develop himself mentally, morally, spiritually. He is capable of fulfilling his destiny or of rejecting it. He may make the effort or he may refuse to make it. There are forces within him which urge him to rise through moral effort to higher levels, and there are also forces which tempt him to sink to a lower level in greed, in lust, in indolence. In other words, man can be saved by his own moral effort, by his own moral aspiration from betraying the best that he is capable of, from the temptations which beset him, or from the burden of guilt which his sins may have put upon him. If he makes the effort, God will help him. All men are liable to sin, but all men are also free to repent. No one is totally disabled morally. God is ready to forgive: "God does not desire the death of the sinner but that he should return and live." God is gracious. He is the God of forgiveness.

God is gracious and forgiving, long-suffering, and full of kindness and of truth. God will do more for man than man deserves if only man makes the initial effort to rehabilitate himself. Man does not require the atonement blood of another to save him. Man does not need saviours. Man needs teachers, guides, and his own strong will. Nor is a particular belief, any particular belief, not even Judaism, a condition of salvation. Salvation is open to all men, even to those who do not accept Judaism. The rabbis declared: "The righteous among the gentiles will inherit the world to come." If men only avoid the immoral practices of murder and incest, of adultery, of robbery, of the eating of the flesh of living animals, of idolatry and blasphemy—the so-called Seven Laws of Noah—they are in the same category with the most pious among the Jews who observe the 613 commandments.

Judaism maintained that salvation is not achieved by faith alone or through the mediation of anyone. Man needs help in his struggles, in his efforts—encouragement, hope, confidence. If man needs any help from faith in his struggles to save himself from his lower self and to rise to higher levels, it comes from faith in God himself. "I cried unto Thee, unto Thee alone, O God." It is by deeds and good works that a man rises. It is by them that a man is brought nearer to God. "Your deeds will bring you nearer to God and your deeds will estrange you from God." It is deeds, it is the good life which make atonement for man.

Here I should like to point out that it is characteristic of Judaism to lay the greatest emphasis on doing, on conduct, on practice. Learning is important, but not as important as leading a good life. Thus, one of the great rabbis said, "A man who has learned much Torah and has good deeds is like a horse which has reins. The man who has the first, but not the second, is like a horse without reins; it soon throws the rider over its head." How true that is of the intellectual and the sophisticated person whose life is not held steady by moral purpose, by moral conduct, by sound moral guiding principles. How true that is of our whole world today, so learned, so advanced scientifically, and yet so morally anarchic. The rider has been thrown time and again because of the lack of a sound moral foundation.

Another great teacher declared, "Let a man first do good deeds and then ask God for knowledge of the Torah. Let a man first act as righteous and upright men act and then let him ask God for wisdom. Let a man first grasp the way of humility and then ask God for understanding." Learning is important, but not as important as conduct. Faith is important—faith in God is vital—but it is not the supreme ingredient in the life of the faithful. There is a startling statement of the rabbis which sums up this characteristic outlook of Judaism. God is made to declare: "Would that they would forsake Me but keep My law."

If a man has sinned—and what man does not sin?—he is redeemed from sin by repentance and by acts of righteousness, by *teshubah*, by *tzedakah*. They are the conditions of salvation. It is not acknowledging God or confessing a sin which are the conditions of a man's being saved from the consequences of his action, but the changing of his way of life—reparation, restitution, redirection of his way of life. "If a man is guilty of sin," declared one of the sages, "and confesses it and does not change his way, unto what is he like? He is like unto a man who holds a defiling object in his hand even while he is immersing himself in purifying waters. All the waters in the world will not avail him. He remains unclean because he clings to his defilement."

Sometimes the people of Israel, facing grave dangers, were taught to pray for deliverance in utter humility and complete recumbency on God. "It is not for the sake of our righteousness and the good deeds we possess that Thou wilt save us, but deliver us for the sake of Thy righteousness." This is a poetic expression of trust in God's goodness and compassion. It is not to be taken as a theological formula for obtaining salvation. The classic position is that Israel or any people must repent and improve its way before it can enjoy God's favor and help.

Now, you may think I am discussing ancient ideas which have no relevancy to the world today and to philosophy today. You would be mistaken in so believing. The doctrine that man is helpless to save himself reappears in our own day, in the philosophy of what has come to be called existentialism, which received its formulation in the early part of the nineteenth century at the hands of the brilliant Danish religious philosopher Søren Kierkegaard, and has won many disciples in Christian circles in recent decades, and, more recently, even among some Jewish theologians of the type of Martin Buber. A writer by the name of Will Herberg has recently written a book called *Judaism and Modern Man,* in which he sets out to give an existentialist interpretation of Judaism. Now, what is this existentialism? It is a philosophy grounded in deep pessimism and disillusionment, holding that man is trapped helplessly and cannot escape the predicaments in which his existence is involved. By his own capacities man cannot redeem himself. He is a bundle of contradictions. Man is the slave of boundless desires which he cannot satisfy. His mind is constricted by inescapable paradoxes which he cannot resolve. He must make choices time and again, but heredity and environment make it impossible for him to make free choices. Man should be just to his neighbor, and yet his self-interests are in conflict with his altruism. Man cannot help himself; only divine grace can save man from his evil nature and redeem man from himself. Man needs a redeemer. For the Christians it may be Christ; for the Jew it is God. This same pessimism and disillusionment with the scientific, social, and political movements of our day, which promised so much for man but which have resulted in such fear and anguish and human suffering, underlie the secular branch of this philosophy of existentialism of the school of Jean-Paul Sartre, which approaches spiritual chaos and nihilism.

All this is rejected by Judaism. Judaism rejects this exaggerated pessimism with regard to man's nature and man's endowments. Man can, to a large extent, make his own world; and man has, to a large degree, made his own world. In spite of setbacks and throwbacks, it has been a progressive world. Man has moved forward to more knowledge, to higher standards of living, to greater justice, to better health conditions, to greater and more energetic efforts at the eradication of poverty and exploitation in the world. The pace is frequently slow and frequently checkered and frequently reversed, yet, if you take the long view of history, man has risen from the jungles of barbarism and bestiality to higher levels.

Judaism maintains today, as it has maintained all along, that man is a co-worker of God in creation. Man is finite and yet not helpless. Man is conditioned; yet he is free. Man cannot think as God, but man can think about God. Man does not know the ultimate answers, but in faith he can work with relative truths and find satisfaction and happiness in his work, provided it is sincere work and well-intentioned and directed toward God and toward man.

"Thine is not the duty to complete the task—neither art thou free to desist from it." "Share your burden with the Lord and He will sustain thee. He will never suffer the righteous to be moved." Share your burden with God, but above all, work, strive, seek, and as you work, pray. "Establish Thou the work of our hands; yea, the work of our hands, establish Thou it." In other words, on the subject of whether a man needs to be saved, Judaism has differed with many, if not with all the great religions of mankind. Man need not be saved from any imputed guilt of the past. A man does not require anyone else to atone for him for his sins. A man is saved from his own sins and from his own lower self by moral aspiration, by seeking to lead the good life. "He who seeks self-perfection, he will be saved."

Where Judaism Differs

Part II: "That Man Should Not Enjoy Life"

SERMON, THE TEMPLE
FEBRUARY 17, 1952

Judaism has as distinctive an approach to the subject of man's happiness and enjoyment of life as it has to the subject of man's salvation. It differs as sharply with many of the religions and philosophies of mankind on whether a man should enjoy life as it does on whether a man needs to be saved, and how. To many of us it seems strange to raise the question, Should a man enjoy his life on earth? Yet that is the question that is at the heart of many of the religions and philosophies of mankind, and I dare say that their predominant answer is in the negative, negative in two ways: that man does not, and that man should not, enjoy life.

When you come to think of it, man has always been afraid of life, and there is much in life to make him afraid, much that is darkly baffling and unknown, much that is evil and wrong, much of pain and sorrow, and overshadowing all and everything is the sure and ineluctable end of all—death! Man was never quite equal to the tribulations of life and never quite able to master the forces which determined the course of his life. He could not understand himself or his world; his origin or his destiny; what is above, what is below, what is before, what is behind. The vast impersonal occurrences in nature—floods, storms, droughts, earthquakes, plagues —frequently crushed and overwhelmed man, and the destructive social forces which he could not control—wars and invasions, tyranny and oppression—undermined his confidence in himself and filled him with anxiety often bordering on a sense of doom and of veritable terror. Now this apprehension was not limited merely to primitive societies or primitive cultures. Enlightened civilizations, even sophisticated civilizations, experienced it. It was known in the ancient classical world, and it is not alien to our modern world. The mood of pessimism is widespread in our day, induced by the disillusionment born of the failure of science and intellectual advancement to bring man that security and that order and that peace for which he had hoped.

No wonder, then, that so many of the great systems of human thought and belief stressed the sadness of life and the futility of life, and urged men to escape life if possible, to transcend it. Some religions, like Buddhism and, at certain stages, Hinduism, from which Buddhism derived, regarded the very fact of life itself as evil and the cause of all human suffering. There can be no happiness for man because life itself, being, existence as such, is evil. Therefore, not only is the love of life, its physical as well as intellectual attachments, to be renounced by man, but also the very idea of existence itself, of self. Self-disintegration, in other words, is, according to these philosophies, the highest law and the highest duty and the highest privilege of man. His task is, so to speak, to regain that state of perfection which was his before he fell into this world.

Other systems of religion and philosophies did not find the root of all evil and of all unhappiness in life itself, but in the duality which exists in life, and in the conflict which this duality induces in the life of man. In other words, there are two realities in the world—matter and spirit, body and soul, darkness and light, good and evil. They are two powers, if you will, two gods who are in eternal and irreconcilable conflict one with another, and man is torn between the two.

Matter is all evil. According to these philosophic speculations and religions, the body, the physical body, is all evil, irremediably evil. The human soul is imprisoned in this body, held in thrall by its passions and its desires, its instincts. The human soul seeks escape from this bodily enthrallment. Therefore, the more you curb your physical self, your passions, your desires which are sinful, the more you assist in the freeing of the soul. The higher part of man, of course, is his soul; and for the sake of its freedom, man, according to these philosophies, should resist all pleasures, all earthly ambitions which keep the soul in chains. Holding the body in contempt, subduing the flesh, repudiating all the urgings and the promptings of the body, practicing poverty and fasting and self-castigation, removing yourself, if need be, from society itself—this is the way which leads to the free and exalted spiritual life. The ideal man, therefore, is the saint, the man who has renounced the material world completely.

This dualism was a widely accepted doctrine in many of the religions of antiquity. In Zoroastrianism, for example, the religion of the Aryans of Persia, you find this dualism represented as the two cosmic forces of good and evil. One was the good god, Ahura Mazda, the god of light and of love; the other was the god of darkness and of evil, Ahriman. Among the enlightened Greeks, Plato made this dualism of matter and spirit and of matter and mind, of the sensible and the ideal, central to his philosophy, and later systems of thought, such as Neo-Platonism, expanded this idea. You have heard of the Cynics, that interesting school of Greek philosophers of the fourth century before the Common Era, who looked upon all the pleasures of life as evil, including intellectual pleasures such as the study of philosophy. The Stoics, who in a sense derived from the school of the Cynics and were so numerous in the Greco-Roman world for so many years, maintained that health and wealth and a good name did not contribute to happiness. They advocated rigorous self-restraint and a repressive regimen as the ideal way of life.

In the first centuries of the Common Era a religious philosophy much in vogue in the Mediterranean world was called Gnosticism. Gnosticism influenced Christianity. At the root of this philosophy was the self-same contrast between matter and spirit, the conviction that the material world was altogether evil. It was not even the handiwork of the true God, but of some inferior cosmic deity. Man should escape from the fetters of this bodily existence to the true world of the spirit, which was the true world of the spiritual God. And the way of escape is the way of asceticism. Paul held this doctrine of dualism, of the pure spirit and of the sinful body. "So, brothers, we are under obligations," he declared, "but not to the physical nature, to live under its control, for if you live under the control of the physical, you will die, but if, by means of the spirit, you put the body's doings to death, you will live." The way to put the body's doings to death was to subdue them by strict ascetic practices.

There were two reasons why Christianity in the early centuries was overwhelmingly ascetic in its outlook. In the first place, it was firmly rooted in this doctrine of the dual nature of man; also it believed in the immediacy of the end of the world, or in the second coming of the Redeemer, who would usher in a new order into which only the utterly pure and righteous would enter. All others would perish. The way of life, therefore, which Christianity offered was for a world *in extremis*; the crash and doom of the world was at hand. Christianity called upon men to disencumber themselves of all those things which are likely to keep their minds and their souls entangled in the affairs of this perishing world. Even marriage was derogated, or at best only tolerated, for it tends to divide man's interests. "If you are united to a wife," declared Paul, "do not seek to be released, but if you are not, do not seek a wife." To remain unmarried is to secure one's undivided devotion to the Lord. If, however, a man's passions are too strong, let him marry, for it is better to marry than to be on fire with passion. Marriage was a concession to human weakness.

More extreme views were also held. Some proclaimed celibacy as the only correct way for the faithful Christian. In the second century, Marcion, whose extreme Gnostic views influenced the early church and at times threatened to submerge it completely, was an extreme ascetic. He condemned marriage and insisted upon celibacy. To bring children into the world was only to perpetuate this sinful world. A holy man was he who disregarded all family and earthly ties, became a recluse from human society, and practiced severe austerities to purify his soul. These ideas captivated many minds and gave rise to those institutions which we call the hermitages, the monasteries and nunneries, to religious orders of itinerant beggars, to saints who lived in caves and cemeteries, in deserts or on solitary mountains or on pillars, to strange practices of bodily mortification and all forms of ascetic extravagance. One finds such ideas in the early Christian church, in Buddhism, in Hinduism, and among the Greek schools of philosophy, and also in Islam.

Thus, in the laws of Marim, which gives the regimen of practice for the ideal man in the Hindu religion, the following way of life is assigned to him:

> The ascetic (the saint) in summer let him expose himself to the heat . . . during the rainy season live under the open sky, and in winter be dressed in wet clothes, gradually increasing his austerities. When he bathes at sunrise, noon and sunset let him offer libations of water to the manes and the gods, and practicing harsher and harsher austerities, let him dry up his bodily frame . . . let him live without a fire, without a house, wholly silent, subsisting on roots and fruit . . . sleeping on the bare ground, dwelling at the roots of trees. Having thus passed the third part of life in the forest, he may live as an ascetic during the fourth part of his existence, after abandoning all attachment to worldly objects . . . after offering sacrifices and subduing his senses. . . . Departing from his house . . . let him wander about absolutely silent, and caring nothing for enjoyments that may be offered.

Let him always wander alone without any companion, in order to attain his final liberation. . . . He shall neither possess a fire nor a dwelling, he may go to a village to beg for his food, indifferent to everything, firm of purpose, meditating and concentrating his mind on Brahman. An almsbowl, the roots of a tree for a dwelling, coarse worn-out garments, life in solitude and indifference towards everything, these are the marks of one who wishes to attain complete liberation.

Judaism rejected all these ideas and all these practices. There are no ascetic teachings in our Bible. Here and there is a stray reference to some Nazarite or some Rechabite, but they represented no considerable groups in Israel, and left no impression at all upon the authoritative religion of our people. There are no monasteries and no nunneries in Judaism. There are no ascetic prescriptions in the Shulchan Aruch. The law of Judaism on the subject is very clear. Maimonides, in his code, clearly defines the authoritative and the legal position of Judaism on this entire subject.

Perhaps a man will say: inasmuch as jealousy, passion, love of honor, etc., are evil and bring about a man's downfall, therefore, "I will remove myself from them," to the point where he will refrain from eating meat or drinking wine or marrying or living in a pleasant dwelling place or wearing an attractive garment—nothing but sackcloth and coarse wool—just as some Gentile priests and monks do. This is an evil way and is forbidden! He who follows these practices is called a Sinner! . . . Our sages ordained that a man should refrain only from those things which the Torah prohibits and he should not, through vows and oaths, deny himself those things which are permitted. . . . This applies also to those people who are continually fasting. They, too, are not doing the right thing. Our sages forbid a man to afflict himself through fasting. Concerning all these and similar matters, Solomon declared: "Be not righteous over-much and do not make thyself over-wise—why shouldst thou destroy thyself. . . ."

While, for example, the church encouraged or extolled celibacy, Judaism maintained that the first of all mitzvot, the first of all commandments, was that a man should build a home, marry, beget children. "Any man who is not married is not completely a man." "A man who is not married persists in a condition of life without joy, without blessing, without goodness." No High Priest could hold that office or could officiate in the Temple unless he was married. The mutilation of one's body was forbidden by the Torah, and the hideous practices which one can still see among many ascetics in India today are abhorrent to Judaism.

According to Judaism, one need not and one should not renounce what is lawful. Food and drink are given by God to man to sustain life. "Thou preparest a table before me. . . . My cup runneth over." One should partake of the gifts of God in gladness and bless Him for His bounty. Judaism taught men not to despise the gifts of God, but to offer thanksgiving for them. *"Boruch atto adonoy"*—"Blessed art Thou, O Lord" for bread and wine, for fruit and oil, for spices, for fragrant plants, for a beautiful tree or a rainbow, for all the goodness and the beauty and the joy that is in the world.

Rabbi Judah declared: "In the spring when a man goes forth and beholds beautiful trees swaying in the air, he should stop and offer a prayer: Blessed is the Lord for having created a world in which nothing is wanting and for having fashioned living things and beautiful trees and plants to delight the heart of man."

The famous Abba Arika, Rab, who with Samuel established important schools and academies in Babylon and made Babylon a center of rabbinic studies, declared: "A man will some day have to give an account to God for all the good things which his eyes beheld and of which he refused to partake." And it was Rab who composed this beautiful prayer, which is characteristic of the balance, the sanity, the good sense, the essential humanity which is Judaism, and is incorporated in our prayer books and recited on the Sabbath ushering in a new month:

> May it be Thy will, O Lord our God and God of our fathers, to renew unto us this coming month for good and for blessing. O grant us long life, a life of peace, of good, of blessing, of bodily vigor, a life marked by the reverence of God and the fear of sin, a life free from shame and reproach, a life of prosperity and honor, a life in which the love of the Law and the fear of Heaven shall cleave to us, a life in which the desires of our heart shall be fulfilled for good. Amen.

This is an Amen to life itself. This is a great affirmation of life; as such, it is characteristic of Judaism.

The wise physician Ben Sirah declared: "Defraud not thyself of the good day, and let not the part of a good desire pass thee by, for there is no seeking of dainties in the grave."

The rabbis of the Talmud were not monks or anchorites. Here and there one comes upon one who practiced austerities, for one reason or another. But he is a rare exception. These rabbis did not seclude themselves in religious austerities or pledge themselves to poverty or celibacy. They worked and earned their living and lived and moved among their fellow men in the normal pursuits of life. Only they made a study of the Torah an especial task, a privileged enterprise of their lives. They did not go through the communities with a staff and a bowl as did some religious mystics and dervishes and friars, begging alms to sustain themselves while they were practicing austerities for the sake of their souls. The teachers of our religion have few kind words to say about poverty generally, except to urge its eradication through social justice and loving-kindness. "Poverty in a man's home," they said, "is worse than fifty plagues." Here and there we find a teacher like Philo, who, under the influence of Greek philosophy, extols asceticism. Here and there in the Middle Ages we find a philosopher like Bachya, who, under the influence of Arabic pietism, extols asceticism. Occasionally in times of dire persecution and deep longing and during expectancy of the coming of the Messiah to redeem them from exile, a mood of sadness would settle over this or that section of our people, and they would resort to a regimen of penance and fasting to hasten the coming of the Messiah. We find such practices among the Chassidim of Germany, who are not to be confused with the Hasidim of eastern Europe in the eighteenth century. We find such practices again among the Cabalists of Safed and their followers in the sixteenth century and among the Jewish communities of eastern Europe who suffered so terribly as a result of the Cossack uprisings in the middle of the seventeenth century, when nearly one-third of European Jewry was destroyed.

But this mood was not a permanent mood and was not sustained by any basic religious doctrine. There was never a time when the tree was enveloped and hidden by the creepers which clung to it. In eastern Europe, a mood of sadness and depression had settled upon our people as a result of wars which had destroyed hundreds of thousands of Jews. It was not long thereafter, at the beginning of the eighteenth century, that a movement arose among these selfsame Jews, led by a marvelous personality, Israel Baal-Shem Tov, that put an end to this languishing spirit of melancholy and despair which was pervading Jewish ranks, and restored the spirit of joy and faith and confidence among the people. This was the movement of the Hasidim. The cry which swept over the war-ravaged communities was not to let go, not to yield to despair, but to endure, to worship the Lord in joy. If you have trust in God, you need not despair, you need not be sad, you need not be afraid. "The Guardian of Israel sleepeth not nor slumbereth." God is at work in history. The faithful one is patient and perseveres, unafraid. Hasidism put an end to this mood of despondency and to these practices of austerities and asceticism.

It is told that a young man came to a Hasidic rabbi to be ordained. The rabbi inquired regarding his daily conduct, and the candidate replied, "I always dress in white, I drink only water, I place tacks in my shoes for self-mortification, I roll naked in the snow, and I order the synagogue caretaker to give me forty stripes daily on my bare back." Just then a white horse entered the courtyard, drank water, began rolling in the snow. "I observe," said the rabbi, "this creature is white, it drinks only water, it has nails in its shoes, it rolls in the snow, and it receives more than forty stripes a day. Still it is nothing but a horse."

It should not be assumed that Judaism offered men hedonism or that it taught that pleasure was the be-all and the end-all of human life. Epicureanism was disallowed and viewed by Judaism as a deviation. Man exists to fulfill himself in the service of God. That is the philosophy of Judaism. The aim of life is defined in the Torah—to serve God through a life of goodness and justice and love. "Thou hast been told, O man, what is good and what the Lord doth require of thee—to do justice, to love mercy, to walk humbly with God." This calls for a life free from all forms of excess, which weaken and undermine a man's powers and keep him from functioning most effectively in the attainment of these objectives. In Judaism there is neither hedonism nor quietism nor escapism nor asceticism. Judaism is the religion of a virile people, of a life-loving and life-affirming people, prophetic and this-worldly in its basic emphasis and outlook, conscious of a vital mission and a high destiny. This world is not evil. What is evil in man's world can be set right by man, and God will help man to set it right if man will make the effort.

There is a future, a bright future, for the human race. There is the hope of the end of days, when wars will cease and poverty will cease and fear will be driven from the habitations of man, and men will dwell under their vines and under their fig trees with none to make them afraid.

To achieve all this, man must train himself for moral action through a life of virtue, which is not a life of austerities but a life of balance, of moderation, not suppressing his instincts and his desires but controlling them, guiding them. The contrast which Judaism drew was not between desires and freedom from all desires, but between good desires and evil desires, or the abuse and perversion of desire. The strict monotheism of our religion held in firm check this tendency toward dualism and toward belief in two powers, which we saw was at the root of all the extreme ascetic movements in the world. "The soul is Thine, O Lord and the body, too, is Thy handiwork." Judaism taught a way of balance and moderation. It asked not for the repudiation of life but for its sanctification, not for asceticism but for purity.

Concerning the whole mystic approach to life, there is a remarkable saying of one of the rabbis: "The mystical doctrine can be compared to two paths, one of which leads into Fire and the other into Ice. Whoever strays into the former perishes in Fire, and whoever strays into the latter perishes in Ice. What should a man do? He should walk in the middle."

In the Book of Proverbs we read: "Hast thou found honey? Eat as much as is sufficient for thee, lest thou be surfeited and vomit." If you have found honey in life, do not reject it, do not turn away from it. It is good nourishment for a man, but good nourishment only when partaken of in moderation.

The pleasures of life are not to be rejected, but on the other hand they must not be permitted to enslave us to the point where we become surfeited and glutted and, through overindulgence and consequent enervation, come to hate life. To yield indiscriminately to our appetites is to destroy ourselves. To be unsatiable—that is the great sin of life. To be unsatiable—in sin or in virtue—and to think of enjoyment of life merely in terms of physical pleasures is to reduce ourselves to the level of the animal.

The lasting satisfactions of life come from home, from friends, from the good repute which we enjoy among our neighbors and in our community, from learning which helps to keep us young, from joining with our fellow men in building the good society which gives purpose and dignity to our lives—these are the things which contribute pre-eminently to the enjoyment of life. Unfortunately, many people forget this fact.

Again, there are things which we as human beings must do in the world which do not at the moment give us pleasure. There are duties we must perform which at times involve sacrifice and suffering and struggle. These things are not to be included in the category of pleasures, but they are the essential ingredients of the worthy life, and they yield man the deep and lasting inner satisfactions, the pride of being a human being, of acting as if he were indeed fashioned in the image of God. To speak of the enjoyment of life, we should ask ourselves what we mean by enjoyment. What life are we talking about—the total life of man, mind and body, the full development of all of our capacities, physical, mental, and spiritual, or are we thinking merely of the enjoyment of life in terms of food and drink and the things we put on our backs?

Self-discipline is essential to a sane and wholesome enjoyment of life, but that self-discipline does not come through asceticism. That self-discipline comes through observing the law of God as it is defined for us in our Torah, in our ethical code.

So here again in one of the basic problems of human existence, Judaism had an answer which differed in an essential way from that which was given by many of the great religions and philosophies of history, but one which modern psychology and the deepest knowledge of which man has been capable in our day is vindicating and reaffirming. When we talk of psychosomatics, we are talking in modern terminology of that simple but profound truth which Judaism proclaimed so many centuries ago. The body and the soul make up one unity. The abuse of the one or the neglect of the one contributes to disharmony, to lack of balance, and therefore to unhappiness—sometimes to pathological suffering. A balance contributes to wholesomeness of living. Religion was given to man, according to our philosophy, to help him live a happy and satisfying existence upon this earth, and to prepare himself for a future beyond his ken and beyond his world, a future known only to God.

VI. THE RABBI

At THIS sacred hour I would pray to Him who is my strength and my fortress and my refuge, that I might prove worthy of the service to which I have been called, and deserving of the faith which men have placed in me; that His spirit might descend upon me, granting to my work and my ministry an abiding value and an enkindling enthusiasm and a power which will enable me to touch the lives of some of you, win some soul to higher aspirations, and guide some hand in its outreachings for the higher gifts of God. I would pray for the men and women of this congregation, and for their earnest efforts to rise to ever higher altitudes, to widen the circle of their life's interests so as to include a segment of the infinite. I would pray that their loyalties and sincerities may reveal unto them the purposefulness of life and the glory of service, that they may drink deep of the waters of contentment at the fountains of spiritual salvation; and I would pray that Tifereth Israel, rededicated and reconsecrated, may in a still larger measure serve the cause of Israel and Israel's faith, that it may continue to be a blessing unto men, reaching out into their lives, mellowing their higher ambitions and inspiring their finer motives; that the young men and women who shall be reared under its influence may grow into splendid manhood and womanhood, and into a supreme and transcendent devotion to their people and to its great, imperishable mission.

PRAYER OFFERED BY RABBI SILVER
ON THE OCCASION OF HIS INSTALLATION AT
THE TEMPLE, OCTOBER 14, 1917

In the spring of 1963, before a meeting of the Central Conference of American Rabbis, Abba Hillel Silver and Solomon B. Freehof engaged each other in a public dialogue. The packed hall was utterly still as these two leaders of the American rabbinate reflected aloud on their lives.

Rabbi Silver spoke about the duties and problems of the American rabbi who was called on to be "pastor of his flock, tribune of his people to the non-Jewish world, defender of social justice"—but who must be principally "a teacher," teaching young and old the spiritual and ethical doctrines of Judaism. In this task, the rabbi would encounter obstacles—"the inertia of people, the sluggishness of progress, downright opposition. . . . But these need not destroy or even retard his true career. They could even temper and strengthen him. The greatest obstacle which a rabbi may encounter is himself. Lack of character or courage or tact or sensitivity; false objectives, like a desire for excessive publicity, or the eagerness to be well liked by everybody—such inner deficiencies will in the long run corrode a rabbi from within." So went Rabbi Silver's thoughts that evening.

"Now, Abba," Rabbi Freehof then asked his former classmate and lifelong friend, "a man can't help saying occasionally a word about something he has done—*Zeh chelki mikol amoli*—'this is my portion from all of my labor.' Suppose you had to go over Abba Hillel Silver's career. What would you consider your best achievements of everything you have done?"

"The contribution which I made toward the establishment of the State of Israel," was Rabbi Silver's reply. "This is not, of course, technically speaking, a rabbinic achievement. But it was never separate or apart from my profession as a rabbi. Zionism has always been a part of my conception of historic Judaism, and I came to it not as a secular nationalist but as a devout Jew, and I never permitted my Zionist activities, even when they were most intense, to push aside or to overshadow my activities and duties as a rabbi."

"And what, if anything, would you count as your chief failure?"

Silver smiled with the audience at his friend's question.

"Sol, I would rather have my enemies speak of my failures. They can do it much better than I."

Then he offered his answer.

"I am conscious of many failures in my life, but of no chief failure. In things worthwhile, my reach almost always exceeded my grasp; and in every human relationship, I think I could have done better. And if I were to live my life over again, I would correct the mistakes which I made, and I am sure I would make many others."

There was a pause in the dialogue, and in the large hall, after this reply. Rabbi Silver had given his answer quietly, simply. Everyone knew that he had spoken the truth he felt in his heart.

But the pause expressed something else. It was the pause of recognition before a life that all knew had been lived with remarkable faithfulness to its own truth. Before them, the rabbis saw a man whose personal religiosity, devotion to Zionism, activity in behalf of his people and his land, and response to the social and economic needs of his day were all expressions of his core commitment as a rabbi. Prayer, and study; the needs of individuals and community; synagogue, school, and seminary—the full gamut of obligations devolving on a rabbi in America— Abba Hillel Silver valued, defended, and tried to lift to their highest level. The final selections of this book reflect the intensity of Abba Hillel Silver's devotion to the profession which he served and honored with his life.

The Synagogue

ADDRESS AT THE SEVENTIETH ANNIVERSARY OF
THE WASHINGTON HEBREW CONGREGATION
MAY, 1922

The two noblest achievements of the Jewish people are a Book and an institution—the one the Bible, the other the synagogue. I do not wish to speak this evening about the Bible, that marvelous and authentic record of all the varied and fretted moods of human life, a human document which is divine because it is so profoundly human; but I do want to say a word about the institution of the synagogue.

No other institution in Jewish life so adequately and so completely expresses the genius of the Jew. It was born, as you well know, in the Babylonian exile. It was the creation of Jewish laymen. It was never dominated by a priestly hierarchy. It never had a cult of sacrifices. It is the most democratic institution which the genius of the Jew evolved in three thousand years.

When the Jew returned from exile, he brought the synagogue back with him, and the synagogue gained the position of affection and devotion in the hearts of the people even during the Temple's existence. In the synagogue the youth were taught; the rabbis expounded the law to meet the advancing needs of life; the stranger was welcomed, and succor was given to the needy and distressed. When the Second Temple was destroyed, the synagogue gained complete possession of the life of Israel. And throughout the dark centuries of exile and wandering and oppression the synagogue was the refuge and sanctuary of the soul of our people. Having been born of the people it wandered with the people, and because it was a wandering tabernacle, the synagogue was never comparable in its physical aspects to the marvelous cathedrals and mosques which other peoples and other reli-

357

gions builded. In the Jewries of the Old World you do not find synagogues
that are resplendent in their physical form; most are bleak and small and
unadorned. You will find them in out-of-the-way places. Tourists are not
attracted by them, because there is little in them to attract the eye, unless
it be the eye of him who knows in what shabby garments the world always
clothes its most precious ideals.

I can understand why a painter like Sargent would represent the
synagogue as an old, haggard woman, sitting among the ruins of life, while
he represented the church as a radiant young maiden, full of beauty and
spiritual charm. Sargent, not being a Jew, saw only the physical synagogue.
He could not find there those towering domes and spires, those marvelous
columns pillared in grandeur, those naves suggesting the spaciousness and
aspiration of unencumbered lives, and those stained-glass windows which
hold within their imbued passionate glory all the creative hopefulness of a
free people.

Those things one cannot find in the gray sanctuaries of the Old
World. It is only in recent years that our people, enjoying a bit of freedom and prosperity, have begun to erect synagogues which in their physical expression body forth the grandeur of the spirit within. It is altogether
proper that we Jews who have been favored by God with freedom and
prosperity should express our overwhelming gratitude for these gifts of
benign Providence and our deep reverence for the sanctities of our faith by
building shrines whose bodily form is worthy of the spiritual splendor of
our faith. Shall we dwell in houses of cedar and the spirit of God dwell
behind curtains? The rabbis wisely said that a city whose housetops are
taller than the roof of the synagogue is doomed to destruction. The synagogue should, by its physical aspect, symbolize the prominence which it
occupies in the life of the community.

But whether our synagogues rival in beauty the religious houses of
other peoples or not, the synagogue is a thing quite apart from the house
which enshrines it. Throughout the Middle Ages and in many parts of the
world to this day, within these bleak houses, unattractive to any eye except
to the eye that can see into the heart of things, within these dank walls
and beneath these dark ceilings, the Jew raised for himself a spiritual synagogue of matchless artistry. Where others sought to express their faith in
Gothic column or in classic frieze, the Jew expressed his faith in spiritual
contours. The hunger for the beautiful in his life found satisfaction in
hymn and psalm and liturgic chant. His intellectual vigor and energy ex-

pressed themselves in the study of the Talmud and the sacred law of his people, and his passion for justice poured itself into his sacrificial loyalties to all that was true and noble in life. The world without could see only the drabness, the little structure in the dark ghetto alley; but the Jew within could exclaim, "How beautiful are Thy tents, O Israel!"

The Hebrew poet Bialik asks in one of his poems: "Do you wish to know, my brother, whence your people drew that courage to endure the hatred and cruelty of twenty centuries? Do you wish to know how the spirit, amidst the agony of all the centuries of your race, remained young? Do you wish to know what saved the spirit of your people from breaking under the crushing blows of ceaseless adversity? Come with me, my brother, and I will take you in the quiet hour of some setting day into a little village, perhaps on the faraway steppes of Russia, or in some forsaken spot of Poland or Lithuania, and there taking you by the hand I will lead you to a little ramshackle structure, and there in the gathering gloom you will find perhaps three or four of the sons of your people, wearied with age, bent with the burdens of life, poring over some ancient tome or intoning in a melancholy chant some Psalm of David, and there, my brother, you will stand on the threshold of your people's immortality; there you will see the temple of your people's eternal life."

The synagogue witnessed through the long centuries all the heroic moments of our people's experience, from the day it left Palestine and was scattered over the face of the earth. Whether it was the crypto-synagogue in Spain, or the Rhenish Synagogue during the Crusades, or the nameless synagogues in the five hundred towns devastated in the Ukraine this last decade, the synagogue saw the pathos and the tragedy, the suffering and the loyalty, the undaunted courage and the resplendent faith of its children, and treasured those memories. Out of those memories the synagogue is fashioned.

Let me tell you the story of the synagogue of Sokolovka. It happened in 1921, not in the Middle Ages. It was Yom Kippur Day, and the Jews, man, woman, and child, were assembled in the synagogue. Word came that Kosakov, the leader of a band of Cossacks, had entered the town. Kosakov came to the synagogue, followed by his tribe of assassins, and commanded the Jews to take the scrolls from the Ark and march around the synagogue, dancing and singing as is the custom on Simchas Torah, the Day of the Rejoicing with the Law. It amused this Cossack to see these Jews dancing before him in forced merriment. Then he commanded them to march to the public square. The rabbi, divining what was about to happen, commanded his flock to turn toward the Ark and together with him repeat the verse "The Lord, He is God" seven times, as is the custom on the Day of Atonement—that battle cry of the weak and the helpless who have been called upon to wage without arms the battles of the Lord of Hosts. Then with brave step he led his congregation to the square of the city. They were lined in a semicircle, men, women, and children—the men in the center dressed in white, for it was Yom Kippur—and at a signal they were all shot down.

The synagogue heard that cry, "The Lord, He is God!" and treasured it along with other cries from the ages. It is of these cries and these sights and these scenes, of these sanctities and sublimities of a people's life, that our synagogue is builded. That is why wherever a few of the sons and daughters of Israel find themselves, almost instinctively they come together and build, with their humble means, a synagogue.

The synagogue is dear to us, not only for its historical associations and memories, but also for the things it represents, for the immortal phrases which it uttered during its long career, for the ideals of which it speaks to us. The synagogue speaks to us first of God. In the beginning, God! In the end, God! In the change and transitoriness of life, God! In sin and death and suffering and pain, God! The source of all, the goal of all, the creative purpose, the all-wise intelligence, the good friend, the beloved, God! The synagogue speaks of man, the child of God; of man made in the image of God, of man's life, holy because God is holy. The synagogue speaks of all mankind, of one brotherhood of human beings, because our Father is one, and all are His children. In the beginning and in the end, God!

I wish that we would open the doors of our homes and the doors of our hearts a little more and let God enter. I wish that our children would grow up a bit more conscious of that never-failing friend who walks beside them on the road of life, always whispering in their ears the word of courage and hope. In the midst of the trials and tribulations of their lives, they will need God. Some day they will find themselves standing before an open grave, the grave of a dead hope, or of something dearer even than hope, bereft of all, and they will need God, the comforter and the consolation. Of Him the synagogue spoke first, and will speak now.

Then the synagogue speaks of freedom. I said a moment ago that the synagogue was a democratic institution, the creation of the masses of

Israel. It is. It most accurately represents the democratic passion of the Jew. I have often listened to people who have tried to explain why some non-Jews do not like Jews. I have heard people say that the Jew is disliked because he is too bright, and others because he is too dull; too rich, or too poor; too callous, or too sensitive. Somehow, I did not hear the one true explanation of anti-Semitism. We are hated as much for our virtues as for our vices. We are hated because implanted within us from the beginning of time there is a passion for freedom which we ourselves cannot repress, even as the prophet could not repress the word of God, which was like a burning flame within his bosom.

From the days when Abraham smashed the idols of his father; from the days of Moses, who emancipated the slaves; from the days of the prophets who sought to lead the imprisoned out of the prison houses; right through the Middle Ages, when the Jew was the harbinger of intellectual freedom to Europe; to the days when the sons and daughters of our people, the political exiles of Russia, are incarcerated on the angry steppes of Siberia, the Jew has been the slave and the master of an overwhelming passion for freedom. It was inborn in him when our ancestors were nomads in the wilderness. Among them there were no kings, no princes, no potentates. Each was the equal of the other. In the great wilderness our people was nurtured in freedom. When they came into Palestine they had no king. When, driven by the emergency of an invading army, they cried, "Give us a king," their priest, Samuel, denounced them for a lack of faith. After the return from the Babylonian exile, the Jews for hundreds of years had no kings. Their priests governed them. Since the destruction of the Second Temple, for almost nineteen hundred years the Jew has lived in all parts of the world, a fairly unified people without ruler, without king, without pope—free men, who have submitted to authority only when that authority was based on scholarship and spiritual primacy.

That is why the world hates us. Wherever you find Jews, there you will find a group of people who resist repression and tyranny. There you will find sons and daughters of Israel crying for the breaking of chains; there you will find intellectual people who call upon their fellow men to destroy all privilege. That is why the dark forces of reaction, the forces of illiberalism, hate him. They fear the two-edged sword of prophecy in his hand, his passion for justice and freedom.

Another great ideal which our synagogue preached was peace. We hear a great deal about peace nowadays, and yet the church, which always claimed to be the peacemaker, is not leading in the work of peace. It is my firm conviction that the church today has two alternatives. It must assume either a role of aggressive leadership or a role of pious irrelevancy. And the church will assume leadership only when it will rise above the state, and regain its own prophetic voice. The church has been the lackey, the servant of the state. During the Middle Ages it competed with the state for supremacy. Since then the church, having lost its role as competitor, assumed the role of ally. It has in many countries become a state church. During the last war, almost every church was a state church. The Christian church of Germany was German first, and only secondarily a church of God. And so with the English church, and the French church, and the American church. Only as the church breaks from its entanglements with the state, from being compelled to underwrite the policies of the state, will the church assume the role which the prophet once held. Then will the church be able to enkindle the will of the peoples for peace. The synagogue, which from the days of Isaiah preached peace and called upon men to turn their swords into plowshares, continues to this day the champion of international justice and peace.

It would be wrong to offer a selection of Rabbi Silver's statements which does not include a glimpse of his skill and perhaps delight in polemical controversy. While never seeking controversy, he did not run from a good fight—and he had his fights. Given his depth of conviction, his strength of personality, and the dozens of controversies which raged in Jewish life during his time, it could not have been otherwise.

As the following two pieces will show, he could be a formidable opponent. Both statements are rejoinders to attacks made on rabbis and the synagogue, particularly on the Reform movement. Elliot Cohen, Horace Kallen, and Henry Hurwitz—the trio Dr. Silver takes on in the first piece —were proponents of a "cultural" Judaism which they felt could be free from traditional religious "parochialism." Their attacks on the liberal religious movement were not gentle. Neither is Rabbi Silver's reply. Maurice Samuel's attack was more personal and took the form of a bitter criticism of a "modern" rabbi whom readers had no trouble in identifying with Abba Hillel Silver. Rabbi Silver minced no words in his reply, suggesting that Samuel's real motive was personal malice rather than concern for Judaism.

The exchange was hot and exciting, in its day. Rabbi Silver's response reveals much of his feeling about the nature of the American Jewish community and the role of the American rabbi.

*Why Do the Heathen Rage?**

ARTICLE IN THE JEWISH TRIBUNE
SEPTEMBER, 1926

I

The latest attempt to salvage poor shipwrecked Judaism in America is on.
The *Menorah Journal* summoned the doughtiest intellectuals to this heroic
task. These came highly equipped with trenchant pen, with Jovian thunder and unmistakable boldness. They labored valiantly; they plumbed the
very depths, and brought to the surface—a bucket of water.

There is an element of the Purim-spiel in this most recent drama of
national salvation. Dr. Kallen, whose distaste for the "Judaistic religion,"
except as a soporific for the unenlightened, is notorious, sets himself the
task of reviewing the curricula of the Jewish theological schools of America.
He even suggests a new type of rabbi—a cross between a Freudian clinic
intern and a graduate of the New School for Social Research. Mr. Cohen,
who to this day has successfully hid his scholarly achievements under a
bushel, becomes the valorous champion of Jewish scholarship, and fairly
devastates with the breath of his scorn the unlettered rabbis of our age.
Lastly, comes Mr. Hurwitz, mediatory and reassuring, and joyously an-
nounces that as a result of the Menorah Organization's activities, its summer school and its lecture bureau and its proposed Foundation for Jewish
Research, the terrible night which had descended upon American Israel,
and which was so graphically described by the above-mentioned writers, is
about to end. "Our day dawns," he exclaims, in sanguine anticipation of
an "adequately financed and endowed" Menorah movement.

* This article is based on the papers of Elliot E. Cohen, "The Age of Brass," *Menorah
Journal,* October, 1925; Dr. Horace M. Kallen, "Can Judaism Survive in the United States?"
April and December, 1925; and Henry Hurwitz, "Watchman, What of the Day?" February,
1926.

II

A periodic inventory of a people's cultural assets and liabilities is a necessary and commendable service. But clearly, if it is to have any value, it must be undertaken in a dispassionate and scientific spirit, and by men qualified through knowledge and experience to pass judgment. Prejudices are obstructions to inventories. Broad denunciation and cynical flouting of what one does not happen to relish cannot be regarded as adequate stock-taking. One is entertained or outraged by them according to one's prejudices, but one is not enlightened. Above all, whoever presumes to approach the sanctities of a people's life must do so in a spirit of reverence. Thoughtful men do not employ a cheap and easy cleverness in discussing spiritual values which might be the very lifeblood of men.

From the essay of Mr. Cohen I cull the following few specimens to indicate the quality of the newer criticism to which American Judaism is being subjected:

> The Elders of Zion myth is a by no means distant cousin of the "Jewish mission" myth (p. 439).
> The little respect our culture receives is that paid to a people who stumbled [sic] on some spiritual ideas capable of being incorporated, in a greatly improved form of course, in the culture of the West (p. 448).
> Lacking wisdom, our leaders take refuge in speech. Good Watsonian behaviorists, they discover the springs of thought in the voice box (p. 427).
> Speeches and sermons are born of the air and destined to vanish with the breath that gave them birth (p. 430).
> But they [the rabbis] are guilty certainly of a too weak acquiescence in the degradation of the rabbinical function to that of a spokesman—i.e., mouthpiece—of the ignorance, ambitions, and fears of the influential Jewish laity (p. 440).

We submit that for sheer "brass" in this sad Age of Brass one need not look elsewhere . . .

III

Mr. Cohen is rendered furious by the fact that some Jewish writers and public men have praised the Jew and Judaism excessively. This seems to be the sum and substance of his twenty-five-page indictment. Seemingly it is good taste, and altogether proper, to proclaim to the world that the

Menorah Journal is "the best-printed, best-edited, and best-written periodical" and that its advent marks a turning point in American Jewish history, but it is nothing short of "bluster, braggadocio," etc., to assert that Israel has been the monitor of monotheism in the world, the pathfinder in moral idealism, or that the Jews may be justifiably proud of their history and of their contributions to mankind.

With what avidity Mr. Cohen belabors his theme of the Jews' self-praise! He offers a collection of anonymous quotations as Exhibit A and some extracts from the writings of such distinguished authors as Roth, Leiser, Gewurz, Browne, and Samuel as Exhibit B. Using these as his *pou sto,* Mr. Cohen proceeds to move the world. Himself not lacking that voice of brass which he so deprecates, he uses it to excellent advantage in an onomatopoetic characterization of the quality of our age. The voice of our age is the voice of "the brass horn, rotund and hollow, the scream of the trumpet, the imposing bray of the trombone, and the ear-piercing blasts of the cornet," and so on to the limits of Roget's Thesaurus. And having accomplished this feat, the critic delivers himself of the following pronouncement:

> There are two facts immediately apparent about this modern voice of Israel. It is new—and it is false. A Jew raised in the direct line of Jewish tradition, trained in the old Jewish discipline, will be puzzled to know what to make of this curious and un-Jewish "Religion" of the American Jew. . . . The Jews of his time, he says, were too busy studying the old books to cry their worth in the marketplace (p. 433).

And yet, sad to relate, this is exactly what the Jew did do consistently and continuously through the ages. One could fill more than one volume of the *Menorah Journal* with citations from Biblical, Talmudic, Midrashic, and medieval Jewish literary sources to show that the Jew *did* praise, and often very extravagantly, his faith, his Torah, the community of Israel, the land of Israel; in fact, everything which was dear to his heart. He spoke proudly and glowingly of them, being stranger to the subtle artifice of diffidence which characterizes some of our modern Jewish intellectuals. Had Mr. Cohen taken the trouble to consult some handy concordance such as the Yalkut Eliezer under the caption "Israel," the Sefer Ha-Agada or Eisenstein's Ozar, he would have been amazed at the way those early rabbis, "raised in the direct line of Jewish tradition," extolled the excellencies, the uniqueness, the primacy and superiority of the Jewish people—quite in keeping with the older tradition of the Bible, wherein Israel is spoken of as a light unto the nations, a holy people, an eternal people, and the chosen people. We shall permit ourselves but one rabbinic quotation. "Just as oil brings light to the world, so Israel brings light to the world—just as oil is superior to all other liquids, so Israel is superior to all other nations" (Shir Ha-Shir R.1: 21). There is no concordance of our post-Talmudic literature to which the writer may be referred, but it might not be amiss to point to a few opinions out of the hundreds held by leaders of Jewish thought in ages other than this Age of Brass concerning Israel and Israel's spiritual greatness.

Maimonides, the rationalist, declared: "Our nation is wise and perfect, as has been declared by the most high through Moses, who made us perfect: 'Surely this great nation is a wise and understanding people'" (*The Guide of the Perplexed*, Part 2, Chap. 11). Jehuda Halevi, the poet and philosopher, held that Israel was the heart of the world (*Kuzari*, II:36), that the gift of prophecy was bestowed upon Israel alone (I, 101 ff.), and that all mankind exists for the sake of Israel even as Israel exists for the sake of the prophets (II: 44)—a remarkable exposition of the doctrine of the "super nation." One is also tempted to mention Judah Loew ben Bezalel's (Austrian Talmudist and preacher, d. 1609) stirring work *The Eternity of Israel*, whose entire purpose is "to establish that God bestowed eternal life upon Israel" (p. 16); that "Israel is eternal because its existence is of God and in God" (p. 22), and that "Israel is the essence and goal of all creation" (p. 18). And is not this prayer, which is echoed and reechoed in our liturgy, quite significant in this connection: "Thou hast chosen us from all peoples; thou hast loved us and found pleasure in us, and hast exalted us above all tongues." The whole mystic literature of our people wherein the concept of Israel is transfigured into that of a mystic spiritual communion, indissolubly bound up with God and the Torah, abounds in exaltations of the people and of its heroic destiny.

A phrase of the rabbis comes to mind to which we are sure Mr. Cohen would not subscribe: "God said to Moses, 'Praise and extol Israel as much as thou possibly canst, for I shall in the days to come be extolled because of them, as it is written'; and He said: 'Thou art my servant, Israel, in whom I shall be praised'" (Lev. R. II: 4).

If in recent years spokesmen of our people have found it necessary to stress anew the moral excellencies of their faith and to remind men of the decisive contributions which Israel has made to the cultural assets of mankind, should not these facts in all fairness be attributed to the desperate emergencies with which Israel was suddenly confronted in the recrudescence of anti-Semitic propaganda, rather than to conceit and vainglory? In the face of the numerous traducers of our race who suddenly appeared here and elsewhere, bent upon maligning the Jew and Judaism, depreciating our worth and defaming our name, should it be accounted a sin in these spokesmen if they sought to counteract this propaganda by calling attention to the services which the Jew has rendered the world, and by dwelling upon the true inner worth of their faith?

IV

Had this vocation of counterpropaganda been the only interest of American Israel during the last decade, the critic's indictment would have had validity, but the latter knows quite well that this was not the case. The last ten years have witnessed a remarkable renaissance in Jewish life and an intensification of Jewish activities in nigh every field. The World War, the desperate plight of our brothers abroad, the challenging opportunity of our National Homeland, the threat of organized anti-Semitism, and, by no means least, the inner urge toward self-expression combined to stir American Israel to a remarkable pitch of alertness and enterprise. One need not dwell upon the truly herculean efforts made by the American Jew for the relief of his war-stricken fellow Jews abroad—an effort which is even now being renewed. But one ought not to miss the vital implications of this albeit purely humanitarian enterprise. In the hour of crisis, Israel was not found wanting, either in loyalty or generosity. This is evidence of an inner soundness which ought not to be disregarded. Again, this major philanthropic effort, in which all elements of Jewry participated, tended to draw the disparate groups of our people closer together and to establish numerous contacts which, fortunately, have increased rather than decreased with the years.

In the field of Jewish education marked progress has been made. Countless schools, Talmud-Torahs, yeshivas, and religious schools, have been established, in many instances with splendid buildings erected to house them. A growing sense of community responsibility in the matter of the religious and cultural training of our youth has been manifested in the organization in some of the larger cities of bureaus of Jewish education, headed by competent educators. Side by side with the increase in facilities has gone an improvement in curriculum and in standards of instruction. Teachers' training schools have sprung up, and the serious lack of textbooks has been partially met. The vast problems of Jewish education in America have by no means been solved, but American Israel has during recent years wrestled with them earnestly, and, to a degree, successfully.

The number of higher institutions of learning has been augmented by the addition of two new academies within the last five years. The older rabbinic seminaries have increased their facilities, their faculties, and their student bodies, and enriched their libraries.

Educational work among Jewish college students, which was so splendidly initiated by the Menorah Organization, has gone on apace. There have now been added two new agencies, the Hillel Foundation and the Avukah. Recently the larger religious bodies of American Jewry met and resolved to pool their resources in an effort to carry on a more extensive program of Jewish education among college men and women. There is promise in all this and an indication of a general awareness touching the magnitude and importance of this work.

Truly phenomenal has been the increase in the number of centers, community houses and Y.M.H.A. buildings which have been established within the last decade. Clearly they have come into existence in response to a real demand. Were these institutions not wanted by the American Jew, and more especially by the young American Jew, they would not have been built, or financed, or used. The quality of their work depends, of course, in the last analysis upon the quality of the leadership which each institution enjoys, but it cannot be gainsaid that in the main they have performed a salutary service in the physical and cultural development of our youth, in their moral guidance and in fostering a sense of Jewish loyalty among them. Now that American Israel is making an honest effort to provide wholesome recreational and social facilities for its young people, one is surprised to hear derogatory remarks about them from critics who twenty years ago would undoubtedly have lamented the lack of such facilities.

And, lastly, American Jews have built and are building synagogues and temples at an astounding rate. Judging from the jeremiads of our critics, this is to be taken as positive proof of Jewish decadence and disintegration. We beg to differ. Not so long ago one heard the justifiable complaint that our synagogues were physically unattractive, and that they were repellent to the esthetically minded young American Jew. It was said, and rightly said, that these shabby structures were uncomplimentary to a people as prosperous as the American Jew. The plaint of David was repeated: "Shall we dwell in houses of cedar, but the Ark of God dwell within curtains?" Now that American Israel is erecting sanctuaries which in their outer form seek to body forth the beauty of the faith which they enshrine, now that we are bringing a bit of the charm of Japheth into the tents of Shem, the cry is raised, "The Stone Age!" In building spacious and beautiful synagogues American Israel is following an authentic Jewish tradition. For wherever Jews found peace, security, and prosperity, they raised noble religious edifices and attempted to express their religious life esthetically.

Had the American Jew built his synagogues at the sacrifice of other worthy causes he would be deserving of the severest censure, but he has been equally liberal with his philanthropic institutions and in his foreign relief. He has been contributing increasingly larger amounts to Jewish educational purposes, to Palestine, and to causes not specifically Jewish. If there are worthy movements to which he has not yet given sufficiently, it is due to the fact that he has not yet been completely convinced of their importance. The American Jew is not niggardly, nor does he withhold his hand from any cause once he is convinced of its value.

And these synagogues are used! This might sound strange to those critics who seldom enter one. People do come to worship. Not all, of course. Neither do all go to symphonies, or art museums, or to any place where they are likely to be stimulated and enlightened. But in every community one may find men and women, God-fearing and worshipful, who long for the courts of the Living God. These come, and they are the heart of every synagogue. Many more come for the sake of the sermon or lecture, and others come out of habit. Some come regularly and some sporadically, as the desire or need prompts them. One cannot really gauge a man's loyalty to the synagogue or its influence upon his life by the regularity of his attendance at divine worship. Besides the religious services, congregations conduct their schools, elementary, high, and in some instances, normal schools. They have their sisterhoods and brotherhoods, with their numerous social and educational activities, their adult study groups, extension courses, forums, libraries, etc. In many cities the synagogue is the very hub of Jewish communal life.

So that American Israel has been engaged in many other activities in recent years besides blowing the loud bassoon of self-praise.

V

And American rabbis, too, have done much more than preach, although preaching the word of God is still, by some, regarded as an honorable profession, and, if done in consecration and sincerity, one of life's supreme privileges. The organization of the religious life of American Jewry, the establishment of schools, synagogues, theological academies, and the training of teachers has been almost entirely the work of American rabbis. Some of our important national institutions, such as the Union of American Hebrew Congregations, the United Synagogue, the Jewish Congress, the Jewish Publication Society, the Jewish Chautauqua, the National Farm School, etc., owe their existence to the initiation of American rabbis. Many charitable institutions, many Jewish centers and community houses, owe their inception to the leadership and untiring work of these men. The Zionist Organization of America has consistently through the years drawn from the rabbinate some of its most devoted leaders, executives, and officers. Such activities plainly do not come within the category of "speeches and sermons which are born of the air."

It should be borne in mind that the most pressing tasks which confronted the Jewish ministry heretofore have been those of organization and upbuilding. Millions of Jews in the brief period of a generation or two were transplanted from the four corners of the earth to these shores. Communities, some small, some enormously large, sprang up, as it were, overnight. They were structureless and disjointed. They possessed neither philanthropic agencies, nor schools, nor synagogues—in fact none of the facilities which go to make up a community life. All these had to be built, and it fell largely to the share of the American rabbis to build them. Accordingly most of the thought and energy of these men went perforce into this indispensable groundwork of organization—a tiring and exacting employment which is not yet completed.

If, therefore, the American rabbi has not been more of the scholar, if in many instances his preaching has not measured up in intellectual quality to that of his European confrere, it is due not to his inherent mediocrity but to the nigh endless time- and energy-consuming community responsibilities which the conditions of Jewish life forced upon him. The European rabbi, as a rule, is head of an old established community, possessing its full quota of religious, educational, and eleemosynary institutions, and in which the necessary functions of congregational life are well distributed. This has not been the case in America, and in most instances is still not the case. Our communities are recent and unformed. New schools, new synagogues, and new centers are needed, with all their attendant needs of program, curricula, coordination, etc. Drives must be launched, and it seems almost daily, for new hospitals, new orphanages, and new homes for the aged; drives for foreign relief, local relief, Falasha relief; drives for Palestine, for Hadassah, for the Jewish National Fund; drives for the Union of American Hebrew Congregations, for seminaries, for yeshivas, for dormitories, for libraries; drives for the Menorah Organization, for student congregations, for bureaus of Jewish education, for the Chautauqua . . . in each instance the rabbi is appealed to first for his active cooperation. In some cases he is compelled to initiate these drives himself; in others he becomes their propagandist, and in still others he is the actual solicitor.

Furthermore, Jewish congregational life, far from being departmentalized, is sadly centralized. The rabbi, especially in the Reform congregation, is darshan, melamed, chazan, and shamos all in one. In view of these multitudinous and harassing responsibilities, it is not surprising that the rabbi's hours of study and meditation are few in number, and that this paucity reflects itself in the quality of his preaching and writing.

Still, a creditable list may be drawn up of American rabbis who have done meritorious work even in the field of Jewish scholarship. There is, of course, no Zunz or Geiger among them as yet, but Zunzes and Geigers are rather rare throughout the Jewish world today, and American Israel will require a considerably longer period of germination before it will produce scholars of such magnitude. Two hundred years of semination preceded the first efflorescence of Jewish genius in Spain. "America has not yet produced one great poet," is the criticism which Thomas Jefferson undertakes to answer in his "Notes on Virginia." "When we shall have existed as a people as long as the Greeks did before they produced a Homer, the Romans a Virgil, the French a Racine and a Voltaire, the English a Shakespeare and a Milton, should this reproach be still true, we will inquire from what unfriendly causes it has proceeded." Still, fine and valuable work in Jewish scholarship has already been done by some of the graduates of the American theological schools, such as Finkelstein, Kaplan, Efros, A. Newman, Epstein, Waxman, Levinthal, Enelow, Frisch, Blau, L. I. Newman, Englander, Philipson, Linfield, Calisch, Morgenstern, Cohen, Max and Jacob Raisin, Rhine, Rosenau, Bettan, Cronbach, Freehof, and others, whose work cannot be dismissed with a supercilious shrug of the shoulder.

When the press of community work eases up, when Jewish laymen in larger numbers take over the administrative tasks which are rightfully theirs, and when congregational life becomes more departmentalized, American rabbis will be able, as they are eager, to devote themselves more definitely to their essential prerogatives—"to learn and to teach."

In passing, we wish to remark that when we speak of American rabbis we do not refer to the vaudevillians in the pulpit. Unfortunately there are some rabbis who have cheapened and vulgarized the Jewish pulpit, by sacrificing the timeless for the "timely" in their discourses, by pandering to Jewish morbidities in the choice of their themes, by weekly recourse to struts, antics, and noise. On the bulletins of some of the larger synagogues of America it has become increasingly rare to find a subject which does not have a distinctly "Christian" angle, a savor of the ever-palatable "prejudice" theme, or the "kick" of the latest play. Fortunately such pulpits are not typical, and some day, when a few conscientious laymen in the pews will bestir themselves sufficiently to express their disgust, the heroic occupants of these pulpits will beat a hasty retreat.

VI

In the catalogue of Jewish self-laudations, Mr. Cohen places the idea of the "mission of Israel."

> The claim of Israel to a prima donna role among the nations is totally presumptuous and is, as a matter of fact, ignored by the world. To a mind with the least regard for truth it is obvious that Israel is not the primal moral force to which all the peoples look for guidance, the spring of all modern philosophy, science and letters, the intellectual aristocrat in a heathen world, the exclusive repository of the spiritual resources of mankind. There are only the slimmest evidences of fact to support these hifalutin pretenses. To maintain these notions is to be guilty of the most preposterous nonsense; to believe them is to cherish the most palpable delusions (p. 434).

Per contra one would like to give the conclusions of a *non-Jewish* intellectual—Matthew Arnold: "As long as the world lasts, all who want to make progress in righteousness will come to Israel for inspiration, as to the people who have had the sense for righteousness most glowing and strongest." And of still another *non-Jewish* writer—Leo Tolstoi: "The Jew is that sacred being who has brought down from heaven the everlasting fire and has illumined with it the entire world. He is the religious source, spring and fountain, out of which all the rest of the peoples have drawn their beliefs and their religions."

In order to make out a case, Mr. Cohen subtly smuggles in a few prerogatives which the Jew never claimed. No sane Jew ever maintained that Israel was "the spring of all modern philosophy, science, and letters, the intellectual aristocrat in a heathen world, the exclusive repository of the spiritual resources of mankind." Erasmus' phrase comes to mind: the gentleman "is raising devils only to have the credit of laying them." The Jew has maintained that his racial genius has expressed itself most fully in moral and religious values, and that it is his historic obligation to teach them by precept and example to the world. In these he has been teacher; in all else he has been disciple. Every great historic people from the ancient Greeks to the modern Anglo-Saxons has been conscious to a greater or lesser degree of some particular potency with which its corporate life was endowed, and which constituted its supreme though not exclusive contribution to mankind.

Mr. Cohen errs when he assumes that the ideal of the mission of Israel is a recent discovery. He suspects that he is in error, and he seeks refuge in a footnote, hoping to prove by means of dexterous *drush* that the ancient ideal of the mission and the modern are the same but different. The shibboleths of the newer psychology are all mustered: inferiority complex, defense mechanism, etc., etc. But the rooted and disconcerting fact nevertheless remains, that consistently through the ages for more than twenty-five centuries the Jew has stressed and underscored his mission to the gentiles. There is a certain sacred objectivity to a fact which even clever intellectuals ought not to tamper with. It was not Geiger or Holdheim or Einhorn who invented the phrases:

> "And ye shall be unto Me a kingdom of priests and a holy nation" (Exod. 19:6).

> Or, "The remnant of Jacob shall be in the midst of many peoples as dew from the Lord, as showers upon the grass" (Mic. 5:7).
> Or, "Behold my servant, whom I uphold; mine elect, in whom my soul delighteth; I have put my spirit upon him. He shall make the right to go forth to the nations. . . . I the Lord have called thee in righteousness, and have taken hold of thy right hand, and kept thee and set thee for a covenant of the people, for a light of the nations. To open the blind eyes, to bring out the prisoners from the dungeon, and them that sit in darkness out of the prison house" (Isa. 42:1, 6–7).

Our apocryphal and apocalyptic literature fairly rings with this theme. The great missionary activity carried on by the Jews in the centuries immediately preceding and following the beginning of the Christian era was inspired by this idealism, and the whole Messianic saga of our race is surcharged with this imperial faith.

The leaders of modern Reform Judaism simply re-emphasized this ancient Jewish ideal. Their error was in assuming that this ideal was opposed to Jewish nationalism, whereas in reality it is inextricably intertwined with it. Deutero-Isaiah, who of all Jews most eloquently vocalized this missionary aspiration, was of all Jews the most nationalistic and "Palestinian." A people need not expatriate itself in order to be apostolic, and universalism and nationalism rightly conceived are, of course, never antithetical.

Religion was the sole reason why the Jew persisted in maintaining his identity in the world. I have searched high and low in Jewish literature to discover evidences that the Jew struggled to remain a Jew amidst adverse circumstances in order that he might develop a great "synagogue architecture, mural paintings and frescoes, and sculpture in wood and brass, works in silver, gold, and other metals . . . and the old signboards of Polish Jewry" ("Watchman, What of the Day?" p. 15). I find nowhere that the Jew objected to intermarriage with other peoples (a practice which would of course have destroyed him) on the ground that the resultant racial admixture would produce less gifted musicians or scientists or writers. There was but one reason throughout the ages "Lest he will turn away thy son from following Me, that they may serve other gods" (Deut. 7:3). The Jew persisted in racial uniqueness in order to preserve the integrity of his faith. Loyalty to the faith spelled loyalty to the race. When the American Jew abandons his faith he will swiftly and surely assimilate. He will intermarry with the peoples about him, and he will destroy himself racially, and no quantum of Jewish music and Jewish art or books on Jewish literature and philosophy will be potent enough to save him. The anti-religious Jew will be the first to go, as he always has been. The religiously indifferent Jew will linger on by sheer force of inertia until the relentless assimilative forces scatter and overwhelm him too. The secular nationalist will endure until such times as his ideology derived from the segregated and compact Jewish community life of eastern Europe is dissipated by the dissolving influences of American life. Even the strong appeal which Palestine is making today to many of our people will not prove sufficient to command their loyalty in the days to come. The establishment of a strong Jewish commonwealth in Palestine will not accomplish the miracle of preservation for the

American Jew. The existence of a great German fatherland has not kept the Germans in the United States from assimilating. The Jew in the United States will not long remain either a Yiddishist or a Hebraist, in the technical sense in which the proponents of cultural pluralism understand the terms. Only the religious Jew who will continue steadfast to his faith will conserve and carry on the culture and the traditions of Israel. The rest will disappear, as they always have, as they inevitably must. In other words, Judaism, far from being "a small part of the total fulness of the life of the Jewish people which I [Horace M. Kallen] am accustomed to call Hebraism" (p. 557), is in reality its very heart and lifeblood.

This ideal of the mission sustained and inspired the Jews throughout their troubled and checkered career. To what degree they remained faithful to it, let their martyred dead bear witness; let all the great social movements of mankind which felt the impact of Israel's dynamic spirit, surging and creative in living men and women through two thousand years, bear witness; let the cross and the crescent bear witness—for they kindled their torches at the sacred fires of our altars; let the Renaissance and the Reformation bear witness, for in the intellectual preparation for the one the Jew played a not inconsiderable role, and in the ideology of the other a most decisive role; let all the mighty movements for social righteousness of the last century bear witness: "Whatever there is in modern civilization that is making for human fraternity, whatever religious aspiration is calling men to a higher sense of duty, wherever men and women are toiling to prove that humanity is a great brotherhood, there we find men living, acting, thinking under the influence of these leaders of Hebrew thought" (Baldwin, *Our Modern Debt to Israel*, pp. 202–3). And there, too, the writer might have added are to be found *today* Jewish men and women who, propelled consciously or unconsciously by that same racial urge towards *malchuth shamayim*, are carrying in a hundred fields of human endeavor the message and the mission of their people.

What is to be gained by pooh-poohing this ideal, by cheapening it in our own eyes and in the eyes of our children? What have we to substitute for it? Will an argument like the following prove more effective in arousing Jews to heroic self-preservation and self-fulfillment? "We are a pretty ordinary lot; we have no particular mission to the world; we are possessed of quite commonplace virtues, and therefore—let us write histories about ourselves, endow foundations for Jewish research and establish chairs of Jewish learning in American universities in order to inform the world about these middling qualities and these indifferent contributions of our race."

Do not wisdom and policy rather dictate even as truth warrants a renewed accentuation of this ancient motif in modern Jewish life? Ought we not to challenge our people today, as they were challenged of old, to nobler living and thinking, to personal righteousness and community service, on the basis of this historic mandate? Will not an enkindled desire to serve and to help bring with it an impassioned will to live? Is not Spinoza's proposition as valid for peoples as for individuals? "No one can desire to be blessed, to act well, or live well, who at the same time does not desire to be, to act, and to live, that is, actually, to exist."

The mission ideal of Israel is neither apology nor vainglory. It concerns the non-Jew only as the object; it concerns the Jew as the subject of the service. The *Jew* is to serve. The Jew is called upon to undertake the burdens, the self-discipline, and the crucifixions of moral leadership. Leadership is a crown, to be sure, but a crown of thorns. It is not by strutting and declaiming that a people leads, but by the forceful example of sacrificial loyalty to great ideals, by holy lives and consecrated purposes. Is there a worthier ideal to hold up before our people?

VII

Both Mr. Cohen and Mr. Hurwitz lament the indifference of the Jewish intellectuals to Judaism. They are not very clear as to who these intellectuals are who have thus drifted away. One is inclined to think that the whole concept of the Jewish "intelligentsia" in America needs a great deal of "deciphering." One suspects that, like the "American proletariat" and the "American peasantry," they simply do not exist. All three terms are borrowed from other civilizations, and from totally different social stratifications. Presumably, the writers refer to the educated Jews, principally the college-bred men and women. It has not at all been established that the adherence of these men and women to the synagogue and to Jewish communal life in general is weaker than that of any other class in Jewry. We cannot judge of the Jewish community of New York. There all problems are frightfully complicated by the sheer size and unwieldiness of the group and by its amorphous character, and one cannot readily get at the facts. Even there one is likely to find large numbers of educated and professional Jews in the synagogue, in the Zionist movement, at the head of educational enterprises, in community centers, and elsewhere. One is in a position to judge a little more accurately of the smaller and less chaotic centers of Jewish population, and one is likely to find there that college men and women have affiliated themselves with the synagogue in numbers relatively greater than those of other classes. The Jewish community of Cleveland is the fourth largest in the United States, containing some 90,000 souls. I speak of Cleveland not because it is different but because it is *not* different. It has been reliably estimated that nearly 75 per cent of the Jewish professional men—doctors, lawyers, teachers, architects, etc.—are members of some temple or synagogue, their number relatively far exceeding that of other Jewish groups. Many of these professional men and many other non-professional college men are on the boards and on the important committees of religious institutions of Cleveland, on the boards of the Bureau of Jewish Education, the Zionist organization, the B'nai B'rith, and numerous Jewish social agencies. Many college women are leaders in the activities of the temple sisterhoods and the Council of Jewish Women. There is no outer compulsion forcing these people to affiliate themselves with the synagogue; such affiliation yields no monetary returns and is not effected by the insistence of public opinion. One cannot, of course, measure the quality of the religious sincerity of these men and women, nor the intensity of their Jewishness. It is enough that they *wish to belong* to a Jewish religious institution, to send their children to its school, to support its activities, and to attend its services whenever the spirit moves them. Wherever Jewish community life has had a chance to organize itself, it has not failed to attract the Jews of higher educational and cultural attainments to a degree comparable to and in many instances surpassing that of any other class.

To be sure, there are many educated Jews who are not members of the synagogue, just as there are tens of thousands of Jewish workingmen and Jewish businessmen who are not; but it is not necessarily their education which has estranged them from Judaism, nor, as the critics are inclined to believe, the absence of good textbooks on Judaism or authoritative Jewish scholarship. Many educated Jews, quite like their confreres who have received no academic training, are too busy grubbing for a living or making money or wallowing in the pleasures and excitations of our age to think of anything outside of their vocation, their ambitions, and their delectations. Still others find membership in a distinguishable and protestant minority too difficult a burden to bear. It is not easy to be a Jew. Under the most favorable conditions, the road which the Jew must travel is a thorny one, and thousands seek, as thousands have sought, the primrose path which leads to assimilation, partial for themselves, complete for their children.

It is therefore idle to believe that, given more books on Jewish law, history, philosophy, and art, these fair-weather gentlemen who cannot bear the strain of Jewish individuality will eagerly return, shouting in joyous refrain: "Hallelujah, we have seen the light!" German Jewry has had the advantages of *Juedische Wissenschaft* for nearly a century—great scholars, great teachers, and great books—and yet apostasy, intermarriage, indifference, and cynicism are more rampant among its intellectuals today than ever before.

The alienation from Jewry and Judaism resulting from the deprivations inherent in the lot of a disfavored minority is particularly in evidence in the case of that smaller group of Jewish intellectuals to whom the writers may be referring—the authors, journalists, artists, philosophers, professors, etc. Many of these have eschewed Judaism and the Jew not because they do not know their people (for a goodly number of them hail from good old-fashioned Jewish homes, from distinctly Jewish environments, and some of them actually received Orthodox Jewish training), but because they do not *wish* to know. There are richer pastures elsewhere—higher rewards, both social and monetary. It is only after these intellectuals are disillusioned, after they discover that the anticipated rewards are not forthcoming, that they return to the welcoming fold of Israel, a bit saddened and embittered and a bit overzealous.

One of the strange notions of Mr. Cohen is that writers like Robert Nathan, author of *Jonah,* and Lawrence Langner, author of *Moses,* misrepresent the Jew in their writing; or that such men as Alexander Goldenweiser hate Jewish culture and scorn the hope of Jewish renaissance because, forsooth, "we have neglected to make easy of access to searchers such as these the treasures of our tradition." There seems to be a confusion in metaphor here. *Searchers for truth* are not retarded in their pursuit after truth by the fact that truth is not easy of access. They *search* for truth. On Dr. Goldenweiser's venality Mr. Elisha Friedman has already thrown a very revealing light (*Menorah Journal,* August, 1925). More need not be said. But concerning the others, one wonders whether Schechter could not have illumined the author of *Moses* on the true meaning of Jewish legalism if the latter had taken the trouble to consult his works: or could not Ahad Ha-am's *Moses* or Cornill's *Moses* or even Philo's *On the Life of Moses* (all available in English), or numerous other essays which any Jewish librarian would have put at his disposal have given him the truth if he had really sought to know the truth instead of popularizing a stupid fiction. But then Mr. Langner gives his own case away when he frankly acknowledges that he built his character of Moses "not upon the actual life of Moses as told in the Old Testament, but upon the preconceptions of the theater audiences" (Introduction to *Moses,* page ix). And is not this also true of Mr. Nathan? It has evidently not occurred to the critic that the mere publication of books does not ensure their being read.

But the height of grotesqueness is reached by Mr. Cohen when he states that Mr. Mencken, of the *American Mercury,* who recently declared that "the religion [of the Jews] is probably the most murderous ever heard of in history," was driven to this conclusion because the latter "never found available in a form palatable to a gentleman of his intelligence accounts— or the originals on which they are based—of the history, literature, and religion of the Jews." Poor Mr. Mencken, more sinned against than sinning! Dare one ask whether the books of the prophets and the Psalms in their English version were acceptable to this gentleman's aristocratic palate? And did these give him the impression that the Jewish religion is the most murderous ever heard of? Would a reading of Schechter's *Studies,* Kohler's *Theology,* Lazarus' *Ethics of Judaism,* Abelson's *Immanence of God in Rabbinic Literature,* Buttenweiser's *Prophets of Israel,* or Graetz's *History* or the Jewish prayerbook, or even the numerous articles on the history, religion, and literature of the Jew in the Jewish Encyclopedia (all available in English), have given this eminent critic that exalted opinion of our faith? Or must these writings first be recast in the style of the *American Mercury* and *The Smart Set* before this sybaritic theologian will deign to bestow upon them a passing glance? Again, Mr. Mencken undoubtedly reads German, and in the vast Jewish literature written in that language he undoubtedly could have discovered some material by which to test his scholarly conclusions. The fact of the matter is, that in the face of blissful ignorance and boundless mendacity, the Almighty Himself is helpless.

VIII

Dr. Kallen's review of American Jewish life is no less superficial. His argument runs something like this: Judaism can hardly survive in the United States, for all the three classes into which he divides American Jewry show clear signs of decay. The working classes are not interested in the transmission of Judaism to their children. The middle classes, largely composed of eastern European Conservative or Orthodox Jews, because they take greater chances in business and are therefore in greater need of the grace of God, are more religious. They are to be credited with whatever of Jewish activity there is in the United States; but their children do not follow in their footsteps. And the prosperous native Jews of western European origin, among whom are to be numbered the Reform Jews, show least promise. According to Dr. Kallen, the Reform Jewish group hardly ever sends one of its sons into the rabbinate (although on the authority of Dr. Morgenstern, president of the Hebrew Union College, we have it that nearly sixty per cent of the student body of the Hebrew Union College come from Reform Jewish homes *). Its children graduate from the Sunday school, says Dr. Kallen, into an indifference to Judaism (although the large majority of them seem to find their way into congregational affiliation. Of the forty-five members on the boards of the two Reform congregations of Cleveland, twenty were educated in the religious schools of these temples. This is true of many of the older congregations).

Dr. Kallen's summary is very dark, indeed. "The Jews of America fall with respect to Judaism into three broad divisions, none of which shows any seeds of a vital future Judaism." And what is the remedy, if any? Make Judaism more relevant to modern life (the battle cry of the earlier reformers!). All the educational institutions of Judaism should be given "a specific contemporary relevancy." The rabbis and teachers should become aware that they are living "in a world of which industry, trade, science, the movies, the radio, and the press are the dynamic substance, immediate and compelling." And what a shock this will prove to those

* Dr. Morgenstern writes: "You will understand that it is not easy to determine exactly whether a student of the College comes from a Reform Jewish home or Sabbath school, or not, since there are various gradations from Orthodoxy, through Conservatism, to Reform. However, I have gone over the present enrollment of our students carefully and find that approximately 65 out of about 105 students come from what I feel justified in calling Reform homes and environments. Furthermore, of this year's entering class I have looked up the records and find that 18 students were born in this country and 9 were born abroad, one of them in England. This last student comes from a typical Reform Jewish home. Of course not all of the eighteen who were born in this country can be said to come from strictly Reform homes, but the great majority unquestionably do so.

"I find this: that each year, as is quite natural, the percentage of students born abroad decreases steadily, and correspondingly, the percentage of students born in this country increases. Furthermore, with this development there is likewise a steady, though not a rapid, increase in the percentage of students who come from Reform homes. The percentage is now approximately 60% from Reform homes, whereas a few years ago it was, I am sure, not over 40 to 45%."

innocent, cloistered American rabbis who are so utterly unaware of these amazing facts!

And who is responsible for this intellectual isolation of the American rabbis, thus discovered to be so naive and unconversant? Why, the rabbinical seminaries! They are "intellectual morgues dedicated to the anatomy of the dead past of language and law and history." All these subjects should be scrapped or relegated to professional scholars. The rabbinical seminaries where "Judaistic ministers" are trained should become in a manner annexes to the New School for Social Research; Jewish scholarship should be separated from the ministry (Dr. Kallen, to my knowledge, is the first man to complain that American rabbis suffer from too much scholarship); they should be instructed more in the Jewish present and less in the Jewish past. They should be taught the structure and functions of Jewish communities and their institutions (although specialization in this field belongs more logically, it seems to me, to the profession of the Jewish social worker, and these subjects should occupy the chief place in the curriculum of the Training School for Jewish Social Work and similar institutions). The rabbis should also be trained in psychopathology, so as to understand, we assume, why Jewish literati must first become amateur *goyim* before they become professional "Hebraists." "A training school for Judaist ministers, in a word, would familiarize its trainees with that total fulness of the life of the Jewish people which I am accustomed to call Hebraism, and of which Judaism is a part and but a small part."

But just what this sadly attenuated Judaism is, or is to be, or why it is at all, Dr. Kallen does not take the trouble to state. The impression one gains is that Dr. Kallen's Judaism is expressed in terms of a modicum of knowledge of Jewish history, literature (principally modern), and of the structure and needs of modern community life. From a rather difficult sentence at the close of his article one may also infer that the sole function of this Judaism in the "total fulness of the life of the Jewish people" is to assuage pathological disturbances within the Jewish group whenever such disturbances occur—in other words, to dispense a sort of patent soothing-syrup. "He [the rabbi] will be able to bring it [Judaism] relevantly to bear on that device for the enhancement of security and the assuagement of fear which is the Jew's own, and which is peculiarly suited, therefore, to the idiosyncrasy of whatever pathological condition of mood arises within the structure and behavior patterns of Jewish groups."

We have already indicated what our conception of the role of Judaism in Jewish life is. We insist that it is not peripheral but focal. Furthermore, in common with all other "Judaists" we find that at the heart of our faith certain essential doctrines touching God and man's relation to God, and providence and prayer—doctrines which do not even appear on the farthest horizons of Dr. Kallen's dissertation. Whatever else Judaism may be, it is surely first and foremost a faith and a theology. Its message is primarily to the individual and then to the community. It concerns itself with the fundamental spiritual needs of human beings, the need of God, the need of communion with God, and the need of an invincible hope in the ultimate triumph of the moral order. It seeks to organize the life of man around a central motivating faith in a Supreme Intelligence, who is source and sanction of all the moral aspirations of man; it defines the ritual of God's worship as justice, love, and piety, and points to the rewards of His worship—peace, strength for life's struggles, confidence in the midst of defeat. It has a vision, too, and a program for the whole community of Israel, "to perfect the world according to the pattern of the Kingdom of God." It also presents an international code of morality based on brotherhood and peace.

Institutions, therefore, which undertake the training of ministers who are to preach these ideals must first apply themselves to the inculcation of these ideals among their students; they must convince them of the reality of these spiritual values, and they must inspire them with glowing zeal to live by them and for them, to shape their own lives after their pattern, and to help others to shape their lives accordingly. To this end the whole sacred literature of Israel is to be utilized as text, the whole range of Jewish experience, the complete records of the searchings and gropings of the mind and soul of Israel as revealed in the writings of our philosophers, poets, and preachers. "Behold within thee the long train of thy trophies, not without thee." This is basic. But it is not exclusive. Whatever of truth bearing upon these tremendous purposes may be gleaned from the literature of other peoples, from science, art, and philosophy, must be utilized for correction, clarification, and interpretation. To be sure, rabbis who are to carry on their ministry of spiritual leading in a modern world must have a sound understanding of the problems of modern society and of the specific problems of Jewish society, in order that their work may be relevant and efficient. From our acquaintance with the existing theological institutions we are convinced that serious attention is being increasingly given to these subjects. The seminaries are supplementing the economic and sociological studies which their students take in the universities by special courses in the specific problems of the Jewish community. Perhaps there should be more of these courses, but certainly the more ought not to loom so large as to crowd out the basic theological, historical, and literary studies. The aim must always be to prepare the men not for executive positions in social agencies, a task which rightly belongs to other institutions, nor for the position of arbiter in specific economic disputes which daily arise in American life, concerning which only the expert economist or sociologist can today speak with any authority, but for the prophetic preachment of the basic spiritual truths of human experience, for the all-important work of morally sensitizing men and women to such a pitch that when a situation arises involving a clear moral issue, whether in their private life or in their civic, national, or industrial life, they will be moved to choose the good and eschew the evil.

IX

Dr. Kallen's ill-tempered criticism of the modern rabbi deserves only passing notice. We submit that an assertion such as, "They [the rabbis] develop into public flatterers of the powers on which their livelihood depends," is unfair and utterly unbecoming the scientific temper of a seeker after truth. This is spleen and venom and the settling of old scores—not truth! It would appear from this statement that the American rabbis, whose average incomes are less than those of a moderately successful junk dealer or pants manufacturer, are so crippled and incompetent that they could not earn a living elsewhere but must depend on the ministry for their livelihood, even at the cost of spiritual degradation. It seems to grieve this professor that the prosperous Jewish communities of America are, in some instances, making it possible for a rabbi and his family to maintain a tolerably decent standard of living. Even Moses in his day seems to have had his Kallens. Whenever he entered the Tent of the Meeting, the rabbis say, there were men who were wont to cry out: "Look at his fat limbs and the sleekness of his body! His food and drink are of the Jews, and all that he has are of the Jews" (T. Jer. Shek. 5:2).

   Similarly puerile is the slur cast by the writer on the young men who are attending the various theological schools in order to prepare themselves for the ministry: "They have been bribed into the rabbinate." The fact that learning to be a rabbi usually costs nothing, and that the profession calls for no great physical or intellectual exertion, and that the income is relatively high are the reasons given why these young men have chosen their vocations. Judging from the low estimate which the professor has of his fellow Jews, one wonders why, in the face of all these alluring inducements, our theological schools are not overrun with students . . . . Were the emolument so high and the "ease and security of a rabbi's life" so certain, "bribes" would not be necessary. The fact of the matter is that the ministry does not offer the ease and security and the rich incomes which the average young man choosing a career quite naturally considers. It holds out none of the glamorous financial prospects which the successful practice of law or medicine or business does. The professor is perhaps misled in his financial barometer by the relatively high incomes of a few metropolitan rabbis (who probably would have done quite as well, if not better, financially, in other walks of life). The average is not at all so attractive. One need but visit the homes of American rabbis—Orthodox, Conservative, or Reform—from one end of the country to the other, to realize how very modest these homes are and to what stinting and scraping these men are often reduced by the necessity of keeping up a standard of living which their communities demand of them. And as for "ease and security," a veritable tyro in the ministry could give the professor some pointers . . . .

The children of well-to-do Jews are not going into the ministry today any more than they are going into the profession of teaching or social work or the arts. Very few of them are now going into any profession except the law, which has its "business" angle. It would be of interest to know whether the students of the New School for Social Research are recruited from the ranks of America's multimillionaires. Well-to-do parents want their children to enter into their own established business concerns or into some other business in which they can help them. Nothing so fantastic as the ministry occurs to them. It is the children of the poor who are sometimes attracted to the ministry or to social work or to teaching or to the career of an artist. This has always been so. "Take care of the children of the poor, for the Torah emanates from them."

X

In conclusion, a word about Jewish unity and Jewish leadership in America, the lack of which is so sadly lamented by many.

Throughout the writings of Cohen, Kallen, and Hurwitz, one finds

a pathetic hankering after organic unity in American Israel. Each one
blandly assumes that the differences which exist are slight, and could be
easily composed if the rabbis were not such bunglers, or if the seminaries
were not such morgues, or if some great leader would arise who by the
wave of some magic wand would reintegrate the scattered life of our
people. Thus Mr. Hurwitz writes: "Third, and this is the basic evil—
there is no real leadership in American Jewry; no leadership that, trans-
cending all the various prevailing sects, parties and propagandas, possesses the intelligence to see Jewish life steadily and as a whole, with
all its genuine needs and stirring potentialities; religion and culture and
philanthropy and industry, Diaspora and Zion; or possessing the intelligence, has the courage and energy to bring American Jews to serve all of
these needs integrally together."

Rabbi Joel Blau, in his thoughtful paper "The Case of Jewish
Education," which appeared in the *Menorah Journal* of February, 1925,
is moved by a similar mystic faith: "I look forward to the time when some
great leader in Israel, be he rabbi or layman, will recall our people from
this (as historic reckoning goes) momentary aberration, will recall it to
sanity and wisdom. And then, if we cannot entirely abolish our religious
differences, mainly centering in questions of religious etiquette, we will
look upon them with an eye so steadily directed to truth that these minor
points will cease to count. After that we shall be ready to build a real
Jewish Educational Institute, to serve as a center for Jews of all varieties.
One House for the entire Household of Israel!"

But all this is frightfully naive. There is no Jewish community
in the world, unless it be in the small backwater centers, untouched by
modern life, where such a unity exists. There is much less unity in the
great centers of Jewish life, in Poland and in Russia, than there is in the
United States. The Jewish communities there are split most decisively
along numerous nationalistic, economic, and religious lines. At times the
political emergencies of a minority group will weld them together into a
temporary truce, but they possess neither a central authority, an acknowledged leadership, a common purpose, nor a common program. This
is true also of the countries in western Europe. Everywhere Jewry has its
nationalists and its assimilationists, its Yiddishists and its Hebraists, its
modernists and its fundamentalists, its pietists and its atheists, its radicals
and its bourgeoisie, its Bolshevists and its bankers; and as the process of
secularization on the one hand and religious individualization on the other

continues, there will be still greater differentiation among the groups in
Jewry. This is true of all peoples. It is also true of the Jewish people.
It is very surprising that men who, like the distinguished editor of the
Menorah Journal, correctly understand that Israel is a *people* and not
merely a religious community do not bear this fact in mind. A religious
sect may have *a* leader; a people has *leaders,* with various and opposing
programs in all the departments of national life and thought. A people is
divided fifty ways as regards the leaders it chooses and the ideals it chooses
to follow. The Yiddish Bolshevists of Russia and the Russian Zionists
alike recognize that the Jews constitute a distinctive ethnic group. But
what a gulf there exists between their purposes and programs—and what
hostility! The Mizrachi and the Agudath Israel have the same Shulchan
Aruch in common, and yet even in Palestine they need must have their
own communities and their own leaders—and no love is lost between them.

The plain duty of the thoughtful American Jew today is to discover for himself the particular interpretation of Jewish life which appeals
to him, and affirmatively to follow it through, joining with others of like
mind in an effort to make that view and that tendency as dominant in
Jewish life as possible. There will never be "a comprehensive vision and
compelling leadership in American Jewry," any more than there is in
American life in general or in the life of any civilized people.

There will take place from time to time a pooling of resources
when common interests, chiefly political and economic, are at stake, when
anti-Semitic propaganda or unfavorable legislation threaten the security
of all the groups, or when humanitarian sentiments make a common
appeal. At times the various religious groups in Jewry will meet in conference to foster educational agencies whose programs are acceptable to
them all. But beyond this commendable "opportunism," it is folly to
expect solidarity and unity in American Israel.

Rabbis and Their Critics

SERMON, THE TEMPLE
APRIL 17, 1932

To be criticized or attacked is quite a regular and commonplace experience in my life. In the course of a very active public ministry of more than
a decade and a half, in which I have stood for and tried to champion
some very positive ideas and movements in Jewish life and to express
some very positive and definite views on issues both local and national,
I have, of course, made some enemies, and have, of course, been criticized
and attacked. I suppose that all men in public life who are not satisfied
merely with being pampered idols or straddlers or just good fellows have
similar experiences.

Sometimes these attacks are in the realm of ideas. They are inspired
by legitimate differences of opinion and are restricted to the amenities
of public discussion. But oftentimes these attacks are motivated by personal animosities and envy. They then take on the character, naturally,
of slander, innuendo, and plain mud-slinging.

Mostly I ignore such criticism. Never do I consciously initiate
controversy. Occasionally, when an attack is especially virulent and personal, I do take occasion to expose the critic and the real motive behind
the criticism, so that those who are uninformed may understand the
peculiar malice and viciousness which prompted the attack.

Recently I felt constrained to expose the author of a published
attack and to make public the personal malice of his attack. I was also
moved by another consideration not quite as personal as this. His attack,
which centered upon me, was part of a wholesale onslaught upon the
American Jewish ministry, particularly the Reform Jewish ministry whose
symbol he believes I am.

Maurice Samuel pays me an unconscious compliment by declaring

388

in his article that my "example has done more to mold the aspirations and ideals of young rabbis than any other single influence of this decade."

I had to rub my eyes when I read that.

And then he proceeds to indict these young rabbis throughout the land on every conceivable charge. They are insincere. They are poseurs. They are self-seekers. They are poor scholars. They are poor everything. And because I was publicly singled out as the symbol of these men and their spokesman, I felt called upon first to reveal the utter lack of qualification of this gentleman to make such criticism.

That was my first reason for writing a reply. And the second was to defend the men in the ministry against unjust and ill-tempered denunciations.

I was gratified at the response which came to me from my colleagues throughout the land on the publication of my reply. I was fairly deluged with letters expressing warmth and appreciation for the service which these men believe I rendered the profession and the cause of Judaism in hurling back this vicious onslaught from an envenomed and envy-consumed dilettante.

Here and there, of course, as much here as there, a rabbinical colleague of mine who beguiled himself into the belief that somehow Samuel's attack was not intended for him because he was different, or here and there, as much here as there, some colleagues who somehow believed that the attack on Rabbi Silver automatically raised the value of their own stock made a pathetic attempt to defend the writer. But men saw quickly through the maneuver.

Samuel belongs to a whole group of men who in recent years have made the rabbinate the target of their shots. These men are mostly journalists and writers who have attempted to establish themselves in the non-Jewish literary world and have failed. They have accordingly brought their literary wares over to the Jewish world, and here, too, they have not been as successful financially and otherwise as they had hoped to be. They wanted recognition, acclaim, leadership, and rewards. Since these were not forthcoming, they have become enraged and vindictive, and they are venting their wrath upon all men in Jewish public life in the United States who have achieved some measure of standing, influence, or success.

The vehicle of this group for some years was the *Menorah Journal*, a periodical published in New York City. And this periodical would blast forth from time to time with cynicism, with recklessness, with what we

Jews call *chutzpah,* about Jewish leaders, both lay and of the parish, and Jewish institutions. "Jewish lay leadership is bankrupt," was their cry. Also, "The Jewish rabbinate leadership is bankrupt." "The rabbis are uninformed. They are flunkeys. The rabbinic seminaries are intellectual morgues."

I took it upon myself, knowing these people, to expose them some years ago in a series of articles called "Why Do the Heathen Rage?" The catch phrase of these gentlemen was "Jewish Culture." Jewish Culture was to be a substitute for Judaism. They were not entirely sure what was meant by Jewish Culture, whether it was *milchig* or *fleischig* or whatever. But they were sure that they were hostile to the religion of the Jewish people.

They resented the position of importance which the synagogue was occupying in Jewish life. They also resented the position and influence of the rabbis in Jewish life. They wanted to be the spokesmen and leaders. Because I made it my business to dissect their credentials, to investigate their scholarly equipment for the task which they had set for themselves, to scrutinize this program of Jewish Culture and to lay bare this sham and charlatanry to the American public, of course these gentlemen have never forgiven me. Samuel's attack is only one of a number which have taken place and which will take place. Those of you who take pleasure in these things may rest assured that there will be other attacks and perhaps other replies.

The position which I have taken throughout my ministry and which many of my colleagues have taken, which runs counter to this so-called Jewish Culture as a substitute for Judaism, is simply this: I believe that religion is the sole reason why the Jew has persisted throughout the ages in maintaining his identity. I have searched high and low in Jewish history and literature to discover evidence to support the thesis that the Jew struggled desperately to survive through the ages against great odds, because he wanted to produce great art, literature, or drama. The Jew strenuously resisted intermarriage, for example, a practice which would have destroyed him in the long run, not on the grounds that such intermarriage would result in a racial admixture and would produce less gifted poets, musicians, or writers among the people, but simply for the reason given already in Biblical times: "Lest he will turn away thy son from following Me, that he may serve other gods."

The Jew persisted in racial loyalty because of his loyalty to his faith. When the Jew in the United States or elsewhere abandons his faith, he will quickly assimilate, and no quantum of Jewish art or music and no amount of books on Jewish history and philosophy will be able to check the inevitable process of assimilation. The anti-religious Jew will be the first to go, as he was always the first to go. The religiously indifferent Jew will linger on by sheer force of inertia until the relentless assimilationist forces scatter and overwhelm him too. The secular nationalist Jew will endure until such time as his ideology, which is borrowed from the Old World, from the compact and segregated community life of Europe, becomes dissipated and scattered in the new scene of American life.

Even the magnificent appeal which Palestine is making today to our people will not be strong enough in the years to come to command the unfaltering loyalty of the Jewish youth. The upbuilding of a strong Jewish commonwealth in Palestine, however much desirable, will not achieve the miracle of preservation for the Jews in the United States.

The existence of a German fatherland, strong and powerful, has not kept the eight or ten millions of Germans in the United States from assimilating.

Cultural pluralism, the idea that America must become a crazy quilt of numerous cultural groups, is a vain and hopeless dream. The United States would not permit itself to be Balkanized culturally. So we know that from any reading of the Jewish scene in the United States, only that Jew who remains steadfast to his faith (keep that in mind: not merely to the set of abstract theological principles which are inherent in Judaism, but to the rich, abundant faith which is our people's, a faith which carries with it Jewish practices, Jewish habits, Jewish modes of life, Jewish customs, the Hebrew language through which the genius of the race expresses itself, and the synagogue and hosts of common loyalties which all come with Jewish religious life) will carry on the destiny of our people in this country. All others will assimilate as they always have, as they inevitably must.

Only in Palestine is a secular Jewish life possible, or in those countries where a Jew possesses a distinct group life, possesses distinctive minority rights—a nationality within an empire of nationalities.

This is not and cannot be the case in the United States. So that we who love both Judaism and the Jewish people (and the two are not synonymous) wish to preserve Judaism through the Jewish people and the Jewish people through Judaism. Therefore we are vigorously opposed to, and are fighting consistently against, attempts to reduce Judaism to a secular nationalism or humanism. And because of that it is likely to be the battleground of the next decade or two, and you may expect your rabbi and all other rabbis to be in the midst of the fight of polemics.

As regards the criticism of the rabbinate, no right-thinking man resents well-directed and instructive criticism. In fact the rabbis are their own severest critics. If you have ever attended a meeting of the Central Conference of American Rabbis, or if you have ever read the reports in the yearbook published by the Conference, you would realize how unsparingly the rabbis criticize their own profession and themselves. There is no spirit of smug complacency among the rabbinate in the United States today, I assure you. The difficulty is with the layman, that he is not profound enough in his criticism and does not reach down to the basic problem involved.

I believe that it was Professor Mordecai Kaplan who recently said that the profession of the modern rabbi is really a new profession bearing an old name. In the olden days the profession of a rabbi was well defined. The functions of a rabbi were clear-cut. A rabbi in the Old World was the religious head of his community. He was the repository of Jewish law. To him civil and ritual questions of law were brought, and he handed down a decision on the basis of tradition and law. He was also a scholar in his community; his chief task was to study at home or in the synagogue. He studied the Torah, the Talmud, and rabbinic literature. Only occasionally did he perform weddings and officiate at funerals. These were the tasks of other religious functionaries in the community.

The role of the modern rabbi is totally different. People no longer go to him for a Kashah or a Shelah in matters of Kosher and Trefah. His role as judicial head of the community is gone and his new role is not defined. Is he to be primarily a teacher, an adviser of his people, an active propagandist of social reform in keeping with the traditions of the prophets of our people, or primarily a Jewish scholar? No one can perform all of these functions and do justice to any one of them. Hence the difficulty and hence also the root of much of the criticism launched against the rabbis.

An attack is made upon the men in the ministry in the matter of Jewish learning and scholarship. And yet here, too, there is confusion in the minds of those who make the attack. The contrast is made, in the field of religious study, between the old-time rabbi and the modern rabbi. That is a false contrast to make. The rabbi of old needed to study only the Bible, the Talmud, and rabbinic law; knowledge of any other branch of learning was not expected of him and was frequently resented in him if he had it. Occasionally a great rabbi arose who combined both great learning in

Jewish sources and also learning in secular sources, but by and large the rabbi of old specialized in one sort of learning and devoted his years to that, and of course he became master of it.

But of the modern rabbi much else is expected, a much more varied learning. He must know not only his Biblical science and something of Talmudic literature; he must not only be thoroughly at home in Jewish history, he must be at home in other branches of learning, in other languages, in other literatures, in some of the sciences, in economics, sociology, philosophy, psychology, history. He must be alert to what is going on in the world around him and be well informed; otherwise he cannot lead and instruct a modern congregation who are themselves not reared in rabbinic or secular learning. A rabbi in an age such as ours, which is characterized by doubt and skepticism, must be able to command a scientific knowledge, to combat skepticism and doubt. I am inclined to believe that the intelligence and mentality of the rabbi today is not inferior to that of the rabbi of old, but the latter was compelled to restrict himself to one specialty of learning, while the rabbi of today must branch out and command many types of knowledge and learning.

Then, too, this fact is overlooked: the rabbi of old had little else to do but study. He was expected to spend his time in the "tents of the Torah," studying over volumes of Jewish law. The communities were old communities, well established and well organized, and the religious life was very well departmentalized. They had their quota of charitable institutions, and a definite niche was carved out for the rabbi, and a definite function. But that is not and was not the case in the United States. As far as Judaism and the Jewish people are concerned, this is a new world. Jewish communities in America had to be built *de novo*—from the ground up, as it were. Synagogues, schools, charitable and philanthropic institutions, Jewish centers and Y.M.H.A.'s had to be built. Jewish societies and lodges were called into existence. A vast program of construction and organization has been laid at the doors of the rabbis of this generation, a program which consumes their time and energy. This generation of rabbis is a generation of builders. I mean that in a physical sense, if in no other sense; this is a role which the rabbis of the Old World did not have, and much of the time and energy of the modern rabbi has to go into this exhausting process of building.

And then there is this other task which has been thrust upon them, especially since the war, of fund-raising and campaigning. A plague of drives has descended upon the rabbis. Funds for hospitals, orphanages, homes for the aged, the Union of American Hebrew Congregations, seminaries, yeshivas, dormitories, laboratories, bureaus of Jewish education and what-not; for local relief, national relief, Falasha relief, and Palestine relief. And in each and every instance the rabbis throughout the country have been called upon to assume the role of actual leadership in these drives. These tasks have consumed much of their vitality and energy and time.

The synagogues in the United States, unlike the synagogues in the Old World, decided to become community centers, to serve the community not only religiously but also recreationally; not merely to be a house of worship and study but to be a place of entertainment for young and old, of dances, plays, parties, cabarets, and so on. So the rabbi was called upon to be a director of a large recreational program for his people, who wanted the synagogue to become their social as well as their religious center; the rabbi today in many instances is not only a rabbi, a pastor, but a melamed and a chazan.

I frequently hear people say, "What does Rabbi Silver have to do? He only has one sermon to prepare and preach for Sunday morning." They envy me my profession. I wish they could spend a week with me, not simply with me but with any rabbi of a large congregation. For I assure you that they would not be so envious. Not that I am complaining: I am not complaining and I never have. I love the profession too much to complain, and if it were five times as difficult I would still love it. But I should like you laymen to have an idea of just what a modern rabbi has to do which often brings down upon him a variety of criticism.

I have nothing to do during the week but attend four or five noon meetings for various kinds of organizations, civic, charitable, and educational. I have nothing to do but lecture three or four times a week in the evenings, sometimes at noon, before organizations, societies, schools, universities, both at home and outside of Cleveland.

I have nothing to do but teach four or five classes a week.

I have nothing to do but to plan programs and meetings for various organizations within The Temple; to arrange lecture courses and do a certain amount of supervision and instruction in a large religious school.

I have nothing to do but officiate at funerals and weddings, sometimes as many as eight or ten a week.

I have nothing to do but meet with any number of people who come to my study for advice and for help.

I have nothing to do but cooperate with national Jewish organizations which require my time for lectures or for attending out-of-town meetings of boards and committees.

I have nothing to do but to conduct two or three services a week in The Temple and to prepare one sermon a week, which ought to be of some interest and literary merit and scholarship.

In my spare time I have nothing to do but to make a few occasional visits to the sick and aged and carry on at least a minimum of social life in my own home. And then if I still have nothing to do, there is still the big thing left undone that one wants to do—namely, to spend hours at one's desk in study, learning and seeking new knowledge and new inspiration, recharging oneself. And frequently only the very late hours of the night and the very early hours of the morning are left for study, which in the early days was the main function of the rabbi.

It is clear that the present generation of rabbis has not the time for the creative scholarship which some wish him to do. Here and there a rabbi does succeed in forcing himself to set aside some time for scholarly pursuits —*rara avis*. Of course, occasionally you find a rabbi who sets publicity to work, advertising that he is a great scholar and is going to write an epoch-making book and persuades some morons to believe it. But that is publicity and politics, not scholarship.

The next generation of rabbis for which this generation is building will benefit from the work of this generation. It will perhaps be able to take the advice and profit from the criticism and will, it is hoped, devote much time to Jewish scholarship.

And then there is the criticism that rabbis do not visit their people. Pastoral work for a rabbi is not a Jewish custom of old. The old-time rabbi did not call upon his people. His people called upon him for advice and consolation. But it is a good custom that the Protestant and Catholic ministers have found very useful and helpful. In a small community the rabbi is able to do pastoral work and finds it helpful, the best way for the rabbi to enter the homes of his people. But in a large congregation it is practically impossible. I once figured out that in this congregation of over sixteen hundred families, it would take a rabbi who wanted to visit each family one evening about four years to make the rounds. Perhaps the fault is with our large congregations; but there is the reality of the situation which we must face.

There is a criticism made of rabbis that they turn their pulpits into book- and play-review platforms. I have heard that criticism made of certain of my colleagues who prefer the cheap and vulgar and sensational and easy rather than the difficult way of preparing an original sermon on vital religious or moral themes. The reason that some rabbis do it is that the laymen like that sort of thing. They are popular subjects and they draw. When *Mourning Becomes Electra* was playing in Cleveland, I venture to say that at least twenty people asked me if I was going to review the play. I was tempted to put into The Temple Bulletin that *Mourning Becomes Electra* is playing in Cleveland next week and Rabbi Silver will not lecture on it.

There is a certain sensationalism, a certain cheapness and vulgarity in some of the pulpits of this land, but fortunately these pulpits are not typical. As soon as some conscientious individuals in these temples will bestir themselves and express their disgust, those loud and blustering rabbis will beat a hasty retreat.

The charge is also made that rabbis are not courageous in advocating social ideals and do not speak their minds. In some instances this is a just criticism. But I think the Jewish rabbis are more liberal than the clergy of any other religious denomination in the United States; in fact the non-Jewish clergy frequently marvels at the liberal utterances expressed by the rabbis in this country. In some cities the rabbi is the sole individual raising his voice for liberalism and social righteousness. On the other hand, you and I know how frequently the rabbi is attacked for doing just that; how frequently he is attacked for being too outspoken and for meddling in what the layman thinks is not his business. Criticism comes from both angles: the radical thinks the rabbi is not radical enough and the conservative thinks the rabbi is too radical. And there you are.

To sum up, the Jewish people never looked upon its rabbis as saints or supermen. They looked upon them as men, some of them more gifted than others, but men of the people, chosen by the people to perform certain religious duties and provide certain religious guidance and leadership in Jewish religious life. And I think that by and large, working under these difficulties, the American Jewish ministry is possessed of earnest, sincere, hard-working, faithful men, who by following their best judgment are serving the cause of Judaism and the Jewish people.

Perhaps in the years to come, when our life is better organized, when our institutions have been longer established, when Jewish responsibilities have been properly divided and assigned, much of this criticism which is today being made of the rabbi will of itself disappear. Meanwhile may I advise all Jewish laymen to bear with their rabbis even as their rabbis have to bear with them.

I Go Through My Files:
1914–1918

SERMON, THE TEMPLE
OCTOBER 29, 1939

It is good for a man to keep a record of his public utterances and to review them from time to time. I assure you it is a sobering and humbling experience. One is brought face to face with the impartial judgment of time. And it is a relentless judgment. Time, history, life frequently make a mockery of our best-reasoned judgment and frustrate our verdicts and our hopes. I am sure that there are men today—writers, journalists, lecturers—who are just as sure of their opinions about things happening today and their consequences as men and women were during the First World War, twenty-five years ago. I am inclined to believe that they will be disillusioned when they come to read the record of their present utterances twenty-five years from now.

The fact of the matter is that no one really foresaw the events of the last half-century. No one really foresaw the tragedy of the First World War; the entrance of the United States into the First World War; the Bolshevik Revolution of 1917; the rise to power of the Fascists in Italy; or the rise of Nazism to power in Germany. No one really foresaw the attack on and the annihilation of German Jewry. Here and there, there were writers who alluded to certain possibilities, but mankind as a whole, I mean thoughtful men and women, did not expect these things actually to happen and were not prepared for them.

History does not follow any logical syllogism, because history follows life and life is illogical. The move of one pawn on a chessboard reorients all of the pieces. No one can foresee the infinite number of pawns on the chessboard of history. All this is brought home to you when you go through your files covering a period of years.

It is also impressively borne upon you how modest a man ought to be in his opinion and how modest he ought to be in expressing opinions on matters not within his control, and how much a man ought to avoid a certainness, a dogmatism, a cocksureness in expressing his opinions on world events.

I was closing my college career when the First World War broke out in 1914. The war touched us then as sensational news. We were tremendously excited, of course. We watched the war fascinated, as one watches a great show, a colossal drama. We speculated about it. We took sides. We estimated its possible duration—but always as something quite removed from us, on the other side of the ocean, as a European affair. Only as the war was prolonged and the frightful toll of human victims kept mounting, day by day and month by month, only as the shattering tragedy unfolded before our eyes, only as it kept getting nearer and nearer to us through relief agencies and reports and propaganda did we really try to evaluate it and ask ourselves: What does it all mean? Can any light come out of that darkness, and any sanity out of that madness?

The issues in the World War were then not yet clearly defined. My sympathies were with the Allies from the beginning. We understood the militarism represented by the Kaiser's Reich, the implications of the invasion of Belgium and the sinking of the *Lusitania*. I spoke of these things often in the harassed early days of my ministry.

Steadily, as the war lengthened and became more desperate, our sympathies for the Allies became increasingly more active. We did not want the great democracies of France and England to be defeated. When the Russian Revolution finally overthrew Czarism, the last inhibition was removed from the advocacy of American military aid to the democracies. By the time I came to this pulpit, the United States was already in the war.

In looking over my files, I find that I advocated the war. This was in a farewell address to the Jewish soldiers and sailors who were departing for war in August of 1917:

> As a child of the Jewish race, I am not a war advocate. The prophets have proclaimed that there would be a permanent peace and we have always spoken for eternal peace. But the present war is not a war of victory for us. We are not looking for gain. We are in this World War to do away with the reasons for war. We are not fighting the Germany that gave us the poets, the philosophers, the musicians, the artists, but against the German autocrats who are entirely responsible.

I find myself endeavoring to persuade myself that with the entrance of the United States into the war, the issues had been clarified. In a New Year's message in September, 1917, I said the following:

> If it shall please God that the coming year mark the Neilah of the Great Atonement of humanity, then Israel, too, will behold the close of its day of affliction. If this war which began in sin is to end in redemption; if, after this deluge of blood and tears, the rainbow of promise is to appear over a ruined world, then the rights of peoples must be firmly established and absolute equality must unreservedly be granted unto all the children of men. This war will prove to be the most futile, the ghastliest tragedy of the ages, if at its close one vestige of political or economic bondage remains, if one group of men is kept shackled in disabilities and discriminations. The moral and spiritual gains of this struggle must be commensurate with the terrible sacrifices it has entailed. Out of the crucible of burning pain, humanity must come forth purged of all its dross, its weaknesses and its prejudices, its lusts and its follies.

> The war began in sin, in the greed of dynasties, in the lust of empires; there was not a moral value at stake when the war began! But so stupendous did the struggle wax, so gigantic in its proportions, so harrowing in its toll of human misery, that out of its own volcanic soul a new motive and a new purpose has been evolved. Humanity, bleeding and tortured, in the fury of despair, has seized the reins from the hands of the masters and is guiding the forces which they have loosed into new channels of moral reconstruction.

> Already this new motive has been proclaimed in no uncertain terms by a great people—democracy. And democracy means equality of opportunity for people and peoples, for individuals and for the groups.

> And if the resolution of America is as firm as its protestations are loud, then humanity will not lay down its sword until the world is free.

President Wilson said: "Make the world safe for democracy!" I felt one with all other people of my generation who were standing on the threshold of a new epoch. I was not aware of the frightful complexity and obdurateness of events. I was not fully aware of the limitations of all human life, particularly of organized human life. I did not realize then as one comes to realize in later life the heartbreaking pedestrian crawl of human progress. I was not aware of the reality of the legend of Sisyphus, who was condemned eternally to roll to the top of a hill a large stone which no sooner reached the summit than it fell again back into the plain. I did not bear in mind the wisdom of that legend of our own sacred text that at the gates of Paradise there is an angel with a flaming sword, a revolving sword, which forever bars mankind from entering. The war, I was sure, would achieve a fresh new stage in the moral advancement of mankind.

My first cold plunge into reality came at the Front. I went to Europe in the summer of 1918. I was in France and I saw the war as it was, not from a safe and glamorous distance, but in the mud and filth of dugouts and trenches which I visited; amid the reek and chloroform of field and base hospitals and in the organized drab business of killing and mangling men and then trying to put them back together again.

I recall the New Year's sermon I preached when I returned, in September of 1918. It was something of a shock to my congregation. They expected me, I am sure, to talk of the glory and the heroic sacrifices of the people at the Front, to deliver a patriotic address full of fervor for the war and the promise of victory. Instead I spoke of the dead and the dying, of suffering and misery in the world of Hell, of the aches in the hearts and minds of men, women, and children.

I did not turn pacifist. My religious tradition is not that. It never was that. I did not lessen my service to my country. I gave a good deal of my time to the selling of Liberty Bonds in all parts of the country. I felt that the war must be won, inasmuch as we were in it. But more than ever, I desperately clung to the hope of building something amidst the ruins. I clung to the hope that perhaps these tears would wash away some of the sins of mankind, that somehow, after the war, when our men returned, they would set about cleansing and purifying their own lives and destroy all that was ugly and unworthy of sacrifice:

> After our men are through crushing forever the menace to human peace and national comity they will come back and set about deliberately and determinedly to smash the lines here at home, and they are going to smash every line that confines and limits the onrushing spirit of freedom-seeking men and women.

> They are going to smash ruthlessly and relentlessly every line of social injustice, every line of economic wrong, every line of political reaction, every line of religious prejudice and intolerance that exists here in this land, and that confines and stultifies the spirit of onsweeping ambitions of freedom-loving men and women.

Why should we permit life to be starved and shriveled in little groups because of lack of opportunity; why should not each son of God be given a chance to develop himself, the chance of education, the chance of infinite opportunity to make of himself the best that he is capable of; why not smash the line and permit the sons of God to become great with the greatness of life?

As I review my files, I find myself thinking in those days that somehow, some good would come out of this evil, that out of the ravages of hate and revenge would come reconstruction for mankind.

Then came the Armistice, and the long heartbreaking drag of the peace negotiations. It became clear that while some problems might be solved, the most urgent problems would not be solved. A frightful reaction set in. I saw how the hopes of mankind were being destroyed, one by one, and how old-time diplomacy, imperialism, and political corruption were entrenching themselves again all over the world. I find myself, as I go through my files, speaking on "The Sins of the Allies," and "Is the Treaty of Peace a Peace Treaty?"

In place of that emancipation that I had looked for after the war, I saw a stampede of bigotry and intolerance, riots, raids, Red-hunting, and Red-baiting. It became difficult in those days to express one's free opinion in this city, even as it became difficult anywhere in the United States. The country was afraid of Bolshevism. All liberalism was trampled under by this fear of an all-conquering Bolshevism. And so I find myself, in the months immediately following the Armistice, trying to organize in this city, with the aid of some friends, the City Club, and to reopen public forums in high schools and on Cleveland's Public Square, in order to re-establish the principle of free speech in a free country, after the victorious consummation of a war which was to have made the whole world safe for democracy. In those days there swept over this land a fear and distrust of all immigrants and foreigners, a movement to suppress foreign languages in the United States, a movement called "Americanism," which had the same emotional wellspring as Hitlerism. I find myself speaking before temples and civic organizations on the subject "Immigrant versus Foreigner," trying to stress what Americanism really is, trying to justify the immigrant who had just finished serving in the war. I tried to stress that an immigrant is not necessarily a foreigner, nor is a native American necessarily an American. A foreigner is one who remains forever hostile to the ideals of Americanism. A native-born American who is similarly hostile remains fundamentally a foreigner. An immigrant who comes here and throws his destiny and his life into the life and hope of America—he is the American.

There came to me slowly through those searching years, when the world had been rocked and its foundations laid bare, the realization that war never builds man's dream world, that it does not ennoble man, and that even if the war is won it often achieves the very opposite of what it intended to achieve. I saw clearly then that the reconstruction of our society must be achieved by the slow work of patient planning and peacetime building, by patient and unemotional workers. I realized then, as I realize now, that it is sometimes necessary to resort to war to curb a ruthless aggressor if there is no other way out. But war remains an evil. War blacks out civilization not only during the period of the actual conflict but for long, long periods thereafter. When war was declared in 1914, Sir Edward Grey said: "This day will mark the beginning of the going out of lights in Europe, and I am afraid that we shall not live to see the day when those lights will be rekindled." His words were prophetic. In 1918, when I crossed the Atlantic to go to the Western Front, I crossed on the *Rochambeau*. One of my first experiences was the blackout. No man dared to smoke a cigarette on deck. When I entered Paris it was at night. I had never been to Paris before; my impression was that it was a city of ghosts. Twenty-five years later, I fled from a Europe again overtaken by war, and again all around me there was the man-made midnight. And through these twenty-five years—this is the saddest of sad things—the world has evidenced, because of the World War, one blackout after another of thought, human freedom, tolerance. What we have in the world today is blackness, with only a few slender tapers keeping their lonely vigil in a darkened world.

It is, therefore, from my own files, from my own experience that I must draw my attitudes to this new World War. It is a necessary war. It could not be otherwise as long as that power-drunk madman reigns in Europe. There is but one way of stopping him, and that is war. But it is an evil, an unspeakable evil. And knowing my experience of the last twenty-five years, I cannot put my hope on this war, much as I would like to. I do not see it through apocalyptic eyes. It speaks to me no words of promise. I realize today what I did not realize then, that "there is no seeking of dainties in the grave."

And I must think now not so much of this war, but of what will follow the war, of how Europe will have to begin anew where it left off; not this year, or last year, but where it left off in 1914, after nearly a half-century of peace. The world will have to begin again. Pray to God that it will not repeat the mistakes of 1919. After the war, it will be the task of those who eat the bread of understanding and drink the water of wisdom to set about building habitations fit for human beings. It will be the task and the opportunity of the American people to cooperate in this building, not by giving that kind of leadership which some self-righteous, altogether too righteous, Americans would like to give to the Europeans, based on the assumption that they are the wicked ones and we are the blameless ones; but by pointing the way and by setting out on the way ourselves.

Ideas, ideals, thank God, there are aplenty in the world. What mankind needs is the willingness and the determination on the part of great nations to give noble cooperation in the realization of these ideals. It is not worthy of Americans to speak of the desirability of a League of Nations and then to refuse to enter it.

I shall not sit in judgment upon the people abroad. I shall commiserate with their suffering. I shall hope and pray for a righteous outcome of this war. When it is over, I shall summon the American people to join a real war in a real way by backing up their sacrifices. I shall join again in another effort to build an international society based on mutual understanding, law, justice, and peace.

Perhaps if you were to go through the files of your minds, your thoughts would be very much like mine.

Problems and Prospects of American Judaism

FOUNDER'S DAY ADDRESS
THE HEBREW UNION COLLEGE
MARCH 12, 1950

In establishing the Hebrew Union College seventy-five years ago, Dr. Isaac Mayer Wise made a major contribution to the preservation of Judaism in the United States. No Jewish community in any part of the world has ever survived which relied exclusively on philanthropy and on places of worship, and which did not sink its roots deep into the nourishing soil of Jewish learning and scholarship. Judaism is an adult religion for mature men and women, and it calls for the deepest of insights and for the most profound and continuous study. It is more than a faith and a code of conduct. It is the intellectual quest of God; and what the best minds and the most inspired souls in the unique and bold religious enterprise called Judaism have had to say, and the records of their spiritual experience, constitute not only the priceless treasures of Judaism, but its indispensable means of survival.

It is not only when a Jerusalem is destroyed that a Jamnia must be built; but the builders of Jerusalem must likewise plan for a Jamnia. King David is represented in our tradition not only as the conqueror and builder of Jerusalem, but as a devoted teacher who instructs and inspires many pupils. It was because of his zeal in the study and the propagation of the Torah that David received the kingship.

Isaac Mayer Wise had the clear vision to see this. "Judaism is not a faith," he wrote in 1858, "a mere belief in certain doctrines, nor is it a compendium of observances; it is a divine science, a body of knowledge.

Therefore, we say, Reform must begin with the spreading of light, more light, as much light, indeed, as the age can bear. Instruction, more instruction, as much of it as the intellect is capable of receiving."

Dr. Wise realized early that if a strong Judaism was to be built in the New World, it must be founded upon learning, upon a learned rabbinate and a learned laity. He was remarkably little concerned throughout his long life with eleemosynary projects, not because he did not recognize their importance, but because he knew that Jews being what they are, *rahamanim b'nai rahamanim,* "merciful children of merciful ones," would not ignore such projects, while they might very easily come to ignore the most fundamental project in Jewish life, and the most important factor in its survival, *Talmud Torah,* "the study and teaching of the Torah."

On the occasion of the opening of the Hebrew Union College in 1875, addressing himself to his students, Dr. Wise declared: "The student's combat is in his studies, and his triumphs in his learning. You are making war upon ignorance, and the more courageously and efficiently you do it, the more glorious will be your victory. . . . Judaism must be studied in the products of the Hebrew mind, and these are preserved in Israel's great literature. As little as one can possess an adequate knowledge of a country without surveying it, so little can one form a correct idea of Jewish history, ethics, metaphysics, and theology without an intimate acquaintance with the original sources in which the Hebrew mind has actualized itself. As for the scientist, no object of nature is without interest, so for us, not a line of Jewish literature is without significance."

In the matter of the priority which should be given to Jewish learning in the American Jewish community, Dr. Wise's hopes, I am afraid, have not been realized. Because of it, American Jewish life today ominously lacks balance. It has overconcentrated on philanthropic institutions as against religious institutions, and on religious institutions as against schools and academies for the training of our youth and our leaders in the faith, language, and literature of their people. The indifference of the Jewish layman increases as he passes from the social agency to the synagogue to the school. In the long run this practice of putting first things last, so alien to the historic attitude of our people, might well prove disastrous to American Judaism. "My people is destroyed for want of knowledge," warned the prophet Hosea.

The recent re-establishment of the State of Israel makes even more imperative the strengthening of our religious institutions—synagogues, schools, and academies in the Diaspora. The hope of national restoration which was a potent factor in Jewish survival throughout the ages must, in its realization, be compensated for by an intensification of the purely religious and cultural agencies of Jewish life.

It is clear that a considerable part of the Jewish people—perhaps a majority—will continue to live outside of Israel in the indeterminate future. The Prime Minister of the State of Israel a few days ago predicted that there would probably be a Jewish population of 3,000,000 in Israel in the next ten years, and spoke of four to five millions as the ultimate population of that country. There are more than that number of Jews today in the United States alone. It is to the interest not alone of the State of Israel, which will have to draw replenishment and economic and political support from the Diaspora reservoir for years to come, but of the Jewish people as a whole and of Judaism, the noblest creation of the Jewish people and its supreme gift to mankind, that Diaspora Jewry should remain vital, vigorous, and spiritually sound. All talk, however patriotically motivated, which derogates Diaspora Jewry or altogether writes it off is meaningless and harmful in the extreme.

What our people possesses today of cultural and spiritual treasures is not exclusively the creation of the Jews of Palestine. The 4,000-year-old drama of the Jewish people was enacted on more than one world stage. Some of its principal actors, from Abraham to Moses, never lived in Palestine. Even when there was a flourishing Jewish life in Palestine, there were also flourishing Jewish communities in other lands. Babylonian and Palestinian Jewry, for example, re-enforced and enriched one another, and both made significant if not comparable contributions to the sum total of Jewish life and thought.

What is clearly indicated today is the setting in motion of the liveliest possible spiritual and cultural intercommunications and interactions between Israel and the Diaspora, similar to that which existed during periods of the Second Commonwealth. The Zionist political program has now been achieved. It was unfortunate that so much of the energies of Reform Judaism and of some of its most distinguished leaders was diverted and spent in opposing it. Even the genius of Isaac M. Wise—proud, militant, and uncompromising Jew that he was—faltered in this instance. One can readily understand the reason why. Dr. Wise lived in "fair, well-spoken days," at a time when human hopes ran high. The very year in which he founded the Hebrew Union College, he wrote, "Before our very eyes the world moves onward into the golden age of redeemed humanity and the fraternal union of nations, as our prophets thousands of years ago predicted. We are fast approaching the universal democratic republic, with civil and religious liberty cemented by the world's advanced intelligence. This century settles old accounts. It is progressive."

He could not foresee—as indeed very few did foresee—that the new century which he was facing would open a "purple testament of bleeding war." He could not surmise the political, economic, and spiritual collapse of Europe not many years after his passing, the breakdown of democracy, the rise of Fascist and Communist dictatorship, the resurgence of paganism, and the gas chambers where millions of his people would be done to death.

And being unable to foresee it, he could not conceive that any normal person could believe that Jews would leave "the great nations of culture, power, and abundant prosperity in which we form an integral element to form a ridiculous miniature state in dried-up Palestine."

Dr. Wise lived his creative years in America—free, prosperous, tolerant America. Early in his *Reminiscences* he reports the fact that he was "an enthusiast on the subjects of America and freedom." Those of you who have read his moving and penetrating essay on Moses will recall the resonant strophes, the almost rhapsodic outburst toward the end of the essay: "The loudest and mightiest of all sounded that one great and powerful word of the Almighty, freedom, freedom, freedom! Freedom sounded from Sinai; the mind is free, the spirit is free, Jehovah is the God of freedom; and now it re-echoes from ocean to ocean; the mind is free, the spirit is free, man is free; break the yoke, break the shackles; man is free."

In the Declaration of Independence and the Constitution, Dr. Wise saw reflected the central Mosaic idea of a state and its citizens, and he was moved to declare that "the political side of the Bible is realized in the United States. We live in a perfectly Jewish state and under a Jewish government in the strictest sense of Moses."

In America Dr. Wise saw not alone the fulfillment of what he called Mosaic ethics, but the great opportunity for Judaism to use this country as a base for the propagation of Judaism as the universal religion of mankind. He was persuaded that the triumph of Judaism was not far off. He entertained not the least doubt that "before this century will close, the essence of Judaism would be the religion of the great majority of all the intelligent men in the country."

In such an environment of pleasant freedom and in such a climate of high Messianic expectancy, it is not to be wondered at that Dr. Wise was extremely impatient with "those who wanted to establish a Jewish state in Palestine," and declared them to be "pessimists who despaired of human reason, the progress of humanity and the solidarity of mankind."

It was, of course, most fortunate that these pessimists, who may have despaired of reason, progress, and the solidarity of mankind appearing in sufficient time to save them and their people from extermination, did not commit the graver sin of despairing of themselves. All the maledictions of the *tochayho*, "the catalogue of curses" (Deut. 28), did indeed come true in our day, all but one—*v'lo taamin b'hayyecha*, "thou shalt not believe in thine own life." They *did* believe in their own lives, in their own powers, in their own destiny—and believing, they toiled, fought, and triumphed.

But now life has closed the long debate which never should have been opened. It is closed for all Jews except for those frustrated few who delight *crambem recoquere*—to recook stale cabbage. The principle of progress in Judaism in no way contradicts the historic necessity of the Jewish people for national restoration, which was always a basic tenet of historic Judaism. All the prophets of Israel were patriots, and they were all "political." They, however, wanted Israel to be different within the family of nations, an *am s'gulah*, "a distinctive people," distinctive in its spiritual caste, in its ethical conduct, in its faith and idealism.

Similarly, the ideal of the mission of Israel was never alien to the best minds among the proponents of the Zionist ideal. It was never their dream to recreate just another Levantine nationality, to increase the congeries of political states by one more.

In fact, now that Theodore Herzl's political program has been triumphantly consummated and the work of state-building and the ingathering of our people is proceeding apace, the restoration movement may now well move into the spiritual and cultural orbit which was defined for our day and which is identified with the name of another great Zionist, Ahad Ha-am. The ultimate objectives both of Herzl and Ahad Ha-am were the same, though in practical life they frequently clashed. Herzl was impressed primarily with the physical and political problem of the *galuth*, and sought a political solution for it in the creation of a Jewish State. Ahad Ha-am saw the spiritual problem of the *galuth* in terms of the threatened cultural and spiritual disintegration of our people, and he sought a solution for it in the creation of a spiritual and cultural center for our people in Palestine.

It was fortunate that the sound political vision and program of

Theodore Herzl governed the course of the movement until the State was established. A premature overemphasis of the concept of a spiritual or cultural center would have found the Jewish people unprepared for the final political and military struggle without which the State could not have been established, and without which the ingathering of myriads of our people could not have been accomplished. Ahad Ha-am discounted too much the value of practical work in Palestine and of political and diplomatic action. He was too skeptical of the capacity of Palestine to absorb large masses of Jews and to absorb them quickly.

But Herzl's political triumph now paves the way for the vision which was Ahad Ha-am's—that of the radiating center in a reconstituted Jewish State which would also serve as a unifying influence for world Jewry. Ahad Ha-am did not believe that a total *kibbutz galuyoth,* "a total ingathering of all Jews," was feasible or necessary for the spiritual influence which a reconstructed Jewish State, true to the essential genius and character of historic Israel, could come to exercise in world Jewry.

The Jewish communities of the Diaspora will look eagerly for all stimulating influences which might emanate from Israel. But Diaspora Jewry need not remain a mere passive recipient of outside cultural influences. It can become, as indeed so often in the past it did become, creative in its own right, wherever the religion, language, and literature of the Jewish people were fostered.

In 1909 Ahad Ha-am wrote in the *Hashiloach:* "It is necessary to improve and deepen our life as a people to the utmost possible degree in the Diaspora and, at the same time, to seek the complete and perfect solution beyond the Diaspora, in Palestine."

This is a good program for Jewish survival from here on. Israel and the Diaspora should remain interdependent, spiritually inseparable though politically separate and apart. Both should be helped to become strong and creative.

In the days of King Hezekiah, when the Jews of Jerusalem anticipated the siege of their city by the Assyrians, they built a tunnel from the Spring Gihon in the Valley of Jehoshaphat to a reservoir called Siloah, in order to secure the water supply for the city. Some years ago an inscription was discovered not far from this pool of Siloah hewn in rock, written in ancient Hebrew characters and telling how the tunnel was hewn through the rocks in order to bring water to Jerusalem. It is the famous Siloam Inscription which is now in the museum of Istanbul. "This is the story of the tunnel," reads the inscription. "The axes of one group were opposite to those of the other. When they were but three cubits apart, it was possible for one to call to the other, for there was a fissure in the rock to the right and to the left. On the day of the completion of the tunnel the diggers struck, facing one another, axe facing axe, and then the water flowed in the spring to the pool of Siloah for a distance of 1,200 cubits."

Moving from opposite directions but facing one another, axe facing axe, thus concertedly the Jews of Israel and the Jews of the Diaspora should strike through the rocks of separation to build a two-way connecting spiritual and cultural conduit which will cause the waters of life and healing to flow uninterruptedly for the salvation of our entire people.

Was not this also the restoration vision of Zechariah, although limited to the concept of a one-way stream of influence? "It shall come to pass in that day that living waters shall go forth from Jerusalem, half of them toward the eastern sea and half toward the western sea. . . . And the Lord shall become King over all the earth. In that day the Lord shall be one and His name, one."

It is to be noted that the hour of the physical restoration of Israel, or the eager hope for it, was always bound up with profound spiritual anticipations. It was to be an hour of regeneration, of spiritual renewal. Recall that exquisitely tender and compassionate prophecy of reconciliation and restoration in Chapter 31 of Jeremiah in which the prophet speaks of a new covenant which God will make with Israel at the glad, healing time, a stronger and an enduring covenant. "I will put my law within them and will write it on their hearts, and I shall be their God and they shall be my people." Another prophet of the restoration, Ezekiel, proclaims, "I will take you out of the nations and gather you from all lands. I will give you a new heart and will put within you a new spirit. You shall be my people and I will be your God." Deutero-Isaiah's heart rings with a "new song." Exaltingly he speaks of "a new heaven and a new earth." In the hour of vindication Israel shall be called by a new name which the mouth of the Lord shall determine, and Israel will be "a glorious crown in the hands of the Lord, a royal diadem in the hand of your God."

Is there any reason why this great hour in our history, this present Messianic hour of vindication and salvation should not lead to a resurgence of faith and should not become a summons for rededication and spiritual renewal for our people here, in Israel, and throughout the world?

The establishment of the State of Israel has contributed a large measure of dignity and confidence to Jewish life. It, therefore, has brightened the prospects for a spiritual renaissance among our people. Upon surer foundations, the Jewish world community of tomorrow, inside and outside of Israel, may be able to build a more affirmative religious life and recapture perhaps that revolutionary religious leadership which twice in the past molded the civilization of mankind.

Exile made the mission of Israel impossible because the mission of a defeated people is automatically discredited. Exile was defeat for God as well as for Israel. The people of Israel, the prophets were convinced, brought exile upon themselves because of their sins, but in exile the name of the God of Israel was profaned because the gentiles said that the God of Israel was helpless to save His own people. "When they arrived among the nations to which they came, they caused My holy name to be profaned in that men said of them, these are the people of the Lord and yet, they had to go forth from His land." As long as they remained in exile, the glory and majesty of the Lord were contemned by the nations. The God of a defeated and conquered people has little to recommend Him. God, therefore, will redeem Israel, declared Ezekiel, and restore them to the land because He was grieved for His holy name which the household of Israel has caused to be profaned among the nations to which they came. "It is not for your sake that I am about to act, O household of Israel, but for My holy name. . . . When I restore my holiness in their sight through my dealings with you, the nations shall know that I am the Lord." No successful proselytizing for Yahveh among the nations was possible as long as the people of Israel were in exile.

One is reminded that the notable period of Jewish proselytizing activities in post-exilic times languished and petered out with the final scattering of the people following the collapse of the Bar Kochba uprising and the Hadrianic persecutions.

The restoration of the State of Israel has in no way revoked the spiritual mandates or altered the religious destiny of our people. "Let no one imagine," declared Maimonides, basing himself on the Talmudic authority of Rabbi Samuel, "that the coming of the Messiah will alter anything in the accustomed order of the world." *Ella olam k'minhago nohayg.* The world will go on exactly as before. The only significant difference will be the removal of the yoke of oppression from the shoulders of our people, *shibud malchuyoth bil'vad,* and the Jewish people will be free to devote themselves uninterruptedly to the Torah.

The restoration of the State of Israel with its tremendous psychological implications has freed our people from the spirit of depression and forlornness, the fears and the confusions of the long, weary, and homeless centuries. It is now possible, if so we will, to move forward on our appointed tasks as a covenanted people with a new heart and a new song.

Isaac Mayer Wise's vision of a liberal, courageous, militant Judaism, unafraid to proclaim itself as the true universal religion of mankind, can now come into its own. Wise was admirable in his championing of Judaism. He was fearless in his criticism of Christian orthodox dogmas, both Catholic and Protestant, and of the whole Christian mythology. In this regard he was in the classic tradition of Profiat Duran, Yom Tob Lipman, and Isaac Troki, and in this regard he has had few important followers in the American Reform rabbinate. Unlike many of his later disciples, when Wise spoke of a universal religion, he meant Judaism, and when he spoke of the mission of Israel, he meant just that—to convert the world to his faith. When in 1874 he made another one of his powerful appeals for that which was closest to his heart—the establishment of the college—he declared, "We unfurl the banner of Judaism as the light of the nations. . . . Judaism and progress, Judaism and moral freedom, Judaism and liberality, light and unity are identical." He did not make overtures for a theological truce, and he did not suggest that since religion was, after all, only a matter of personal taste, everyone could well afford to be broad-minded and latitudinarian about it.

He even dared to qualify the slogan, "Americans first and then Israelites." It was one of those commonplaces which he could accept only with due modification. "If Congress would enact laws," he declared in 1872, "imposing upon the citizens atheism, or upon the Jew the Christian dogma, I would be an Israelite first, and in rebellion against my country, whatever means I would select to have that law or laws revoked . . . . As things stand now, I am also an Israelite first and a citizen then, because my duties as a man and an Israelite are continual, almost without interruption, while my duties as a citizen are but temporary and periodical. I am a loyal citizen because it does not prevent me from being an Israelite according to my convictions."

Dr. Wise was not intimidated by the higher Biblical criticism which blossomed forth in his day. "Scientifically," he declared, "it does not stand as high as the old Talmud, which had its fixed rules of interpretation, while the modern Talmud does not; no fixed laws of hermeneutics; it is still in its pilpulistic state. Kuenen, Welhausen, Renan, Ewald or Smith are no more reliable authorities than the Jochanans, Gamaliels, Jehudas or Rabbina and Ashi." Like Rabbi Meir, he reserved the right to eat the kernel and to throw away the shell. He anticipated that a more mature scholarship and, more especially, the future discoveries of Biblical archeological research, would undergird the authenticity of much that was being frivolously challenged, and would expose the tendentious activities of some of the Biblical critics of his day whose purpose seemed to be, above all else, to prove that the God of Israel was either borrowed or objectionable, that the institutions of Judaism were shoplifted from some Babylonian or Egyptian emporium, that the great men of Israel were either myths, tribes, or Aryans, and that that which was old in the Bible was really recent, and what was recent was inferior to the perfections of Christian teachings.

Dr. Wise was not taken in by this higher anti-Semitism, to use Dr. Schechter's phrase. He may have been too orthodox in his attitude toward Biblical criticism, relying too much in the formulation of his Reform theology upon the unimpeachable authority of the Pentateuch, which higher criticism endangered. He may have been faulty in his political evaluations. He may not have been a great systematic theologian or philosopher. But he *did* understand the real essence and spirit of Judaism. He did believe in its invincible destiny. He did have the courage to defend and to champion it. He did have the surpassing love to dedicate his life to it. He did have the insight to seek its perpetuation through the spread of learning and the establishment of schools and a rabbinical seminary. He did possess a gift, bordering on genius, of organization, of overcoming opposition, of giving direction and unity to an inchoate and anarchic Jewish life in the New World. Herein lies his immortality.

Through the Hebrew Union College, Dr. Wise and his eminent successors in office and the distinguished scholars who have labored here have, for three-quarters of a century, carried on the basic tasks of "progressive" Judaism, a term which Dr. Wise preferred to "Reform" Judaism. They carried on the tasks by stressing essential Judaism, and the importance of Jewish scholarship.

The re-forming of the external accouterments and ritual practices of our ancient faith loomed very large and very important in Wise's day. It was, so to speak, a *mitzvath asay she-ha-z'man g'ramah*, "a positive command required by the occasion," but that work is fairly well accomplished now. There is really very little left to reform. Judaism has now been "modernized" and "streamlined" to suit the most radical and the most fastidious of tastes. However, it is doubtful whether the modernization of Judaism has made our people more spiritual or more pious. Certainly it has not filled our temples with devout worshipers who should come there *be-ragesh,* as the Psalmist said, "in throngs" or "in ecstasy" or "eagerly," whichever way you translate *be-ragesh.* Nor has it filled our schools with youth thirsting for Jewish knowledge.

Our task in the days to come, I am persuaded, will be much more difficult than in Wise's day. For, after all is said and done, it was not too difficult a task to urge Jews in the New World to abandon certain antiquated and burdensome religious customs. Some, of course, did resist, but the many did it quite readily, even when unbidden and uncoaxed. They were grateful for the official sanction which Reform Jewish leaders gave to a course of practice which they had already adopted quite independently and without first consulting them. It seems that certain Conservative Jews today are asking for a similar official sanction from their leaders—or rather, that certain Conservative rabbis are seeking to thrust such official sanction upon a way of life which their Conservative flock has already adopted without waiting for authorization either from the *yeshivah shel ma'lah,* "the Court on High," or from any *yeshivah shel mattah,* "a court below"—a way of life which differs not one whit from what their Reform fellow-Jews had adopted as recently as 100 years ago.

Today, however, our tasks are much more difficult. We must make stern demands upon our people if Judaism is to survive. Great religions have always made great demands upon their devotees, and have called for tremendous commitments. Fashionable theosophies may offer a minimum of discipline and a maximum of peace of mind. Judaism has always offered man the *ol malchuth shamayim,* "the burden of the Kingdom" of God, a burden, however, which lifts all other burdens from the human heart, and gives man's soul enfranchisement and the supreme satisfactions of life. The commandments of Judaism, to be sure, are not beyond the reach of man. They are not far off in heaven or beyond the seas. They are very near, *b'ficha u-vil'vav'cha laasoto,* "in thy mouth and in thy heart to do it." But they are not very easy!

Today it is no longer a question of more ceremonies or of fewer ceremonies, of going backward or of going forward in things external, but of going inward. It is upon the inwardness of Judaism, upon the intellectual quest of God through the time-honored techniques of Jewish religious life and learning and study, upon the disciplines of the devotional life and the ethical life that we shall have to concentrate in the days to come. It is with these heavy obligations that our laity must be confronted. It is no longer a question of the competitive values of orthodoxy, conservatism, or reform. None of them has scored any significant victories in our day for Judaism. Nor will any significant victories come about through any physical mergers or through any artificial combinations of administrative apparatus. This is not the way to meet a spiritual crisis; and it is a spiritual crisis of the gravest kind that Judaism and all spiritual religions in the world are facing today.

Progressive Judaism from now on will have to think of progress not in terms of external reforms, but in terms of deepening and enriching classic Jewish concepts. It is in the re-definition of essential doctrine, not in surface ritual reform, that the historic progressive motif in Judaism abides.

Prophetic Judaism gave new definitions to the concepts of God, people, temple, sacrifice, kingship, property, slavery, labor, family, stranger, brotherhood, peace. They are new definitions; all *yashan mipnay hadash totziu,* "bring forth the old before the new." They replaced the old with the new. They made progress by going inward. They sank deeper shafts to mine new gold. What was progressive and therefore permanent in their contributions was not that they were "up to date" or responsive to the "state and inclination of their day," but that they went deeper and challenged the spirit of their age. They sought to inform, affect, and alter it; for the spirit of no age ever attains to the spirit of God.

Rabbinic Judaism continued this process. What was progressive and, therefore, permanent in their contribution were not the necessary "hedges" which they built around the Torah and which the times required, but the deepening of essential concepts of Judaism—Talmud Torah, the disciplines of study, Torah Lishmah, Kiddush Ha-Shem, Yesurin shel A-havah, the noble ways of prayer, the higher ranges of charity, the spiritual evaluation of the Sabbath, the wider spiritual scope of the synagogue, and how to train for a life of faith, how to be *arum be-yirah,* "skilled in faith." They were in the noble and progressive tradition of *m'galeh amukoth mini hoshech,* "uncovering depth from utter darkness," making transparent what was opaque.

Medieval Jewish philosophy likewise contributed new definitions and new insights—the interplay of revelation and reason, the meaning of freedom in man and in God, and the way to build a confident life for man in a world created and governed by an unknowable and indescribable God. A medieval Jewish philosopher, Halevi, gave a profound and new definition to the concept of Jewish nationality.

Jewish mysticism, likewise, revealed new depths and new penetrations, more especially in the field of probing the inner meaning of the sacred text. In its latest manifestation, in Hasidism, it gave us new concepts and new techniques: *hithlahavut*, "enthusiasm," *hishtapchut hanefesh*, "outpouring of one's soul," the sacredness of joy in the practice of faith, and the importance of personality in spiritual leadership—the concept of the inspired guide, the Tzadik.

The progressive and permanent element in Reform Judaism was not the abandonment of certain outmoded and incongruous customs, but the substitution of scholarship for scholasticism, of liberty for authority, and the replenishment in modern terms of an ancient concept not yet fully grasped, the mission of Israel.

This is the kind of progress and spiritual adventure with which this great institution, its teachers, students, and graduates, will have to concern themselves in the days to come in a century wherein radicalism in science and radicalism in forms of social and economic organization and political authority are confronting the individual with radical new problems of adjustment, and religious and ethical traditions with their most serious challenge. What is social justice today? Is the Jewish concept of *tzedek*, "justice," fully expressed in the evolving forms of socialism and communism and in their methods? Are there basic principles of human status, rights, and freedoms endangered in them as in a capitalist society which religion must be on guard to defend? To what extent can the concentration of political power in the state in the name of social progress be sanctioned without completely submerging the individual whom God created *y'hidi*, "one," integrally *one!*

There is no longer any nourishing food for the coming generations of Jews in any program of revision of surface customs and practices. If, however, at the behest of a faith of boundless horizons, of a Torah of which it was said, *"Hafoch bah va-hafoch bah d'cholo bah"*—"Turn it and turn it over and over again, for everything is in it," of a God who proclaimed, *"Dir'shuni vi-h'yu"*—"Seek me and live," and of a tradition which gave primacy to study and scholarship, we are resolved to carry on, not catering to modernity, but questing renewal, not reaching out for discarded paraphernalia but for depth and inwardness, we shall serve the coming generations of our people sincerely and faithfully in the deepest reaches of their needs, and we shall remain true to an heroic and impregnable religious tradition which has had many noble and inspiring champions in the past, of whom Dr. Isaac Mayer Wise was one and certainly not the least.

The Ancient Paths

ADDRESS, GRADUATION EXERCISES
THE HEBREW UNION COLLEGE
MAY 23, 1936

Virgil concludes the fourth book of his *Georgics* with an epilogue in which he says: "Thus I sang of the care of fields, of cattle and of trees, while great Caesar thundered in war by deep Euphrates, and gave a victor's law unto willing nations and essayed the path to Olympus." While vast political events were sweeping by him, and mighty changes affecting men and nations were taking place all around him, the poet was content to sing of tillage, of planting, of the rearing of cattle and the keeping of bees. This was due not so much to his love of "inglorious ease"—as he himself modestly suggests, but, we suspect, to his intuitive surmise that here, in nature —in fields, trees, and cattle, in the revolving seasons, in the eternal life-hunger of living things, in death and resurrection—were the abiding realities of life, the facts which endure though all else changes, the things which survive the rise and fall of empires and mighty Caesars thundering by deep Euphrates.

Virgil's judgment seems sound. It is good for all men, and especially for leaders of men, in periods of ferment and upheaval, to keep steadily before their eyes and before the eyes of other men not so much the things which are timely as the things which are timeless.

One of the great gifts which a historic religion like ours brings to mankind is that it carries in its deep channels, steadily, safely, and undeviatingly, certain timeless, quintessential truths, regardless of the roiling and foaming of the waters on the surface which may be lashed by the sudden gusts of winds or storms. The teachers of our religion, whether prophet, priest, or rabbi, spoke of "the ancient paths," "the dark

418

sayings of old—that which we have heard and known, and our fathers have told us," "the former things of old," not because they were slaves of tradition, but because they surmised that in them was a pattern of life and ideas not hastily or carelessly sketched by a passing day or a transient mood, but fashioned out of a vast millennial experience, a long and profound searching, one which had stood well the wear and test of time, and one which had been found by unnumbered generations to be the "good way," the way which gives rest to the tried souls of men and nations.

Our days are swept by revolution. Our world is not only restless with change, but the changes are sudden, swift, and seemingly devoid of any informing principle or definite goal. It is not at all clear whether these changes are prophecy of a new political and social cosmos or only the throes of a painful disintegration into chaos. Men and nations seem unable to find any strong, simple moral certainties to which to render their eager loyalties and upon which to build a positive and tranquil life. The air is filled with the din of many confused and confusing voices shouting their strident, violent messages. Everywhere there is great thundering by deep Euphrates . . .

At such times, the rabbi who wishes to serve men in their deepest needs will do well to stand fast by the classic traditions of his faith. I mean, the things which are unchangeable and perdurable in it, the values which are from everlasting to everlasting. Each age must have a spiritual leadership whose predominant occupation is responsive to its predominant need. At all times it is in the realm of emphases where the genius of true leadership lies. The role of the rabbi, broadly speaking, remains fairly constant through the ages and that role is fairly well defined. He is the expounder of the theology and ethics of Judaism, the interpreter of its law, and the spiritual guide of his people's communal life and institutions.

But each age has its own crisis and urgency. Each generation has its own particular set of perplexities. This is particularly true of Jewish life. How frequent and sudden and radical are the changes which come over Jewish life in the Diaspora. Between 1914 and 1934 alone—in twenty short years—the life and fortunes of more than half of the Jews of the world have been altered in such an amazing and drastic manner as to set at naught all former calculation and prognosis. Think of the transformations, political, economic, and cultural, which have come over the lives of the three million Jews of Russia in the last two decades, and of the half-million Jews of Germany, and to a lesser degree, of the millions of Jews in

the other countries of central and eastern Europe! Think of the new
Diaspora which is fast being created today in countries and continents
where Jewish settlements heretofore had been meager or hardly known!
Contrast the fact of Palestine and of the Jewish national renaissance in
the life of world Jewry today with what it was before the World War.
Recall, if you can, American Jewish life of a generation ago—and contrast
it with the magnitude, the complexity, the ferment and turbulence of it
today!

And think with what desperate problems of survival—sheer political
and economic survival—our present generation of Jews is being confronted
in many parts of the world. There are powerful governments today which
are bent upon the systematic destruction, or, as they would have it, elimination of their Jewish—not citizens any longer, but unwelcome aliens.
They have a full-blown program of anti-Semitism, an anti-Semitic metaphysics, an apologetics and an elaborate technique. And Nazism, be it
remembered, is not confined to Germany, though in Germany it has had
its freest play and its most shameful victories. It is a plague of lethal ideas,
sweeping over the world today, victimizing the Jew wherever it reaches,
comparable to the centuries-lasting madness which was let loose upon
Europe by the Crusades, and equally menacing to the peace and security
of our people.

No government is quite secure today. No people is quite certain
of its tomorrow. Nations have simply despaired of planning their future.
They live, as it were, from hand to mouth. Each day is a day which brings
them nearer to war or revolution. And in the midst of this universal insecurity and instability, the lot of our people is the most insecure of all.
The times are desperately critical for all mankind, but most of all for that
most sensitive seismograph of all mankind's earthquakes and disturbances
—Israel.

A rabbi, therefore, entering upon his career in such a time of
tribulation will, I believe, best fulfill his mission if he will set about
to discover just what the predominant need of his age is, in the realm
which he has made his own, and, upon such findings, determine what the
predominant occupation of his leadership shall be. What does the world
stand most in need of today? What does his people stand most in need
of today? How can he, with that power of heart and mind with which he
has been endowed and with that equipment of knowledge and insight
which he has secured in this academy of learning, most directly, most

relevantly, and most helpfully respond to those needs? What will be the burden of his message, the cry of his lips, the plea of his heart to his fellow men in these darkening days?

I regard the answers to these questions so paramount that I shall not dwell upon any of the other themes which a baccalaureate address to a graduating class of rabbis normally is expected to dwell upon. I will not moralize about the qualities of character which are requisite for success in the ministry. I do not know what success in the ministry means. One of the most successful men in the ministry that I know of died of a broken heart. I will not admonish you to be strong and courageous in your advocacy of industrial justice and political integrity. You are already too old to have that quality grafted on to you if you do not already possess it. If one is at all morally sensitive—and if one is not, why, of all professions, should he choose the ministry?—he will soon discover for himself that the bitterest moments in a man's life are those which find him desecrating with his own hands the beautiful altars of his own moral integrity and quenching the proud fires of his own spiritual stateliness. I might be tempted to direct your attention to a bit of wisdom which most of us acquire only after we have badly bruised ourselves and others—that there is such a thing as "speaking the truth in *love*." Occasionally, the hot, impatient word will leap to our lips. Occasionally our hand will reach for the scorpion whip at the sight of outrageous wrong. But we should bring ourselves to remember that in the spiritual order it is the law of kindness which yields the ultimate victory. Our task is to persuade through reason, and, through love, to win men over to our vision. And if we fail—and most of one's ministry is failure, and the nobler the ministry, the greater the failures and the more precious and exalted the rare victories—we shall at least not have sanctioned by our example the technique of hate, bitterness, and spiritual violence which has gained such currency and approval among men and nations today.

I might also be tempted to dwell upon the pastoral element in your ministry, which in the eyes of many laymen in your future congregations will be regarded as your most important service to them. You will be admired for your eloquence, your scholarship, and your achievements, but you will be loved and blessed by grateful hearts for the helpful way in which you personally will bring light to them directly in their dark hours, for what you personally will mean to them and theirs as friend, counselor, and guide.

These and other themes are tremendously important and deserving of comment on an occasion such as this. But uppermost in my mind today are not these thoughts but thoughts of the temper of the world into which you are entering as ministers, the desperate spiritual crisis in our civilization, the life-and-death struggle which is raging today between the classic religious and moral tradition of mankind as represented by Judaism and the new paganism of power, dictatorship, state totalitarianism, militarism, and racialism which is sweeping the world. I cannot help but be apprehensive also concerning the quality of crisis and emergency which has entered Jewish life today. And I ask myself at this moment, watching the ordination of new rabbis in Israel, what shall a rabbi preach in these times? What shall be the center of gravity in his message and mission? Out of the treasure-trove of historic Jewish ideas, which shall he select to raise on high for ensign and banner to his troubled age?

The answer, it seems to me, is to be found in what I suggested a moment ago, in the *timeless* ideas of Judaism, in those truths which are from everlasting to everlasting. There are certain ideas or principles which are indispensable to any age regardless of its intellectual, political, or economic complexion. Just as there are qualities of personal character which were precious in the sight of man five thousand years ago, and which will hold their identical worth among men ten thousand years hence—integrity, courage, loyalty, self-restraint, so there are values in the social life of the human race as a whole which are eternally precious, paramount, and permanent.

And these values—unfortunately ignored, spurned, and denied by large sections of the world today, but which must nevertheless be defended and conserved at all costs if civilization is to endure—are, in very truth, the ancient paths of Judaism; and today, in their hour of betrayal, these ideals call for their spokesmen and champions as never before.

Let me point to one or two of these essential and indispensable values. A sovereign thought in Judaism has been the supremacy of the moral law. There is a law—eternally valid, written by God in the hearts of men, binding alike upon all men, and all nations. No one is exempt from the operation of this law—no state, no class, no party, no government. Against that law, nations as well as individuals can and do sin—"A sinful nation, a people laden with iniquity"—its kings and noblemen and priests, and rich men, yes, and the poor and the proletariat . . . . In the name of this supreme moral law, universally mandatory and exacting, a prophet could denounce a king. A Samuel could attack a Saul. Nathan could point the finger at King David and cry out, "Thou art the man!" Elijah could summon Ahab to a dread accounting; and Jeremiah could pronounce doom upon Zedekiah, because "he humbled not himself before Jeremiah speaking in the name of the Lord."

But the fearful heresy of our day proclaims not the supremacy of the moral law but the supremacy of the state or the nation. The state or nation can do no wrong. The party in control of the state can do no wrong. The party boss, the *duce,* the *Fuehrer,* the commissar, can do no wrong. The eternal cry of the Jew through the ages has been not "There is no king but Caesar" but "There is no King but Thee!" The new paganism recognizes only one mortal sin for which a nation should do penance, the sin of having been defeated in battle, and recognizes only one impartial judge above the nations, as one of the military experts of the Nazis declared—*success!* Since the Renaissance and the Reformation, since Machiavelli and Luther, the concept of state autonomy and self-sufficiency has fearfully advanced. Since Hegel and Fichte, the state has been apotheosized. The state is itself the right. It is the origin as well as the goal of all morality, and conformity with state ends is conformity with the moral law. State absolutism is steadily degrading morality to political strategy, and is robbing man of his freedom and his dignity.

There is here, as in other fields, an irreconcilable antithesis between the classic Jewish tradition and the new paganism. The perspicacious among the new pagans know it. That is why the Nazis, for example, have centered their bitterest attacks upon the Jew and Judaism, and upon the Old Testament.

Under our tradition the function of the state is to preserve law and order and to insure the largest measure of justice among men. Under the new dispensation, the function of the state is conquest through war. Its spirit is the *Wehrgeist.* The goal of all education is *Wehrhaftigkeit.* "Battle is the divine business of every German." In Italy children are trained from infancy in the science of soldiering. "In pre-war days, in Europe," writes Franz Werfel, "soldiers marched because they had to; now boys of twelve march for the fun of it." In contrast to this mystic adoration of force, of *Schrecklichkeit* and of brandishing of fists, our tradition proclaims, "not by might and not by power."

Our tradition proclaims the redemptive and healing power of love. "Love thy neighbor." "Love the stranger." The new paganism proclaims the principle of hate, of class struggle, of irreconcilable national ambitions, of xenophobia.

Our tradition speaks of humility, individual and collective. "The humble shall inherit the earth." The new order is blatantly and vulgarly arrogant in its conceits, claims, and pretensions. Dictators everywhere are inflating their peoples with the most boorish and indecent sort of national chauvinism, racial vanity, and class intransigence.

Our tradition speaks of the dignity of the individual. Our Torah begins with the creation of *one* man and ends with the death of *one* man. The first man was fashioned in the image of God. The second was one whom the Lord knew face to face. Man is significant in our tradition. Every individual has the right to say, "For my sake was the world created." Every man is a unique event in the world. When one sees a great concourse of people, he should thank God for not having made them all of one mind. In the new emergent world, men are being driven back into herd mores, into dread conformity. They are being reconditioned into mass reactions. A fearful robotism is the clear objective of the modern totalitarian state.

Thus the very basic doctrines of our faith, the salient principles of our spiritual and moral tradition, are being challenged in our day by powerful, ruthless, and determined forces who are again worshiping the unclean spirit. And these forces are scoring one victory after another.

The rabbi, therefore, who is heir of prophet, priest, and Psalmist, who chooses to walk with them, will in this hour of dread decision for mankind preach, teach, and proclaim most of all and above all these ancient truths with an earnestness and a vigor, with an eagerness and exaltation as if they were new revelations just come down to man, calculated to shake the very foundations of the world.

There is an untamed and amazingly dogmatic romanticism abroad in the world today. This turgid, headlong romanticism, born out of the maranatha complex, out of excessive Messianic expectations in the fields of politics and economics, has a tendency to make the classic ideals and standards of mankind seem old indeed, in fact, antiquated. That has happened before. The nineteenth century believed that the laboratory would yield all truth. The twentieth century believed that the machine would achieve all good. Both hopes have proved vain, but ere life exposed their vanity, they had a way of making the old codes and convictions of historic religions look outworn and slightly ridiculous. But they were not outworn. They were not old. They were not young. They are eternal. And they are unsensational, quite as unsensational as a mathematical formula, quite like the mathematical formulae to which physicists are now attempting to reduce this whole complex and exciting universe of ours. To these unsensational and eternal truths of his religious culture the rabbi should most fervently address himself today, and proclaim them with renewed emphasis to the world.

And to his own people, the rabbi would do well to bring today a message of comfort and confidence. There is a time to chide and a time to soothe. The harassed soul of Israel today needs the healing, comforting word. It needs morale. It needs the reassurance of a resplendent destiny, of ultimate victory, of the sheltering wings of God. In the hour of Israel's prosperity and power, our ancient prophets castigated their people, but in its dark hour of sorrow, defeat, and exile, they spoke with a compassionate tenderness. They spoke of resurrection, of vindication, of restoration. Their banner over their people was Love. The synagogue should, in these days, be a place of spiritual refuge and heartening. From the pulpit should come to our people not querulousness and censoriousness and partisanship and spluttering polemics and the bitterness of an impatient or disappointed spirit—"we walk no better for abusing our crutches"—but the strong, confident faith, the gladdening word of hope, and the wise, practical guidance and instruction. In such times as these, I suspect that our people stands in greater need of sages than of prophets.

The rabbi today should quietly and patiently strengthen the strongholds of Jewish life and the bulwarks of Jewish survival agencies. We do not need today a new philosophy of Jewish life, a new set of concepts and definitions to play around with. It is not Judaism which needs reconstruction today but ourselves. Of course, we are in an age of transition. We always have been. The gloomy Dean Inge opines that when Adam and Eve left the Garden of Eden, Adam turned to Eve and said: "My dear, we are now definitely entering upon an age of transition." Of course we must make adjustments to changed conditions. But Jewish survival owes far more to our people's refusal to make hasty and temporary adjustments, to their obdurate insistence upon the eternity and unchangeability of the basic teachings of Judaism than to any facile and accommodating adjustability. We need today planned and intensive cultivation of the marvelous spiritual and cultural legacy which is ours, energetic dissemination of our eternal teachings. We need training, upbuilding and organization.

The rabbi today should strive not for unity in Israel—a task quite impossible of achievement among our people or among any other people —but for a maximum measure of cooperation on the basis of common needs and obligations. He should foster among his people the larger loyalty to the whole house of Israel—here and abroad—and the sense of a common destiny. Provincialism and protective isolationism are no longer possible for any Jewish community in the world today. The rabbi should encourage the cooperation of his people in the upbuilding of the Jewish National Homeland in Palestine, not because that is *the* solution of the Jewish problem—there is no one solution, for there is no one Jewish problem—nor because he is enamored of nationalism, which has more or less run riot in the modern world, nor yet because he feels that the *galuth* is liquidating and that there is no longer any hope for Jewish communities in the Diaspora. That is a too-hasty reading both of past and of contemporaneous Jewish history as well as of the history of mankind. He should encourage their cooperation because a Jewish homeland will help to normalize the status of our people in the world, because it will remove the element of desperation—of fighting with our backs to the wall—from our renewed struggle for equality and emancipation which the world has again forced upon us, because it will serve as a haven for hosts of our people who must now seek new homes in a world where doors are everywhere closing, and because this Jewish National Homeland may become in the days to come a vast dynamo of creative Jewish cultural and spiritual energies.

A great hour awaits you, my friends, and you will be matched with this hour. It is a time when kings go forth to battle and mighty armies close in desperate combat. But you are to be rabbis, leaders of a people whose very name—Israel—means wrestling with angels and demons and mastering them. You are to be the teachers of the Torah, and of such it was said long ago: "Whoever devotes himself to the Torah, he shall triumph in the end."

The rabbis interpreted the phrase *"Ashrecho v'tov lach"*—"Blessed art thou and it is well with thee"—to mean "Blessed art thou" in this world; "and it is well with thee" in the world to come.

It is a saying which can come to mind as one reads this address delivered in 1952 to the graduating class of the Hebrew Union College–Jewish Institute of Religion. For the man who spoke these words had tasted a measure of accomplishment and recognition such as comes to very few. Thirty-seven years after his own ordination, he was acknowledged as the leading rabbinic figure on the American scene. He was recognized as one of his land's most distinguished citizens. He was a leader of world Jewry, the man whose labors and talents in behalf of Zionism had naturally made him chief spokesman for his people at the United Nations on the eve of the decision which established the State of Israel. As a young rabbi he had confessed his dream: "The one ambition of my mortal days would be to break through all the confining circumstances of my world to rise above the dead level of mediocrity and to raise others. . . ."

The dream had been more than fulfilled. But the achievement of hopes and success does not always make a person blessed. To be able, thirty-seven years later, to affirm the same article of prophetic faith that he had quoted on the day of his own ordination; to be able to say after a lifetime of labor in times so filled with trial that "there is yet room for vision"—this is to know the meaning of the words, "Blessed art thou." To be further able to address these words to a class of rabbis, one of whom was his own son—this is to taste the meaning of the words, "and it will be well with thee in the world to come."

There Is Yet Room for Vision

COMMENCEMENT ADDRESS
THE HEBREW UNION COLLEGE–JEWISH INSTITUTE OF RELIGION
JUNE 7, 1952

Shortly before his death, Judah Hanasi summoned his elder son, Gamaliel, who was to succeed him in the patriarchate, and said to him: *"Nehog nesiutka beramah"*—"Conduct your office with eminence, with greatness." There is a difference of opinion among scholars as to the meaning of the word *beramah*. Some would read *beramim*—"with men of high standing." The Aruch reads *bedamim,* "with something precious, of great value." The first interpretation appeals to me most: "Conduct your office with greatness."

Judah Hanasi was a very humble man, although he occupied the most exalted office among his people. The rabbis declared: *"Mishemet rabbi, batlah anawah"*—"With the death of Rabbi, humility passed away." His advice to his son, therefore, could not be taken to mean: "Be haughty and of a lofty bearing, maintain a domineering attitude towards your fellow men." It was greatness of another sort that he undoubtedly had in mind: spiritual stateliness, a mood of authority which derives from sure confidence in one's status, one's mandate, one's mission, and one's future. He spoke of a high courage with which one, especially a leader, should face all the evil and all the evildoers of the world, knowing that in the end goodness will prevail. This quality of greatness was always dear to the heart of our people. They preferred to associate it with their teachers, their leaders, and their prophets. As a symbol of his newly acquired high estate and eminence, it was the practice in rabbinic times to spread a cloak of gold, *golta dedahabah,* over the ordained at the ceremony of his ordination.

428

It is of such greatness that I would like to speak to you today, on the day of your ordination; for ours is a time for greatness, and the need is for great men.

We are too near our times properly to appraise them. One requires distance in order to see great objects in their proper perspective. We ourselves are too much involved in the turmoil, the fears, and the conflicts of our day to see objectively the amazing new pattern of life which is emerging.

Many people are quick to describe our age as materialistic, as lacking in idealism, in aim and purpose, and as drifting helplessly to disaster.

A mood of crisis is abroad in our world, and there is fear in the hearts of men. Men talk of economic collapse, of a third world war, of an irrepressible conflict between the East and the West which will completely shatter our civilization. There is much violence in our day, all the unleashed mendacities and vituperations of a cold war, *b'ikbot meshika hutzpa gisge*. It is not only in Messianic times that arrogance and brutality increase, but in all times of upheaval and social convulsion.

There are very few people who see this age of ours as a great age. I am persuaded that it *is* a truly great age. Historic events, great in amplitude and consequence, are coming to pass in our day. I am not thinking at the moment of the new worlds which science is continually disclosing, the new insights into the nature of matter and energy, the new sources of power and wealth, the new methods of production, distribution, transportation, and communication. I am not referring to the amazing progress in the medical sciences which has so markedly improved the health of the human race and increased the average length of life, nor to the marvels of engineering and the miracles of construction.

In characterizing our age as great, I am thinking in terms of social progress and welfare, in terms of human advancement and civilization. More is being done in our day for the improvement of the conditions of the common man, for the raising of his standard of living, his health, his education, and for his protection against the disabilities of sickness, unemployment, and old age than in any generation, than in any five generations, in the past. Never have more determined efforts been made to bring about a fairer sharing of the wealth that is produced and a better way of life for all.

Never have the submerged races and peoples of the earth risen as they have risen in our day to demand and to achieve, as they have to a large measure achieved, freedom and self-determination. Within the last six years one-fourth of the earth's population—more than five hundred million non-self-governing people—have obtained their political freedom. Imperialism and colonialism are in their death throes. Backward peoples are pressing forward into the light of a new day, and the exploitation of the dark races of the earth is rapidly drawing to a close.

What we are witnessing in our day, if we have eyes not only to see things but to see into the heart of things, is not social disintegration, but a radical new reintegration of humanity, a profound change in the social evolution of man, a change not free, of course, from dangers—for there is no progress without danger—but one of boundless and immeasurable potentialities. We are witnessing one of those sharp, decisive turns in the road of human progress comparable to the catastrophic metamorphoses observable in nature as in the case, for example, of the caterpillar which, at a certain stage, is transformed into the chrysalis and the chrysalis into the butterfly.

I do not wish to overdraw the picture. I am not suggesting that our age is approaching idyllic perfection, or that the millennium is just around the corner.

The important thing to consider is not whether we are on the eve of the millennium, but whether the major trends of our age are in the direction of the hoped-for good society, or away from it. Is our age breaking chains, or not? Is it trying to eradicate poverty and illiteracy and to raise the standard of living of people, regardless of race or color or creed? Is it trying to satisfy the legitimate aspirations of peoples to national freedom and independence? Is it trying to organize the world for peace and for international cooperation? I believe that in all these major trends, our age has given welcome evidence of great determination and of considerable progress. It is moving purposefully in the right direction—the abolition of war, the reduction of poverty, and the elimination of racial inequality. These are the three major trends of our century, and they are the major trends both in the East and the West, in the Communist as well as in the non-Communist world. What is tearing these worlds apart is a difference not of ideology or objective, but of method.

In the solution of the problems of this great, but greatly troubled age of ours, Judaism has a vital role to play. It is the ideals of Judaism which are really at stake in the struggle today, and Judaism's method for human progress. The importance of the individual, his inalienable rights, freedom, democracy, equality, brotherhood, peace—what are they but the offspring of Judaism, reared and nurtured by it? And what method is available to mankind to replace the bitter methods of violence, suppression, and terror, which have led to such mounting disasters in our generation, other than the method which Judaism proposed long ago, the method of inner reformation—the inner revolution of compassion and reconciliation, a method which has never been fully tried in the world and which today is being ignored more thoroughly than at any other time in human history.

Judaism has the true spirit with which to confront this upreaching age of ours, wild with spiritual confusion; for it has unswerving faith in man, in mankind, and in human progress. In this regard Judaism is quite unique among the religions of mankind—as unique in this as in its God concept, its prophets, its synagogue, and its prayer worship. With the possible exception of Zoroastrianism, faith in man and in human progress is not present commandingly, if at all, in Hinduism, Buddhism, Confucianism, Taoism, Christianity, or Islam. Indeed, belief in human progress belongs only to a very small portion of the human race. The predominant mood of most historic religions is pessimism. Most religious philosophies, from ancient Gnosticism, Stoicism, and Cynicism to modern existentialism, are grounded in deep pessimism and disillusionment. Man is hopelessly trapped and cannot escape the predicament of his own existence. He cannot hope to solve the entangled ethical paradoxes of his life. The world is not a good place to live in. It is evil. No real happiness is possible in it. The good society cannot be established on earth. Man is lost in original sin or homeless in an infinite and impersonal universe. He cannot help himself. He needs redemption and a redeemer. His salvation can be achieved not by personal merit or moral effort, but by an act of faith in the vicarious atonement of a saviour and by the grace of God. Man is not free to change himself or his destiny. There is really no purpose in resisting evil. The more one strives to develop his personality, the more enmeshed one becomes in the toils of painful existence. The very will to live is at the root of man's suffering and unhappiness. Man should forego all desire, all ambition, even good ambitions, and await the blessedness of release from the weary and pointless cycle of change into self-disintegration and non-existence. Death is better than life.

It is not doing injustice to the great religions of mankind to suggest that their predominant motif is pessimism, resignation, and other-worldliness; nor, in so doing, are we denying the spiritual grandeur or the high elevation attained by some of them. Nor is it to suggest that similar moods are not to be found anywhere in the far-flung domains of Jewish literature wherein, through the ages, ritualists and pietists, rationalists and mystics, traditionalists and reformers, priests and prophets recorded their views. Numerous sects flourished among our people, especially during the Second Commonwealth. "Israel was not dispersed," declared one of the rabbis, "until it broke up into twenty-four heterodox sects." Some of them were undoubtedly influenced by the Oriental theosophies prevalent in their environment. Some overemphasized one or another tenet of Judaism, and in so doing upset the spiritual balance, the unique ethical equipoise which distinguishes our historic faith. In most instances it was a case where sound ideas were followed through relentlessly to their logical conclusion, and, by that very consistency, they became illogical and unwholesome, reduced to absurdity. But they never constituted elemental ideas in Judaism, and, in spite of the variety and at times contradictory religious views and opinions recorded in our literature, it is not difficult to discern the outlines of the major trends in Judaism, the key ideas which were occasionally hidden beneath the luxuriant growth and creepers of subsequent commentary and exposition. It is not difficult to discover beneath the restless surface eddies the deep and steady channels of the permanent attitudes which carried on undeflected through the ages.

The great insights of Judaism are easily recognizable in all the stages of its development, and especially its concept of man and of human progress. They derive from a unique religious humanism which sifted and screened the copious beliefs of the Oriental world and rejected all that was extreme and excessive, all that was overgorged either with sensuality or spirituality, all that denied reality or was blinded by it, all that deified man or degraded him. Judaism was a movement of purification and of equilibrium, achieving for the religious life of man what Greece achieved for his artistic and intellectual life, a sobriety of measure and order which we are wont to call classicism.

In the unique construction of Judaism, man, for example, was indeed conceived as fashioned out of the earth, but in the image of God. He is certainly bound by his physical and mental limitations, but he is boundless in moral aspiration and is possessed of adequate instruments with which to change the face of the earth, the structure of society, and his own personal life. Man is finite and yet not helpless. Man is very important in God's scheme of things. There is evil in the world, but it can be overcome through repentance and aspiration, and therein lies the true meaning and adventure of life. Life is good and a gracious gift from God. To love God one need not hate the world. Life should not be feared or contemned or renounced, but sanctified and enjoyed through wholesome living in which the whole of man—body, mind, and soul—is fulfilled. Man is exalted through his struggles for the establishment of the Kingdom of universal justice, brotherhood, and peace on earth. Evil must be fought and eradicated, and justice must be established in the gate, and man may be sustained and inspired by the convictions that the major processes of history move purposefully toward a definite and benign goal. Man's principal concern should be with life this side of the grave, since "the hidden things belong to God, but the things that are revealed belong to us and our children." These are the all-suffusing ideas of Judaism, its inner fluid and its inner force.

Other religions possess one or more of these ideas. Some adopted them from Judaism; but Judaism has woven them all into a unified and unique pattern, has coordinated them into a dynamic religious philosophy and ethical code which, when applied, powerfully influenced the civilization of mankind in the past and must continue to influence it in the future. That other faiths and groups have accepted some of Judaism's teachings and are working today in the same direction should greatly hearten us. It would be a strange logic, indeed, if such endorsement of our faith by others were to be used to justify the surrender of our own religious and group identity.

It is with high confidence, therefore, *beramah,* that the teachers of Judaism today can confront this exciting, promising, but spiritually turbulent and confused age. They have in their keeping the medicine for the healing of the nations. What they have to say is free from inner contradiction, incontrovertibly relevant and indispensable, sound in program, sound in technique, sound in spirit, and directed to a world which God created not for chaos, but one which He formed for an abiding and pleasant dwelling place for man.

Nor need they fear any more the hostility of science. The physical sciences are no longer battering at the besieged citadel of religion as they did in the nineteenth and the early twentieth centuries. The mechanistic view of the universe has been largely abandoned. Physics is no longer committed to a law of determinism. The philosophy of materialism has suffered severe discredit in our day at the hands of science. If it is not an avowed ally of religion, science is certainly no longer its formidable antagonist. Science itself stands face to face with many unsolved and unsolvable mysteries. In science, as well as in religion, one has to operate with basic terms which cannot be defined and with basic propositions which cannot be proved, and in science, too, with every new insight comes a new obscurity.

Thus, within the framework of their acknowledged unknowables, both science and religion are proceeding today uncompetitively to develop, on the basis of their experience, insights and intuitions, power and wisdom for the greater glory of man.

The religious teacher has every ground for proclaiming his message to the world today *beramah*, boldly, with assurance and authority, and without fear that the findings of science may tomorrow shatter the very foundations of his faith.

The religious teacher in Israel may find additional confidence and strengthening in his ministry in the fulfillment in our day of a great historic hope which for so long seemed to be unrealizable, and in the righting of a millennial wrong which seemed to be irreparable.

The hope of national restoration was always an integral part of Judaism. Our faith nurtured it and was, in turn, nurtured by it. Providentially, this long-deferred hope came to fruition in our day. It is a blessed and glorious consummation which our generation was privileged to behold. It should greatly exalt us. Our people always looked forward to the time of its restoration as to a time of greatness, elation, and hope. "When the Lord will bring back the captivity of Zion . . . they will say among the nations: the Lord hath done great things with thee: the Lord hath done great things with us. We shall rejoice." What has so unexpectedly transpired in our day should recharge our courage for the greater tasks which lie ahead. For the Messianic hope of our people has been realized only in part. The *galuth*—exile—has come to an end and *shi'bud malkuyot*, "the servitude of foreign powers." But in its profounder and universal sense of *aharit ha-yamim*, the establishment of the good society of universal justice, brotherhood, and peace on earth, the Messianic hope of our people is, of course, far from having been consummated. The ultimate goal of Judaism reaches beyond all national restorations and sovereignties to the time "when they shall not hurt nor destroy in all my holy mountain, and the earth shall be full of the knowledge of God as the waters cover the sea." This Messianic hope Judaism must continue to proclaim. It can do so today more hopefully as a result of what has transpired in Jewish life. In a new, buoyant mood of achievement and vindication, the leaders of Israel may now devote themselves to the totality of Judaism's Messianic message which, in spite of the establishment of the State of Israel, remains unfulfilled. The great work is yet to be done.

The spiritual leader in our day may also be enheartened by the fact that men are turning to religion more and more as to the last sanctuary of man's freedom and dignity.

The religious shrine has from time immemorial served as sanctuary for men who sought escape from persecution or the punitive arm of government. When all else failed, man's last refuge was beside the horns of the altar. Today the church and synagogue are, in an even more vital sense, man's last refuge from the all-demanding, all-coordinating, and all-subjugating state.

Man is being made small in our day by the very systems which undertake to serve and exalt him. His rights have been curtailed by the very governments which avowedly seek to extend them. He has been denied his freedom on the plea of greater freedoms to come. It is a passing phase, I am sure, a by-product of wrong methods which are being employed to achieve good results. But in the meantime, man is being beaten down into littleness and rightlessness. Every precinct of his life is being invaded. Where is escape? Where shall the dove find resting place while the flood waters cover the earth, except in the ark of faith? Where shall man find shelter for his self-esteem and dignity, sanctuary from the relentless collective rhythms of his world? Where but in the courts of the living God! Where man is never subordinated except to God, where he is thought of as "a little lower than the angels"—where he is held inviolate in his spiritual dignity as a child of God. "How lovely is thy dwelling place, O Lord of hosts! My spirit longs and pines for the courts of the Lord." "For in Thee doth my soul take refuge, and in the shadow of Thy wings will I take refuge until the calamities be over-past."

It is not so much for peace of mind that men and women are turning to religion today but to escape the frightening attrition of their spiritual independence and to find sanctuary from the violent forces which threaten to liquidate their inherent human dignity and to submerge and nullify them as sovereign personalities.

To reassure them of their inalienable human worth and greatness, the spiritual teacher comes to men today with the comforting message of his faith: *"Wekabod wehadar te'atrehu"*—"God crowns man with glory and honor." It is a welcome message, indeed! And men hunger for it. It appeals to the greatness in man, to his full status and stature, and by so doing, it helps to make him great as well as to demand greatly of himself.

You are being ordained into the rabbinate in times dangerous and convulsive, and yet, into great and prophetic times; and I would urge you to strive to match your hour. Strive for greatness! How?

Have a high regard for your calling! It is a great calling. Give to it unreservedly your enfranchised minds and your understanding hearts. Honor it with your full substance and let your substance grow with increasing knowledge garnered through the advancing years and with the experiences which life will engrave in your hearts. How much of the basic vocabulary of our faith stems from the root terms of learning and teaching: Torah, Talmud, Mishnah, Gemara, Midrash, Tana, Amora, Sabora, Talmud Chacham! You, too, will be teachers—teachers of the Good Book, the good life, the good society. Our profession is not necessarily one of the specialized scholar, but most assuredly it is one of the faithful and avid student and learner.

Throughout our lives we must be men of the Book and men of books. Religious mystics of other faiths at times came to despise learning and books. "Books!" exclaimed the famous Sufi of Islam, Abu Sa'id. "Ye are excellent guides, but it is absurd to trouble about a guide after the goal has been reached." He also said, "The first step in Sufism is the breaking of ink-pots and the tearing up of books and the forgetting of knowledge."

This mood was practically unknown even among the mystics of Judaism, for their very mysticism was grounded in literature, in the occult and recondite interpretation of the phrases, words, letters, events and characters of the Book of books—the Bible.

In order that we may speak with authority and with an inner quickening and bring knowledge and insight to those who will turn to us as to trusted teachers and guides, we must be equipped maximally. Whatever else our ministry is called upon to do for our fellow men, it must certainly instruct the ignorant, *edut adonay neemanah mahkimat peti*. It must bring light to those who cannot see into the heart and the meaning of things, *mizwat adonay, me'irat enayim*. Without knowledge, gathering and expanding, blending the old and the new, and maturing into a wisdom adequate for ministration, we cannot instruct, and without replenishing our own inner light, we cannot enlighten the eyes of others.

We hold our calling high, *beramah,* when our spoken word is carefully weighed and carefully prepared. *"Imrat adonay zerufah"*—"The word of the Lord is refined of all dross." Words come easily, especially to those who are glib of tongue, but they are not always the responsible words or the helpful words. Words spoken in haste and unpremeditated, or opinions and judgments expressed which are not fully tested and substantiated, or true words spoken in bitterness without love are unworthy of our high calling, which must depend so much on the word, the dowered, the appropriate, the timely, and the timeless word. Like every other profession, ours, too, has its firm canons of craftsmanship and its exacting and meticulous standards of technique. Isaiah praised God for enabling him to acquire *leshon limmudim,* "a cultivated and trained speech," so that he might most effectively encourage with words those who were weary and beaten down.

It is easier to grow careless, dowdy, and slovenly in the preaching profession than in any other profession on earth, and we must be warned against it. *En aniyut bimkom ashirut.* There must be no patchwork poverty of form and expression in places where spiritual wealth is to be exhibited. To step into a pulpit inadequately prepared in content and form and face a congregation of God, to dash off a paltry sermon out of a passing headline, to force a puny homily out of a shy and unwilling text, or to set about exciting a congregation into admiration rather than persuading them into a conviction is to speak to men and women who need to understand the message of God *belaage safah ubelashon aheret,* "with contemptuous lips and with a strange and estranging speech."

There is also in evidence a growing tendency to lower the standards and canons of good taste in our synagogue programs and activities matching the prevalent degradation, in order to compete for attention with radio and television and other forms of entertainment. The synagogue cannot, in the long run, maintain itself through vulgarization. When it does succeed, for a spell, in bringing larger numbers to its halls by some strategem of unallied and unrefined spectacles or attractions, ought not the words of Isaiah disturb and confound us? "Who hath required this at your hands, to trample My courts?" Certainly, in our tawdry world of increasing slag and grime, a few precincts ought to remain inviolate sanctuary for human fellowship and the upreaching heart and mind of man where the clear atmosphere remains unfailingly one of the beauty of holiness and where everything always speaks of glory, *uwehekalo kulo omer kabod.*

We hold our calling high *beramah,* when we underwrite what we say by what we are. *"Torat adonay temimah"*—"The law of the Lord is perfect." The rabbis add: *"Eymatay hi temimah besha'ah shehi yoz'ah mippi tamim"*—"When is it perfect? When it comes forth from the mouth of a perfect man," or rather, from the mouth of a man who strives after perfection, since no man is perfect. A man must come into a court of equity with clean hands. Into the courts of the Lord, a rabbi must come with clean hands and a pure heart.

Very little that we are likely to say during the course of our ministry will have been said for the first time. Even the greatest utterances of men have had their ancestors, and all ethical doctrines have passed through several cycles of existence. The most famous teachers among our people were proud to attribute their teaching to illustrious predecessors and to hang their teachings, as it were, on what they called "the majestic trees" of the past. The fact is that we are dealing with an order of thought wherein basic new ideas are rare and infrequent. Speaking of the remarkable advances in science in our times, a recent writer declared: "The best doctor of a century ago would need a rigorous training to be fit to act as a modern hospital attendant." But assuredly, that is not the case with the best artist, poet, musician, or religious leader of a hundred or a thousand years ago. Progress in our field is not to be measured in terms of discovery, but in terms of application and fulfillment.

Wherein, then, will your originality lie? In the courageous timing of your message, in the inspired and compelling phrasing of that which men have known all along but have not taken to heart, but, above all, in the way in which your life will surround, pervade and re-enforce the utterances of your lips. These will lend distinction to your career. *"Yirat adonay tehorah"*—"The worship of God is pure." The rabbis add: "A man may be at home in the entire range of the Law, but if he is devoid of high moral principles, he has nothing—his hands are empty."

Men, as a rule, are quick to detect those who come to them bearing the gifts of learning or charm, or brilliance or salesmanship, but with empty hands and empty hearts. It is the sincere heart which alone provides the resonant music to the spoken word, which, when heard by men, deeply moves and exalts them.

We hold our calling high, *beramah,* when we speak the truth.

"Mishpete adonay emet"—"The judgments of the Lord are true." The *mishpatim* embrace those regulations and ordinances which define man's relations with his fellow men.

Our prophets and teachers were warned not to be afraid of men, but to speak the word of God fearlessly. *"Al tehat mipneyhem"*—"Do not be afraid of them."

The things, however, to fear most are not the persecutions of men, but the seduction of adulation, the temptation to be in with the right people and to bask in their sunshine, the wish to be unvexed and undisturbed, and not to face that which must, in all conscience, be faced. The Psalmist, whose superb Psalm 19 I have been quoting, prays that he be delivered from the persecutions of the wicked and presumptuous men—*mizedem hasok abdeka*—but he also prays to be cleansed from his own hidden faults which we do not like to acknowledge in ourselves which destroy us with a subtle inner corruption, so subtle that we are often not even aware of the deadly process of disintegration which is going on in us.

One need not be perennially querulous and cantankerous in the sincere service of God. One can serve God with joy and come before Him and His creatures with singing. When the High Preist, declares the Zohar, was to stand before God in the sanctuary, he had to enter the holy place with joy, and all things about him were to express joy; for in God's service there is no room for sadness. Serving God and man is a *simhah shel mizwah* —a service of joy. To be *m'urob im habriat,* cordial and pleasing to men, is no betrayal of conscience. In our vehement days with their violent ways, the spiritual guide serves his sacred calling best when he avoids all harshness of judgment and expression, and when he speaks the word of truth with love and compassion. Some of our greatest teachers and prophets— Moses, Elijah, Isaiah—were condemned and punished by God because they berated their people too severely, or doubted them too much, because they struck with the rod of their mouth when they should have employed the gentler speech. Our message will be far more welcome and fruitful when it comes "as the dew unto Israel"—and not as a raging storm. Was it not the Lawgiver Himself who prayed: "May my doctrine descend as the rain, my speech as the gentle dew." The mood of our faith is not always that of tempest and thunder. It is also a mood of green pastures and still and restful waters.

"Pekkude adonay yesharim, mesamhe leb"—"The precepts of the Lord are right, rejoicing the heart." It is to increase the happiness of the

world through an acceptance of the precepts of God and to bring joy to the tired hearts of man that we have undertaken our religious ministry, not to vindicate certain ethical abstractions. It is not enough to worship God— one must worship Him *besimhah uwetub leb*, "with joyfulness and with gladness and goodness of heart."

There is so much tragedy in our world today, and sorrow and anxiety, that the faithful shepherd of men will strive to comfort and reassure men, encourage and strengthen them—rather than increase their consternation. The prophet Ezekiel prophesied against the shepherds of Israel because they had not strengthened the weak nor healed the sick nor bound up the wounded nor brought back the strayed nor sought out the lost, but with rigor and harshness ruled over them. *Ubehazakah reditem otam ubefarek.*

Our careers should be guided always by the threefold love—*ahabat ha-makom, ahabat ha-adam, ahabat Yisro'el*. Without the love of God, man, and Israel in our hearts, we shall be offering through our ministry strange fires upon the high altars of God.

But there are times when even the kindly shepherd must lead with a firm hand. There are times—and they come not infrequently in the life of a rabbi—when at the behest of his sacred calling and in defense of his own immortal and undishonored soul, he must stand up and bear witness to the truth that is in him regardless; when he must be like "an iron pillar, like brazen walls," against king and princes and priests and people. The sincere and faithful rabbi will know, beyond any peradventure of doubt, when those challenging and undeniable moments arrive, for the hand of God will be heavy upon him, and he will step forward then with all the power and authority that is in him "to declare unto Jacob his transgression and to Israel his sin."

But let us not confound religious truth with political or economic partisanship, with total identification with one or another system of politics or economics. The role of the religious teacher is not to be the partisan or apologist for any system. No system completely meets the exacting demands of religion. Whether it be capitalism, socialism, or communism, or any of their numerous overlapping forms, there are basic principles of human rights and essential social ideals which are at stake in each, and the religious teacher must at all times remain free to defend these rights and ideals for which no system is adequate guarantee. We have seen in our day that even the rule of peasant and proletariat does not protect society against abuse of power, the exploitation of man, and the defeat of the spiritual promise of human life.

My dear friends: Thirty-seven years ago, on a Sabbath afternoon in June, I was ordained rabbi at the Hebrew Union College at the hands of my revered teacher, Dr. Kaufmann Kohler. For the valedictory, I took as my text the verse in Joel: *"Ziknekem halamot yahalomun bohureykem hezyunot yir'u"*—"Your old men shall dream dreams, your young men shall see visions." It was during the first year of the First World War that I was ordained. Much has occured in our world since that time—wars and revolutions and the most appalling cataclysm in the annals of Jewish history. These have been years of conflict and disaster, but they have also been immense and creative years. Nearly four changeful and eventful decades have elapsed since that time, and were I to choose a text today to enfold my message to you who are about to be ordained as rabbis—to all of you, and to one of you—I should choose the identical text from the book of the prophet Joel. For *"Od hazon layamim"*—"There is yet room for vision in the days to come." *"Od hazon lamo'ed"*—"There is yet a vision for the appointed time which will not deceive. If it tarry, wait for it. For it will surely come." There is every reason for you to look forward confidently into the future—to see visions of better things to come, to plan and build with all the ardor of your lives bridges into the future athwart impassable gulfs for the eager feet of men, and ladders betwixt heaven and earth. The days to come will surpass all the achievements and the grandeurs of the past.

You are entering not quiet or reposeful times, nor yet stagnant times, but great times of new plowing and sowing. You are entering a profession which will enable you to render great service. In spite of the bafflements and vexations which you will inevitably experience in your careers —for no human life and certainly no worthy human profession can escape them—I feel that your lot has fallen in pleasant places, and that you will have reason to be content with your portion in life. *Habalim naflu li ban'imim, af nahalat shafrah alay.*

You are adding your names to the roll of a goodly company of men who, through the ages, dedicated their lives to a service which was worthy of their life's dedication. With your endowment and training, you may move forward *beramah,* intrepidly and in high spirits into the tasks and opportunities of the coming years, like "those that go their own gait, erect, stepping with freedom and command, leading, not following." Go forth, dear young colleagues, possessed of yourselves, up-bracing your fellow men, instructing, and learning from those whom you instruct, humble yet fortified in confidence and self-esteem. You will be nobly rewarded in ways in which God rewards His chosen ones. You will find freedom in His service and dignity in walking humbly with Him, and the bread of life will be yours and the wine of the spirit, as you help to build His Kingdom. There will be a goodly harvest, and you will be content.

THIS of all things I can conceive of least—my own death. I have seen death in others many times. Even in them death seemed to me an intrusion or an interlude rather than a finality. Perhaps it is because I have never been able to think of anything as ending—or for that matter as beginning. I know being. I have never experienced non-being. I do not refuse to think about death. I do not know how to think of it.

I have no particular longing for immortality; but I am in the stream of life and I cannot escape it. My life began with the life of the universe and can only end with it. It has surged through infinite cycles and phases of being. It will continue its appointed course uninterrupted. All things are alive and in their transformations only pass into new forms and new ways of life. Death is the peak of a life wave, and so is birth. Death and birth are one.

Of all life forces, thought is the most marvelous and baffling. Of it I am continually and sharply aware. In me it is my essential self, my unity and my uniqueness. At the close of its present cycle it may combine or it may scatter and reorganize into a new integration. It cannot disappear.

I would not lose my zest for living or my purpose in life if there were no immortality, but I would be deprived of the only intelligent conception of life of which I am capable.

If we were strong enough to face death without sorrow, we could come to face immortality without joy. For the life we enter through death, if it be conscious life, must of necessity have its pain as well as its peace, its defeats as well as its victories. Death is not the last station of the soul's calvary: "The righteous have no repose either in this world or in the world to come . . ."

My comfort and my sustenance is not immortality, but God. His universe is perfect and my destiny is part of His perfection—even my tears and all my broken hopes.

WRITTEN FOR AN ANTHOLOGY ON
IMMORTALITY, 1928